BLUE WATER PATRIOTS

The American Revolution Afloat

JAMES M. VOLO

ROWMAN & LITTLEFIELD PUBLISHERS, INC.
Lanham • Boulder • New York • Toronto • Plymouth, UK

ROWMAN & LITTLEFIELD PUBLISHERS, INC.

Published in the United States of America
by Rowman & Littlefield Publishers, Inc.
A wholly owned subsidiary of The Rowman & Littlefield Publishing Group, Inc.
4501 Forbes Boulevard, Suite 200, Lanham, Maryland 20706
www.rowmanlittlefield.com

Estover Road
Plymouth PL6 7PY
United Kingdom

Distributed by National Book Network

Blue Water Patriots: The American Revolution Afloat, by James M. Volo, was
originally published in hardcover by Praeger, an imprint of Greenwood Publishing
Group, Inc., Westport, CT. Copyright © 2006 by James M. Volo. Paperback edition
by arrangement with Greenwood Publishing Group, Inc. All rights reserved.

British Library Cataloguing in Publication Information Available

The hardback edition of this book was previously cataloged by
the Library of Congress as follows:

Volo, James M., 1947–
    Blue water patriots : the American Revolution afloat / James M. Volo.
        p.   cm.
    Includes bibliographical references and index.
    1. United States—History—Revolution, 1775–1783—Naval operations.
    2. United States. Continental Navy—History.   3. Great Britain.
    Royal Navy—History—Revolution, 1775–1783.   I. Title.
    E271.V65   2007
    973.3'5—dc22   2006026031
    ISBN-13: 978-0-275-98907-1 (cloth : alk. paper)
    ISBN-10: 0-275-98907-0 (cloth : alk. paper)
    ISBN-13: 978-0-7425-6120-5 (pbk. : alk. paper)
    ISBN-10: 0-7425-6120-8 (pbk. : alk. paper)

Printed in the United States of America

⊗™The paper used in this publication meets the minimum requirements
of American National Standard for Information Sciences—Permanence
of Paper for Printed Library Materials, ANSI/NISO Z39.48-1992.

Contents

Introduction

In peace, in war, united still they move;
Friendship and Glory form their joint reward....
"What god," exclaimed the first, "instills this fire?"
Or, in itself a god, what great desire?

—Lord Byron

We will put to hazard the fortunes of war in America to insure the safety of the British Isles.
—John Montagu, Lord Sandwich, First Lord of the Admiralty,
1775–1782

Soon after the end of the Seven Years War (called the French and Indian War in America, 1754–1763), Anglo-American colonials began to revitalize those maritime activities that had been threatened by the French during the eighteenth century. Technically at peace with France and most of Europe for the first time in decades and protected from pirates, corsairs, and raiders by the demonstrated might of the British Royal Navy at sea, American trading vessels, whalers, and slavers soon inundated the trading ports of the world, especially those among the rich islands of the West Indies. The British government in London, and especially the Board of Trade that was given oversight of the economic life of the colonies, noted the increase in this activity with some apprehension.

Although Americans shared a common history, culture, and religious tradition with England, they nonetheless began evidencing a general

dissatisfaction with British rule and the Royal Navy almost before the ink
on the Treaty of Paris (1763) had dried. Many areas of contention existed
between the colonies and the ministry in London at the time including
disagreements over expanding the boundaries of the provinces, strained
relations with the Indians, political control of the provincial governments,
illegal levels of trade with the French and Dutch islands of the West
Indies, and the avoidance of taxes by smuggling. The home government
viewed each complaint with growing annoyance and increasing frustra-
tion passing legislation that closed the frontiers to settlement, dispatching
new governors to the colonies, and enforcing the trade regulations with a
new-found vigor.[1]

The Anglo-American colonies were generally restricted to a thin strip
of settlements along the sea, and a considerable portion of the population
lived by the sea, were at home upon the sea, or worked in the maritime
trades. Of the twenty largest cities in Anglo-America in 1775, only one
(Lancaster, Pennsylvania) was not a port, and it flourished as a feeder city
for goods and produce from the interior destined for the largest colonial
port, Philadelphia. Lacking both improved roads and an adequate bridge
building technology, inter-colonial communications, trade, and travel
were best carried out by water in small coasting vessels. New England
provided almost half of British shipbuilding capacity worldwide. In
Maine and New Hampshire more people were engaged in shipbuilding
than in agriculture, and in Massachusetts it was estimated that there was
one ship for every one hundred inhabitants.[2]

Until challenged by the Americans, the British trading empire was a
closed and highly profitable economic system that reached halfway round
the earth, and if not highly efficient in modern terms, at least its lawful
side seemed so at the time. The foundation of the British economy and
the Empire itself was based on a form of regulated trade known as
mercantilism. Colonial shippers and merchants supposedly made their
profits by moving raw materials to England and returning finished goods
to the colonial markets, while the British government took its part of the
wealth generated by this activity in the form of taxes, port fees, and customs duties. By law the colonials were denied the privilege of partaking
in many forms of manufacture or in any trade practiced extensively in
England and specifically protected by Parliament in order to maintain a
moderate level of employment in the home islands. However, in the
1760s colonial trade with foreign markets in the Mediterranean and West
Indian was growing faster than that with British ones. The stockholders
of legitimate trading and manufacturing companies in Britain were appre-
hensive at the loss of a large proportion of their profits to the colonials,
and they complained bitterly to the ministers of government whenever
the colonials skirted the regulations through illegal manufacturing, clandestine trading, or outright smuggling.

As the colonies grew so did the volume of their trade with foreign nations, and it became obvious to the Crown that its colonies were slowly approaching economic independence. Yet many Americans were fearful of making an irrevocable break with Britain. During three-quarters of a century of wilderness warfare the colonists had demonstrated their ability to stand against both European and Native American enemies on the frontiers, and many cast dispersions on the role played by the red-coated regulars, considering each wilderness victory to be their own personal triumph. Yet whenever matters of economic independence were discussed by reasonable men, it was pointed out that the colonies needed the protection of Britain at sea, specifically that of the Royal Navy. The colonies were thought too weak at sea to maintain independent merchant or fishing fleets in the face of French, Spanish, or Dutch pirates and commerce raiders should the newly won peace fail. Britain had waged an almost continuous naval war with one or more of these aggressive nations since the 1580s (and would continue to do so until 1815). Moreover, if the colonies left the orbit of the trading empire, London merchants might press the passage of domestic legislation closing the empire's ports to American tobacco, grain, fish, slaves, and naval stores. This, it was thought, would ruin the mainland colonial economy and plunge most Anglo-Americans into poverty.[3]

Britain was jealous of its trade with America and had attempted to reassert its authority over the colonies by imposing heavy duties on foreign imports as early as the 1730s. Some form of trade regulation had existed since 1660, but the ministers in London began to strictly enforce them for the first time in 1764. It was the vigorous enforcement of the principles underlying the collection of the duties rather than the actual financial burden that the taxes imposed that was the cause of much of the colonial alienation. London deployed a small army of customs and revenue officers to most major American ports displacing the authority of the local agents of government. The colonials viewed new regulations such as the Sugar Act (1764) and Townsend Revenue Act (1767) as violations of fundamental political principles rather than as simple instruments of revenue collection or trade regulation. Violation of the acts was no longer considered a mere breech of the law drawing a small fine, but was now considered a crime punishable by seizure of both ship and cargo or by fines that represented a full year's profit.

Hostility quickly grew towards the representatives of the Crown, especially in the New England ports, where enforcement was most vigorously prosecuted. In the 1760s and 1770s Boston underwent the greatest number of customs seizures among major American port cities, which may help to explain the depth of the radicalism that flourished there. Spontaneous demonstrations erupted at the sight of a revenue cutter, and Royal Navy press gangs looking to man a shorthanded vessel met with unprecedented levels of non-cooperation and even violence among the people. The colonials made no distinction between the vessels and officers of the Revenue Service and those of the Royal Navy. Although most of the references to arrogant and intrusive officials before 1764 actually concerned the deputies of the customs and not naval officers, the colonists "considered both pirates and dealt summary justice to both."[4]

As relations deteriorated between New England and Britain, the Crown repeatedly responded with the worst possible moves, inexplicably further restricting export trade to English ports and barring New England mariners from the rich fisheries of the Grand Banks. It is not surprising, therefore, that the centers of the American revolutionary movement should be found in northern port cities such as Newport, Providence, and Boston. Moreover, the signal acts of overt rebellion against British authority were carried out by colonial mariners and seafarers on the blue waters of the Atlantic many years before colonial militias faced down redcoats on town greens or over intervening gray stonewalls.[5]

Initially, the maritime conflict seems to have centered on Rhode Island's Narragansett Bay, while the land war simmered in nearby Massachusetts. Every school child knows that the American Revolution began on Lexington Green in 1775, but how many are aware that in 1764 a Royal Navy cutter, *St. John*, engaged in the suppression of smuggling, was fired upon by Rhode Islanders; that in 1769 the revenue sloop

The peacefully busy colonial port of Boston in 1722 with its "long wharf" protruding into the harbor. A half century later the city was to be the scene of hostility to government, mob action, and open violence.

Liberty was seized and burned by the people of Newport; or that in 1772 the navy cutter *Gaspee* stationed near Providence was attacked and burned in the night by armed men in small boats for no ostensible reason beyond their apparent distaste for the arrogant attitude of the cutter's commanding officer.

The government in London was outraged by these attacks on its vessels, by isolated acts of violence carried out against its taxing agents in the streets, and by resistance to the proclamations of its governors and officials. Yet it was not the burning of British vessels by a few disgruntled radicals but the massive public demonstrations like the Boston Tea Party of 1773 that drew the ire of the politicians in London. The ministry closed the entire port of Boston as a punishment for destroying £18,000 worth of tea belonging to the influential lords and members of Parliament who were stockholders in the East India Company.

It is of no little consequence to history that the first retaliation taken by the Crown against Americans was to suspend their fishing and shipping rights. These actions led directly to an enhanced support for the Bostonians throughout the colonies, and it unified the Americans as never before save during the Stamp Act crisis of 1765. The "Child Independence" may have been born during the Stamp Crisis, as John Adams once proposed, but it was drawn forth from the coastal waters of North America in 1775 just as surely as Moses was taken from a floating basket in the Nile in Biblical times.[6]

In 1770 a few Bostonians, deemed radical street demonstrators, were killed in a club-swinging clash with British regulars known as the Boston Massacre, but as the day-to-day situation worsened, the outbreak of more serious and widespread violence became increasingly likely. The Americans felt that they were being treated as second class citizens by a group of peevish ministers and their deputies, and they rightly resented it. Ultimately, the colonials took the stance that conciliation was impossible and that open warfare was necessary to maintain their liberty. The incidents on Lexington Green, at Concord Bridge, and on the roads to Boston on April 19, 1775, immediately led to a real shooting war that resulted in a continuous effusion of blood throughout the colonies from which there was no honorable retreat.

These circumstances led the Continental Congress to provide immediately for an army based on the existing provincial militia structure, but the colonial representatives doubted the practical value of forming a colonial navy. Not even the shadow of such a force existed in the colonies beyond a few scattered privateers left over from the French wars. It was inconceivable that America could deploy a fleet with any chance of matching the sixty warships that the Lords of the Admiralty promised to post to its shores. Nonetheless, the chairman of the embryonic Naval Committee of Congress in 1775 could visualize a half dozen American cruisers sweeping the colonial coastline and the Caribbean of British merchant vessels while the battleships and frigates of the Royal Navy were busy blockading Boston harbor.[7]

The Continental Congress, therefore, adopted a strategy that would defend the deep-water ports of America from intrusion by the Royal Navy. To this end they envisioned cordons of armed boats, floating batteries, row galleys, and land-based fortifications guarding cities like New York, Baltimore, Philadelphia, Norfolk, Charleston, and Savannah. Yet the enterprising Americans were not prone to miss an opportunity to embarrass the ministers in London or to profit from a little "blue water" privateering. They quickly planned to begin their naval war, therefore, as commerce raiders on the sealanes they knew the best, those connecting Europe, North America, and the West Indies.[8]

Colonial consciousness of the military value of prosecuting a war at sea was fueled largely by necessity. The rebel army was woefully short of gunpowder and arms, and it was hoped that American ships could run to Europe or the islands of the West Indies to procure a supply. Both George Washington, as commander-in-chief of the Army, and the individual colonies, in the guise of local committees of safety, commissioned a number of cruisers to act in the cause of American independence before the Congress stirred itself to action. These vessels, and others ultimately commissioned or built by the Congress, were active in both American and European waters, and they captured hundreds of British merchant vessels (valued at tens of millions of pounds sterling by war's end). They also defeated several British vessels of war in single ship encounters.[9] Serious consideration must be given to the proposition that the American rebellion would have collapsed without the timely intervention of these events at sea.[10]

Notwithstanding their joint desire for independence from Britain, the colonies initially deemed themselves nothing more than a loose confederation of discrete political states united only for protection from a common enemy. This led each to act independently during 1775 and early 1776. The immediate result was the establishment of eleven separate state navies. Only New Jersey and Delaware of the thirteen united states were excepted. The state vessels were usually smaller than those of the Continental Navy, being composed mostly of boats, barges, and row galleys adapted for work in shallow waters. They varied widely in quality and number, and were under orders from the several local committees of safety rather than a more comprehensive national agency. Although a few state ships were vessels of considerable size, the main effect of the state navies was to deny the scant supply of cannon, gunpowder, shipbuilding facilities, and crews to the Continental Navy.

At the same time the pressing logistical demands of the rebel army investing Boston caused George Washington to undertake a quick remedy to the problem of military supplies in the form of a handful of private cruisers sent to raid British provision transports. This ad hoc naval force was deemed an immediate success, and the Congress, elated by the consequences of Washington's efforts, quickly appropriated money to buy or build additional warships. The Congress' new found commitment to a naval war can be measured by the fact that a total of almost $1 million was appropriated for the Naval Committee to provide for a Continental Navy.

Yet the committee quickly found itself waging a war at sea with an empty treasury, an exhausted credit, and a depreciated currency. Shortages of experienced officers, seamen, and supplies dogged the American naval effort throughout the war. In part, this was due to its inability to attract available cash and able seamen away from the potentially more lucrative privateers. Moreover, the committee had to invent a naval command structure and an administration—providing for not only vessels, officers, and crews, but also for food, cannon, gunpowder, rope, sails, repair facilities, chandlery, medical services, and a legal system for processing captured vessels and cargoes, securing prisoners, and dealing with the needs and complaints of its own naval personnel.

Unlike the Americans, who needed to invent the whole administration of both their army and their navy from the outset of the Revolution, the British had an established and experienced administration in the Board of War for its army and the Board of Admiralty for its navy. The whole scheme of British strategic thinking emphasized the prevalence of the naval arm making the Board of Admiralty the most powerful administrative office in the empire. The Lords of the Admiralty controlled the lion's share of all military expenditures, and they directed the world's greatest fleet of warships. The Admiralty Board had established procedures for promoting offices and rating seamen. It controlled everything from arms, ammunition, and rations provided to both soldiers and sailors, to the production and repair of warships, the detention of prisoners of war, and the functioning of military hospitals. The Ordnance Department at Woolwich provided all the artillery and gunpowder for both the army and the navy. More importantly, the men of the Royal Navy cherished a tradition of victory that had been reinforced several times during the wars of the eighteenth century. With such a formidable organization arrayed against them, it is a wonder that America's "blue water patriots" attempted to fight a naval war at all.

The purpose of this book is to document the naval operations that took place during the American Revolution. These can be divided into two parts: those that took place before the French intervention of 1778, and those that took place thereafter. From spring 1775 to summer 1778, the Americans undertook to engage the Royal Navy with a handful of frigates, schooners, privateers, and whaleboats. The Royal Navy quickly found that if it did not take steps to curb these activities, the rebels would appropriate the colonial sealanes to their own use and interfere with their strategy for the land war. Although a few British vessels fell to American "seapower" at the onset of hostilities, the Royal Navy was never really threatened by the rebel effort at sea. By the end of 1778 all the major warships of the Continental Navy had been driven from the sealanes. Only the privateers remained active.

After the alliance with France in 1778—and then Spain (1779), and finally Holland (1781)—the American war became a worldwide naval conflict with campaigns carried out on a grander scale than the Americans could muster. The war at sea spread from the Atlantic Coast, to the West Indies, to the Straits of Gibraltar, to the West African coast, and even to the Indian Ocean. After 1778 the land war in America also shifted its focus from New England, New York, and Pennsylvania towards the south. Thereafter major land operations moved to the Carolinas, Georgia, and Virginia, and the French and Spanish threatened the Gulf coast and the islands of the Caribbean with invasion. In fact, the last major land battle of the Revolution north of the Mason-Dixon Line was fought at Monmouth, New Jersey, in June 1778, almost at the exact moment that France declared its alliance with America.

America's new-found allies at sea endeavored to draw out the British fleet, meet it in formal line of battle, and generally put it on the defensive; yet the Americans were anxious that the French, in particular, concentrate their naval strength on the Atlantic coast of North America, thereby supporting the rebel armies on the seaboard. Moreover, French naval assistance was valued as much for commercial reasons as for military ones. The revolutionary economy could not continue to function with British cruisers intercepting more than 40 percent of American merchantmen and commercial fishermen that left port. Congress believed, perhaps incorrectly, that the continuing decline in the value of Continental currency was directly linked to this drag on the maritime commerce of the country, and it spent several months in 1776 debating what the ideal model of American trade with Europeans other than the British should look like.[11]

Throughout the war the major gateway ports of America were the target of British strategy, to be seized in an effort to strangle the colonial economy. True to form, whenever a regional port fell to British arms, the economy of the local hinterland collapsed for a brief time, but water-based transportation and trade never completely ceased. The resilience of the American maritime economy lay in its secondary port cities. The city of Providence "leapt to the forefront of Rhode Island's trade" in the place of British-held Newport; and Baltimore and Wilmington replaced Philadelphia and Norfolk as destinations for cargoes to the middle states. The inland water routes between Philadelphia and the upper Chesapeake and Delaware bays remain relatively safe, and the short stretch of land between Head of Elk and Christiana Bridge posed no great obstacle to the movement of trade goods or military supplies between the bays. The Patriot hold on Boston and on the many ports on Long Island Sound throughout the war years offset to a great extent the eight-year-long British occupation of New York with New London and New Haven providing river transportation to interior Connecticut and Massachusetts with good land connections to the Hudson highlands of Westchester, Albany, and the rest of the state. Tertiary seaport towns like Salem, Gloucester, Plymouth, Bridgeport, Westport, Norwalk, Egg Harbor, Chester, New Castle, and others provided safe havens for small cargoes carried in shallow draft schooners and sloops bypassing the risk entailed in trying to land in major cities.[12]

Much of the naval effort after the 1778 alliance consisted of months of boring vigilance as both the French and British fleets rode quietly at anchor in American bays and estuaries truculently eyeing each other. The Americans, outclassed by the size of the European naval establishment, held their breath expectantly, but the fleets rarely came out to fight. Meanwhile the European powers planned a series of baffling combined arms operations in the southern colonies and the West Indies. Most of the ensuing naval battles between the Allied and British fleets were indecisive. Nonetheless, it must be remembered that it was the French fleet commanded by Francois Jean Paul Comte de Grasse that sealed the fate of America in the War for Independence by winning the Battle of the Chesapeake in 1781.

The primary focus of this work is the period before 1779, when the Americans confronted the Royal Navy alone, but a wider period is considered in terms of the consequences of the war for France, Spain, and Britain. Due to the overlapping nature of events during the Revolution, the author has provided a short account of the organization and effectiveness of the American naval effort in comparison to that of Britain and France in order to orient the reader. Moreover, the author has decided to place events under common categories related by topic rather than by chronology, as in a chapter concerning Washington's efforts in forming a fledgling navy, or another dealing with the European operations of John Paul Jones and Nathaniel Fanning. The author hopes the reader will find the resulting history useful, comprehensive, and precise.

1

The Enforcement Crisis

The ... militia drums beat to arms, not to quell the mob collected in defiance of all law and allegiance to their sovereign, but to increase it.
—Capt. James Hawker, RN[1]

For they, 'twas they unsheathed the ruthless blade,
And Heaven shall mark the Havoc it has made!
—Lt. Nathaniel Fanning, CN[2]

Parliament under George II, the grandfather of King George III, had attempted to reassert its authority over trade practices in Anglo-America with the Molasses Act of 1733. Protection of British sugar interests in the Caribbean drove many of London's dealings with Anglo-America, and the restrictions and heavy duties levied on molasses from non-British sources should have eliminated the illegal trade. Instead the practice flourished because it remained extremely lucrative, surviving even the colonial wars of the mid-eighteenth century. The prevailing winds and currents made anything other than a clockwise transit of the North Atlantic very difficult for sailing ships. Stops along the bulge of Africa and in the West Indies were almost always on the most practical, if not the most direct, route from Britain to Anglo-America, and shippers from both sides of the Atlantic traded in the islands and along the coast of Africa on their way from Europe.

The three-way traffic in molasses, rum, and slaves, which historians call the Triangular Trade for its stops in the Caribbean, New England,

and Africa, was fundamentally supported by the fisheries of the Grand
Banks off the coast of the Canadian Maritimes. The fisheries provided the
less-than-romantic dried cod used to feed the plantation slaves who produced sugar and molasses in the West Indies. Half the molasses brought
into New England was used in cooking or food preservation, and the
other half was distilled into a very satisfying rum. Distillers in New
England made tidy profits changing the molasses into liquor, yet only
about 5 percent of the rum was exported to be bartered for slaves, ivory,
palm oil, or other items from Africa. The simplicity of the molasses, rum,
and slaves concept makes it popular with historians, but it is somewhat
misleading. Only a tiny fraction of colonial trade actually followed the
pattern suggested by the trading triangle, and coastwise trading among
the colonies and with the Caribbean was certainly more significant both
in terms of its volume and value. Profits were to be had with every
exchange, and each transaction helped the Americans to offset an annual
deficit in commodity trading with Britain that amounted to nearly
£1.5 million before the Revolution.[3]

There remains, moreover, a common misconception that all colonial
Americans lived in log homes cut from the standing forest, ate from
wooden bowls fashioned by hand from the living tree, or ran about in
animal skins or homespun produced before the kitchen hearth. As one
historian of the period has noted, "Life in those days was not so simple
as is sometimes imagined." The American colonials exhibited a great lik-
ing for sophisticated imports of all kinds. Among these they consumed
annually 75 tons of pepper and more than 1.5 million bushels of salt.
They imported each year more than fifty different fabrics, a quarter million hats, and an untold number of shoes, boots, silk garters, laces, and
fans. Almost one hundred different drugs and medicines have been identified among the most common imports as well as fine china, wallpaper,
dyes, pigments, files, saw blades, tools, hinges, cutlery, gun parts, and
manufactured items of many descriptions.[4]

The most lucrative profits to be realized through this trade, however,
proved to come from the genial addictions, "a quiet smoke, a nice cup of
tea, a sweet tooth . . . exotic rarities converted into cravings."[5] The consumption of alcohol, in particular, had not yet taken on the negative asso-
ciations commonly voiced by temperance advocates in nineteenth century
America. Besides domestically produced rum and beer, there were
imported wines, brandies, and liqueurs of many types. Whiskeys, gins,
and other distilled beverages were not particularly popular except as
home brews intended to deny import duties to the Crown for the mere
privilege of enjoying a temporary intoxication. Imported coffee and choc-
olate, especially from the Dutch, were also highly valued. Better homes
stocked a fairly generous supply of these items, and business establishments such as taverns and coffeehouses that catered to the "addicted"

were common sights in most towns. Colonials willingly spent a fair penny for their favorite extravagances, but they greatly resented paying import duties on them. They therefore depended in large part on smugglers to provide low cost, high quality products. Ironically, the disputes that would result in the American Revolution would revolve to a great extent around these luxury items, while coffeehouses and taverns would become the seedbeds of discussion, dissention, and rebellion.[6]

EVADING THE CUSTOMS

Before 1764 the Royal Navy had been of little service in suppressing smugglers, although it was often suggested in Parliament that it should have taken a more active roll. The Customs Service of the Exchequer, the department of government that levied taxes and duties, was the only governmental agency directly charged with their collection, but the colonials had a long and successful history of evading customs officials. Customs houses were generally established only in major ports, and the agents had only a few small vessels with which to patrol the coastlines. In fact, customs vessels were required to focus their patrols to within two leagues (approximately four miles) of the coast, while naval vessels were generally restricted to patrolling out of sight of land. Nonetheless, both services could seize a vessel in blatant contravention of the law wherever it was found.

Shippers were required by law to report their cargoes for inspection at the customs' wharf before unloading in the colonies. Of course, this regulation could easily be ignored by simply landing contraband elsewhere along the coast before reporting to the customs wharf. A common ploy of smugglers was to load with a small cargo of enumerated goods in Holland or France destined for a legitimate port in the West Indies, and then stop in some out-of-the-way British port such as the Orkney or Shetland islands and compound the cargo with legitimate, duty-free British goods for which they received proper clearance papers and manifests. Upon arrival in America they would openly unload some of the items, pay any duties on the landed cargo, and then depart, seemingly in accordance with all the procedures of the law. With no authority to inspect the holds of legally licensed vessels, the best the customs agents could do was to carefully supervise the unloading of the cargo. Having run the gauntlet of the customs once and having the clearance papers to prove it, the vessel was virtually no longer suspect, and the smuggled items could be covertly landed elsewhere. It was often not worthwhile for an officer of the customs to seize these small batches of contraband because of the generous bonds demanded by the courts and because of the personal liability to which the arresting officer was placed if the case was not proven. Smugglers often used the threat of lawsuits for supposed damages in such cases to avoid prosecution.[7]

The ministers of government in London considered every colonial seaman and shipper a potential smuggler, and the natural coastline of New England with its many small coves and shallow inlets made enforcement of customs very difficult.

It became clear to the government in London that if customs revenues were to be collected with regularity, the Royal Navy would have to help enforce the law. In 1764 Parliament passed legislation that was meant to assist the shore-based customs officials with the enforcement of the decades old Molasses Act. Written by George Grenville, the Sugar Act (or Revenue Act of 1764) served as an immediate occasion for giving the Royal Navy a more active roll in enforcement. All commissioned officers of the Royal Navy were made deputy customs officials, and they were empowered to search through the cargo of suspicious trading vessels at sea. They were encouraged to vigorous enforcement of the law through a system of generous rewards in the form of a part of the value of the cargoes and vessels forfeited. In a single year, Lt. Abraham Crespin received as his share of reward money £231; Lt. William Dudingston garnered £88; and Capt. Thomas Jordan collected £61. This was a great deal of added income for a serving naval officer. A captain's nominal salary, depending on grade, was at best £360 per year and a lieutenant's only £110. Moreover, the admiral commanding the station received one-eighth of the value of all seizures made in his area of operation, making the position of station commander highly profitable.

Unfortunately, the involvement of the navy in customs enforcement seems to have engendered more competition than cooperation between the two services, and it placed the station commanders at odds with the colonial governors over just who deserved to collect the monetary rewards for enforcing the law.[8] Previously the colonial governors received a third part of all seizures made by the customs agency in their colony. Up to one-quarter of this was now claimed by the navy. The legislation itself carefully defined the share that went to the king, but it was sufficiently vague about the governors' rights to cause a controversy. The dispute was ultimately resolved in favor of the navy, yet as late as 1771 Governor William Tryon was still pleading with the crown for shares of the navy's seizures for the colonial governors.[9]

Under the Sugar Act, enforcement was extended to almost all coastwise traders including the smallest inter-colonial mariners who might move cargoes only a few miles along the shoreline in sailing skiffs. The skippers of vessels greater than 10 tons were required to obtain documentation of their cargoes at the customs before shipping out and to do likewise when they landed even if going from one colony to another. "If any goods are shipped without such sufferance ... the officers of the customs are empowered to stop all vessels ... which shall be discovered within two leagues of the shore of any such British colonies or plantations, and to seize all goods on board."[10]

An accused shipowner or master was not allowed to present a defense until he had posted a cash bond of £60 (or equivalent in colonial money). Then, presumed guilty from the outset, he was required to prove his innocence in a Vice Admiralty court. This was somewhat like defending a present-day parking ticket before a military court martial. Even when acquitted the defendant was required to pay all the court costs if the court decided that there was probable cause for the original seizure.[11]

It has been estimated that American ships brought 4 million gallons of molasses into the colonies annually. Half of this total was smuggled. From 1764 to 1766, when the tax was reduced, the three penny tax per gallon of molasses was high enough to make smuggling profitable. Thereafter, with the tax reduced to one penny, the revenues actually increased because the smugglers abandoned the trade in molasses for more highly taxed items. Whereas in the previous year it was estimated that half a million gallons of contraband molasses had been seized, in 1767, the first year of the tax decrease, not a single vessel was libeled by the West Indian Squadron for smuggling molasses out of the Caribbean. Moreover, there is little evidence of smuggling into the major colonial ports in this period. The Royal Navy libeled only two vessels as smugglers in Massachusetts Bay in two years, and only four were libeled in the port of Philadelphia in the same period.[12]

Nonetheless, the ministers in London were convinced that every American afloat was a potential smuggler, and hundreds of vessels were needlessly searched annually. Passage of the Sugar Act resulted in more rigid enforcement along the coasts of New England than elsewhere because it was thought that it was there that most cargoes of molasses were destined. It has been estimated that there were sixty rum distilleries in Massachusetts alone. The southern colonies with their sparse populations and isolated plantation economies imported very little molasses by comparison to the vast amounts used in New England.[13]

The taxes collected on legitimate shipments of molasses remained the single greatest source of revenue from the American colonies, yet they were insufficient to cover the cost of the establishment needed for their collection. The Office of the Exchequer estimated the cost of enforcement at almost £40,000 each year. Ironically, the additional effort employed in collecting duties from the Americans may have been misapplied. Not only did it sour the relations between London and the colonies, but in the 1780s, after a great reform of the revenue service, the British government estimated that the empire was still losing over £1 million a year to smugglers worldwide.[14]

THE NORTH AMERICAN SQUADRON

In 1764, Rear Adm. Alexander Lord Colvill was posted to Halifax with a North American squadron of twelve naval vessels. Colvill had previously served at this post from 1759 to 1762 as Commodore. Halifax was not the most desirable posting for a lord, but the port had the only Royal Navy dockyard and naval supply storehouse in North America and was thought a fitting command for an officer only recently raised to Admiral of the Blue. Ships on the North American Station went there when in need of a refit, thereby saving an arduous crossing and recrossing of the Atlantic. Halifax would remain the primary base for the Royal Navy in North America throughout the remainder of the century.[15]

Colvill's area of responsibility on the North American Station stretched from Nova Scotia to Florida. The sugar islands were generally protected by the ships of the West Indian Squadron, which had been formally divided into a Leeward Island Station and a Jamaica Station in 1742, and the fisheries of the Grand Banks and Newfoundland were considered a separate station because of continuing disputes with France and Spain over colonial fishing rights. Colvill subdivided his command into nine separate postings along the Atlantic coast each with at least a frigate under a senior captain in the most active American ports. Capt. Archibald Kennedy, the senior naval officer at New York in HMS *Coventry*, was second-in-command of the squadron under Colvill.

All the ships of the North American Squadron came out from Britain in 1764 with Colvill. Those previously assigned there were returned home. Ultimately Colvill requested a number of additional armed cutters to be used along the generally peaceful but rugged Atlantic coastline. These diminutive vessels promised to be more useful than men-of-war in apprehending smugglers who were the main focus of the station's responsibilities. Their fore and aft rig enabled them to sail close to the shore in weather too severe for square-rigged warships, and their shallow draft allowed them to get into coves, inlets, rivers, and creeks impossible to navigate in larger vessels. Ironically, the Admiralty approved the purchase of six sloops and schooners built in America for this purpose. Each was provided with a crew of British Jack-tars, a file of Royal Marines, and a cadre of young Royal Navy officers. The cutters were named *Chaleur, Hope, Magdalen, St. John, St. Lawrence,* and *Gaspee.*

Colvill stationed his largest ships at New York City, New London, and in the Chesapeake where the waters usually remained open in winter. Norfolk, Virginia, was the northernmost port that was free of winter ice on the Atlantic coast. Colvill deployed a number vessels to sea off the

This is a typical Royal Navy cutter as portrayed in a period illustration. Note the long bow sprit and square top-sail yardarm that distinguished the type from a simple single-masted sloop. The Union Jack at the bow was the British national flag. The flag astern, mostly red with the Union Jack in the quarter, was the Royal Navy ensign of the period replacing a white naval ensign with the red cross of St. George from earlier times.

coast of Maine because he knew from experience that many American rivers, bays, and inlets were difficult to navigate and would be frozen over or filled with floating ice in winter leaving his vessels stranded. HMS *Rainbow*, with Walter Sterling as senior captain, was posted to patrol the coasts of Virginia and Maryland; HMS *Squirrell*, Capt. Richard Smith, and *Sardoine* (pronounced sardine) to cruise from the Delaware Capes as far north as Sandy Hook, New York; and HM sloop-of-war *Hornet*, Capt. Jeremiah Morgan, and *Viper* to cruise from the mouth of the Cape Fear River off the coast of North Carolina south to Georgia. The remainder of the squadron were posted to Long Island Sound and Massachusetts Bay.

POPULAR RESENTMENT

Prior to 1764 American colonists had generally accepted the doctrine that Parliament could pass acts regulating trade and imposing duties on imports. They had merely nullified any act that proved too irritating by smuggling, by producing enumerated goods clandestinely, or by simply ignoring the law. After 1764 the voice of a new, more radical group of politically active colonials was raised above the normal background of discontent common to the middle classes. These radicals proposed for the first time the idea that only the colonial legislatures could tax Americans because they were not properly represented in Parliament. Clandestine political grumblings quickly became open confrontations with calls for liberty and the rights of Englishmen permeating the air.

The people of the colonial waterfront took an active roll in the increasing public disorder. The natural rowdiness of the waterfront denizens ranged from mere mischief such as tavern brawls to sometimes bruising battles between large groups of men. Flowing rum, loose women, and pent up frustrations from being confined aboard ship for long periods made seamen prime candidates for inclusion in any public demonstration. Repeatedly resistance to British officials and the enforcement of customs regulations included the type of crowd action that commonly appeared on the waterfront. Sometimes the participants thought in terms of the theoretical concept of political "Liberty"; sometimes they acted in terms of their personal freedom to do as they wished; most times there were several ideas about liberty swirling through their heads simultaneously. "Whatever definitions of liberty appeared on the waterfront, the maritime world's understanding of liberty helped to shape the struggle for American independence." Any effort to restrict trade or limit smuggling threatened the livelihood of a whole segment of the waterfront population, and maritime workers of all types provided the mobs for the earliest calls for liberty in America.[16]

American dissatisfaction with the prevailing system of enforcement could also take on more subtle forms. During the three winters on station

Those identified as enemies of American Liberty were often treated to less-than-careful rousting, as shown in this British illustration from the period. Note the prominent place of the sailor in his petticoat-breeches, knows as slops, and round hat in the forefront of the mob.

in New London aboard HMS *Cygnet* British naval officers Charles Leslie and Philip Durell found the citizens disrespectful of their office, disobedient to the law, and discourteous to their persons. Most of the population refused to be seen in public with Royal Navy officers or to attend private functions where they were openly received. Townsmen initiated brawls wherever the British Jack-tars settled down to drink or eat while on shore leave, and many sailors were waylaid and beaten after trying to spark the young ladies of the town. Before there were Sons of Liberty and Liberty trees there were the Sons of Neptune—as the sailors and former privateers called themselves—who rioted in the streets for the rights of Englishmen.[17]

The sea officers and seamen on other stations experienced similar episodes. When Lt. Thomas Allen, commanding the cutter *Gaspee*, put into Casco Bay, Maine with a pair of smugglers in tow in 1764, he was shocked to be met by a local customs agent who, through fear for his own safety, refused to prosecute the owners or to even hold the vessels. While in port Allen and his press gang were attacked by a mob and made to release the mariners. Lt. Thomas Laugharne of the cutter *Chaleur* received similar treatment in New York in July 1764. *Chaleur* had stopped several vessels off Sandy Hook at the entrance to New York Bay, and Laugharne had pressed five mariners from among the merchantmen in the harbor because he was always short of hands. When he next appeared with his longboat at the city wharf, he was mobbed and made to surrender the men he had pressed. He was then compelled to watch as his own longboat was removed from the water and burned in front of city hall.[18]

Capt. James Hawker sent a boat from HMS *Sardoine* to the wharf at Charleston to inspect a suspicious schooner. He recorded that "a mob collected [that] immediately threw stones, logs of wood, staves, and any other thing they could lay hold of into the boat, wounded the officer and men and obliged two of them to jump overboard to prevent worse." Hawker then armed all of his crew on *Sardoine* save a skeleton watch and made for the merchant schooner in several of the ship's boats standing "in the bow of the foremost myself, with the British flag in my hand." He was met by the mob "armed with cutlasses, axes, stones, clubs, etc. to resist me forcibly." A violent clash was but a heartbeat away when the owner of the vessel, with a cooler head, brought forth the vessel's clearance papers and cargo manifest, which showed that it was "regular" and ended the confrontation.[19]

Notorious among the naval postings was Capt. Jeremiah Morgan of HM sloop-of-war *Hornet*. His activities off the coast of North Carolina caused the legislative assembly to vote that he be arrested if he again set foot in the colony. In February 1767, the *Virginia Gazette* noted of Morgan, "[He] is very assiduous, and lets nothing escape him...was he to stay, we should be ruined to all intents and purposes." In September 1767, the people of Norfolk, Virginia, led by the mayor of the town, physically attacked Morgan and his men when they came ashore looking for deserters. The Royal Navy men had to fight their way back to their boat. A warrant was later issued for Morgan's arrest by the local magistrate.[20]

Whether openly brazen, like Morgan, or bravely romantic, like Hawker with flag in hand, these sea officers embodied both the best and worst features to be found among the men of the Royal Navy. Devoted to the best interests of their sovereign and their empire, most Royal Navy commanders stationed in America suffered from a common misconception of the colonials as crude, avaricious, and innately disloyal. In following their instructions concerning the customs in too literal a manner, these naval officers drove the otherwise loyal colonials from private grumbling to active resistance, if not open rebellion. Had every Royal Navy officer carried out Lord Grenville's legislation to the letter as did Morgan and Hawker, the American Revolution may have begun a decade earlier.[21] The populations of the port cities of Connecticut and Rhode Island were notorious for their resistance to the customs. As charter colonies rather than royal ones, neither colony exhibited any desire to vigorously enforce the trade regulations. With the support of colonial governors like Thomas Fitch and Samuel Ward, and under the sympathetic scrutiny of judges like Richard Morris and John Andrews, both colonies regularly erected legal impediments to the prosecution of smugglers and the forfeiture of their vessels and cargoes. This was often accomplished through the active interference and contravention of the law by the governors and the judges themselves, who would purposely throw Vice Admiralty cases into the civil courts where they could drag on for months.[22]

Capt. John Brown of HM brig *Hawke*, for example, was thrown into jail by Judge Morris when he tried to libel the merchant ship *New York* but could not post an outrageously large bond of £10,000 imposed by the judge for possible damages to the ship and cargo. Brown, a £30-per-month captain, could not amass such a vast sum, nor would the local customs official, Charles Apthorp, aid him. This set of circumstances resulted in a five-month-long adjournment of the case, a suit brought against Brown by the shipowners, and the ultimate release of the vessel. This case illustrates the lack of cooperation between the services, the hostility of the courts, and the tactics used by American merchants all of which plagued the enforcement mission.[23]

THE STAMP ACT CRISIS

The French and Indian War (1754–1763) created a vast debt for the British, and the Grenville ministry decided to extract at least some of the money from the colonies in the form of a stamp tax on all legal and business papers. Previously any legislation laying *internal taxes* had always come from the colonial assemblies, and the stamp tax was clearly an attempt to levy an internal tax from outside the colonies. Along with the passage of the Stamp Act, Parliament renewed the Mutiny Act, which required the colonial assemblies to house and feed the British army and to provision and water any British naval vessels sent to America.[24]

Grenville sought to minimize the reaction to the stamp tax by appointing American stamp agents rather than English ones. This turned out to be a crucial mistake that insured the failure of the stamp policy. Colonial stamp distributors, their property, homes, and families were simply too vulnerable to the displeasure voiced by their neighbors in the mob to carry out their obligations. This factor caused most of the agents to resign their posts as soon as the level of protest over the stamps rose above tavern mutterings to become street demonstrations. Grenville also miscalculated both the potential economic effect of the tax and the breadth of the reaction to it. Colonial shippers and merchants were required to take out numerous public documents while conducting their everyday business affairs including bills of lading, clearance permits, insurance policies, rental agreements, mortgages, attachments of property, and all kinds of contracts. The Stamp Act also affected lawyers, newspaper editors, printers, municipal employees, and an army of ordinary persons who signed indentures, produced public documents, or ran licensed businesses. The tax stamp on packs of playing cards was particularly irksome as almost everyone played cards as a form of diversion.[25]

The Stamp Act was designed to take effect on November 1, 1765, and in October, a Stamp Act Congress met in the city of New York with representatives from nine colonies in attendance. The governors of Virginia, North Carolina, and Georgia prevented any delegates from attending, and the legislature in New Hampshire simply sent word of its support. The congress prepared a resolution asserting that the basic rights of the colonials had been violated by Parliament's attempt to tax them without their consent. Many merchants pledged not to import British goods until the offending acts were repealed, and those who did not pledge faced open intimidation by the mob, which fashioned itself into a high-sounding Continental Association. Yet even in the face of growing discontent London went forward with the printing of thousands of stamps and dispatched them to the colonies.[26]

Almost everywhere colonists refused to allow the use of the stamps. Those stamp agents who had not already resigned their posts, hid in their homes or aboard ship, and refused to appear in public. In Massachusetts, Andrew Oliver had his home destroyed by the mob, and he fled to the protection of British troops garrisoned in Boston. In Connecticut, Jared Ingersoll was surrounded by more than 500 angry demonstrators. He instantly resigned his post, threw his hat in the air, and cheered for liberty. In New York, violence broke out when a mob gathered to burn the lieutenant governor in effigy and harassed the troops with a surprising lack of regard for their own safety in the face of fixed bayonets. Several homes were invaded and looted. Windows were broken and fires set in the streets. Only the restraint practiced by the regulars and their officers prevented an exchange of gunfire. In March 1766, after being warned of a possible armed revolt, Parliament repealed the Stamp Act.

The Royal Navy played a significant role during the height of the crisis. With the legislatures and many of the governors on the side of the colonials, the ships of the Royal Navy were often the only practical instruments of British authority left in the colonies. The pattern for resistance to the stamps was set in Boston, and it was in Boston also that the Royal Navy attempted to fashion a practical response to the problem. When the local stamp agent, Andrew Oliver, was intimidated into resigning his office, the governor, Francis Bernard, took steps to save the stamps from the populace. This seems slightly ridiculous to us today, but the governor was aware that the mob had designs on the stamps themselves for the purposes of propaganda. Turning the stamps over to the colonials, or allowing them to be destroyed, would have been "greatly humiliating and derogatory to His Majesty's government."[27]

Bernard asked Capt. Thomas Bishop of HMS *Fortune*, then the senior naval officer in Boston, to take the crates of stamps aboard his ship and secure them until they could be unloaded at Castle William on an island in the harbor. He also asked that the navy intercept any ships from England carrying additional shipments of stamps for other colonies. For this last purpose Bishop deployed *Jamaica* and *Gaspee* to the approaches to Boston, and he sent the sloop-of-war *Tryal* to Halifax to receive further instructions from Admiral Colvill. Several days later *Gaspee*

Vessels like this Royal Navy brig were often the only outposts of Royal authority left in the colonies during the Stamp Act Crisis. Two-masted vessels of 20 guns or less like this one, commanded by junior officers such as lieutenants, were often referred to as Sloops-of-War even though their spar and sail plan had little similarity to the single-masted commercial vessel known as a sloop.

intercepted the ship *John Galley* arriving from London with additional packages of stamps, which were also deposited at Castle William. No one dared to even open the packages for inspection. In a letter to the Admiralty, Bernard highly praised Bishop for his cooperation.

By way of contrast the colonial protests against the stamps and the stamp agents in Rhode Island quickly turned violent, rivaling the armed outbreaks seen against the revenue service. At the time HMS *Cygnet* (Capt. Charles Leslie) was the largest warship in the harbor at Newport. The local stamp agent, Augustus Johnston, the chief customs agent, John Robinson, and several of their friends retreated to the warship in fright when riots broke out. Leslie ran out *Cygnet's* guns and made a great show of clearing the ship for action and preparing to repel boarders by raising the nettings and distributing cutlasses and pikes to the crew. This ploy kept the rioters at a distance.

Robinson's absence from the custom's office effectively closed the port because no outgoing shipping could leave nor could any incoming vessel unload without his assurance that they had the properly stamped clearance papers. Moreover, Robinson absolutely refused to leave the protective confines of *Cygnet*, and he also refused to issue any documents that were unstamped. He maintained this position for three solid weeks. The governor of the colony, Samuel Ward, was enraged by Robinson's stance, but there was little he could do to force the issue because the customs was independent of his authority. No one seems to have questioned the unstamped papers that began appearing along the coast during the crisis except Captain Antrobus of HMS *Maidstone*, who voiced his concern to Governor Ward in a letter but took no action against shippers.

In late November Robinson yielded. With his income dependent on the volume of trade that passed through his office, and with life aboard an overcrowded ship less inviting than his own warm hearth and home with winter coming, the customs chief resolved his dilemma through the use of a mild subterfuge. He officially requested the stamp agent, Johnston, who was sharing his exile aboard ship, to issue stamps to the customs office for its use. Johnston, in all feigned innocence, denied the request because he had never actually seen the stamps sent to Rhode Island. These had been waylaid in Boston. Yet, it is abundantly clear that HMS *Viper* (Captain Lobb) had arrived at Newport with all of Rhode Island's supply of stamps some time in October. The packages had been transferred to *Cygnet*, but the packages had been left unopened in the expectation that they would never be used. Robinson, thereafter, began issuing customs documents without a stamp but with a clear conscience.

New York was always a hotbed of anti-government protest. The struggle for political dominance in New York, however, was no unevenly matched contest between mobs of like-minded citizens and a few customs officials as it was in Boston or Newport. No place in America was so evenly split in its loyalties. From first to last, rebel sympathizers and government loyalists were in constant conflict and turmoil. Even the colonial legislature was split between the powerful pro-Loyalist DeLancey and pro-Patriot Livingston families.[28]

Capt. Archibald Kennedy was posted to New York in HMS *Coventry*. He was the son of a customs collector from New York, had lived there most of his life when ashore, and had large property holdings in the city. He had used his equity in these properties to help his brother officers weather financial rough spots or to provide them with bail-bonds when all other sources had been exhausted. Kennedy's familiarity with the population of the city should have better prepared him for the crisis that was about to break over the Stamp Act, but it did not. Instead his property became a pawn in the hands of the mob led by New York radicals like Isaac Sears and Alexander McDougall, former privateers and Sons of Neptune, who now became leaders of the Liberty Boys, or Sons of Liberty.[29]

The New York stamp agent, James McEvers, immediately resigned leaving the colonial lieutenant governor, Cadwallader Colden, responsible for the stamps until the newly appointed governor, Sir Henry Moore, should arrive. Unlike many colonial officials, Colden was openly dedicated to implementing the Stamp Act, and he was sure that the Liberty Boys intended to seize the stamps. He asked Kennedy to intercept the shipments outside New York Bay and convey them to Fort George on the tip of Manhattan. To this end Kennedy deployed *Guarland* (Captain St. John) and *Hawke* (Captain Brown) to patrol off Sandy Hook.

The ship *Edward* was subsequently met and brought to Fort George at the tip of Manhattan Island. Unfortunately, the stamps had been loaded beneath other cargo, which had to be off-loaded before they could be reached. Fort George had no facilities for handling cargo, and the city wharf was filled with protestors waiting to descend on the *Edward* should it be brought near. Kennedy ordered the cutter *Gaspee* to warp alongside the merchantman to serve as a receiving vessel for the cargo, and unloading proceeded at anchor in the bay. Armed boats from the *Guarland* patrolled the bay during the process, and they escorted the stamps to Fort George where they were secured.

Meanwhile, William Franklin, royal governor of New Jersey, requested that Colden also store the stamps for his colony in Fort George. Franklin asked that Kennedy be ordered to send a vessel and a detachment of marines to transport them. Colden blocked the first request claiming that there was no space at the fort to store more stamps, and he also opposed Franklin's subsequent suggestion that New Jersey's stamps be placed aboard Kennedy's ships. The latter decision was completely within the naval vice commander's purview, and Kennedy refused to involve himself with New Jersey's problems. It should be noted that the Admiralty gave its naval commanders much greater freedom of action than the Board of Trade allowed governors or army commanders. Moreover, the naval and military commanders, the customs officials, the stamps agents, and the governors were not part of a continuous chain of command. This was one of the weaknesses of the empire's bureaucracy with each reporting to his own distinct superior. All that was expected was polite cooperation between the services and the branches of colonial government.

Repulsed at New York, Franklin turned to Captain Hawker of *Sardoine*, who was on station in the Delaware River opposite Newcastle (Delaware) on the western border of the Jersey colony. Hawker accepted New Jersey's stamps on his own responsibility, and he also accepted those of nearby Pennsylvania. When winter ice began to build in the river threatening his ship, Hawker took *Sardoine* from the water, placed it in a cradle above the normal high tide mark, and made a fortress of it bristling with cannon and swivel guns. He let it be known that anyone attempting to take the stamps would be fired upon, and no one tried. Like most other naval officers in the colonies, Hawker made no attempt to close any ports or demand that documents have stamps upon them.

Meanwhile on November 1, 1764, the Liberty Boys in New York staged a particularly effective demonstration massing several thousand protestors and penetrating the outer defenses of Fort George. This gave Colden great concern, and he immediately asked that Kennedy remove the stamps from the fort and place them aboard his own ship, HMS *Coventry*. Kennedy refused fearing, correctly, that his own property in the city would be held hostage to the demands of the protestors. Colden then deliberated with the city council and decided to hand over the stamps to representatives of the mob before their persistence brought on a bloody conflict with the garrison of the fort. The protestors burned ten boxes of stamps as an example to the government of their power and then retired. This incident was a major blow to Royal prestige in New York and elsewhere in the colonies.

In December the customs house in New York began to issue unstamped documents to shippers, but Governor Moore, finally arrived from England, refused to advise Kennedy as to whether or not to honor them. Kennedy took it upon himself to declare the port closed until the Stamp Act should be obeyed or repealed. He kept the port closed for a month. Finally, word came from Admiral Colvill advising his subordinates that the stamps were a "shore matter" and that the navy no longer needed to deal with them. This freed Kennedy at last from his dilemma, and he opened the port for business as usual without the stamps.

The southern colonies also had a strong reaction to the Stamp Act. Captain Sterling, on station as senior captain in Chesapeake Bay, transferred Virginia's stamps to HMS *Rainbow* as soon as they arrived, and the Virginia customs agents avoided violence by immediately issuing unstamped clearance papers, which Stirling wisely acknowledged. None-theless, in May 1765, seven anti-stamp tax resolutions were proposed in the Virginia House of Burgesses. The Virginia resolutions claimed that only the colonial legislature had the right to tax Virginians. "Taxation of the people by themselves, or by persons chosen by themselves to represent them ... is the only security against a burthensome taxation." The first reaction in the colonies to the unprecedented *Virginia Resolves* was one of shock, yet many Americans found themselves in accord with their primary thrust of no taxation without representation. In Virginia, at least, the argument over specific customs regulations and tax stamps had quickly evolved into an all-out battle concerning British constitutional principles.[30]

The people of Maryland immediately requested the resignation of their designated stamp agent, Zachariah Hood. Fearing violence, Hood fled to New York where he demanded that Kennedy order one of his ships to Annapolis as a floating stamp distribution station. Kennedy absolutely refused to sanction the idea, but he sent *Hawke* to Annapolis anyway to insure the peace of the colony and to serve as a place of refuge for loyal colonial officials should they need it. The only violence seen in the colony was a tavern brawl involving a group of Jack-tars from HMS *Hornet* that resulted in the outnumbered sailors being thrown into the Chesapeake Bay after receiving a minor battering at the hands of some local toughs.

In North Carolina, the stamps were delivered to the colony by Lt. Constantine J. Phipps in HM sloop *Diligence*. In compliance with his orders from Stirling as senior captain on station, Phipps placed the stamps into the hands of the governor, William Tryon. In the absence of a stamp agent, who had resigned, Tryon ordered that the stamps be transferred to HMS *Viper*, Capt. Jacob Lobb, who was on station at Wilmington. Lobb accepted the stamps and then unwisely attempted to enforce their use, seizing three vessels for having unstamped papers as they approached the mouth of the Cape Fear River. The people of Wilmington took their revenge by stopping all provisions and water to the Royal Navy ships in the harbor and by jailing a boat's crew from *Viper* that came ashore. In February 1765, a thousand protestors surrounded the customs house to demand the release of the seized merchant vessels. Three days later boats from both *Viper* and *Diligence* combined in a nighttime amphibious operation to secretly infiltrate Fort Johnston that overlooked the harbor and to spike all the colonial cannon found there. With the ships' guns run out of their ports the next morning, Lobb and Phipps released the three merchant vessels thereby diffusing further unrest in the colony.

The stamps for South Carolina and Georgia reposed for some time in the hold of HMS *Speedwell*, Capt. Robert Fanshawe. Thereafter, South Carolina's stamps were permanently deposited at Fort Johnson in Charleston never to be used. Upon receipt of Georgia's stamps, however,

Governor James Wright actually attempted to issue them and put the Stamp Act into practice. Wright was notable as the only governor to actually have issued documents with the stamps attached. Although Fanshawe supported the governor with a detachment of marines, Wright backed down as soon as a mob of protestors appeared before his home. The stamps were quickly returned to the hold of *Speedwell* for their protection.

In every colony the stamps spent at least some time under the protection of the Royal Navy; and, with the exception of those few stamps burned in New York or issued in Georgia, none were destroyed or taken. The navy had done its part during the crisis, but the Stamp Act had been a total failure as a source of revenue and as a government policy. Although the act had failed miserably everywhere in the colonies, London considered what happened in New York the worst failure of the whole Stamp Act affair. Kennedy was initially blamed for this, but he survived the controversy to be appointed commander of the North American Station from November 1766 until July 1767. Of all the Royal Navy officers in America, only Lobb and Kennedy had attempted to enforce the Stamp Act on shipping. Admiral Colvill, who cleverly waited to see how the colonies would react before taking a position on the enforcement of the act, should probably have provided a less ambiguous form of leadership early in the crisis.[31]

THE TOWNSHEND ACTS

In 1766 Charles Townshend became Lord of the Exchequer. He immediately proposed a series of drastic revenue measures to help pay for the administration and security of the colonies thereby relieving the burden on the British taxpayer in England.[32] There was a good deal of resistance in Parliament to the passage of the bill, and although Townshend died suddenly in 1767, the Townshend Revenue Act "stole through the House; no man knew how."[33] The duties were reissued and expanded in 1769 over the protests on a vociferous Whig minority, which generally supported the colonial position on taxation for its own political purposes. The act set taxes on a vast number of "goods and commodities of growth, produce, or manufacture of the British Colonies." These fell into two groups distinguished as *enumerated* (taxable) or *non-enumerated*.[34]

The list of enumerated items encompassed almost all the yield of colonial production on the North American continent and in the islands of the Caribbean. A number of the articles—tobacco, indigo, ginger, dying woods, and cocoa among them—were subject to duties even when they were simply shipped between colonies. In other words, a shipment of tobacco moving between Norfolk in Virginia and Baltimore in neighboring Maryland would be taxed even though they never left the Chesapeake

Bay. Similarly a tin of ginger was to be taxed if it passed from New York to New Jersey 1,000 yards across the Hudson River.[35]

No course of action by the government in London could have been calculated to more arouse colonial resentment. As enforcement of the acts increased, "the colonists resisted with greater stubbornness." Legitimate imports from Britain fell from £2.2 million to £1.3 million in a single year (1768–1769). In Philadelphia imports from Britain were cut in half from £400,000 to £200,000, and in New York they fell from £500,000 to a mere £75,000. Not only was the royal exchequer denied its increased revenue, but merchants, manufacturers, and shipowners throughout the empire were denied a great deal of business. The result was a severe depression of the British economy that added to unemployment and underemployment among the maritime workers on the waterfront and increased the call for political change and enhanced economic opportunity elsewhere.[36]

Many Americans claimed that the customs officials tried "to use the revenue laws as a cloak to set up in America a centralized authority over domestic and foreign commerce."[37] It would be an error to consider these attitudes concerning the customs mere expressions of colonial pique. The new rules were so burdensome that they could not feasibly be followed. Many seaside towns had no customs facilities. Gloucester, for example, was a trading port of some size, but it did not have a single customs office. Obeying the new law required that a trading vessel from downeast Maine travel many miles off its course to stop at Salem or Boston to clear the customs before beginning its voyage to Europe.[38]

Among its provisions the Townshend Act established an American board of customs commissioners to be located in Boston so as to provide closer control of the revenue service. The greatly enlarged customs bureaucracy annoyed the Bostonians, and when the board composed of five commissioners arrived on November 5, 1767, they were met by protests and jeering crowds.[39] A Patriot pamphlet referred to the officials as "miscreants, blood suckers, whores, and Cossacks."[40] The board took fright expecting that there would be an outbreak of violence directed at themselves. They petitioned Governor Bernard for troops to protect them, but he proved a politically timid man and refused to call in the redcoats. The board then requested help from the Royal Navy in the form of a letter to Commodore Samuel Hood, who had taken over command of the North American Squadron in July 1767. Hood responded with his own 50-gun flagship, *Romney*, Capt. John Corner commanding, attended by the sloop-of-war *Beaver*.[41]

Corner, who arrived in Boston in May 1768, was ordered by Hood to anchor his vessel where it would provide the most aid to the governor and the customs officials, but he was to limit his activities to "the water." Nonetheless, Corner immediately began impressing seamen from merchant vessels entering the harbor. The Massachusetts General Court protested *Romney*'s presence and declared the impressment of seamen in peacetime illegal. Lieutenant Governor Thomas Hutchinson, a noted Tory sympathizer acting in place of Bernard, proffered his opinion that impressment was legal throughout the empire at any time, but even he found Corner's actions ill-advised in light of the tenuous peace that was holding in the city.[42]

On June 10, 1768, the commissioners seized the sloop *Liberty* belonging to John Hancock for a technical violation of the customs. Hancock, a respected merchant, was also thought to be a notorious smuggler. When his sloop was seized a supposedly spontaneous riot broke out among the people of Boston in his support. The mob was probably incited by Samuel Adams, who, it was thought, could organize a riot among his mob of followers on a moment's notice. The houses of the commissioners were ransacked, and they and their immediate subordinates took refuge aboard *Romney*. Corner reported that the town was in an ugly mood and that he anticipated additional trouble.[43]

Meanwhile, Lord Hillsborough, the Colonial Secretary, had dispatched four regiments of regulars to Boston, the first redcoats deployed to the colonies in peacetime. Their presence was intended to intimidate the colonists and to suppress dissent. On October 1, 1768, the troop transports arrived escorted by a small naval squadron led by Capt. James Smith. Commodore Hood thereafter arrived at Boston to judge the situation for himself. Finding the spirit of opposition among the colonials as high as ever he decided to post at Boston HMS *Hussar (28)*, the frigate which had escorted the troop transports, and HMS *Rippon (60)*, the man-of-war that had recently transported Governor Lord Botetcourt from London to Virginia. The board of commissions consented to remain in Boston only because of the presence of the warships in the harbor. Ironically, the warships had little effect on the radicals ashore largely because almost no one in Boston thought they would actually fire on the city.[44]

Fearing open rebellion, Hood now changed the focus of his operations from Halifax to Boston in order to stay on top of the potentially explosive situation. Colonel James Dalrymple, the British regimental commander noted, "I don't suppose my men are without fault but twenty of them have been knocked down in the streets [of Boston] . . . and no more has been heard of it, whereas if one of the inhabitants meets with no more than just a kick for an insult to a soldier, the town is immediately in an alarm." Hood immediately began to lose forty to fifty seamen per month to desertion, and he blamed the increase on the Boston radicals who would try to persuade the Jack-tars and redcoats to desert by offering them money for their arms and equipment.[45]

Subsequently, Ebenezer Richardson, a customs official and friend of Lt. Governor Hutchinson, inadvertently killed a young Bostonian, eleven-year-old Christopher Snider, during a protest on February 20, 1770. Hutchinson allowed Richardson to avoid immediate prosecution by claiming self-defense. The Boston radicals were outraged. They vowed to prosecute the official for murder and robbery, and to wipe out the entire system of customs houses and customs officials. Unfortunately, the colonists, mistaking British restraint for undisputable license, came to believe that they could harass the troops with impunity. Two weeks after the death of Snider, on March 5, 1770, a group of radicals carrying clubs headed by a free African-American named Crispus Attucks confronted a squad of soldiers near the customs house. The British soldiers, frightened by the threats and taunts of the mob, opened fire at point-blank range. Attucks and two others were killed instantly and two more men were mortally wounded. Two of those who died were mariners and one was a ropemaker.[46]

The Patriots in Boston labeled the incident a massacre and demanded the arrest of the soldiers and their commander, Capt. Thomas Preston. Consequently, the soldiers were confined, but no one could be found to act in their defense at trial. Finally, John Adams and Josiah Quincy of Braintree, Massachusetts, provided a defense sufficient to acquit Preston and all of his men of murder, save two who were convicted of manslaughter and branded upon the thumb as a punishment. Thereafter, Hutchinson prudently withdrew the troops from the city streets to an island garrison in the harbor and the town became relatively quiet.

Politically a Whig, Hood mirrored the position of his party in London with regard to the colonies. Although he privately questioned who was responsible for the massacre, Hood immediately offered Hutchinson his full cooperation and the support of his squadron. HM sloop *Beaver (14)* and HM sloop *Senegal (14)* were called back to Boston from their recent postings to New Hampshire and Rhode Island, respectively, to support the larger and less maneuverable warships of the fleet. Near the end of his tenure as commander of the North American Squadron, Hood warmed somewhat to the people of Boston. He turned over the squadron to James Gambier, his senior captain, who would hold the position until permanently relieved by Rear Adm. John Montagu. Hood had served as the squadron commander from July 1767 until October 1770, an extremely contentious period in American history.

According to some historians, John Montagu should head the list of naval officers responsible for the outbreak of the revolution because he constantly characterized the Americans as rascals, smugglers, and disaffected rebels. Yet every previous commander of the North American Squadron had sent home similar, if less exaggerated, reports. Possibly Montagu became a natural target for colonial ire because the *Gaspee* incident, the Boston Tea Party, and the closing of the port of Boston all happened on his watch. Events made his tenure a very trying time, but the nature of his personality seems to have made things worse. John Adams considered the admiral coarse, low, and vulgar. Adams wrote, "His brutish manners are a disgrace to the royal navy and to the King's service."[47] Moreover, Montagu was openly opposed to any form of conciliation with the colonials believing that intimidation rather than cooperation should be the primary tool for maintaining the order of the empire. "They are almost ripe for independence," wrote Montagu to the Admiralty, "and nothing but the ships prevents their going to greater lengths."[48]

THE BURNING OF *GASPEE*

One of the loudest complaints made by the residents of Rhode Island in 1772 was against the commander of the cutter *Gaspee*, Lt. William Dudingston. He was stopping and searching all shipping in Narragansett Bay including rowboats, which did not have papers to produce and were not required to have them when moving goods within the bounds of the colony. It seems certain that his activities were a pure form of harassment rather than an overzealous enforcement of the regulations. The colonial newspapers called Dudingston "cowardly and insolent" and a "disgrace to his commission."[49]

In 1772 *Gaspee* intercepted the colonial packet *Hannah*, Benjamin Lindsay (Master). Lindsay, inbound to Providence from New York, refused to heave to and have his papers examined. Annoyed by Dudingston's arrogant and officious manner, he took advantage of a fresh wind, an ebb tide, and the shallow draft of his own vessel to avoid the cutter, which made chase for more than twenty miles before running fast aground on a sandbar off Namquit Point. A frustrated Dudingston sat aboard the stranded 102-ton cutter, waiting for the flood tide to float it off as the *Hannah* sailed safely away.[50]

Lindsay continued on to Providence seven miles away where word spread of the cutter's predicament. Eight whaleboats under the direction of captains Abraham Whipple, Simeon Potter, and John Brown were launched, each filled with vengeful colonists armed with staves, stones, and a few firearms. In the dead of night, the colonials overwhelmed the crew of the *Gaspee*, and burned the vessel to the waterline. Dudingston, who was wounded by a single shot through his arm and into his groin during the encounter, was arrested on a specious charge, fined by a local magistrate, and held in jail by the local sheriff until his superior officer paid his fine. The British government was outraged by the burning of its vessel and the detention and wounding of its officer, but a Royal Navy investigation failed to make any recommendations for avoiding similar events in the future.

The burning of *Gaspee* serves to highlight the deteriorated state of central control and the ambiguous nature of authority that came to characterize colonial government in this period. Commissioners from New York, New Jersey, and Massachusetts were appointed to inquire into the case in 1773, but there was so much open animosity shown for them that the body was dissolved when no witnesses were forthcoming. However, it still remains unclear why so many colonials should have so quickly taken advantage of this particular opportunity to express their resentment toward the Royal Navy. The Rhode Islanders gained nothing from the burning. In fact, enforcement of the law over the next two years became even more vigorous. Dudingston, having recovered from his wound, was acquitted for losing his command at a court martial, promoted to Post-Captain, and survived the war to enjoy his half-pay navy pension.

THE BOSTON TEA PARTY

Although the government rescinded all the other Townshend duties, it hoped to reaffirm the right of Parliament to tax the colonies as Americans submitted to the payment of the duty on the tea for the sake of their pocketbooks. Parliament passed the Tea Act in 1773. Its ostensible purpose was to grant the East India Company a monopoly on the sale of tea, but its hidden purpose was to maintain the 3-penny tax on every pound that had been in effect for almost six years.[51] Benjamin Franklin noted, "The British Ministry have no idea that any people can act from any other principle but that of [self-]interest, and they believe that three pence in a pound of tea, of which one does perhaps drink ten pounds in a year is sufficient to overcome all the patriotism of an American."[52] While the dedication of Americans to tea drinking may have been overestimated by the ministry, it is safe to say that tea leaves had certainly become a symbol for deeper grievances than a mere dispute over taxing beverages.

Parliament authorized the shipment of half a million pounds of tea to the colonies and demanded that the tax be paid by the importers when the cargo was landed. On the night of December 16, 1773, as many as 8,000 people massed to listen to a speech given by Samuel Adams, which targeted the tea on ships in the harbor as a symbol of British tyranny. After the speech a group of men, loosely disguised as Mohawk Indians, joined the crowd. They boarded one of the three East Indiamen in the harbor and threw 350 chests of tea into the water. The demonstration, which was anything but spontaneous, has come to be known as the "Boston Tea Party."

Once again London was outraged, but this time the ministry responded with a series of retaliatory bills. The first that passed Parliament was the Boston Port Act, which closed the entire port as a punishment and as a warning to the other colonies. On May 13, 1774, HMS *Lively* arrived in

The Boston Tea Party is possibly the best known event of the period before the outbreak of war. Yet New York held its own tea party on the city's wharf some time later, and other tea ships sent to other colonies were turned away at the entrance to their destined ports. Many of the stockholders of the company were high government officials, which may help to explain the intensity of the government's response.

Boston with copies of the Port Act and a new military governor for the colony of Massachusetts, Lt. Gen. William Gage. It was Admiral Montagu that initiated the blockade of the port, and he quickly became one of the most disliked men in America. One month later Montagu, himself, was relieved by Vice Adm. Samuel Graves.

From town meetings and provincial congresses throughout America came words of support for the Bostonians. Among those who exhibited a common cause with them were the people who made their living from the sea. Fishermen, mariners, shippers, shipbuilders, and ship chandlers quickly recognized that their livelihoods could be cut off just as easily in Newburyport, Portsmouth, or Providence as they were in Boston. Those who made their living afloat in Philadelphia, New York, Baltimore, or Charleston could just as quickly be barred from the sea as those in New England.[53] From every quarter came resolves to scorn the British actions. Besides moral support, aid in the form of money and food flooded into Boston, and a call went out for a great congress of colonial representatives to be held. Many colonists loyal to the Crown declared the country to be in a state of rebellion from this time.[54]

SUMMARY

The role played by the Royal Navy in bringing about the American Revolution is controversial and difficult to assess. Obviously the shooting war began as a land engagement, but it is clear that many of the major points of contention between the rebels and the government had nautical matters at their core. Yet no rational theory has come forth showing that the Revolution could have been avoided had the Royal Navy only been more or less vigilant in enforcing the customs. The sea officers of the Royal Navy were simply caught up in an effort to uphold a series of bad policies set by a group of unremitting politicians 3,000 miles away.[55]

Purely as a revenue measure, the Sugar Act of 1764 was the only colonial tax passed by Parliament before 1775 that was successful, and that success must be credited to the Royal Navy. It easily outstripped the customs service in terms of the efficiency of its enforcement. While the navy had the law on its side, its officers, by their actions and attitudes, undoubtedly helped to make colonial protestors into American Patriots every time they came within sight of land. The Royal Navy's continued dependence on the mainland for provisions, especially drinking water, complicated its efforts at enforcement. With the increasing rancor of the political rhetoric, these sources of supply were no longer deemed secure, creating shortages that also affected the king's troops. In response the navy started stripping New England's coastal islands of livestock, ransacking shoreside farms for produce and forage, and seizing coasting vessels carrying provisions and merchandise. The navy became so embroiled in this escalating struggle that many coastal communities considered that they had been under attack well before April 1775.[56]

In 1773 Benjamin Franklin described the nature of the enforcement problem and its consequences in a piece entitled *Rules by Which a Great Empire May be Reduced to a Small One*. Herein he paints a picture of Gestapo-like tactics better attributed to a repressive and despotic tyranny than a society of free citizens living under a constitutional monarchy, a theme echoed by many radical publications of the period.

Convert the brave, honest officers of your navy into pimping tide-waiters and colony officers of the customs. Let those who in the time of war fought gallantly in defense of their countrymen, in peace be taught to prey upon it. Let them learn to be corrupted by great and real smugglers; but (to show their diligence) scour with armed boats every bay, harbor, river, creek, cove, or nook throughout your colonies; stop and detain every coaster, every wood-boat, every fisherman; tumble their cargoes and even their ballast inside out and upside down; and, if a pennyworth of [dressmakers'] pins is found unentered [on the cargo manifest], let the whole be seized and confiscated. Thus shall the trade of your colonists suffer more from their friends in time of peace than it did from their enemies in war. . . . Oh, this will work admirably![57]

Parliamentary Governments of Britain

From 1760 to 1782 the British government went through seven prime ministers. The almost constant change in leadership disappointed and polarized Parliament, and the apparent weakness of each prime minister left them subject to political challenge. Only one of these prime ministers was a Tory, and he remained in office less than two years. Party designations with regard to policy in Britain often proved complex and ambiguous because the Whigs were divided into two warring camps. Only their mutual hatred of the Tories allowed Whig government to proceed.

Dates in Office	Prime Minister
1757–1762	Thomas Pelham, Duke of Newcastle
1762–1763	John Stuart, Earl of Bute[a]
1763–1765	George Lord Grenville
1765–1766	Charles Watson-Wentworth, Marquis of Rockingham
1766–1768	William Pitt (the Elder), Earl of Chatham
1768–1770	Augustus Henry Fitzroy, Duke of Grafton
1770–1782	Frederick Lord North
1782	Marquis of Rockingham[b]

[a] The only Tory administration of the period.
[b] Rockingham's second administration lasted six months and was replaced by a coalition government.

2

The Rebels Under Sail

These people show a spirit and conduct against us they never showed
against the French, and everyone has judged of them from their former
appearance and behavior...which has led many into great mistakes.
                                            —a British officer, 1775

Almost all the people of Parts and Spirit are in the rebellion.
                                            —Adm. Lord Richard Howe

Beyond the general characteristics that distinguished them from one
another in 1775, both sides in the American war did almost everything
wrong during their initial encounters at sea. Certainly the Americans had
never before waged a naval war, but it must be remembered that the
British also had never attempted to suppress a widespread colonial rebellion through the concentrated application of their sea power. American
skippers displayed an arrogant self-confidence and excessive focus on
prize money throughout the conflict, and their British counterparts
evinced an overabundance of conceit and a meaningless dedication to
protocol. Moreover, both generally failed to learn quickly how to adapt
their tactics and strategies to the circumstances of a rebellion fought at
sea.

It took about a month after the outbreak of hostilities for Adm.
Samuel Graves to order that Royal Navy vessels forcibly seize their provi-
sions from American ports, but individual British sea officers like Capt.
James Wallace of HMS *Rose* had acted more promptly. His raids on the

islands in Narragansett Bay began as early as April 27, 1775, only one week after the fighting at Lexington and Concord. Wallace also acted on his own authority when firing upon the towns of Stonington, Connecticut, and Bristol, Rhode Island. A Patriot witness of the October 7, 1775, attack on Bristol noted the effect of the surprise attack by the frigates *Rose*, *Glasgow*, and *Swan*. "The night was dark and rainy and people were in terror and confusion. For an hour 120 cannon and cascades [mortars firing incendiary rounds] were discharged upon us, [and] kept up a constant fire on the people." A formal policy of bombarding towns into submission appears to have begun as early as September 1775, but its application was not ratcheted up until after 1779 in response to the French alliance.[1]

During the course of the war British vessels bombarded or burned every colonial seaport of appreciable size with the exception of Baltimore and Salem. Besides creating a good deal of local terror, the bombardments had little positive effect on the British war effort. The policy served better for the Patriots as anti-government propaganda than for the British as a means of cowing the public. By generally steeling the determination of the rebels to resist, the bombardments utterly failed to meet the expectations of the strategic planners in London. Word of the fate of Falmouth, for instance, arrived at a critical juncture in the deliberations of Congress and actually insured the establishment of an American navy by the otherwise uncertain delegates.[2]

MACHIAS LIBERTY

The honor of who struck the first successful blow against the Royal Navy has never been definitively determined, but there are several likely candidates. On May 27, 1775, a group of American whaleboats struck at British shipping in Boston Harbor, and burned a Royal Navy vessel, *Diana (4)*, that had run aground. This raid was certainly the first aggressive act taken by Americans afloat. In June 1775, Abraham Whipple of Rhode Island put out into Narragansett Bay in the sloop *Katy (10)* fitted out by the state of Rhode Island. His opponent, Wallace of the *Rose (20)*, was the senior British naval officer in the area commanding two 20-gun frigates, an armed sloop, a brig, and several armed tenders. In company with the row galleys *Washington* and *Spitfire*, Whipple ran a British tender aground on Conanicut Island. Wallace could do nothing to prevent the grounding of its consort. Also in June, the armed sloop *Commerce* of South Carolina with twenty-six men under Lieutenant Clement Lemprierre stopped and ransacked a Royal Navy supply vessel in Florida, stripping it of more than 100 barrels of gunpowder (6 tons) within sight of its armed escort, which was prevented from interfering by a large sand bar at the mouth of St. Augustine harbor. These episodes are often identified by historians as the first official naval acts of war committed by any of the colonies, but they hardly rate as a traditional naval engagement.

The most significant early clash between the rebellious colonials and the Royal Navy took place in August 1775 in Machias, a small town in Maine on the Machias River, then the eastern district of Massachusetts. If this affair was not the first naval battle of the Revolution, it should have been. It has all the characteristics and drama of a popular uprising against tyranny.

The Royal Navy cutter *Margaretta (4)*, commanded by Midshipman James Moore, was sent to convoy the cargo vessels *Unity* and *Polly* with a load of timber to Boston. Moore fully anticipated that he would meet with local resistance. His intuition was confirmed when he was greeted by a "liberty pole" set prominently on the wharf. Many of the citizens, opposed to any action that might aid the British, agreed to provide the timber only because the *Margaretta* was lying in the anchorage with its gun ports raised, its 3 pounders run out, and springs[3] placed on its cables in anticipation of firing on the town.[4]

The timber vessels were warped up to the wharf and loaded under the threat of Moore's guns. Initially all seemed to be going well, but some of the residents of the surrounding towns of Mispecka and Pleasant River attempted to seize Moore while he was at Sunday services ashore at Machias. Moore barely escaped by jumping into a waiting boat and pulling for the *Margaretta*. Shocked by the violent spirit of the populace, but actually loathe to fire on the town, Moore immediately raised anchor and allowed the cutter to drift further down the anchorage toward the bay. During the night irate citizens fired at the schooner from the high surrounding cliffs and endeavored to board it from boats and canoes. After beating off several attempts, Moore made it known that he would fire on the town if there were any further attacks.

On the next morning the young naval commander decided to remove his vessel from the confining waters of the inlet. In his haste to come about in a stiff breeze, the boom and gaff of the cutter were carried away. Moore pulled alongside a local sloop moored in the anchorage belonging to Captain Robert Avery and had his men strip this vessel of its spars in order to affect repairs on his own. He also impressed Avery to act as an unwilling pilot. In less than an hour *Margaretta* was under way with a jury-rigged repair.

Meanwhile the residents of Machias had decided to apprehend the limping cutter. Forty armed men led by Jeremiah O'Brien and Benjamin Foster boarded *Unity* and *Polly*, respectively, and fell to work lightening the vessels and getting away from the wharf. Foster, unfortunately, ran *Polly* aground, and he and his men took no further part in the subsequent action. O'Brien, however, quickly closed the gap between the British cutter and *Unity*, coming under Moore's stern near Round Island and demanding his surrender in the name of America. Moore refused and fired

Often considered the first sea battle of the Revolution, the lumber sloop *Unity* (right) and the Royal Navy cutter *Margaretta* entangle in Machias Inlet (Maine). The Patriot forces under Capt. Jeremiah O'Brien won the day by boarding.

his 3 pounders and several swivels into the Americans, who had taken refuge behind a barricade of timber planks erected on the deck. *Unity*'s sails and rigging were cut up somewhat, but this did not diminish the return fire of its musket men, who killed the British helmsman with a single ball to the head. The Americans then closed with Moore's vessel, and, by running close enough alongside to entangle the rigging and lash the vessels together, they made a concerted attempt to board in the face of *Margaretta*'s file of Royal Marines. The British made a bayonet charge, and Moore himself was seen to throw several hand grenades onto the deck of *Unity*. Yet the colonials rallied, leapt across the gap between the vessels, and with clubbed muskets, axes, and swords drove the British below decks.

The *Margaretta* was taken with heavy losses on both sides. Moore was mortally wounded with a ball to the chest and another to the stomach. He died after two agonizing days ashore. Of the British compliment of approximately thirty, eight marines and sailors were killed. Among the two dozen Americans involved in the actual combat, three died and a dozen were wounded besides the luckless Capt. Avery, who was killed in the crossfire.

O'Brien decided to transfer the cannon from *Margaretta* to *Polly*, which he renamed *Machias Liberty*. Some accounts say that it was to *Unity* that the guns were transferred, but recent scholarship suggests otherwise.[5] Scarcely was the transfer completed when two British vessels appeared in the harbor. The armed cutter *Diligent (8)*, and its tender *Tattamagouche*, on a hydrographic mission for the Admiralty, were surrendered without a fight when the commander of the expedition was captured as he rowed ashore totally unaware of the outbreak of hostilities. Capt. Foster was thereafter placed in command of *Diligent*, and the two armed American vessels established themselves as sentinels over the harbor. In a single stroke the colony of Massachusetts had gained for itself the nucleus of a tiny navy.

Despite the cost in lives, the victory at Machias was momentous. A vessel of war of the Royal Navy, albeit a tiny one, had fallen to the Americans in pitched battle and two others had been forced to surrender by a group of disgruntled citizens in an armed lumber sloop. The myth of British invincibility afloat had been dispelled. More to the point, this episode helped to cement in the minds of many Americans the fiction that successful resistance to the might of the Royal Navy was possible.[6]

OTHER FIRSTS

As has been noted, a group of American whaleboats struck in Boston Harbor in May 1775. Ironically their initial objective was a herd of hogs on Noodle Island in the bay rather than the vessels of the Royal Navy. Adm. Samuel Graves, made aware of the raid by the burning of the hay stacks on the island, ordered out the Royal Marines in longboats from the fleet to intercept the rebels. Unfortunately for the marines, the whaleboats were generally swifter than the longboats even when loaded with squealing pigs. The Royal Navy schooner *Diana*, commanded by one of the Admiral's nephews, Lt. Thomas Graves, attempted to cut off the American line of retreat, but it ran aground. The rebels quickly turned on the stranded vessel, swarmed aboard, and killed or captured the crew. Having removed the schooner's 4-6 pounders and some other weapons, the whaleboat men set *Diana* afire.

The admiral's lack of an active response to these events was remarkable. He planned no strategy to deal with the whaleboats other than to rig a series of floating booms at some distance around his warships to prevent them from being overwhelmed while at anchor.[7] Nor did he attempt to secure any of the remaining supplies on the islands. However, he did find time to write a scathing indictment of the British Army commander, General Gage, and to pen a defense of his nephew to the Admiralty. "[I can] assure their lordships of the perseverance and good conduct of Lieut. Graves, the commander of the *Diana* in this action."[8]

British Gen. John Burgoyne responded to Graves' lack of activity, "He is not defending his own flocks and herds, for the enemy has repeatedly and in a most insulting manner, plundered his own appropriated islands. He is not defending the other islands in the harbor; for the enemy has landed in force, burned the lighthouse at noon day, and killed and took a party of marines almost under the guns of two or three men of war ... the King's armed vessels [are] sunk, the crews made prisoner, the officers killed.... He is [not] ... enforcing instant restitution and reparations by the voice of his cannon, and laying the towns in ashes which refuse his terms."[9]

At about this time George Washington authorized Nicholas Broughton to proceed to the port of Beverly, Massachusetts, where he was to take command of the *Hannah*, a schooner fitted out with a few small cannon as a vessel of war. This was the first of eight small vessels that ultimately formed "George Washington's Navy." Each vessel sailed under a white ensign bearing a green pine tree with the words "An Appeal to Heaven" inscribed below it. The *Hannah* is generally considered the first "warship" of the American Navy, and Broughton the first Continental sea officer.[10]

In November 1775 John Manly, Washington's finest captain, intercepted a British storeship that had become separated from its convoy, and made the first major contribution of the navy to the war effort. The *Nancy* disgorged a stockpile of military stores including 100,000 flints, 2,000 muskets, and a 13-inch mortar—"the finest piece of ordnance ever landed in America."[11] Samuel Graves wrote: "It is much to be lamented that a cargo of such consequence should be sent from England in a vessel destitute of arms even so to protect her from a rowboat."[12]

In quick succession thereafter supplies and arms were also taken from the British store ship *Concord* and from four lightly armed troop ships (*Anne, George, Lord Howe*, and *Annabella*) carrying almost 400 Scotch Highlanders destined for service in America. The *London Chronicle* reported that the ships were taken "within sight of the fleet in Boston."[13] Of thirty-six store ships and troop transports dispatched to New England during 1775, only eighteen arrived safely.[14] Although most turned back or were blown off course to Nova Scotia, British Adm. Molyneaux Shuldham wrote: "However numerous our cruisers may be or however attentive our Officers to their Duty, it has been found impossible to prevent some of our ordnance and other valuable stores, in small vessels, falling into the hands of the Rebels."[15]

While the actions of Royal Navy officers like Wallace, Moore, and Graves can be seen as extensions of the pseudo-naval war over smuggling, the offensive attacks by Whipple, Lempierre, Foster, O'Brien, Manly, and scores of unnamed whaleboat men were as audacious as they were unexpected. Notwithstanding academic arguments over the credit for the first blow struck, the seamen of the Royal Navy were learning something about the grit of their colonial cousins, and the Americans were discovering something more of themselves.

THE CONTINENTAL NAVY

In August 1775 the King had opined that "though brave ashore, the Continental forces fear the sea." His view of the situation would be proven wrong as soon as the reports from New England crossed the Atlantic. Americans looked upon their successes afloat with awe, and they rejoiced at each unexpected victory. Celebrations were held in the streets, and illuminations and bonfires in town squares accompanied speeches of praise for the intrepid sailors who had thus faced down the might of the Royal Navy. Congress, elated by these early successes, quickly appropriated $100,000 to buy several merchantmen to be immediately converted into warships. Among these was the *Alfred (24)* the first flagship of the Continental Navy, and its consorts *Columbus (20)*, *Cabot (14)*, *Andrew Doria (14)*, *Providence (12)*, *Hornet (10)*, *Wasp (8)*, and *Fly (8)*.[16]

Alfred and *Columbus* were each about 450 tons. Both seem to have been slow sailers, a weakness credited by some authorities to all warships converted from ship-rigged merchantmen. Brigs, brigantines, and schooners were considered somewhat more effective in their new role. *Cabot* was a good vessel taken into the Royal Navy after its capture later in the war. Admiralty records state that the 189-ton brig was approximately 75 feet on the deck and 25 feet in beam. Of *Andrew Doria* little is known beyond its being a brig. *Providence* and *Hornet* seem to have been fast sailing Bermuda sloops with sharp hulls, while there is evidence that *Wasp* and *Fly* were sharp-built Baltimore schooners.[17]

Of this initial Continental fleet of converted merchant vessels more will be said later, but Congress simultaneously authorized the building of a genuine fleet of thirteen state-of-the-art frigates of 32, 28, and 24 guns. These were no hammer and nail conversions with gunports sawn in their sides to accommodate a few popgun-sized cannon. These frigates were designed to be real warships. Those that made it to the sea proved to be formidable adversaries for vessels of their own size. In 1776 a second series of American vessels, mostly two-masted brigs and single-masted sloops and cutters, were built. Yet it seems that "[t]he limits of financing new ships by the Continental Congress had actually been reached by the Act of 1775, and very little money was left for the program established in 1776." Nonetheless, the additional Continental vessels cruised along the coast of the middle states or back and forth between Europe and the West Indies with some success. The highlights of their operations, although largely indecisive in ending the war in America's favor, make good reading for armchair admirals.[18]

A total of forty-seven major vessels served as a regular naval force during the entire course of the Revolution. These were armed with approximately 1,300 cannon plus a proportional number of swivel guns (man-killing weapons larger than a musket and too heavy to fire unsupported). A number of period documents suggest that the number of cannon in the main battery and the number of swivels deployed were approximately equal. Owing to the loss of official papers, the chaotic administration of the Continental Navy, and a general tendency for informal record-keeping during the stress and haste of war, it is difficult for historians to trace the details of these vessels.[19]

It was the Continental captains and scores of subordinate officers and seamen who carried the naval war to the most sensitive parts of the British empire. Yet the Continental Navy was never very large in terms of its available personnel. Its greatest year was 1777 when slightly more than 4,000 men were serving in its several warships. Not surprisingly the least number of seamen, approximately 600, were serving in 1775 and 1782, the first and last years of active operations. At no time did the personnel of the Continental Navy ever exceed 10 percent of that of the Continental Army. Yet it is difficult to develop accurately representative estimates of the number of men serving. Absolute figures are particularly tricky for the navy because many men signed on for a cruise rather than for a specific time while others signed for the duration of the war. Expressing naval enlistments in full-year equivalents has also proven problematic for historians. Nonetheless, if ten men per gun is assumed to include seamen, gunners, and ancillary personnel ashore, a relatively reliable table of yearly totals can be created based on the number of guns known to be deployed.

Yearly Estimates of Manpower in the Continental Navy

1775	1776	1777	1778	1779	1780	1781	1782
600	1900	4000	2800	2400	1700	1700	600

PRIVATE WARSHIPS

In the immediate aftermath of the battles of Lexington and Concord, Congress provided for an army but doubted the practical value of forming a navy. Nonetheless, enterprising Americans were not prone to miss an opportunity to profit from a little privateering. The bulk of the Patriot naval force was made up of these privately owned and financed commerce raiders that operated under commissions issued by the individual states or the Congress. Loyalists also went to sea as privateers under licenses from the Royal governors of the colonies or from the British

commander in North America. The absolute number of Loyalist privateers is in question, but it may have been as great as that of their
American counterparts. Yet they tended to prey on European and Caribbean shipping, and their effect on the outcome of the war on the North
American coast was somewhat overshadowed by the immense presence of
the Royal Navy.

The annals of armchair seamanship and fictional accounts of daring
single-ship encounters have reinforced the myth that privateers were all
inspired by patriotic motives, but in most cases simple economic self-
interest spurred these Patriots to serve by the hundreds in private warships from 1775 to 1783. So popular was privateering that the regular
navy had trouble recruiting and keeping crews. Nonetheless, as regards
the revolution it is certain that for "the first time in [American] history
the privateer system assumed approximately the shape of a marine militia
or volunteer navy."[20]

Moreover, there was great risk in serving in a Patriot privateer. There
was no guarantee that the licenses issued by the states or Congress would
protect individuals from charges of piracy, and such documents could not
legitimatize rebellion in any case. Both piracy and treason were capital
crimes. At one time or another before the alliance of 1778 American privateers were arrested as pirates in France, Spain, Holland, and several
Caribbean Islands. Strangely several privateers captured in British Jamaica
at the outbreak of the war were freed when they claimed their rights as
Englishmen under the habeas corpus provisions of the British constitution. These rights were thereafter suspended by Parliament. Throughout
the remainder of the rebellion captured Patriot sailors were held under a
bill of attainder charging them with both piracy and treason.[21]

Regardless of the risks, Americans took naturally to privateering, and
many adventurous spirits among the citizenry actually served as part of
the crew. However, most Americans unfamiliar with the sea participated
from the safety of their own homes as mere investors in privateering ventures and let the professional seamen take the risks. A great deal of
money could be realized from a single captured prize. Occasionally, a privateer would take a British merchant vessel loaded with hard-to-get
items, and a seaport might be animated by a supply of Irish lace, exotic
spices, Madera wine, or Jamaica rum for a day while the cargo was auctioned off to the highest bidder.

American shipbuilders and designers provided vessels to the fleet of private warships that were generally superior to those of the British as to
their speed and their ability to sail to windward. Yet privateers were rarely
larger than the smallest class of frigates and even a small British cutter
usually carried more guns and had a larger, better disciplined crew than
an average private cruiser. In a ship-to-ship engagement, a British warship
would simply blow most privateers out of the water or overrun its crew

by boarding with several files of exquisitely trained Royal Marines. Consequently, privateers relied upon their speed to make captures and to make good their escape from patrolling British warships. They paid for this advantage by carrying fewer guns and sacrificing what little cargo capacity they had to essential stores and extra crewmen. The usual plan was to overtake and attack unarmed or lightly armed merchant vessels; force their surrender under the threat of a broadside; and detach a few men as a prize crew who would make for a friendly American or foreign port where both ship and cargo would be condemned as a prize.

A favorite hunting ground for privateers was at the entrance to the Gulf of St. Lawrence where small fishing and trading vessels could be taken with little risk due to the fog and storms that ravaged the region. These often drove the Royal Navy vessels off their station. Another favorite spot was in the West Indies where richly laden sugar transports and rumrunners might be intercepted and brought into neutral island ports or to the southeastern Atlantic coast. However, in Caribbean waters the Patriots had to deal with the Royal Navy's West Indian Squadron based in Jamaica and among the Leeward Islands.

The failure of the Royal Navy in not stopping the privateers from attacking British commerce in American waters was overshadowed only by its equally frustrating inability to drive them from home waters in the English Channel and the Irish Sea. British newspapers were filled with stories of the recurring appearance of Patriot privateers in the eastern Atlantic. Although most of the Continental warships were driven from the sea by 1778, the depredations of the privateers in British waters—more than 100 in 1778 and more than 200 in 1779—were seemingly unaffected. A British naval historian has noted that "lacking sufficient frigates and smaller vessels to chase the agile and well-armed invaders, the Admiralty had, perforce, to supplement their patrols with ships-of-the-line [that] searched awkwardly and rarely successfully for their smaller prey. Not until 1779 were British pursuit squadrons, composed chiefly of frigates, organized to alleviate the scourge."[22]

In just the first two years of the war more than 700 British merchant vessels were libeled as prizes in American admiralty courts. The American prize total fell to a wartime low of seventy-five vessels in 1777, but the continued threat to the British economy proposed by privateers served to fuel war weariness among the population in England. The records of the Continental Congress list 1,697 privateering vessels including: 301 ships; 541 brigs and brigantines; 751 schooners and sloops; and 104 boats and galleys. Many of these were small converted vessels with light weight armament, and their apparent number may have been swelled by the duplication of records. It has been documented that there were at least 792 distinct "full-time" privateers mounting 14,872 guns. American agents in the West Indies and Europe may have issued additional commissions swelling the number of Patriot privateers to 2,000 carrying 18,000 guns. The absolute number of private commerce raiders deployed in any complete single year of the war never fell below sixty-nine individual vessels (1776), and in 1781 there were more than 500. Many cruisers operated throughout the entire eight years of the war. Several states issued commissions to privateers—New Hampshire, Rhode Island, Connecticut, Maryland, and South Carolina among them. Massachusetts alone may have sent out more than 1,000 vessels under its own authority, and more than 600 have been identified that carried Continental papers as well. Oddly New York, under British control for most of the war, is credited with only one state-licensed rebel privateer.[23]

Unfortunately, the successes of the citizen soldier on land and the citizen sailor at sea took on an importance of legendary proportion in future American thinking that blocked out the realities of just how they were accomplished. Privateers flourished only on the fringes of the naval war and kept to sea only as long as they were profitable to their owners. *Holker* (Blair McClenachan), and *General Pickering* (Jonathan Haraden), consistently brought in rich cargoes and valuable prizes. In 1780 *General Pickering (14)* took the British privateer *Golden Eagle (22)* in a monumental battle off the coast of Spain, and then fought off the British privateer *Achilles (42)* for three hours in the harbor entrance to Bilboa while protecting its prize. "Ashore, the Spaniards emptied their wineskins and shouted themselves speechless" while watching the battle. Eventually, Haraden passed safely into the port with his prize intact.[24]

Benjamin Franklin put a high bounty on live captives so that he might have prisoners to exchange for captured American seamen. The success of *Argo* (Silas Talbot) against several armed British privateers demonstrated that the rebels would attack their counterparts if they were offered, besides full rights to any prizes, bounties for the number of cannon captured and the number of live prisoners taken. Talbot collected a great deal of this "head money." *Black Prince, Black Princess*, and *Fearnot*, all privateers sent out by Franklin from France, were specifically charged to bring in prisoners. When his captains—recruited from among Irish smugglers—began ransoming captured men at sea, Franklin let his displeasure be known in scathing recriminations and heart-rending pleas that his captains remember the cruel plight of their fellows held in captivity. From 1776 to 1783 at least 11,000 Patriot seamen died while being held prisoner.[25]

The Continental Navy captured fewer than 200 British vessels worth approximately $6 million. American privateers captured prizes valued at $18 million. Most authorities believe that this is a low estimate with $66 million being a more accurate figure.[26] The figure quoted before the House of Lords in 1778 by William Creighton was an incredible £200 million. This represented 733 merchant vessels lost to the Americans since the opening of the war including a dozen incredibly valuable sugar transports. Although 39 percent of all prizes were recaptured by the Royal Navy or Loyalist privateers, Lloyd's of London listed 2,208 vessels successfully libeled by rebel captors in American or European ports from 1775 to 1783. One of these ships was worth $1 million, but the average value of a prize rests at about $30,000. The real value of these captures, in undepreciated currency such as the Spanish dollar, simply can not be accurately estimated.[27]

Fitting out a privateer was an expensive venture, and those vessels that did not return value for investment were often left in the anchorage or converted to speedy merchandise carriers. Moreover, privateers denied valuable materials, seamen, and officers to the Continental and state navies. Although the owners of private warships encountered the same difficulties in building and fitting their vessels, the strain they placed upon the formal navies in terms of acquiring personnel from among the maritime population was remarkable. Seamen were much more likely to sign for a profitable cruise that might last three weeks than to enlist for a calendar term aboard a warship. Estimates of between 58,000 and 70,000 sailors serving on privateers have been made; but, once again, many of these records are duplications with the same man serving in a number of vessels. Yet when Continental captains attempted to draw seamen from privateers to fill their crews, the Navy Board of Congress required that the men be returned.

Some privateering cruisers were formidable warships, carrying 150 crewmen and upwards of 20 guns. The initial development of these larger privateers is generally credited to Elias Hasket Derby of Salem. Derby set out to create a new type of vessel designed for the service. He carefully computed the sail areas, hull form, and armament so that the privateer could fight off a British sloop-of-war and still be swift enough to run from larger ships. His work led to an entirely new class of topsail schooner that was copied by American shipbuilders throughout the war. Many of these cruisers operated throughout the entire eight years of the war capturing British shipping and defeating in single combat several similarly sized vessels belonging to the Royal Navy. Although the extant records are incomplete or contradictory, the Patriot privateers are normally credited with the capture of eight or nine small Royal Navy vessels of war.[28]

Of course the warships of the Continental Navy had some obligation to stand their ground and make a fight, while the privateers were free to choose their battles. This fact alone made the privateersmen seem more effective than the Continentals. Nonetheless, the Continental captains were constantly challenging the perception of British naval supremacy. In 1777 Lambert Wickes in *Reprisal* sent so much captured British shipping into French ports as prizes that he created a diplomatic crisis between the two kingdoms. In 1778 John Barry in *Alliance (32)* captured five valuable ships of the sugar fleet sailing from Jamaica in a single operation, which set the sugar factors in Britain squealing.

SALUTING THE FLAG

In 1775 and 1776 respectively, Americans sailed under a white "An Appeal to Heaven" banner or a fine yellow flag emblazoned with a thirteen segment serpent and inscribed with "Don't Tread On Me." However, these flags were not national ensigns. On November 16, 1776, Capt. Isaiah Robinson approached the Dutch island of St. Eustatius in the eastern Caribbean in the Continental warship *Andrew Doria*.[29] As he entered the port, Robinson broke out an American ensign styled in red, white, and blue. As was the custom when a friendly ship entered a foreign port, Robinson had the guns of the *Andrew Doria* fire a salute, which recognized the sovereignty of the Dutch government.

The governor of the island, Johannes de Graaf, was accustomed to seeing American vessels in his port. St. Eustatius had been a source of aid for the American rebels for many months, and its wharfs and storehouse entertained a brisk business in arms, munitions, and other warlike stores. However, never before had an American ship broken out a distinct set of national colors. De Graaf, who knew of the signing of the Declaration of Independence, resolved after several minutes of consultation with his advisors to answer the salute with one of his own. As the guns of Fort Orange at the entrance to the harbor barked out a response, Captain Robinson understood that the diplomatic status of the United States as an independent nation had for the first time been recognized by an official act of a foreign power.[30]

The flag that received the salute was not really new. It was identical to the Flag of Union sewn by Philadelphia milliner, Margaret Manny. With thirteen red and white stripes, the Flag of Union had the crosses of St. George and St. Andrew in the corner, much like the all red British naval ensign with its Union Jack in the upper quarter. Margaret Manny's first flag, made of more than 45 yards of cloth, had been raised on board the flagship *Alfred* by John Paul Jones in January 1776. Manny's design was the first approved by Congress, and it was identical to the flag flown by Washington at the siege of Boston. The more famous Betsy Ross flag of thirteen stripes and a circle of thirteen stars on a blue quarter would not be recognized by Congress until 1777. Other flags with red and white stripes sported a wide variety of patterns of thirteen stars on a blue field including a very common 3-2-3-2-3 horizontal arrangement.

3

Naval Administration

If the Continent should fit out a heavy ship or two and increase them
as circumstances shall admit, the Colonies' large privateers, and individuals' small ones, surely we may soon expect to see the coast clear
of [British] cutters.

—Elbridge Gerry, October 1775[1]

I . . . who have never thought much of old ocean, or the dominion of
it . . . am to inquire what seamen may be found in our province, who
would probably enlist in the service, either as marines, or on board
of armed vessels, in the pay of the Continent, or in the pay of the
Province, or on board of privateers fitted out by private adventurers.

—John Adams, November 5, 1775[2]

THE NATURE OF ADMIRALTY

On October 30, 1775, the Congress in Philadelphia committed itself to a
policy of maintaining a naval arm to contend with the British. The effort
was never very large when compared to the size of European fleets. Yet the
colonials were able to put forth a respectable effort at sea over the course of
eight years of war by combining elements of its national fleet, warships
from its several state navies, and hundreds of privateers. This tripartite organization sustained a threat on the high seas with each vessel diverting the
attention of the Royal Navy somewhat from other important tasks.[3]

The patchwork American naval presence was governed and authorized by a hodgepodge of congressional, state, and local agencies. The Massachusetts Assembly was the first to authorize privateers (November 1775). Although the colony had established a small naval force to protect its merchant vessels during the Seven Years War, Massachusetts provided no logistical support, state munitions, or public funding to its privateers. Commerce raiding was not authorized by Congress until March 23, 1776; yet a small number of public cruisers supported by congressional authority were at sea prior to this decision. These were not strictly speaking a part of the Continental Navy serving more like Washington's schooners or the privateers licensed and fitted out in France, Holland, or the West Indies. Unraveling the duplications and deducting both the unlicensed armed boats and freelance commerce raiders that were reported represents a fruitless academic exercise. Despite these exceptions, it is safe to say that most privateers received their authority through the individual states.[4]

STATE NAVIES

During the course of the war all but two of the states formed their own naval arms.[5] State navies seemingly favored vessels carrying 18 to 20 guns. They were big enough to have real firepower but light enough to have some speed. Moreover, they were relatively inexpensive in terms of building, manning, and the cost of long-term operation. Many of the generally parsimonious colonial assemblies also took the overly optimistic view that vessels of this size could be easily converted into useful merchantmen after the war, thereby recouping much of their initial cost to the citizenry.

The Rhode Island Assembly was the first to form a state navy in an attempt to drive HMS *Rose (20)* from Narragansett Bay. The state's force at that time was composed of just two row galleys and one ocean-going vessel (June 15, 1775), the *Katy (10)*, which was later taken into the Continental service as *Providence (12)*. The tiny state ultimately deployed a total of four sloops and three row galleys for which researchers can find definite documentary evidence. *Providence* was one of the most fortunate of American naval vessels. A member of the first Continental fleet *Providence* had a successful Continental career under John Paul Jones during which sixteen prizes were taken. Thereafter it was sent back to the Rhode Island State Navy and placed under the command of Hoysted Hacker, who left the sloop bottled up by the British fleet in Newport in 1777. The vessel's next commander, John Peck Rathbun, escaped the Royal Navy blockade, and after provisioning at Charleston, South Carolina, he made a successful solo attack on Nassau in January 1778. In 1779, once again under Hacker, *Providence* captured HM brig *Diligent (12)* off

Newfoundland. This was considered an important naval encounter between vessels of equal weight and a timely victory for the Americans. The sloop won at least forty sea battles, but it ended its career on a sad note being burned by its crew at Penobscot Bay, Maine. Today a fine, full-size sailing replica of *Providence* can be found anchored in the waters of the Rhode Island city of the same name.

Massachusetts (and its eastern province of Maine) deployed fifteen ocean-going state warships in New England waters. The biggest was the frigate *Protector (28)* built in late 1779. Little is known of its measurements, and no known portrait of it exists. On its first cruise, under Capt. John Foster Williams, *Protector* enraged the 32-gun Loyalist privateer *Admiral Duff* in a long and furious fight that left both ships badly cut up. The *Admiral Duff* sank out from under its determined crew during the fight. *Protector* could rescue only fifty-five of the British crew before setting course for home. On the way, the American frigate was chased by HMS *Thames (32)*, and considering its battered state, it made a fortunate escape after a chase of several hours. Midshipman Edward Preble, noted for his later service in United States naval history, served aboard *Protector* at this time. In May 1781, *Protector* was captured by HMS *Roebuck (44)* and HMS *Medea (24)*. The warship was taken into the Royal Navy as HMS *Hussar (28)* and remained active on the Admiralty lists until 1783.

Almost all of Connecticut's shoreline was protected by extensive marshes, but it was flanked across the sound by British-held Long Island. The marshes made major naval operations along the Connecticut coast difficult for the Royal Navy, but it proved a very active region for whaleboat warfare. Nonetheless, Connecticut launched ten state vessels of which three were row galleys that cruised the Long Island Sound. The largest and best documented Connecticut warship was the *Oliver Cromwell (18)*, armed with 9 pounders and considered a corvette. The French used the term *corvette* to describe a ship-rigged frigate of very small size. The Connecticut brigantine *Defense (14)* played an important role in capturing British troop transports near Boston in March 1776. On April 15, 1778, the pair fought a fierce battle with the Loyalist privateers *Cyrus (16)* and *Admiral Keppel (18)*, the latter of which was carrying the Royal Governor of Jamaica, Henry Shirley. Both British vessels were captured. In 1779 *Oliver Cromwell* was captured by *Daphne (20)* and *Delaware (20)*. It was brought as a prize into New York, sold as a Loyalist privateer, and fittingly renamed *Restoration* by its new Tory owners.

New Hampshire built one 22-gun state brig, *Hampden*, that saw action for only one year (1778 to 1779). *Hampden* may have had lines similar to the famous Continental sloop-of-war *Ranger*, which was built in the same shipyard. Under the command of Thomas Pickering, the brig made a successful cruise in European waters sending in four valuable prizes.

On the way home to Portsmouth, *Hampden* encountered an unidentified British privateer said to be of about 30 guns. The two battered each other for several hours. Ultimately, Pickering was killed and his first officer broke off the fight reporting that his opponent had been totally disabled. The American vessel was also badly torn up. At Penobscot, *Hampden* was one of three vessels captured intact by the British.

Among the southern states, Virginia commissioned a remarkable seventy-two vessels of various classes. However, most were used for commerce rather than for war and very little detail is available for them. One authority says, "Virginia's naval vessels were poorly armed, incompletely manned, and ill-fitted for service." The documentary evidence for these vessels is also very poor, and only one, a galley called *American Congress* is definitely known to have carried 14 guns. Maryland added just one ship of war, *Defense (22)*, to patrol the Chesapeake. In addition there are incomplete records from Maryland for nineteen vessels of indiscriminate class, six row galleys, and a pair of armed boats. Georgia deployed a single armed schooner, and thereafter deployed a handful of row galleys to defend Savannah from attack from Florida.[6]

North Carolina put forth a small fleet of three brigantines and two row galleys besides an undetermined number of armed boats to patrol the Ocracoke Inlet and the Pamlico Sound. Oddly, the colony was considered to have a "safer" coastline than other Southern states. The Ocracoke Inlet was a narrow and difficult channel for sailing vessels to navigate, and in the eighteenth century it was the only practical passage for a warship through the almost continuous string of sand banks and bars (the Outer Banks) that separate Pamlico Sound from the Atlantic Ocean. Cape Hatteras, long noted as a graveyard of ships, made the state's coastline difficult to patrol even in small vessels. The "soundings"—a 100-fathom line defining the deep blue-water edge of the Gulf Stream—passed only 12 miles from Cape Hatteras. At the edge of the soundings the water shoaled rapidly toward the shore. Seamen, lacking the accurate chronometers of later days that would allow for precise calculation of longitude (east-west position), found the approach to the Outer Banks from the Atlantic treacherous, especially in winter or in bad weather when imperfect visibility might cause a sudden grounding. It was for this reason that the Royal Navy limited its regular patrols to the mouth of the Cape Fear River.[7]

South Carolina of all the southern states deployed the finest fleet of state war vessels. Acquired from France and Holland were two warships of 40 or more guns. There were also a handful of 26-gun and 16-gun ships, brigantines, and schooners, and almost a dozen row galleys and armed boats. Twenty-four of these state vessels were noteworthy, and some were larger and better armed than their Continental cousins. Most of the state's vessels were stationed in the waters around Charleston where the Royal Navy would launch two major operations to take the port—a failed attempt in

1776 and a successful one four years later. A great number of American vessels were lost with the fall of the port in 1780.

Two of the largest vessels in the South Carolina Navy were converted French transports. *La Bricole* acquired from Admiral d'Estaing's fleet in 1779 had gunports cut in its sides for 44 cannon, 18 and 24 pounders. *La Truite* fitted as a 26-gun frigate carried 12 pounders. This armament proved too great for the transports making them top-heavy and unstable outside the confines of quiet bays and inlets. When the British attacked Charleston in 1780, the ships were quickly stripped of their guns and sunk to blockade the entrance to the harbor.

The state frigate *South Carolina (40)* was without question the most heavily armed warship to sail the "blue water" under American colors during the Revolution. No warship in the American service fired a greater total weight of metal, 1,152 pounds. It began its career in Europe in 1777 when Benjamin Franklin ordered a large frigate to be built at Amsterdam in Holland from a French design. The ship was completed in 1778, but political considerations involving the continued neutrality of the Dutch kept the vessel, called *L'Indien*, from Franklin's hands. In 1781, with the Dutch alliance completed, the frigate came to South Carolina through the offices of a Franco-American Patriot, Alexander Gillion. Renamed *South Carolina*, the warship made its first successful cruise under Gillion in the North Sea. It next appeared in 1782 in the Caribbean as part of an extravagantly large expedition composed of fifty-six Spanish and American ships thrown against the tiny port of Nassau. The Americans had taken the town twice during the war—the last time by a single sloop-of-war and fifty seamen.

South Carolina carried 28-36 pounders in its main battery and 12-12 pounders ranged along its flush upper deck. Smaller cannon made up a total of 48 guns although the ship was initially rated as a 40-gun frigate. "Experts feel that her size and heavy armament were a direct inspiration for the large, flush-decked [44-gun] frigates *Constitution* and *United States* built in 1794–7." *South Carolina* ended its career after an eighteen-hour sea chase while commanded by Capt. John Joyner. It was run down by *Diomede (44)*, *Astrea (32)*, and *Quebec (32)*. Oddly, the British felt that *South Carolina* was too lightly framed for the Royal Navy, and after its capture the vessel was sold to private parties as a merchantman.[8]

Among the middle states, Pennsylvania fitted out forty vessels in the lower Delaware River between New Jersey and Delaware. These were positioned to protect the approaches to Philadelphia. Of all thirteen colonies Pennsylvania had the smallest coastline exposed to naval attack, but it boasted the largest port city. All except nineteen of Pennsylvania's vessels were armed boats or river barges fitted with cannon to act as floating batteries to support the fortifications built in the river. Five were seagoing vessels, and the remainders were row galleys. The largest was the sloop-of-war

General Greene (16), but the heaviest guns were reserved for the corvette *Montgomery (20)*. Built at Simon Sherlock's shipyard in Philadelphia, the *Montgomery* was too small for its battery of 20-18 pounders and would have been deemed unsafe at sea. On its last deployment as the flagship of Commodore John Hazelwood's tiny fleet of river galleys and floating barges in 1777, *Montgomery* was dismasted in an action meant to contest the British seizure of Philadelphia, and it was burned by its crew to prevent its capture.

The sloop-of-war *Hyder Aly (16)* was part of the Pennsylvania state fleet. A merchantman converted into a corvette, it was named after a Raja celebrated for fighting the British in India. While escorting a convoy of transports in 1782, *Hyder Aly*, Capt. Joshua Barry, took on the *General Monck (20)*, formerly the Patriot corvette *General Washington* that had been taken into the Royal Navy after its capture in 1781. As a British cruiser, *General Monck* carried an assortment of 6- and 9-pound guns. Almost evenly matched in terms of weight of metal, Barry was able to take *General Monck* by boarding only after a prolonged mutual cannonade. The swashbuckling manner of the victory and the recapture of an American-built vessel of war, which reverted to its former name, were wildly celebrated in the states. The *General Washington* went on to a number of victories in the Caribbean. Its capture of a Loyalist privateer after a hard fight off Cape Francois, Haiti, was viewed by hundreds of cheering onlookers from the shore.

New York's small fleet of floating batteries, barges, and sloops attempted to control the waters around Manhattan Island and the Lower Hudson River in 1776, but they were rendered all but useless in the face of a British invasion fleet numbering more than 400 vessels. Several state vessels are known to have served in the Hudson River and Long Island Sound. Among these were the *General Putnam* (schooner), the *General Schuyler* (sloop), the *Lady Washington* (row galley), and the *Montgomery* (row galley). It is not clear that all the vessels serving in the New York Bay belonged to the state fleet. The *General Schuyler* was purchased in New York but was transferred to Washington in April 1776; and the *Lady Washington (10)* was owned by the local committee of safety but was borrowed by General Washington to defend the city.

There were dozens of local and subsidiary state and private vessels that defy placement in any definite category other than miscellaneous because of ambiguities or errors in the historic record. The frigate *General Washington (32)*, for instance, was purchased by private parties in 1782, but it had been built by a group of Philadelphia merchants and had seen previous service as the *Congress (32)* under Capt. George Geddes. This *Congress* was not the Continental medium frigate *Congress (28)* that never left the Delaware River, nor was it the American corvette *General Washington (20)* that was captured and later known as the *General Monck*.[9]

The quality of the state navies, their logistical plans, command structures, and their strategic deployment were matters decided largely by the individual states without consultation with their neighbors. Initially there was no central depot of naval materials, no common source of weapons, cannon, or gunpowder, no overall command structure, and, most importantly, no common set of operational goals beyond informal agreements between neighboring state assemblies or committees of safety. This leaves the historian with the unavoidable conclusion that much of the state navy presence during the war was catch-as-catch-can. Nonetheless, extant documentary evidence suggests that there was an intertwining web of informal sources and mutual understandings in which individuals played a much more important role than organizational infrastructures.

THE ARMY'S NAVY

In 1775 some in Congress thought it "sheer madness to send ships out upon the sea to meet the overwhelming naval force of England."[10] Nonetheless, Washington commissioned eight small vessels in 1775 and 1776 by relying completely on his position as commander-in-chief of the army for the authority to spend public money, detach personnel, and dedicate gunpowder, cannon, and other scarce war materials to an effort at sea. Washington's fleet was the immediate forerunner of the Continental Navy established by Congress, but it was really the "army's navy." All of its commanders and administrators, most of its active duty personnel, and all of its finances came from the army. Those vessels of his fleet surviving wreck, destruction, or capture were ordered out of commission and disposed of by order of the Marine Committee of Congress early in 1777 when replaced by Continental vessels of war.

Nonetheless, it can be argued that the experiences, challenges, failures, and successes of Washington's cruisers had an affect on the future of the Continental Navy that was out of all proportion to their meager number. The general's difficulties in maintaining his fleet also highlighted the need to create a national naval administration to oversee the construction, repair, arming, and crewing of warships; the production or acquisition of cannon, small arms, gunpowder, and projectiles; the libeling of captured cargoes and vessels; the adjudication of prizes and prize money; and a great number of other hidden facets of naval deployment. As late as November 1776, William Ellery of Rhode Island noted, "The conduct of the affairs of a navy, as well as those of an army, we are yet to learn. We are still unacquainted with the systematical management of them." Unfortunately, events were to show that Congress was generally incapable of creating a successful administrative structure for the Continental Navy.[11]

In the absence of a national naval establishment, Washington had initially enlisted a small cadre of trusted men to administer his fleet while he commanded the American land forces surrounding Boston in 1775. These men acquired and armed eight commerce raiders in little more than a year, and they combined their efforts to get them to sea as quickly as possible and to keep them afloat. Prominent among them was Col. John Glover, commanding officer of the Marblehead, Massachusetts, militia regiment and chief player among the general's "naval" staff; Col. Stephen Moylan, mustermaster of the Army of Observation on Dorchester Heights; Jonathan Glover, William Bartlett, and William Watson, the general's civilian prize agents in Marblehead, Beverly, and Plymouth, respectively; Lt. Col. Joseph Reed, Washington's personal military secretary at the army camp; and young Capt. Ephraim Bowen, who seems to have served as the general's personal liaison, go-getter, and on-site representative. It is important to recognize the efforts of these dedicated men, and the other unacknowledged Patriots, who actually organized and managed Washington's efforts at sea.

John Glover has been described as "a tough little terrier of a man" and "one of Washington's most reliable generals." He was among the true heroes of the Revolution, but his extraordinary character as a military leader and battleground tactician were not immediately evident. Trained as a shoemaker in Marblehead, Glover's personal experience with seamanship remains sketchy. By investing his hard earned money in consignments of liquor carried by other shippers, Glover quickly accumulated enough money to buy his own vessels including the schooner *Hannah*, which was named for his wife. By 1774 he had a small fleet of rumrunners and vintners that traded in the Caribbean and the Mediterranean. During the decade before the war Glover was active in the Continental Association and was well placed, at age forty-two, to attract men to his regiment of militia to fight the redcoats. It was Glover who chose the men from among the rank and file of the Army of Observation to man Washington's cruisers.[12]

At age thirty-eight, Irish-born Stephen Moylan was a merchant and shipowner from Philadelphia. He seems to have been completely at home among the denizens of the Massachusetts waterfront making deals with shipbuilders, sailmakers, blacksmiths, coopers, ship's chandlers, painters, and other maritime suppliers. In 1776 he became quartermaster general of the army just in time to oversee the logistical disaster that overtook the army as it retreated across New Jersey. Moylan's frantic attempts to block the Hudson River to British warships with sunken hulks and obstacles known as *cheveaux de fris*, and to supply Washington's troops in New Jersey by water proved fruitless because the Royal Navy quickly gained access to the East River and Long Island Sound. He thereafter resigned as quartermaster and organized a regiment of mounted dragoons in which he served brilliantly.

Joseph Reed, like Moylan, was part of Washington's headquarters staff in the field. In Philadelphia the thirty-four-year-old had been a successful lawyer and leader of the radical element among the colonials. Reed was essentially responsible for establishing all the rules and procedures followed by the headquarters staff of the army. He also drew up the initial set of articles under which the general's cruisers were to operate including therein matters such as the size of rations, rates of pay for the crew, and the scheme for shares of prize money. From his position at headquarters, Reed was also charged with the continued expansion of the general's fleet, approving the acquisition of likely vessels, purchasing cannon, and amassing small arms and munitions through the efforts of his agents in the field.

Jonathan Glover was the brother of Col. John Glover, who recommended him and his friend, William Bartlett, as prize agents to the general. Washington accepted both men even though there may have been some appearance of impropriety in appointing relations and friends to these sensitive positions. The standards regarding conflicts of interest were somewhat less strict than they are today. These appointments, moreover, typified the rather benign nepotism and unavoidable favoritism characteristic of the American rebellion. These men successfully instituted a naval program with virtually no funds, no public port facilities, and no supporting administration. Nonetheless, Reed cautioned, "[W]e have always found that when gentlemen sent upon this business go among their friends, they are apt to stay too long and are induced to favor their friends."[13]

William Watson, prize agent at Plymouth, had been recommended to Washington by the rebel leader Dr. James Warren as "a suitable person to supply 50 men with provisions and to take care of any prizes that may be carried into Plymouth." Warren, later lost to the rebellion as a martyr at the Battle of Bunker (Breed's) Hill, wrote to Watson, "I have such confidence in your honor and fidelity as to presume your conduct will make my recommendation respectable and give full satisfaction to the general." Watson's authority as a prize agent, unlike Jonathan Glover's or William Bartlett's that dealt with the army's finances, was limited to dealing with vessels fitted out at Congressional expense.[14]

Washington chose to make all of the final decisions concerning the deployment of cruisers and the disposition of prizes, and he required his agents and representatives to send all documents and papers to him for his personal consideration. They were also to be on the lookout for vessels suitable for transformation into cruisers. The agents were to provision one vessel and crew at a time and to dispose of prize vessels and their cargoes in an equitable and legal manner. As a matter of practicality, the agents were free to act on their own authority in minor matters, but they were required to keep Reed informed concerning matters of any consequence.

Because the new nation was trying to win foreign support, its agents were expected to strictly follow those internationally recognized rules regarding the jurisdiction of maritime courts and the libeling of prizes. Each agent was to receive 2.5 percent of all monies spent in refitting ships and provisioning them, and an additional 2.5 percent of all legitimate prizes and cargoes that they auctioned or sold. Ultimately, rather than maintaining a redundant system of competing prize agents, those men designated for each port by Congress were given authority to deal with all prizes whatsoever—continental, state, or private.

THE NAVAL COMMITTEE

The chronological development of the Continental Navy is hard for historians to pin down because many proposals regarding commercial maritime affairs and naval operations, each aimed at a discrete purpose, were being considered by the Congress at the same time. There were committees created inside other committees and boards created to answer to more than one superior agency at the same time. The same person often sat on several committees and wrote with overlapping authority about their decisions in private letters that failed to delineate exactly which committee had taken certain decisions. Since accurate minutes of the deliberations of the Continental Congress are "tantalizingly incomplete," a precise chronological account of all its proceedings is difficult.[15]

Nonetheless, it is conceded by most authorities that Congress officially adopted the concept of creating a formal navy on October 13, 1775, and by the end of the next month had authorized $100,000 to be spent in fitting out appropriate vessels. On November 10, the Naval Committee proposed the establishment of a Marine Corps, and on November 28, it adopted "Rules for the Regulation of the Navy of the United Colonies." Herein rations and pay were described, standards for discipline and punishments set, standards for courts martial were developed, recruitment bounties and prize shares apportioned, and pensions for permanent disability or death created. These were all based on long standing British naval regulations. Shortly thereafter $1 million was appropriated for the purpose of building a new fleet of thirteen frigates based on the proposal of the Rhode Island delegation. Yet there was seemingly no end to the debate on legislation concerning the naval arm, and novel concepts and new issues were constantly cropping up.

The most prominent of the agencies created to administer the American naval effort was the Naval Committee formed by the Continental Congress with Stephen Hopkins of Rhode Island as chairman. This committee was founded by members of the Secret Committee of Congress in a private room in a Philadelphia waterfront tavern in 1775 and is sometimes confused with the later Marine Committee of thirteen members. The Marine Committee, which provided the authority and appropriated the funds to raise a Continental Navy, worked through a panel of five members, two of whom were always congressmen, known as the Board of Admiralty.

The Marine Committee was constantly at odds with the state navies, the owners of privateers, and merchant operators concerning the distribution of nautical supplies, munitions, and manpower. They also often held differing views among themselves concerning the deployment of warships, the protection of convoys, and the allotment of prize money. These problems were exacerbated by the constantly changing face of the agencies and of the personnel charged with controlling the national naval effort.

Among the initial purposes of the Naval Committee were "distressing the enemy, supplying ourselves [with war materials], and beginning a system of maritime and naval operations." The Secret Committee, through the Navy Board, also empowered Benjamin Franklin, Silas Deane, and John Adams, its representatives in Europe, to act in its name in commissioning vessels as Continental cruisers, in procuring arms and gunpowder abroad, and in dealing with naval prisoners of war. Ultimately, Franklin took on the sole burden of American naval affairs in Europe.[16]

Formed through the efforts of Adams, Deane, and John Langdon, all of whom expressed "much zeal" for its creation, the Marine Committee ultimately came under control of Thomas Willing and Robert Morris, with the latter being the most active and important person involved in all aspects of naval administration. With the failure of other agencies to deal effectively with naval affairs, Morris, who was the Superintendent of Finance for Congress, gradually assumed their direction in America, and acted as a one-man Agent of Marine throughout the duration of the war.

On December 14, 1775, a Marine Committee of thirteen men, representing each of the colonies, was constituted to execute the resolutions of Congress with respect to the construction of thirteen newly built frigates. This was the second administrative structure to be formed in as many months. The Naval Committee continued to control America's first Continental fleet under command of Ezek Hopkins, but it ceased to exist on January 25, 1776, when its duties relative to the deployment of these vessels ended. The Marine Committee quickly proved too unwieldy in its thirteen-member format, and at its own suggestion a navy board of three members was established in November 1776. The first board, known as the Navy Board of the Middle Department was composed of Pennsylvanians John Nixon and John Wharton, and Francis Hopkinson of New Jersey. A second panel of three—William Vernon of Rhode Island, James Warren of Massachusetts, and John Deshon of Connecticut—was formed as the Naval Board of the Eastern Department in April 1777. These boards were located at Philadelphia and Boston, respectively.[17]

Nonetheless, it soon became apparent that a special level of knowledge of maritime affairs was needed to efficiently administer a navy, and calls went out to create a competent Board of Admiralty based on the British system. William Ellery wrote on February 26, 1777, "The Congress are fully sensible of the importance of having a respectable navy and have endeavored to form and equip one, but through ignorance and neglect they have not been able to accomplish their purpose. I hope to see one afloat before long. A proper Board of Admiralty is very much wanted." Yet it was not until October of 1779 that a five-member Board of Admiralty was established. It was then found difficult to find members willing to serve on the board. Consequently, with a three-person quorum necessary to affect business, "the board was much interrupted" in its proceedings, and when properly formed was "much hampered by half-hearted cooperation on the part of Congress." In 1781 the Board of Admiralty was allowed to pass out of existence, and naval affairs were placed under a single administrator called the Secretary of Marine. No one was found to fill the position before the end of the war.[18]

THE BRITISH ADMIRALTY

The attempts to develop a comprehensive American naval administration generally paralleled the structure used by the British, yet the detailed organization of the Royal Navy was in sharp contrast to the ad hoc character of the American naval effort. The overall command of the Royal Navy traditionally resided solely in the "First Lord Admiral" who was appointed by the king. The First Lord operated through the Board of the Admiralty. This body, composed of the heads of the other departments of state (the Lords), was characteristically efficient, level headed, and quite markedly incorrupt throughout most of its history (a characteristic it seemingly lacked during the Revolution). While the Lords of the Admiralty adopted a number of regulations viewed with disbelief by the ordinary seaman, their foresight in other areas showed a genuine underlying excellence.[19]

The British Admiralty had a staff of sixty bureaucrats and clerks overseen by the Board Secretary, a post held by Philip Stephens from 1763 to 1795. Stephens began his career in the Navy Office in 1739, and he later became an Admiralty Board member serving until 1806. A century earlier the position had been held by Samuel Pepys who had insured by his talented administration that the Board Secretary would wield a great deal of authority although he was a mere civil servant. Pay and working conditions for the board's staff were very good, and many clerks and administrative officers served for long periods. Experience, talent, and diligence were rewarded providing continuity and integrity to the staff and the system. As a consequence by the standards of the period the British Admiralty as a whole was a very efficient bureaucracy.[20]

It was unfortunate that the Admiralty exhibited an uncharacteristic period of weakness and corruption during the American war. Concerning this lapse British naval historians have argued that "however deplorable the weaknesses of administration, the state of the Royal Navy was probably no worse than it had been at the beginning of the Seven Years War and was to be at the start of the French Revolution."[21] Yet it is impossible to wish away the fact that the decade before the American war was a period of "political jobbery and corruption" controlled by King George III's ministers and friends. Under the leadership of Lord Sandwich, John Montagu, the First Lord of the Admiralty, the navy had come to a perilous state and had been systematically sold off. The *Advertiser* of London reported that Sandwich's mistress, Martha Ray, was notorious for selling naval commissions in order to enhance her wardrobe; and Sandwich was lampooned as one of Captain Mac Heath's crooked cronies in John Gay's popular "Beggar's Opera."[22]

Sandwich served as the First Lord three times (1748–1751, 1763, and 1771–1782). He was replaced during the interim periods by both incompetent political appointees and by seasoned admirals such as George Anson, Charles Saunders, and Edward Hawke. Each man viewed the Admiralty's operations and budget differently. It is possible, but difficult, to lay blame for the decline of the navy during Sandwich's tenure on Stephens. From 1763 to 1795 there were dozens of successive secretaries in other cabinet departments such Exchequer or State, but only one for the Admiralty. Stephens long professional service linked the Royal Navy of Admiral Anson during the War of Jenkins Ear (1740–1744) to that of Admiral Nelson at Trafalgar (1805) six decades later. Such service provided continuity, stability, and regularity to the administration of the navy. Nonetheless, while the routine operations of the board remained the province of its secretary, important policy questions were decided by the First Lord; and Sandwich had made the tone of the Admiralty remarkably political.

It was not uncommon to retire vessels even during the course of a conflict, and in the Seven Years War the Admiralty retired, broke up, or sold twelve 60-gun ships, eight 50s, and ten 40s. Nonetheless, in the five years immediately preceding the Revolution, an additional ninety-seven warships had been struck from the Admiralty lists and just fifty-seven added that were of inferior size and weight of metal. Although the navy had been allotted funds, the money had been "diverted to [political] party needs and private pockets all the way from Westminster to the dockyards and back." Money was voted for repairs and the ships went untouched. Stores were ordered and never used. Vessels reported as well-founded and seaworthy were actually rotting at anchor. Conversely, sound vessels were condemned and sold to private parties who charged their names, superstructure, or papers and sold them back to the Admiralty as transports. It has been claimed that 4,000 seamen were kept on the navy payrolls who did not exist—a number approximately equal to all the seamen in the Continental Navy in 1777. There was also a severe shortage of appropriate timber made worse by the loss of the great stands of oak and pine in North America. "Embezzlement, larceny, swindling" and like abuses prevailed almost everywhere from the dockyards to the offices of the First Lord at Whitehall.[23]

The opposition party in Parliament thundered over the condition of the navy's "rotten ships," but the ministry was indifferent to the needs of maintaining the navy. Having humiliated their traditional enemies in 1763, the British seem to have misunderstood the perils that continued to exist and "had been muddling along on a parsimonious peace establishment" ever since.[24] The failure to maintain the Royal Navy in fighting trim was to have devastating consequences during the American Revolution. Many of its vessels had fought in the Seven Years War and were to enter the Revolution as over-aged derelicts. By late 1780 the navy was "on so tight a string that the misdirection of a single ship might mean disaster." From 1776 to 1782 at least seventy-six of its vessels, including fourteen ships-of-the-line, capsized, foundered, or were wrecked.[25]

An analysis of the disposition of the Atlantic Squadron under Admiral Graves in the months before Lexington (1775) shows that of the twenty-four warships on station, more than half were guarding the approaches to New England with seven riding at anchor in Boston Harbor. The remaining thousand miles of coast from New York to Florida were patrolled by a half dozen sloops-of-war and a handful of cutters having only small cannon. By comparison Admiral Howe's fleet that faced the French in 1778 was composed of eighty-three vessels included eleven ships-of-the-line (five Third and six Fourth Rates), forty-three frigates (eighteen Fifth and twenty-five Sixth rates), sixteen sloops-of-war, and thirteen other vessels. Although Howe's command seemed formidable on paper, it was a good deal less imposing in reality. Many of the ships maintained their stations with fouled bottoms, ancient spars, and second-hand rigging. "When ... storms struck, masts, yards, bowsprits, and booms, deprived of their elasticity by age cracked throughout the fleet."[26]

Living conditions and service requirements for the British Jack-tars were intolerable. From 1776 to 1782, almost 42,000 British sailors deserted, and 18,000 more died of disease. Charles Middleton, the comptroller of the navy, noted, "The discipline of service is entirely lost, and to a great measure owing to admiralty indulgence, but still more to admiralty negligence.... One error has produced another, and the whole has become such a mass of confusion, that I see no prospect of reducing it to order. All I can do at the Navy Office will avail but little if the Admiralty continues what it is at present."[27]

Corruption at Whitehall also extended to the British administration in America. When Sir Guy Carleton took command of the New York garrison in April 1782, he opened a vigorous offensive against all kinds of corruption in the city. New York was also the main anchorage for the Royal Navy in America, and British seamen stationed there were given spoiled food and short-weighted rations by dishonest pursers. Their pay was slow in coming, stopped in lieu of nonexistent distributions of clothing and kit, or paid in depreciated colonial currency instead of gold coin or sterling, which was required under Admiralty regulations. The Loyalist population of the city praised Carleton for "cleaning out the entire group of leeches," but it was all too late to affect a proper administration of the city.[28]

THE FRENCH ROYAL MARINE

France also had an extensive naval administration and a world-class fleet. As early as 1669, the French Minister of Marine, Jean-Baptiste Colbert had provided assistance to the shipbuilding industry with port facilities and dry docks—one capable of serving a three-decker. He had organized a merchant service, and had built a fleet of warships adequate to protect French domestic commerce. More importantly he had established formal training for naval architects and had opened several naval training schools for sea officers. This last characteristic of naval preparation was uniquely French. In just a few years Colbert's administration had incorporated the whole theory of national sea power that was to characterize the eighteenth century.[29]

The French Royal Marine continued to grow during the eighteenth century, but it proved no tactical match for the Royal Navy. For example, at the Battle of Quiberon Bay in November 1759, a British fleet lured the French fleet onto a lee shore in a tempest. Here in a single night France permanently lost ten major warships and the temporary use of thirteen more on the shoals, rocks, and sandbars of the bay while the British lost not a single vessel. More than 2,500 French sailors and officers lost their lives in what has been described as "the decisive military event of 1759." It was no accident that Quiberon Bay was chosen by the French as the scene of their first recognition of the American Republic (February 14, 1778).[30]

In contrast to the British, the French continued building warships with greater resolve during the interwar years. It has been said that a French 80-gun warship was "bigger, more roomy, faster and finer in every way than a British 98" with many of the latter's gunports so low to the waterline that they could not be opened in anything stronger than a light breeze.[31] Briefly, under the leadership of Etienne de Choiseul (1761–1774), Gabriel de Sartine (1774–1780), and Charles de Castries (1780–1786) who were successively Minister of Marine, the French actually took the lead in European marine design, restored discipline to their navy, reorganized the artillery of their fleet, and arranged for the training of a body of 10,000 naval gunners. (Many of these improve-ments were lost in the first years of the French Revolution.)

The British viewed the French build-up with a certain amount of dis-quietude, but they were largely distracted by internal affairs, particularly the deteriorating relations with North America. In the long history of the Royal Navy, the American Revolution stands out as the only major conflict in which Britain had no European ally. In consequence, the Royal Navy was unable to assert anything like its customary pressure on its opponents. The almost continuous presence of European fleets in American waters and the availability of a number of American ports and quantities of provisions to the Franco-Hispanic allies was utterly unchar-acteristic of eighteenth-century naval warfare. French and Spanish commanders, often with numerically superior fleets to those of Britain, enjoyed almost complete freedom of movement from their home ports to the other side of the Atlantic, the Caribbean, and the Indian Ocean. Yet the allied navies had one great failing. They lacked a tradition of victory at sea equal to that of Great Britain.[32]

4

The Art of War at Sea

[We will] put to hazard the fortunes of war in America.
—John Montagu, Lord Admiral Sandwich

AMERICAN STRATEGY

Strategy and tactics are related, but they are not equivalent. Strategy is done in a planning room by heads of state, commanders of military forces, or Lords of the Admiralty (usually on maps), while tactics are applied by the on-site commanders at the point of contact with the enemy. In most cases where opposing warships came into contact, the deployment of specific tactics was left to the judgment of the admiral in charge of a fleet or the captain in charge of an individual ship.

Although none of its prominent members were specifically trained in nautical matters, Congress supplied the overall naval strategy for America. This was generally limited to defending the deep-water ports and major coastal towns from insult by the Royal Navy. In September 1775 Josiah Quincy proposed the construction of coastal fortifications "placed to command the channels" so that British warships "could be driven out by [their] fire" or kept out by the deployment of armed barges. "Row gallies must be our first mode of defense by sea," he noted.[1] Naval scholar Alfred Thayer Mahan noted that a strategic reliance on the defense alone harbored an intrinsic inadequacy for any nation with many ports scattered over an extended coastline compelling it "to distribute [its] force so as to be strong enough to stop the enemy on any line of attack that [they might] adopt."[2] It is not clear that the members of Congress understood the consequences of this limitation of their strategy at the time.

The British attack on Charleston, South Carolina, in 1776 was remarkable for the depth of its failure, and it presented a number of strategic lessons from which the Americans might learn in defending other port cities. Unfortunately, the Patriots were never again so successful in defending a port city from naval attack as they were in repulsing Gen. Henry Clinton's combined arms attack. Adm. Sir Peter Parker accompanied Clinton's transports filled with troops with ten warships to attack Charleston. They first had to reduce the rebel fort commanded by Gen. William Moultrie on Sullivan's Island that guarded the narrow passage into the harbor. Known as a chokepoint defense, the fort was made of soft palmetto log cribs filled with sand. These simply absorbed the solid shot and shell of the Royal Navy.

The chokepoint defense of Charleston—as seen from inside Fort Moultrie—was the most effective of the early war years. The soft logs and loose sand of the fortifications simply absorbed the force of the enemy fire. Patriot defenders went about the interior of the fort reclaiming spent shot and firing them back at the Royal Navy.

The explosive projectiles from the bomb ketch *Thunder (8)* were particularly ineffective. The Americans had as many as 7,000 cannonballs and exploding shells fired at them, some from less than 500 yards, yet they suffered only thirty-six casualties. Parker's ships—the frigates *Active (32), Solebay (28), Friendship (18),* and *Experiment (44)*—received a fearful pounding in return, and several others grounded on the harbor sandbar including *Sphinx (20), Syren (32),* and *Actaceon (32).* A number of vessels collided in the cramped confines of the passage. Parker's flagship, HMS *Bristol (50),* which closely engaged the fort for ten hours, was described after the battle as "junk." One of the ship's officers wrote, "No slaughter house could present so bad a sight . . . as our ship." HMS *Actaceon,* which grounded on a bar, caught fire, and surrendered its flag to a boat sent out by the fort. *Bristol* and *Experiment* had together 64 killed and 141 wounded. Because the navy could not get a foothold in the harbor, the British cancelled a planned land attack on the city. This was a singular victory of American land forces over the Royal Navy that might have been repeated at the narrows in New York Bay had similar chokepoint defenses been established.[3]

While many Americans acknowledged the obvious weakness of their naval arm, most retained an implicit faith in the potential effectiveness of the parallel strategy of commerce raiding (*guerre de course*). Robert Morris of the Marine Committee wrote, "It has long been clear to me that our infant fleet cannot protect our own coasts; and the only effectual relief it can afford us is to attack the enemies defenseless places and thereby oblige them to station more of their ships in their own countries, or to keep them employed in following ours."[4] Many Americans, knowing that the colonies lacked a fleet of multi-decked ships-of-the-line, hoped to use frigates, privateers, and smaller vessels against enemy shipping. Many of these vessels could out-sail larger opponents, and in favorable condition could overtake and overmatch the small guns carried by most merchant shipping. John Adams wrote of commerce raiding, "This is a short, easy, and infallible method of humbling the English, preventing the effusion of an ocean of blood, and bringing the war to a conclusion. In this policy I hope our countrymen will join with the utmost alacrity. . . . It is by cutting off supplies, not by attacks, sieges, or assaults, that I expect deliverance from enemies."[5]

The possible intervention of one or more major naval powers, particularly France, played a major role in forming America's operational naval strategy from the onset of the rebellion. Knowing that they could not hope to match even a small two decker of 50 guns on even terms, much less a three-decked 74, Congress sought out the French to act as their champion in that quarter. Ultimately, France, Spain, and Holland came to America's aid forcing the British to create a strategy to counteract the operations of the allied fleets. In fact, the most powerful of the British men-of-war spent a great deal of time patrolling European waters, blockading the French squadron in Rhode Island, or chasing the French fleet about the Caribbean. Thereby the most powerful of British sentinels were removed from many American ports. Nonetheless, British frigates and sloops-of-war, singly and in pairs, never completely abandoned their stations off the largest American cities unless they driven away by adverse weather or lured away by promising prizes.

Francis Lewis summarized the opinion of many delegates in Congress: American warships would best be employed in cruising in squadrons numbering four or five frigates acting in concert, sweeping the Atlantic coast of British merchant shipping and small cruisers. Although small squadrons of American privateers sometimes acted in concert, a lack of equipment and seamen for manning the more powerful Continental frigates suggests that the hope of combining the operations of their widely scattered warships was wildly ambitious. Rarely did more than one Continental cruiser break out into the open sea at a time—sometimes in consort with one or two privateers or state vessels. Cruises by four or more congressional frigates were rare and remarkable events. The largest American naval operation of the war, the Penobscot Expedition of 1779, combined forty Continental and state vessels, including troop transports and privateers. However, the expedition proved an utmost disaster because it lacked both experienced leadership and an appropriate operational strategy.[6]

Nonetheless, as the war progressed the Americans successfully maintained a significant number of cruisers and privateers in European waters. So prevalent were these Americans that the Royal Navy was forced to station its own warships and cutters in the English Channel and Irish Sea to contain them. At one point no fewer than seven British warships were stationed off the French coast near Le Havre relentlessly patrolling the approaches to the port and waiting to spring upon any American cruiser bold enough to stick its nose out into the Channel. The Americans ultimately succeeded in creating a war-weariness among the British public by maintaining a menacing presence in European waters.

In 1777, for example, an Americans squadron operated freely in the Irish Sea. *Dolphin, Lexington,* and *Reprisal* were commanded by captains Samuel Nicholson, Henry Johnson, and Lambert Wickes respectively. A fourth vessel, *Surprise,* commanded by Gustavus Conyngham, was detached to attack shipping off the coast of Holland near Texel. Wickes was made commodore of the flotilla, which had as its major objective the valuable Irish linen fleet. The American presence forced the British to establish an escorted convoy from Belfast, a measure that they had never before been forced to take—not even during the Seven Years War with France. The propaganda value of this policy was greatly appreciated by the American commissioners in Paris who were trying to establish an alliance with France. Such an alliance was the ultimate strategic goal of all the Patriots' operations.[7]

BRITISH STRATEGY

The Lords of the Admiralty, in consultation with the First Lord and the British prime minister, were responsible for all strategic planning for the Royal Navy. The primary strategy throughout the eighteenth century was to bring the enemy fleet to battle and destroy it, thereby preventing a possible armed invasion of Britain, Scotland, or Ireland. Their ultimate goal, bluntly stated by Adm. Horatio Nelson some decades later, was "the annihilation of the enemy." To attain its objectives Britain needed to maintain an overwhelming strength at sea in the form of a fleet of major warships at home supported by several strong squadrons posted to critical parts of the empire. The success of French privateers in the first half of the eighteenth century suggests, however, that the British were less well prepared to deal conclusively with individual commerce raiders or small squadrons of warships than they were to mount an offensive against large enemy fleets.[8]

The British strategy for the American war was to secure or otherwise blockade America's port cities thereby starving the colonial economies into submission while preventing the import of the necessary materials of war for the Patriot army. Initially their plans contemplated only a police action to restore order among a small fraction of their own subjects in New England. No plan was formed to pursue a general conflict along a 1,500-mile coastline populated by hostile inhabitants who might deny the Crown forces all the necessities of war including food and water. It was thought that the North American squadron alone could handle this operation. Additionally they hoped that the loyal colonials, especially those in the American South, would rise up against the Patriot cause and drive the fractious rebel minority from their midst. This expectation never materialized. Britain raised more Loyalist battalions from among displaced New Yorkers than from those in the south.

Yet the ministers in London should not be regarded too harshly for their strategic naiveté with respect to the colonies. The American Revolution was the first major conflict waged for the purpose of political independence, and many of its deeper aspects were unknown or misunderstood. No previous British navy had attempted to support its armies from the distance of 4,000 miles with munitions, reinforcements, and food. Moreover, if the British thought to intimidate the rebels by their mere presence, they were simply demonstrating their lack of understanding of the Patriots, who turned about and attacked British supply lines and captured shiploads of reinforcements throughout 1776.

Some of the responsibility for the strategic mismanagement of the war must be laid at the door of the Secretary of State for the Colonies, George

Lord Germain. Newly appointed in November 1775, Germain was jealous of the autonomy of his department and habitually intrigued to under-
mine the influence of other ministers. To make matters worse John
Montagu, the Lord Admiral, was his personal and political enemy, and
the two men found it difficult to agree on a unified operational strategy.
Responsible for coordinating the American operation, Germain decided
to organize the effort without regard to the ordinary protocols of the Admiralty. By dispatching both his ordnance vessels and his troop transports
piecemeal or without escort, he made them easy targets for America's
miniature warships. In response to the American success Germain urged
the commanders on the North American Station to keep "the coasts of
the enemy constantly alarmed" through bombardments and amphibious
raids. This would at least "prevent their sending out a swarm of privateers, the success of which has enabled and encouraged the rebels to per-
sist in their revolt."[9]

Prior to French intervention, the British secretary of war, William Lord
Barrington, offered the opinion that the suppression of America might be
left solely to the Royal Navy. His view was that the colonies could not be
subdued by the army, and that even if the Patriots were beaten in the field,
the permanent occupation of the cities along the Atlantic seaboard would
necessitate an enormous expense to the government. Barrington's view was
held by only a few ministers in London. Nonetheless, he continued to press
that the army be withdrawn to Canada, Nova Scotia, and other areas loyal
to the crown so that the navy alone could interrupt colonial commerce,
fishing, and every other form of maritime industry, "seizing all the ships in
their ports with very little expense and less bloodshed." A few frigates and
cutters "would probably be sufficient," wrote Barrington, "[but] I think a
squadron of ships-of-the-line should be stationed in North America both
to prevent the intervention of foreign powers and any attempt of the colonies to attack our smaller vessels at sea."[10]

The prime minister, Frederick Lord North; the American secretary,
George Lord Germain; and the king all disagreed with Barrington. They
continued to consider the colonial militias a mere ragtag rabble armed
with fowling pieces and homemade swords that could be swept away by
the British regulars. Their opinion was reinforced by the series of easy
successes during the New York and New Jersey campaigns of 1776.[11]
Moreover, Germain repeatedly requested that Admiral Richard Howe use
his fleet to harass the coast of New England, which had been abandoned
by British land forces in March 1776. Conscious that such operations
would entail an unwarranted dissipation of his forces, Howe showed little
interest in belaboring the Patriot coastline only to remind the colonials
that they were still at war.

Anticipating a French alliance with America during 1778, British strategy changed somewhat. Although the aggressive Germain continued to

espouse the bombardment of colonial ports and towns after the alliance, he noted, "We must hope that the rebels not having reaped that advantage from their new allies which they were taught to expect, and our superiority at sea being again restored, may incline many people to return to their allegiance and to live happy under the protection of Great Britain."[12] The Admiralty Board wrote to Admiral Howe in March, "The object of the war being now changed, the contest in America [must be] a secondary consideration."[13] Preservation of Britain's Caribbean possessions was now moved to the top of the Royal Navy's list of high priority tasks. King George III, himself visited Vice Adm. John Byron's fleet at Portsmouth, England, to show his concern regarding the French menace, and when Admiral d'Estaing's French fleet was definitely reported as being off New York at Sandy Hook, Byron was immediately dispatched to reinforce Admiral Howe so that the French fleet might be crushed by overwhelming numbers. Byron, encountering extreme weather, failed to arrive in a timely manner to do so.

Realizing that New England might be permanently lost to British rule after 1778, Sir Henry Clinton, the army commander stationed in New York, proposed a "southern strategy" that might feed the enthusiasm of Loyalists in Virginia, the Carolinas, and Georgia. Germain's enthusiastic adoption of Clinton's southern strategy required much of the Royal Navy. Sir George Collier, commanding the British fleet in New York at the time, offered the following appraisal of the idea. "The weak enfeebled state of the ships both in point of numbers and of men give me the most painful sensations....I am at a loss as to what to undertake or how to supply the convoys, guards of ports, and various other services which this extensive command necessarily has occasions for.... At least a fourth part of the fleet is regularly blown off their stations."[14] While Germain concentrated on the redeployment of land forces to the south and the encouragement of Loyalist resistance, after 1778 Sandwich increasingly focused on the security of the Channel fleet, his bases in the East and West Indies, and his lines of supply.[15]

With the exception of the tactical disarray its defense created among the war strategists in London, the English Channel was not destined to be the scene of important naval battles during the war; nor were the coasts of Europe to become major theaters of operations with the exception of the approaches to Gibraltar. Most of the fleet actions of the war were to take place on the coast of North America, in the Caribbean, and in the Indian Ocean. Of course, the British had no prior knowledge that this would be true, and in 1778 the ministers in London scrambled to develop a defensive strategy for the home islands. This included the creation of numerous militia camps in the southeast of England and the recall of many of the most powerful men-of-war from foreign posts. The North American Squadron was thereby denied the use of Britain's largest warships.

Furthermore, Britain rarely applied the advantage of its overwhelming naval superiority in America before 1778 in an intelligent manner. Seapower was often dissipated in meaningless coastal raids, pointless diversionary movements, and uncoordinated combined operations that were decisive only on paper. Gen. William Howe's plan to take Philadelphia in 1777, for example, is worth exploring in this regard. From his base in New York Howe planned to attack the rebel capital at Philadelphia, which was ninety miles away overland through New Jersey. He wrote to London, "From the difficulties and delay that would attend the passage of the River Delaware by a march through New Jersey, I propose to invade Pennsylvania by sea; and from this arrangement we must probably abandon the Jerseys." Subsequently, almost 14,000 troops were crammed into the stifling holds of a fleet of 260 transports and warships and kept there for two weeks as the provisions, munitions, and livestock needed to support a land campaign were loaded. A fortnight of preparations were then prolonged by an oceanic voyage of forty-two days and some 800 sea miles with the sprawling fleet experiencing a diversity of weather-related problems. The penned soldiers sickened and ate their way through most of their field rations. When the army landed at Head of Elk by "taking course of the Chesapeake," they were still seventy miles from Philadelphia and were forced to wage a land battle on Brandywine Creek in any case. General Howe could have marched across New Jersey with the same result in little more time than it had taken to provision his brother's fleet.[16]

Likewise General Clinton's second expedition against Charleston became a thirty-eight-day travail at sea. Sailing from New York on the day after Christmas (1779) with almost 14,000 troops, marines, and sailors, the fleet of ninety transports and fourteen frigates had barely passed Sandy Hook when it encountered a fierce winter storm. Some of the vessels foundered; and others, encountering the northward flowing Gulf Stream, were in danger of being swept into the mid-Atlantic. The troop transport *Anna* was dismasted and its regiment of Hessians thought lost until the hulk with its weather-beaten occupants drifted ashore in far away Cornwall, England, seven weeks later. Clinton found that he had to put into Savannah for a refit of the fleet before actually making his ultimately successful attack on Charleston. The unexpected problems experienced by Clinton in this situation suggest that even overwhelming seapower gave the British only a desultory advantage in dealing with the Americans ashore.

Nor did the loss to the Americans of major cities such as New York, Philadelphia, Savannah, or Charleston help to end the rebellion. The strategic taking of places, symbolic of victory in former times, seems to have given way to the greater power of economic and political considerations; and battles and campaigns seem to have become a good deal less decisive in ending conflicts.[17] In response to these operations, Dr. Franklin noted that there would never be enough Englishmen available to subdue, and hold on to, all of America.[18] Moreover, word of the completion of the French alliance with America caused the almost immediate abandonment by the Crown forces of Philadelphia and the ultimate desertion of Newport by the Royal Navy as the British concentrated their forces for a supposed defense of New York. The single-minded focus on defending the port of New York from French naval attack after 1779 may have been the Achilles' heel of British strategy in America.

FRENCH STRATEGY

To the French, strategic control on land was the equivalent of Britain's control at sea. The French objective in maintaining a fleet, from the time of Choiseul, was to protect their trading establishments, island outposts, and colonies. The operational policy of the French admirals was "to neutralize the [naval] power of their adversaries, if possible, by grand maneuvers rather than to destroy it by grand attack." They were generally callous to the idea of controlling the sealanes for long periods of time; but they utilized their warships efficiently to facilitate ulterior objectives on the Continent such as the movement of troops or the distribution of supplies. This strategy, known in naval circles as that of a "fleet in being," allowed them the economy of maintaining a smaller naval establishment than their foes and applying their national resources elsewhere.[19]

Throughout the eighteenth century French war plans included an invasion of the British Isles. It was not that the French and their allies had abandoned the idea of attacking the shores of England, Ireland, or Scotland during the American war. The invasion plans originally developed by the Count de Broglie, brother of the Marshal of France, in the years after the Seven Years War were still feasible and would remain part of French strategic thinking into the Napoleonic Era. Rather than having abandoned the idea of an invasion in 1778, the French simply failed to bring all the requisite parts of a major operation together. The organization of a land invasion force, transports and barges, munitions, field artillery, food, horses, wagons, and escorting warships had to coincide with fair weather and favorable winds for a sufficiently long period to carry it off—all the while with the Royal Navy's attention somehow directed elsewhere. Moreover, France did not have the wherewithal to undertake such an operation without the aid of Spain, which was more than a little reluctant to be drawn into any land-based scheme that did not focus on retaking Gibraltar or other of its former Mediterranean island outposts. The Franco-Hispanic fleet probably came closest to meeting these requirements in the summer of 1779 against Adm. Sir Charles Hardy, but foul water and spreading sickness among the seamen ended the opportunity prematurely.[20]

Those parts of the combined French and Spanish fleets held in European waters contained somewhat more than sixty-five ships-of-the-line. The French fleet, numbering more than half of these, was generally considered more dangerous than the Spanish. One part of the French force, twenty-one of the line and thirty-five frigates, was stationed at Brest under Admiral d'Orvilliers, while the remainder, twelve of the line and thirteen frigates, were at Toulon on the Mediterranean under Admiral d'Estaing. The dual disposition of its warships placed a tactical impediment upon the French, who needed to carefully time the sailings of the separate parts so as to prevent each from being destroyed in detail.

Charles Gravier Vergennes, French Minister of State and chief architect of the alliance with America, seems to have understood the limits of his naval power, and in 1778 he formed a war strategy to compliment it. To succeed in aiding the Americans, according to Vergennes (a former Minister of Marine), the French navy needed only to draw the British fleet away from the American coastline by attacking the fabulous wealth of the British sugar islands in the Caribbean or by threatening British trading interests in India. From 1778 to 1782 the French navy accomplished some brilliant operations in this regard with a remarkable economy of force, especially their ability to obtain naval superiority off the coast of Virginia in 1781 and to counteract the Royal Navy in a series of sharp actions in the Indian Ocean in 1782 and 1783.

ALLIED COOPERATION

The Americans, French, Spanish, and Dutch ultimately joined in the naval war against Britain, but the British had no European allies in the war. The joint allied strategy took this into account and placed the British at a considerable disadvantage by attacking everywhere at once. Each allied nation added its own part to the overall war strategy. The French used their ships to pour troops into the islands of the West Indies and Rhode Island while the Spanish concentrated on the Mediterranean and the American Gulf Coast particularly at Mobile. The Dutch had focused on supplying the Americans with war-like stores since 1775 especially through their island port in the Caribbean at St. Eustatius, but they remained neutral until 1781 when the island was captured by the British. Dutch dominance in the Baltic Sea endangered the main source of badly needed naval stores for the British navy, and both Dutch and French cruisers threatened the tenuous supply of saltpeter (an essential ingredient in gunpowder) coming from India.

Although the Dutch war fleet experienced a rapid growth after 1780, doubling in size in just five years, it was its merchant vessels that most hurt the British. However, Dutch merchant ships proved rich and defense-less targets for British privateers especially in distant waters like the East Indies. It was here that British privateers congregated. Many Dutch ships shifted their registry to that of neutral countries, particularly those of Denmark and Prussia, to elude capture. Dutch convoys to the Caribbean were generally able to avoid the Royal Navy in the vastness of the North Atlantic, but the British presence in the English Channel was another matter that threatened supplies shipped from the Baltic to France. None-theless, the Dutch found the means to move the needed materials through the inland waterways of the neutral Austrian Netherlands into French territory.

Spain's poor showing during the Seven Years War had reinforced its position as a secondary naval power. Spanish naval operations in the American war were generally one-sided and of little help to the Patriots. The Spaniards, lured into the war by French guarantees, generally consid-ered the Americans a potential threat to their possessions in the Gulf and Florida, and they were single-mindedly focused on regaining the island bases at Gibraltar and Minorca, which they had lost in the naval wars of the first half of the century. On Christmas Eve 1779, Adm. Sir George Rodney with a fleet of eighteen warships and a convoy for the relief of the British troops on Gibraltar intercepted Adm. Don Juan Langara with a fleet of eleven Spanish ships-of-the-line near Cape St. Vincent. Out-numbered, the Spanish admiral fled. After assuring the safety of the transports, Rodney ordered a chase during which five of the Spanish war-ships were taken or wrecked. This encounter consolidated Britain's hold on Gibraltar and reinforced its appraisal of Spain's maritime weaknesses.

Spain's operational planning was often faulty, but the blame for this may lie with its individual admirals who still relied on their family con-nections rather than their proven ability to gain positions of command. Adm. Bernardo de Galez, for example, attempted an invasion of Florida from Havana in October 1780 at the height of the hurricane season. The Caribbean storm season was particularly bad that year, but the admiral should have known better. The Spanish had a long history of naval opera-tions in the Caribbean. Galez subsequently lost most of the invasion fleet when two major storms hit in rapid sequence. The British Jamaica con-voy, struck by the same series of hurricanes, lost two ships-of-the-line and six frigates, and suffered damage to most of the fleet.

On the other hand, Adm. Don Luis de Cordoba with the main Spanish fleet intercepted an British convoy outbound from Britain near the Azores. Of sixty-three ships Cordoba took fifty-five prizes and 2,500 pris-oners, half of whom were British redcoats sent to reinforce the garrisons of the West Indies. This unexpected Spanish victory compounded by the serious storm losses in the Caribbean produced a financial crisis among the marine insurance underwriters throughout Europe. Many went bankrupt, and war insurance rates, already remarkably high due to the menacing presence of privateers, were driven to intolerable levels.[21]

CLEARING FOR ACTION

Any ship going into battle needed to "clear for action." The period between first sighting the enemy and closing with them in battle was always one of considerable activity. A thing of beauty when under sail, a large warship was also clumsy and ponderous to maneuver, requiring perfect timing and seamanship of its captain. It was very difficult, therefore, to fight under full sail and maintain the fine control needed to prosecute a battle with some finesse. Therefore, during the closing minutes of the approach the commander would give orders to place the vessel under *fighting sails*—topsails and jib set, the mainsails clewed up, and the royal and topgallant yards sent down if there was time. Duplicate sheets and braces were put in place to insure control of the ship, and the rope slings that supported the great yards were reinforced with chains to eliminated much of the potential injury from falling debris. Nonetheless, there were times when ships went into battle quickly with all their plain sails set.

On deck, hammocks, bedding, and spare canvas were bundled into the nettings along the sides of the railings to serve as some protection from small arms fire and flying wood splinters, as well as to deter boarders. The decks were wetted to resist fire, and sand was scattered about to improve footing. The ship's boats were cast overboard to be towed or retrieved later. Below decks the partitions that formed the officers' cabins were removed, and the furniture, mess tables, and any other loose objects were stowed away.

The carpenter and his crew would prepare their shot-plugs (cone shaped pieces of fibrous wood that could be hammered into any hole near the water line), and the surgeon and his mates would establish a medical station on the orlop deck or in the cockpit. The powder monkeys would bring a limited number of charges up from the magazine for each gun. This was to prevent accidental explosions. The charges would be replenished throughout the battle. Tubs filled with water and sand held the burning slow match with which to fire the charge.[22]

CRUISER TACTICS

American vessels of war almost always operated alone or in small groups, and they usually encountered their opponents unexpectedly. In clear weather two individual ships could see each other over an extended distance, but it was considerably easier to spot any entire fleet of warships spread out over many miles of sea space. A man at the masthead with good eyes and a good telescope could see as far as ten miles.[23]

Nonetheless, it was nearly impossible to tell with any certainty if the sails that appeared over the horizon were those of a friend or an enemy. A fleet composed of ships-of-the-line and a convoy of richly laden merchantman had almost identical sail plans. Differences in the size or the number of guns on a vessel were not obvious at a distance. Many merchant captains painted black squares along the bulwarks of their vessels hoping that they would be mistaken for the gunports of a warship.

A single ship encounter at sea usually brought increased exertions on the part of the commander to ascertain the nature of an approaching vessel before irrevocably committing himself to a fight. The ship to windward (upwind) always had the advantage because it could choose to run down upon an adversary under a following wind or avoid a fight by maintaining its upwind position. The leeward (downwind) vessel could claw its way after an upwind enemy or run from it, hoping in either case to have the fleeter or more maneuverable vessel. A lightly armed merchantman or a slaver would immediately run from the appearance of any unexpected sail, even if it proved to be friendly. Privateers, relying on the characteristic speed of their vessels, might try to run along a parallel course for a time before abandoning a possible prize. Warships, however, were under some obligation to chase, stand, or make a fight with any enemy vessel near their own size. However, it was almost inevitable that even an aggressive commander approached an unknown sail with great apprehension.[24]

Warships were designed to fight, but in practice they did so infrequently. Most close encounters between vessels of war and merchantmen ended in the immediate surrender of the latter. Nonetheless when all of the conditions for a sea battle between opposing warships were established the officers and crew of each faced the supreme test of their readiness and organization. Engagements at sea were bloody and desperate affairs that stressed the courage and resolve of even the best crews, and the officers were under a disproportionate strain to keep themselves and their men steady and under control. While they may have been undisciplined by European standards, the courage of American crews under these circumstances was rarely questioned, and the discipline of the Jack-tars of the Royal Navy and the sailors of the Allied navies was never in doubt.

The *chase* was a tactic used most often by cruisers in running down merchant shipping at sea, and it was here that the Americans held a significant advantage. Most American vessels could successfully run from any enemy warships that they could not match in firepower as long as they had an open sea in front of them. On the other hand, if upwind aboard a fast sailer, an attacking American captain could follow along a parallel course to his quarry until he came abeam. He then steered toward the enemy vessel for a brief period until it turned away, and finally he put himself back on a parallel course. Ultimately these repeated maneuvers brought the enemy prize closer and closer. Only darkness or an adverse change in the wind could keep the distance from closing to within the range of cannon.

Bow and stern guns were assigned the role of "chasers" allowing a vessel to fire one or two balls while chasing or being chased. Well ranged shots could encourage a weaker enemy to yield or discourage a stronger one from further pursuit. Lacking chasers, a vessel would have to slow and yaw to one side to fire a broadside of cannon to the same effect. The vessel thereby lost a good deal of speed and lost the advantage of any intervening distance between it and its opponent. Patience and errorless seamanship on the part of the attacker often made the result inevitable. While taking a surrender, captors generally brought their vessels under the *lee quarter* of a potential prize—generally out of the field of fire of the prize's broadside guns and menacing enough to prevent any sudden surprises.

A long running fight in 1778 between the British privateer *Rosebud* *(16)* and a lightly armed American privateer known as the *General Mercer* can serve as an example in this regard. The *Rosebud* initially demanded the surrender of the under-gunned American vessel, which unleashed a feeble broadside of 3 pounders before taking to its heels downwind. The *Rosebud* chased the American while firing ranging shots from its bow chasers and closing the interval until nightfall. Believing that the *General Mercer* had no stern chasers with which to answer, at dawn the *Rosebud* closed under the stern counter of the American to take its surrender. Unknown to the British captain, however, the American crew had cut a single gunport into the *General's* stern cabin and mounted a small 3 pounder there in the darkness. They added several long bars of iron to a double-shot load that they suddenly fired at point-blank range. The swirling bars carried away the enemy's headsails and sliced through the stays of the foremast. The splintered wooden column was swept overboard causing the *Rosebud* to broach sideways as the tangled mass of rope rigging and shredded sails acted as a sea anchor. With the pursuer thus stopped dead in its tracks, the *General Mercer* made good its escape.[25]

FIGHTING THE SHIP

In an engagement the individual ship commander had several tactics available to him besides participating in a simple slugging match. It was in this area that sea officers could demonstrate their skill and initiative. One tactic was that of *raking* the opponent. Raking was accomplished by crossing the enemy's stern, where few guns were mounted, and firing through the stern counter and down the length of the enemy vessel as the guns of the broadside came to bear. Shot fired in this manner often traveled the full length of the ship, splitting timbers, upsetting guns, and killing the crew. Raking could also be accomplished by passing before the enemy and firing through his bow section. If a skipper had a handier and more agile vessel than his opponent, he could rake with one broadside, tack, and fire the other broadside in a similar manner without taking extensive opposing fire. The process could also be accomplished in light winds by backing across an opponent's wake. Enemy commanders were well aware of what their opponents would try if given the opportunity, and they were quick to react to the potential danger by attempting counter measures. Being raked was almost the worst thing that could happen to a vessel in an engagement short of an explosion in its powder magazine.[26]

All the tactics used by a commander were aimed at one objective—to adversely affect the ability of his opponent to make further resistance. It was never his purpose to sink his opponent. Such a result would adversely affect any prize money, and it was a highly unlikely ending in any case. Military historian John Keegan has noted that "few ships were sunk in these encounters, for the wooden ship was virtually unsinkable

The warship on the right is being raked by its opponent, which is firing a broadside through its stern counter. This was a devastating tactic. Cannonballs might carry the length of the opponent's deck, overturning guns, smashing timbers, and killing the crew.

by solid shot unless it caught fire." Either he had to hold his enemy in
play sufficiently long for his own firepower to take effect, or he had to
sufficiently weaken his opponent so that he might carry the enemy vessel
by boarding. Ship commanders often fired chain- or bar-shot into the
enemy ship's rigging to disable it and prevent it from further maneuvers;
or he could sweep the decks with grape shot—a dozen or so golf-ball-
sized iron spheres fired together—in order to clear the decks of defenders
without shattering the timbers of the vessel.[27]

Centuries of actions at sea in which hand-to-hand fighting decided the
issue were not easily forgotten, and tactics that culminated in slashing,
close-quarters fisticuffs on the enemy's deck were still regarded with great
favor. Attempts to grapple the enemy vessel, entangle the rigging, or ram
the opposing vessels into a conglomerate mass were all based on the hope
that a boarding party might successfully decide the issue. Boarding parties
were often led by the first lieutenant who hoped to establish himself as a
man worthy of advancement to captain's rank. When not formed as part
of the boarding party, Marines were generally sent with their muskets to
the fighting tops from where they could fire down on the deck below or
drop hand grenades on the enemy.[28]

The conditions under which engagements were fought placed the
utmost strain not only on the structural integrity of the ship but also on
the physical resources of the crew. The participants might be engaged for
hours in "grindingly hard physical labor ... much of it within a few yards
of the mouths of thirty or forty cannon." Physical exhaustion, the apprehension of immediate and unremitting danger, and the intense mental
strain that accompanied the control and maneuver of a vessel in battle
left many of the crew believing that they had done all that they could do.
During a prolonged encounter "one did not think too clearly about what
to do next, one collapsed." Although fate sometimes decided the issue, often it was the skipper and crew that rose above these trials that were
favored with victory.[29]

FLEET TACTICS

The tactics employed by the British Royal Navy and the French Royal
Marine defined the art of war at sea in the period. With few exceptions
they were carried forward from the Seven Years War, through the American Revolution, and into the naval wars of the French Revolution and
the Napoleonic era. The major fleet engagements of the American Revolution were classic sea fights fought between European opponents, not
between the British and the Americans. These included fleet actions at
Newport, Rhode Island, Ushant, St. Lucia, and Pondicherry (1778), Grenada, Martinique, and Cape St. Vincent (1779), Martinique, the Azores,
and Mangalore (1780), St. Eustatius, Gibraltar, the Cape Verde Islands,

and the Chesapeake (1781), Ceylon, St. Kitts, the Saintes, Negapatam, and Gibraltar (1782), and finally Cuddalore (1783). Even if American warships in substantial numbers had been able to join the allied fleets after 1778, they would have been relegated by their small size and weight of metal to subsidiary roles outside the line of battle.

Historically, the most common fleet tactic was the *line ahead*, referred to in written records as early as 1653. The development of gunports along the sides of each warship allowed guns to be placed in two or more banks above and below the maindeck. To prevent the ships of the fleet from masking the fire of their consorts and to avoid confusion, ships-of-the-line generally deployed in a single line with the smaller frigates and sloops-of-war standing to windward to repeat signals and provide aid to damaged comrades. The line ahead was essentially a "follow the leader" approach to the control and ordering of the fleet by its admiral, and it dominated fleet tactics throughout the age of sail.

Other fleet tactics moved in and out of fashion with the prejudices of the sea lords. These included numerous variations on line maneuvers such as *doubling the enemy's line*—having your ships on both sides of the enemy at the same time; *passing the enemy line*—a generally indecisive action with two fleets firing as they moved past each other in opposite

An eighteenth-century artist's concept of the Battle of Negapatam fought between the French and British in the Indian Ocean in 1781. The painting illustrates an unrealistically strict adherence to the line-ahead formation on the part of both fleets. The ocean is also unusually calm. Note the frigates and smaller vessels stationed beyond the lines of men-of-war.

directions; and *breaking the enemy's line* by sailing through it in one or more places—an amazingly effective tactic in terms of battering the enemy's warships to pieces by raking. The first major battle between the British and French fleets in the American war (June 1778, near Ushant off the coast of Brittany) was an indecisive passing engagement in which the French uncharacteristically took the upwind position and let the British fleet disappear into the growing darkness. In one of the last major encounters of the war, the Battle of the Saintes in the West Indies in 1782, the British broke the French line and doubled several of their ships, thereby winning a stunning victory.

The French fleet fought in *line ahead* almost without exception throughout the seventeenth and eighteenth centuries. Moreover, French commanders most often chose to fight from the *Lee Gage* (or downwind) of their opponent. They rarely expended their resources in slugging matches meant to sink or capture enemy vessels, choosing rather to happily break off an engagement after dismasting, diverting, or otherwise slowing the enemy fleet. This was most easily done by firing on the up-roll thereby sending the shot into the enemy's "sticks." Once this design was accomplished, the French generally made for port on a downwind run.

British tactics called for the attack to be pressed from the *Weather Gage* (or upwind) and for the guns to be aimed at the hull of the enemy on the downroll—between wind and water—killing the enemy crew and damaging the hull. British tactics, therefore, generally complimented the desires of the French, who favored the leeward position and appreciated the fact that their rigging and sails were not being shot to pieces in the initial stages of the battle. Logically, with fleets of equal speed and weatherliness, the fleet to windward could not be forced to engage, and that to the lee could not avoid an engagement if the wind held steady. Yet this was not always the case.[30]

The British Royal Navy generally failed to adopt tactics that might force their enemy to remain in the conflict until the battle was decided. Until 1782 the British took no steps to deal with a fleeing enemy who did not wish to be engaged, and the choice of the leeward position continued to benefit both French and American ships, which were generally better designed than the British vessels of the period and could be sure of winning a downwind race unless severely damaged. This was to have far ranging consequences at the Battle of the Chesapeake in 1781 where the French initially formed for battle and then suddenly reversed course after exchanging a few broadsides, winning the "footrace" to the mouth of the bay and taking a strong defensive position overlooking Yorktown. Rather than a decisive and bloody engagement, it was this maneuver—very characteristic of the French—that effectively won the American Revolution.[31]

In most naval engagements the commanders of opposing fleets chose to sail along parallel courses rather than drifting about during the conflict.

As warships of the period had no motors, they required a certain momentum in order to maneuver, bring their guns to bear, and maintain their relative positions alongside the enemy. Such fine control of the speed of the vessels was needed that, with time and experience, it was found to be mutually advantageous for the opposing fleets to sail along a line close hauled to the wind. By sailing as much into the wind as possible without being blown backwards, individual captains were able to fill their sails to gain speed or, by backing their sails slightly, to use the wind as a brake. Judicious use of the wind allowed the captain to keep his vessel on its station in the line, and allowed the admiral to keep his fleet in contact with the enemy.

The position between filling and backing was called *luffing*, and the sails took on a flapping mode. Should the vessel lose momentum while luffing, it might be taken *in irons* unable to maneuver or gain speed without resorting to extraordinary measures such as falling away before the wind or sending out its boats to tow it into a proper position to make use of the wind. It could be disastrous for a warship to be taken in irons during a close engagement as it would either be left behind by its own fleet or become a ripe target for boarding or raking by the enemy.

A ship in the mist of battle might turn away and disengage quite easily if in the downwind position, but the captain had to take care not to expose the stern of his own craft to the broadside on his opponent. Turning with the wind was called *waring* the ship. Turning into the set of the wind was *tacking*. Even with damaged rigging, the force of the wind would tend to take a damaged ship away from the battle line, and unless it was engaged by a determined opponent the vessel might make an escape or take time to make repairs. However, for a ship to turn away from the battle line from the weather, or upwind position was much more difficult and required a good deal of preparation. The force of the wind naturally drove the ship in the windward position into the enemy "to fight or surrender; there was little chance of . . . running away."[32] It was generally accepted that a ship could strike its colors with honor if too badly damaged to escape or with too many of its crew wounded or killed to fight effectively.[33]

COMMUNICATIONS

During a single ship action the captain and his subordinate officers relied largely on a powerful voice or a "runner" (usually a junior midshipman with "young legs") to issue orders about the ship. Whistles (like the boson's whistle) and speaking trumpets were also used to signal the implementation of prearranged maneuvers, operations, or tasks. The commander could not be everywhere at once, and his usual station was on the quarterdeck from which he could manage the overall engagement.

During battle in many cases the captain had to rely on the good judgment and leadership of his officers and men in other parts of the ship. For this reason the first lieutenant was usually assigned to the main battery below decks, and the sailing master was given responsibility for handling the ship.

In fleet engagements comprising many ships on each side, the admiral needed to command the actions of his subordinates and of individual vessels as he saw the needs of the overall conflict develop. As there were only rudimentary means of communication by sight, speaking trumpet, or messenger boat, a series of prearranged visual signals were instituted, each with its own meaning. These signals were the basis for the sailing and fighting instructions under which the fleet operated. The admiral's pennant, a long narrow flag colored to suit his rank, was flown from the masthead of his flagship locating him in the center squadron. Signals were made by raising colored flags and pennants in different positions on the admiral's flagship.

These signals were repeated on all the ships throughout the fleet. Smaller warships, usually frigates, were stationed to windward of the battle, outside the pale of the smoke, as signal repeaters to insure good visual contact with the entire line of battleships. The signals were severely limited in scope, most being *Sailing Instructions* that pertained to the movements of the fleet at sea. However, some signals were deemed *Fighting Instructions* for use in combat. For the overall good of the fleet the instructions were to be rigidly followed, yet no one could seriously envision a battle scenario during which individual captains did not have some latitude with which they might react to the tactics of the enemy.

5

Sea Officers

The abilities of sea officers ought to be far superior to the abilities of officers in the Army as the nature of Sea Service is more complicated and admits of a greater number of cases than can possibly happen on the land.

—Capt. John Paul Jones, 1777

AN INDEPENDENT SPIRIT

Until the Revolution, Americans relied completely on the British Royal Navy to protect their commerce and coastlines. During the colonial wars they had successfully manned a few privateers, but Britain had provided all the ships-of-the-line, had appointed all the fleet admirals, and had fought all the great sea battles. Moreover, the seafaring community in America was composed of generally plain-speaking and plain-living people. They would chance upon no great naval leader to parallel the like of George Washington on land, and highly effective frigate captains like John Paul Jones or John Manly could scarcely compare with seasoned and competent admirals like Richard Howe or Francois de Grasse. Admirals like these, who had experience in naval warfare and a history of responsibility in ordering entire fleets, would always trump the qualities of personal leadership and unpredictable audacity of any single-ship captain involved in a worldwide naval war.

Colonial shipyards had built a few small warships during the Seven Years War, but none was bigger than 44 guns. No available American captain had served as the commodore of even a squadron, and no group of colonial ships assembled for the purpose of a naval offensive had been held together successfully for more than a fortnight. Nonetheless, colonial manpower and maritime interests had been tapped as supports for combined land and sea operations sponsored both by the individual colonials or by the ministry in London. Yet in all these cases there were no great sea battles between contesting fleets in which American skippers might gain command experience in a major encounter.

Unfortunately, when working in concert with the Royal Navy, the colonials had experienced only failure or disappointment. Their seamen, impressed into Crown service, had been ill used, or had sickened and died. Up to 70 percent of the 2,000 American volunteers serving with Vice Adm. Edward Vernon's fleet had failed to return from an abortive attack on the French West Indies in 1741, and one seventh of all the colonials serving in the military campaigns of the Seven Years War had died, mostly from sickness, disease, or privation. By 1763 many colonies—particularly Massachusetts, which among all the colonies had best supported the government in London—found themselves heavily in debt largely due to their participation in a number of such operations.

Americans had little in the way of a formal tradition of naval victory separate from that of the Royal Navy. Nonetheless, the colonials had quietly developed a meager seafighting heritage through commerce raiding. The promise of prize money urged many colonials to take up privateering as a trade. As privateers they learned by experience the rudiments of naval gunnery, the elementary evolutions of small squadrons, and the intricacies of ship-to-ship tactics. Throughout the French and Indian Wars the colonial cruisers had a field day indiscriminately hauling in vessels of every description with little regard to their possible neutrality or the nature of their cargo. The Vice Admiralty prize courts in the colonies were swamped with disputes over ownership and insurance, claims for the reparation of unjustifiable losses, and charges of abuse at the hands of the privateering crews. These experiences colored American strategic thinking during the Revolution, and they created an untapped reservoir of experienced, if generally undisciplined and middle-aged seafighters from which to fashion a small cadre of naval officers in 1775. Young sailors from the French wars had become, by the time of the Revolution, experienced seamen, sea captains, navigators, and combat leaders. John Adams noted, "Privateering is as well understood by [our countrymen] as any people whatsoever."[1]

It should be noted that American sea officers, sometimes beginning as privateers or in state navies, often transferred in and out of the Continental service. This was especially true toward the end of the war when the cruisers commissioned by Congress became redundant in the presence of the French fleet. To some extent there was a blending of the service arms in individual officers during the Revolution. For example, one of America's finest sea captains, John Barry, served as an infantry officer during the Christmas attack on the Hessian Barracks at Trenton in 1776. It is with some difficulty, therefore, that historians can parallel the status of individual men with their accomplishments at any specific time as they passed back and forth through the services.

ORDER OF PRECEDENCE

Congress failed initially to seize the opportunity to carefully choose a set of senior naval officers. To the general detriment of the service they turned rather to those willing privateering captains from former days to lead their navy. One of the first choices for a commission in the Continental service was Ezek Hopkins, an old merchant skipper whose only naval experience was as a commerce raider in the French wars. Hopkins initially took the rank of brigadier general in Rhode Island's militia, and he helped to plan the seaward-facing land defenses of the colony before accepting the senior position in the Continental Navy. Hopkins was made de facto commander-in-chief of the navy, an appointment made to please his brother Stephen Hopkins who was at that time chairman of the Naval Committee. The committee styled Hopkins a Commodore rather than as an Admiral. Ezek was described by a contemporary as "an antiquated figure, shrewd and sensible...only he swore now and then."[2]

The Naval Committee also drew up an ordered list of officers to serve in the new navy. Unfortunately, the men on the list were given precedence mainly because of political or social patronage rather than proven ability. Of those officers chosen, only Nicholas Biddle of Pennsylvania, fifth on the list,[3] had received formal training in the Royal Navy. Appointed midshipman in 1771, he had served for several years with another British midshipman named Horatio Nelson. Biddle was a capable officer even though he attained his posting through the efforts of his brother Edward who was a leading member of the Pennsylvania Committee of Safety.[4] An aggressive officer, as captain of the frigate *Randolph (32)* he proclaimed, "I think myself the match for any ship that mounts its guns on one deck."[5]

None of Washington's experienced cruiser captains was listed, except John Manly (second). James Nicholson of Maryland, who topped the list, was one of three brothers (James, John, and Samuel) who would go on to command Continental vessels. Neither James Nicholson nor Hector McNeill (third) had commanded any vessel sent against the British at the time of their appointment. Some months later, John Paul Jones (eighteenth), who had served as first lieutenant on Hopkins' flagship, *Alfred*, wrote to Robert Morris of the Marine Committee of Congress, "I cannot but lament that so little delicacy hath been observed in the appointment and promotion of officers in the sea service, many of whom are not only grossly illiterate, but want even the capacity of commanding merchant vessels."[6] Instead of a frigate, Jones was assigned the sloop *Providence (12)*. Having served as a senior lieutenant in the Continental Navy under Hopkins "he should have stood much higher upon promotion."[7]

In 1781 a congressional committee, investigating how the precedence of these officers was generated, could not "fully ascertain the rule by which that arrangement was made."[8] Nonetheless, a simple guiding principle for appointing captains to their commands by their state of residence can be gleaned from the record. Both Manley and McNeill were well-known Massachusetts skippers and their respective commands, the *Hancock* and the *Boston*, were being built in that colony. The arrangement allowed each to use his established connections with shipyards, riggers, caulkers, chandlers, and sailmakers to the utmost. Most importantly they had earned a good reputation among the local seamen who might be more easily recruited to serve aboard their respective commands. Likewise Nicholas Biddle, John Barry (seventh), Thomas Read (eighth), and Charles Alexander (tenth), all from Pennsylvania, were assigned frigates being built near Philadelphia (*Randolph, Effingham, Washington,* and *Delaware* respectively). New Yorkers Thomas Grinnell (ninth) and John Hodge (fourteenth) were to command *Congress* and *Montgomery* building on the Hudson River. Nicholson, a resident of Maryland, was given the *Virginia*, which was being laid down in Baltimore. The *Trumbull*, on the chocks at Hartford, went to Dudley Saltonstall (fourth) of Wethersfield, Connecticut. Abraham Whipple (twelfth) and John B. Hopkins (thirteenth) were given the frigates *Providence* and *Warren* building in their native Rhode Island, while Thomas Thompson (sixth) of New Hampshire was appointed to the *Raleigh* that was being built by his friend and business partner in New Hampshire. Whatever other rules the committee used to assign precedence to its remaining captains and to assign them to the dozen or so remaining sloops, brigs, and schooners, it is virtually certain that this is how the commanders of the new frigates were decided.

The compliment of American naval officers included many of the friends and relatives of the naval committee's chairman. John B. Hopkins, Ezek's son, had taken part in the burning of the British revenue cutter, *Gaspee*. Dudley Saltonstall, a Hopkins cousin, had been a privateer in the French wars. He was something of an enigma being described by some of his contemporaries as morose, ill-natured, or narrow-minded and by others as sensible and indefatigable. John Paul Jones, whose own temperament was cold-blooded and autocratic, disliked Saltonstall intensely declaring that the man had "a rude unhappy temper."[9]

Saltonstall would oversee the single greatest naval disaster to befallen the early American navy. In July 1779, he sailed as commodore of the largest fleet of Patriot vessels assembled during the war including three

Continental ships, three brigantines, thirteen privateers, twenty-one vessels of the state navies, and a dozen transports. The object of the operation was the British fort at Castine, Maine. The Patriots landed in Penobscot Bay in preparation for an attack with more than 2,000 troops. The American land force was not quite large enough to overcome the 800-man garrison by direct assault, and Saltonstall steadfastly refused to provide naval support to the land attack. After a month of siege warfare, Sir George Collier arrived with ten British warships and 1,600 redcoats to bolster the defense. An American militia general noted of Saltonstall, "The uniform backwardness of the commander of the fleet appeared in the several councils of war at which I was present; where he always held up the idea that the damage that his ships would receive in attempting the enemy's shipping would more than counterbalance the advantage of destroying them."[10]

Fearing an envelopment of their siege lines, the Americans reembarked and retreated up the Penobscot River followed by Collier's warships. Ultimately, Saltonstall was forced to abandon or burn his entire fleet and flee into the Maine woods. The American loss was 474 men; the British only 13. The Penobscot Expedition was perhaps the greatest naval defeat visited on America before Pearl Harbor (1941), and its failure is directly attributable to Saltonstall's reluctant leadership. The fort at Castine, one of the oldest fortified places in America, would be the last on United States soil to be abandoned by the British forces in 1783.

Abraham Whipple, a Hopkins nephew by marriage and a leader of the expedition that burned *Gaspee*, came to Philadelphia in the Rhode Island sloop *Katy*, which was renamed *Providence (12)*. This vessel was chosen for the first cruise of the Continental fleet and given to the command of Capt. John Hazzard (unlisted), a New Yorker, and it should not be confused with the 28-gun frigate of the same name. There is little known of Hazzard except that he was described as "a stout man, very vain and ignorant." Hazzard was dismissed from service immediately after his first cruise for failing to support another Continental vessel in battle.[11]

Whipple, however, seems to have been a competent officer. In July 1779, he had his greatest success at sea in the waters off Newfoundland. Three American warships in squadron, *Providence (28)*, *Queen of France (28)*, and *Ranger (18)* under Whipple as commodore, Capt. John Rathburn, and Lt. Thomas Simpson, respectively, entered a convoy of 150 British storeships and transports in a fog. Although the convoy was escorted by a British 74 and several smaller men-of-war, the Americans made off with eleven prizes. They also captured after a brief action the armed merchantman *Holderness*, one of the escort ships having 22 guns. The propaganda value of the American victory was incalculable. The cargoes included a rich booty of rum, sugar, coffee, and allspice worth a total of $1 million when sold in Boston.

John Barry (seventh), an Irish-born Catholic living in Pennsylvania, may have been the best sea officer in the group on the list. At the outbreak of the war the thirty-year-old Barry, a lifelong seaman and experienced shipowner, sold his merchant vessel *Black Prince* to the government. The ship was renamed *Alfred*, and it became the first flagship of the navy. Captain Barry was given command of the *Lexington (16)* immediately thereafter. In April 1776 he ran down the HM sloop *Edward*, a small warship armed with 10-9 pounders. After a lively exchange of broadsides that lasted more than an hour, Barry captured the *Edward* and brought it to Philadelphia where it was refitted for Continental service and deployed as the *Sachem (10)*. In October 1776 Congress determined that he was to receive command of the 28-gun frigate, *Effingham*; but in September 1777, with the frigate still incomplete, Barry was forced to tow it up the Delaware River and burn it as the British overran Philadelphia.

It was his encounters with the regular Royal Navy that made Barry's reputation. After the loss of *Effingham*, Barry continued in the *Lexington* until October 1778 taking HM schooner *Alert* of 20 guns and two ships loaded with supplies for the British Army. He then transferred to the Continental frigate *Raleigh (32)*. Unfortunately, he was set upon by an overwhelming force on the coast of Maine and forced to beach his ship, which he lost to his pursuers. He then spent some time awaiting a new Continental command by serving as captain of the privateer *Delaware (10)*. In the fall of 1780 he was finally appointed commander of the Continental frigate *Alliance (32)*.

Barry remained with the *Alliance* until the end of the war making numerous captures. Among these was the powerful Loyalist privateer *Mars (26)*. In May 1781 after several hours of bitter fighting, Barry took HM sloop-of-war *Atlanta (20)*. He was wounded in this engagement. Finally in March 1783, he engaged the frigate HMS *Sybylle (28)* in an indecisive running fight that proved to be the last naval engagement of the American Revolution. Barry was listed first among the captains of the United States Navy in 1794, and he is rightfully called the "Father of the United States Navy."[12]

James Josiah (nineteenth) was made senior to several other officers who were given specific commands, but he was assigned no ship. At the time of his commission, he was in command of *Champion*, an 8-gun xebec, one of the assorted sloops, barges, and floating batteries in the Delaware River. During the British attack on Philadelphia, *Champion* fell afoul of the tide, and Josiah was forced to burn it. Little is known of Josiah's naval record otherwise. Soon after the loss of *Champion*, he appeared as a plaintiff in an Admiralty Court case as the captain of the privateer *LeGerard*. In this case he claimed a share of the *Active*, a recaptured vessel taken into the Royal Navy as a supply sloop. Josiah claimed to have been in sight of the prize when four American prisoners on board (Gideon Olmstead, Artemus White, Aquilla Rumsdale, and David Clark) had overcome the officers and recaptured the sloop. Under British law he would have been given a share, but under American law the sailors' claim to the entire value was upheld in December 1778.

BRITISH SEA OFFICERS

The command of a British fleet at sea was the sole responsibility of its Admiral-in-Chief. The organizational control fell to the squadron commanders, usually lesser admirals but sometimes senior captains or commodores, who acted as rallying points for the vessels under their direct command. The actual fighting aboard each ship was directed by the captain, his lieutenants, and his junior officers, while the marines served under their own officers acting under the directives of the ship's captain.

The plain sailing of the vessel and the accomplishment of maneuvers during battle were delegated to the *sailing master* (or *master*) and his mates. The seamen where given either fighting stations or sailing responsibilities according to the organizational structure set by the captain, who was ultimately responsible for everything aboard his ship. Most of the crew were partitioned into task-oriented groups such as gun crews, boarders, sail handlers, or damage control parties. Marines served primarily as a force trained specifically in close combat and special operations. Their station in an engagement was in the fighting tops or as boarders. It was a marine detachment, specially trained to make shore landings from boats, that led the British column on its march from Boston to Lexington and Concord in April 1775.

A fleet was normally composed of three squadrons flying white, red, and blue pennants, respectively. The White Squadron commonly led the line as the Van; the Red took the Center; and the Blue brought up the Rear. The tripartite division of Van, Center, and Rear was common throughout the age of sail among many nations. The Center was the normal position of the Admiral-in-Chief and his red pennant, or flag, could usually be seen flying at the mizzen top of the flag ship. The second-in-command, or Vice Admiral, was normally offered the Van, while the most junior admiral commanded the Rear. An "Admiral of the Red" would thereby be senior to an "Admiral of the White" or an "Admiral of the Blue," better known as a Rear Admiral. These distinctions were somewhat superfluous, however, as admirals of any rank could be given overall command of a specific fleet or station as long as they did not supercede their superior officers without direct orders from the Admiralty.

The leadership of the Admiral-in-Chief remained somewhat remote from the other parts of a large fleet spread at times over many miles of ocean. This resulted in a lack of direct contact sometimes when it was most needed. Admirals, therefore, placed great reliance on prearranged orders and signals. The fleet commander commonly used signal flags, frigates as signal repeaters, speaking trumpets, and messengers in small quick boats to communicate with parts of his fleet. He usually raised his own pennant in one of the larger men-of-war so that his orders could be more easily discerned by his captains; but he could, and often did, command from other vessels in the fleet. This was usually a larger frigate, and it became the flagship (and its captain the flag captain) as soon as the admiral came aboard.

It took no small time to produce a competent naval commander, a fact of which the Americans were acutely aware. In the British service interested youths of good birth and breeding were carefully selected and sent to sea under royal, political, or personal patronage "to learn the ropes."[13] This post, having the title of midshipman, was an intermediate one between seamen known as warrant officers and those given command responsibilities as commissioned officers. Some lads as young as fourteen years were appointed midshipmen, but the majority of serving midshipmen were young men in their late teens and twenties. In all but the most extreme cases, each received a minimum of six years of sea experience before standing for a commission as lieutenant, the lowest rank commonly given a warship to command. Regardless of birth or fortune, only by passing a difficult and comprehensive examination could a midshipman receive his lieutenancy. Although the test was formidable about 95 percent of candidates passed. A "passed midshipman" without a command was often referred to as an *ensign*.[14]

Competent officers progressed by seniority in the British system, and they were given command of appropriate vessels by rank. A *lieutenant* was allowed to command only "unrated" vessels—generally sloops-of-war with less than 20 guns. A *commander* (a worthy lieutenant who had not yet been posted) might be given a Sixth rater, and a *captain* a frigate or any ship-of-the-line. Captaincies were few (about eight to ten became available in a normal year), but the absolute number depended on retirements, deaths, the availability of ships, and the largesse of the Lord Admiral. Any officer in command of a naval vessel regardless of his rank was its "captain." Naval officers that held the rank of captain were said to be *Post-captains* although they were never addressed using the term. Thereafter they were placed on the advancement list toward the rank of *admiral* as long as they stayed in active service. A senior captain, granted the temporary title of *commodore*, might be placed in charge of more than one vessel in a squadron or on a station.

A captain's salary during this period was never more than £30 per month; a lieutenant's £9; and an able seaman's a mere 24 shillings (20 shillings is equal to £1). Although seamen received the same monthly wage regardless of the ship in which they served, officers serving in smaller vessels received substantially less pay than those serving in ships-of-the-line. All naval officers also received additional money (about £1 per twenty-eight-day month) in lieu of the privilege of maintaining a servant. Captains of major warships and admirals, in order to maintain the status that went with their rank, were under some obligation to forego this added income and employ—sometimes from their own pocket—a secretary and cook, as well as a servant.

In British warships the entire value of any prize of war was distributed to the captors. One-eighth was reserved for the commander of the station (who already received £3 10s per day in salary), one-quarter to the commander of the vessel, one-eighth to the master and lieutenants, one-quarter to the warrant officers, midshipmen, and petty officers, and the remaining quarter to the seamen. Inasmuch as each man's share fell with the increasing size of the crew and the number of officers, service in generally smaller and quicker frigates was held at a premium. All naval personnel received their wages, food, and medical treatment in addition to their prize money. This pay scale remained in effect for almost the entire eighteenth century (1708–1794).[15]

Frigates were the eyes of the fleet—scouting, escorting, or relaying orders; but they were also the most likely warship to capture valuable prizes because they had great speed when compared to lumbering ships-of-the-line. Frigates were often detached on independent duty, and the command of one was much sought after by young captains looking to make their fortunes and establish their reputations. A midshipman serving on a frigate on the Newfoundland station during the period recalled the extraordinary activity of his commanding officer.

He appeared to play among the elements in the hardest storms. . . . On gaining the topsail yard, the most active and daring of our party hesitated to go upon it, as the sail was flapping violently, making it a service of great danger; but a voice was heard from the extreme end of the yard, calling upon us to save the sail, which would otherwise be beat to pieces. He [the captain] had followed us up, and, clambering over the backs of the sailors, had reached the topmast head, above the yard, and thence descended by the lift ahead of us—a feat unfortunately not easy to be explained to landsmen, but which will be allowed by seamen to demand great hardiness and address.[16]

Advancement to flag rank by seniority was not a certainty, and a good reputation as a successful captain and competent leader of men was essential. All admirals were flag officers—they had the right to fly their own colored flag. In most cases captains became available for advancement to flag rank in their forties, and many older men, shown to be incompetent, inept, or unfortunate were passed over for flag rank, serving ashore on retirement half-pay for the remainder of their careers. War accelerated the process of advancement, and some captains became fixed on attaining their own admiral's flag to the detriment of their good sense and judgment in tactical situations either being recklessly aggressive or too timid. Others, known contemptuously as "admirals of the yellow" by the Jack-tars, were moved up to flag rank only so the more fortunate or capable captains below them could receive active commands as admirals at sea. Many of the less-than-competent or aging flag officers were given "desk jobs" at Admiralty or positions commanding prison hulks, administering naval hospitals or storage facilities, or serving as naval representatives, diplomats, or colonial governors in isolated places.

An example of this system in action is the career of Adm. Sir Charles Hardy, a generally competent but aged sea officer from the Seven Years War, who was tapped as the Admiral-in-Chief for the Channel Fleet at age sixty-four, just as news of the French alliance with the Americans broke. As a young captain in 1745, Hardy had been knighted for his accomplishments, and during the French and Indian War he served as governor of New York. Sir Charles made his blue pennant in 1756 at age forty-two, but he was generally tied to the shore during the fifteen years that he held a seat in Parliament. By 1771 he had been made the chief administrator of Greenwich Seamen's Hospital. This was a significant post because the Admiralty was very proud of its pioneering medical facility.

Hardy may never again have served at sea except for a political squabble between two other active service admirals. Adm. Augustus Viscount Keppel was a leading sea officer when France declared war in 1778. Having served with distinction during the Seven Years War, it was not surprising when he was chosen to command Britain's main fleet. After an inconclusive action off Ushant in July 1778, mutual recriminations broke out between Keppel and his perennial second-in-command, Vice Adm. Sir Hugh Palliser. Owing to the involvement of both men in opposing political parties, the dispute got out of hand and created great dissension among most of the high-ranking sea officers in the Royal Navy.

Keppel was lukewarm to an aggressive prosecution of the war against America, while Palliser was a toddy to Lord Sandwich. During Keppel's court martial (which Sandwich demanded at Palliser's prodding), Palliser introduced an obviously altered ship's Log as evidence against his superior officer. Palliser's own flag captain, John Bazely of HMS *Formidable*, refused to support the evidence. "The Admiral [Palliser] gave me a piece of paper with some remarks he had made; so ... I made up a Log for that day of what I thought were Facts." The contentious Log, with three missing pages, was produced, and Bazely confessed when asked what had happened to them, "I do not know, so help me God—I hold a ship's Log sacred." After thirty-one days of testimony, much of it by junior captains of the fleet, Keppel was completely exonerated, and Palliser was branded a liar in the popular press. Palliser's own trial then followed. However, Sandwich packed the court with his own people, and he ordered all ships to sea that were captained by officers thought unfavorable to Palliser so that they could not testify. News of Palliser's speedy acquittal caused riots in the streets around the Admiralty offices at Whitehall. Ultimately Keppel withdrew from command in disgust, not to return until 1782 when Sandwich left office.[17]

Hardy was thereafter chosen commander of the Channel Fleet primarily because no other senior officer wanted to assume the post in such a heated political atmosphere. The younger men refused to serve in that important roll under an Admiralty controlled by Sandwich, who most considered incompetent in the role of First Lord. During the summer of 1779 Hardy was given thirty-eight ships to protect the home islands from an invasion by a Franco-Spanish fleet of eighty vessels under Comte Louis d'Orvilliers and Don Luis de Cordoba. Hardy is generally thought to have mishandled the assignment by sailing the entire British fleet past the enemy ships in the dark of night, and finding at daybreak that he was well downwind with the enemy men-of-war anchored within cannon shot of Portsmouth (England). Had invasion troops been immediately dispatched from France there would have been no navy to stop them. Without a fortuitous change in weather, Hardy would have to beat upwind for several days just to annoy the landing barges.[18]

Fortunately, the landings never took place because the enemy fleet became ravaged by disease due to a lack of fresh water and provisions. The British fleet did not fire a shot, but a 64-gun warship, the HMS *Ardent*, blundered into the mist of the enemy ships and surrendered before the enemy left Portsmouth. Hardy had been dangerously lax in not maintaining contact with the enemy after the two fleets had sighted each other in the growing darkness, and he was widely censured in the British press. Only the offsetting incompetencies had saved Britain from invasion.[19]

By way of comparison, the Royal Navy was well served by Adm. Lord Richard Howe who commanded the American station from 1776 to 1778. During the Seven Years War, Howe had scored a signal naval victory near the entrance to the Gulf of St. Lawrence in Canada. As captain of HMS *Dunkirk (60)* he engaged the French *Alcide (64)* and opened such a furious cannonade that the enemy struck its colors—one of the first such results for the Royal Navy in decades. Richard had two brothers who proved equally able soldiers—one older, Lord Augustus Howe and one younger, Gen. William Howe, who would be commander-in-chief of Crown forces in America until 1778. When the eldest Howe brother, Lord Augustus was killed in the forests of New York during the French and Indian War, Richard was made Viscount Lord Howe, but he was popularly known among the Jack-tars as "Black Dick."

Both Howe brothers were depressed and disgusted by Gen. Thomas Gage's bloody victory at Breed's (Bunker) Hill, but they remained in America to command the successful campaign for New York City and the

dogged campaigns in the Jerseys and along the Delaware River that ultimately captured the American capitol city of Philadelphia. The Howes
were moderate Whigs politically, Richard in the House of Lords and
William as an elected member in the Commons. As the respective
commanders of the Royal Navy and British Army in America they
attempted to reconcile the colonials to British rule throughout 1776 and
1777. Ultimately, Richard abandoned the reconciliation meetings, but so
dedicated was William to these negotiations that he was recalled to
England in 1778 to answer charges that he had allowed Washington's
rebel army to escape destruction.

Richard resigned his position as naval commander in America when his
brother William was recalled, and he refused further fleet commands until
1782 when the government administration changed. However, before leaving for England he chased a French naval squadron under the Chevalier
Charles de Ternay into Newport in a series of brilliant maneuvers off the
New England coast. His long naval career thereafter was filled with success. He was made the first naval Knight of the Garter in 1797, and he
served as First Lord of the Admiralty during the Napoleonic Wars.

THE FRENCH ROYAL MARINE

Throughout the eighteenth century the French had the second strongest
navy in the world, Britain's being the first by far. The French Royal Marine
was able to maintain some semblance of equality with the British until the
Seven Years War when it received a series of demoralizing setbacks. These
bitter losses were heartily felt by the people of the coastal provinces
and the French population as a whole. The American war achieved a
modicum of revenge for the French population, rejuvenated the élan of the
French officer corps, and, ironically, sparked a spirit of nationalism that
may have resulted in the French Revolution.

Unlike the midshipmen of the Royal Navy who might be from a middle class or mercantile background, the officers of the French Navy were
almost exclusively the sons of lesser noble houses. An aspiring midshipman (*Eleve de la Marine*) had to apply to the Ministry of Marine with a
certified copy of his family genealogy that went back four generations to
ensure that he had the required aristocratic blood to be an officer. The
selection system, based on birth like that in Spain, had the potential for
grievous consequences in terms of ability, but it worked fairly well in
producing competent officers mainly because the French aspirants, unlike
the British midshipmen who received little training before going to sea,
were highly trained before being put into active service. Consequently,
they entered the navy ready to command; yet at every rank up to flag
the average French officer was almost ten years older than his British
counterpart.[20]

While Minister of Marine in the 1760s, Choiseul had crafted a systematic training regimen in naval science for all young officers as part of his overhaul of the French navy. At the Academie de Marine naval cadets were instructed in mathematics, navigation, naval architecture, gunnery, and diplomacy. Here they studied standard texts on naval tactics such as Paul Hoste's *L'Art Des Armees Navales* (1697), but they also read modern treatises like Sebastian de Bigot Vicomte de Morogues' *Tactique Navale* (1763) or Jacques Pierre Bourde de Villehuet's *Le Maneuvrier* (1765). Although available in translation no similar texts concerning naval science were written in English for three more decades. After graduating, serving officers and seamen were exposed to a genuinely modern series of training cruises, gunnery practices, and fleet maneuvers. Moreover, French sea officers were sent as observers to foreign countries to study the various aspects of shipbuilding, naval administration, and logistical supply. John Paul Jones noted the effective training of sea officers in France, and he formulated plans for an American naval academy immediately after the war based on a regimen and course of studies similar to that used by the French.

By 1775 French naval supply depots were filled with seasoned timbers, masts, spars, sailcloth, rope, pitch, and other nautical materials. Shipyards and dry docks were brought up-to-date, and a great shipbuilding program was initiated with monies both from the king's treasury and from popular subscriptions organized by the provinces and cities of France. Many ships-of-the-line were named for the place that had supplied the finances for their building such as *Marseilles, Languedoc,* or *Ville de Paris.* The entire French nation had come to the realization that naval power was the ultimate key to victory over the British. Moreover, they reveled in twisting the lion's tail by giving the Americans aid in the form of arms, munitions, and safe havens, especially in their island ports of the Caribbean. A British sea officer, having faced the Royal Marine in their first fleet action of the war, wrote, "The French behaved more like seamen, and more officer-like then was imagined they would do, their ships were in very high order, well managed, well rigged and ... much more attentive to order than our own."[21]

FRANCE ENTERS THE WAR

In the whole of French naval history, no family of sea officers was more illustrious than that of Clocheterie. One generation after another proved its skill and courage in battle. Isaac Jean de la Clocheterie, third son of a heroic admiral, joined the navy at age thirteen as an *Eleve de la Marine,* saw action during the Seven Years War, and by age thirty-seven had gained the rank of commandant—a designation roughly equivalent to commodore. Although French sea officers were granted no regular pensions (they were all of noble families), as a Chevalier of the Order of St. Louis, Clocheterie was granted a minimum pension for life from the Crown. In 1776 Clocheterie was posted to the frigate *Belle Poule (30)*. The 640-ton French warship was built in 1768 at Bordeaux, and it carried 26-12 pounders, 4-6 pounders, and swivels in proportion. The crew and compliment of marines numbered 260 men and officers. They were very proud of *Belle Poule*'s coppered bottom that made the vessel one of the fastest in the French service.

On June 16, 1778, Clocheterie sailed up the English Channel in *Belle Poule* in consort with another frigate, *La Licorne*, and a small tender, *Le Coureur*. Clocheterie sighted several warships a short distance to his north. Although France and Britain were nominally at peace, the French commandant immediately signaled a return to the French naval base at Brest. Two aggressive British vessels, a frigate and a cutter (both with newly coppered bottoms), immediately made chase, and Clocheterie scattered his small squadron in response. The captain of *La Licorne* put his vessel on its best point of sailing, but was run down by HMS *Milford (74)*. *Le Coureur*, lightly armed but a slow sailer, was soon hauled off as a prize by the British cutter, *Alert (10)*.

The *Belle Poule*'s vaunted speed seems to have failed Clocheterie in the very light afternoon breezes, and by evening the British frigate *Arethusa (32)*, commanded by Capt. William Marshall, had gained ground on the Frenchman so that the two skippers could speak to one another over the intervening space. At six o'clock in the evening, Fairfax set his course to cross *Belle Poule*'s path and demanded that the commandant declare himself. Clocheterie backed his sails to retain a broadside position and to prevent being raked. The two ships were now within pistol shot, bow to stern, wallowing in a quiet sea. Clocheterie then assaulted Marshall with a series of French epithets, sailor fashion, and refused to otherwise acknowledge his presence.

Marshall, abandoning any diplomatic pretext, finally demanded that Clocheterie surrender his vessel and sail back to the British fleet some fourteen miles distant, presumably as a prize. When Clocheterie refused, *Arethusa* opened a point blank broadside upon him. *Belle Poule* answered, and the fight was on. For five hours the two warships fired on each other while drifting toward the coast of Brittany on the current. The remainder of the British fleet was now well to leeward twenty miles away in a freshening breeze and unable to come to *Arethusa*'s aid. Badly cut up and on an unfriendly coast, Marshall disengaged just before midnight with 44 dead among his crew of 200, and Clocheterie very wisely turned toward the coast to make repairs before any fresh antagonists should make their appearance.

The human battle losses on *Belle Poule* were also very severe. Forty men had been killed. Clocheterie was wounded twice by flying splinters, and his lieutenant was killed outright by a grape shot. Sixty-one other members of the French crew of 260 were wounded, and the ship was badly damaged but salvageable. In fact, the frigate would serve again in both the French and British navies being captured after an uneven fight with HMS *Nonesuch*, a 48-gun two-decker in July 1780.[22]

An early-twentieth-century naval historian has described the reaction in Paris to the unprovoked attack on *Belle Poule* and to Clocheterie's escape.

Great joy and exultation reigned both at court and in the city following the announcement in Paris of this engagement. It was a victory and nothing less ... because whatever may have been the motive of the *Arethusa*'s commander, [the Britisher frigate] had most certainly quit the scene of battle under fire. Le Capitaine de la Clocheterie became immediately the mode [the popular rage]. ... The king summoned the *Belle Poule*'s commander to court for a special presentation and commended him highly for his gallant conduct. His gallantry at Versailles in corridor and boudoir, much more agreeable than being shot at by cannonballs, received abundant recognition also from the fair sex, if the tittle-tattle of the court gossips is to be believed.[23]

The engagement between *Belle Poule* and *Arethusa* allowed France to legitimately wage war on the American side. As such, the names of Isaac Jean de la Clocheterie and *Belle Poule* should be ranked high in America's naval histories. The French alliance with America precipitated a tactical and strategic crisis for the British, but it also served to emphasize the need for French sea officers to show resolve and good judgment.

D'ESTAING IN AMERICA

In anticipation of completing an alliance in 1778, Adm. Charles Henri d'Estaing had already sailed (April) from Toulon with 12 ships-of-the-line, 5 frigates, and some 4,000 troops. He passed Gibraltar in May, and was destined for America a full month before the *Belle Poule-Arethusa* affair. Both the British and the Americans waited to see which way he would spring. The British did not immediately know if his destination would be the Delaware Capes, New York, Halifax, the West Indies, or even India. All of these were strategic possibilities, but it was to the mid-Atlantic coast that d'Estaing set his initial course. The British North American squadron of just eight ships-of-the-line and assorted small frigates and sloops under Admiral Howe was in the Delaware near Philadelphia at the time and in danger of being caught between the American army on land and the French fleet at sea. Yet d'Estaing took an astonishingly slow eighty-five days to cross the Atlantic allowing both the British army and navy to retreat to New York and prepare to receive him.

Once arrived on the American coast in July 1778, d'Estaing found that the outnumbered and outgunned British fleet had taken refuge behind the sandbar that was the threshold to the upper New York Bay. From the lower bay d'Estaing eyed the British for almost two weeks before flatly refusing to take the French warships into the bay to engage Howe. Instead the French fleet raised anchor and sailed away into the open sea. Admiral d'Estaing made several excuses for his failure to engage the enemy. Among them he noted the difficulty of keeping his fleet together at sea, his lack of familiarity with American coastal waters, and the apparent unfitness of some of his vessels after several months to maintain themselves at sea.

D'Estaing may have had more personal impediments to success but a lack of courage was not one of them. As an aristocrat he had begun his military career as a soldier and had not joined the navy until age thirty. The fact that he had been made a vice admiral in just nineteen years, suggests that he had some ability mixed in with his family's patronage. Nonetheless, he seems during his career to have been either overly cautious or recklessly energetic in dealing with the British. In the combined land and naval attack on Newport, Rhode Island, he finished off a flotilla of small British warships quickly enough, but he cut his cables and hurried to sea in haste to engage a British squadron in an indecisive series of maneuvers as soon as it was reported offshore. The American land forces with whom he was to cooperate ashore were stunned by his sudden departure, which was taken without consultation with the land commander. American Gen. John Sullivan was forced to retire in the face of a superior British garrison.

In the Caribbean at St. Lucia some months later, d'Estaing again failed to press an attack against an anchored British squadron of just seven ships under Rear Adm. Samuel Barrington. Twice the superior French fleet approached but their guns had little effect on Barrington's dispositions. Instead of continuing the naval bombardment or getting in among Barrington's ships and overwhelming them, d'Estaing landed some 5,000 troops on the reverse of the island and attacked the British land entrenchments on a low treeless ridge. The French troops, led by d'Estaing himself, were repulsed with heavy losses. "It was Bunker Hill all over again—but this time with the British holding the defensive position."[24]

The French fleet thereafter accomplished a few insignificant victories among the islands of the Antilles, took St. Vincent, and finally captured Grenada. Admiral Byron's tiny squadron arrived with too little, too late to recapture Grenada, but d'Estaing allowed him to escape. After a failed siege of British-held Savannah in September and October 1779 in which the American forces failed to carry the enemy's position, d'Estaing returned home to France with the most of the fleet, reaching Toulon in December 1779. He left behind in the Caribbean two squadrons under

Vice Adm. Francois de Grasse and Rear Adm. Toussaint Lamotte-Picquet, who did a brilliant job of protecting convoys, holding on to newly acquired islands, and engaging in several sharp naval skirmishes, especially the seizure of a number of shiploads of Admiral Rodney's booty from the attack on the Dutch Island of St. Eustatius. D'Estaing's long campaign (almost twenty months) showed the French that the war would be a long one. He critiqued his own accomplishments during 1778 and 1779 when he penned, "From failure to failure, and from one misfortune to another."[25]

6

The Continental Navy

When in sight of a ship or ships of the enemy, and at such other times
as may appear to make it necessary to prepare for an engagement,
the Captain shall order all things in his ship in a proper posture for
fight, and shall, in his own person and according to his duty, heart on
and encourage the inferior officers and men to fight courageously, and
not to behave themselves faintly or cry for quarter, on pain of such
punishment as the offence shall appear to deserve for his neglect.
—Regulations of the Continental Navy, 1776

THE FIRST CRUISE OF THE CONTINENTAL NAVY

In November 1775 the Naval Committee had given Commodore Ezek
Hopkins command of those converted merchant vessels being fitting out
for war by Congress in the Delaware River. Several other Continental vessels were at sea at the time of his appointment, but they were clearly not
placed under his orders.[1] By January 1776 the minimum needs of the tiny
Continental squadron had been met, and the force was made operational.
Commodore Hopkins ordered *Alfred, Columbus, Cabot,* and *Andrew
Doria* to cast their moorings and move down the ice-filled Delaware toward the sea. By February, *Providence, Fly, Hornet,* and *Wasp* had joined
the group. The eight vessels of the first Continental fleet mounted a total
of only 114 guns—the largest being 9 pounders. Besides a cadre of

officers and 700 sailors, more than 200 marines were added to the personnel of the fleet. All were professional seamen or authentic marines who had enlisted to fight at sea.[2]

The Naval Committee gave Commodore Hopkins specific instructions to proceed to "Chesapeake Bay in Virginia ... enter said bay, search out and attack, take or destroy all the naval forces of our enemies that you may find there" and then sail to "the Southward and make yourself master of such forces as the enemy may have both in North and South Carolina." These orders acknowledged Southern support for the creation of the navy in Congress, but they were hopelessly optimistic.[3] The commodore had no intention of nosing into bays and inlets where he might be bottled up by the Royal Navy. Although his own brother was its chairman, Ezek Hopkins considered the Naval Committee, "A pack of fools, ignorant as lawyers' clerks, who thought the navy could help pay for the war."[4]

On February 14, 1776, the commodore called the commanders of each vessel in the fleet to the flagship, *Alfred*, to meet under a fine yellow flag emblazoned with a thirteen segment serpent and inscribed with "Don't Tread On Me." He informed his captains that he would use his discretion to recast the mission entrusted to him by Congress and raid New Providence (Nassau) in the Bahamas to capture a store of gunpowder and arms said to be stored there. He issued orders to that effect and set the immediate destination of the fleet as Grand Abaco Island in the Bahamas.[5]

The fleet sailed from Newcastle, Delaware, on February 14, 1776. By March 1, six of the eight vessels lay at anchor off Grand Abaco. *Hornet* and *Fly* had disappeared during the voyage. For two days the fleet waited for them using the time to further train their men and refill their water casks. Two small island vessels were taken when they blundered into the anchorage filled with warships, and from the prisoners Hopkins received intelligence about New Providence. From this information and his own knowledge of the place, Hopkins drew the specifics of his raid. As the harbor was guarded by two well-situated forts, a direct assault by the fleet seemed ill-suited to the task at hand. Although he had made "no attempt to hide his presence or to take advantage of the speed and surprise that was his," Hopkins decided to employ a subterfuge and send in the marines.[6]

American marines, like their British counterparts in the Royal Navy, were carried aboard naval vessels for several reasons. Primarily they served as a force trained specifically in close combat and amphibious landings. Their station in an engagement was in the fighting tops or as boarders. They also served as a force that the officers could count on to help control the seamen. With this purpose in mind, marines were kept separate from the crew, sleeping and eating in an area between the sailors and the ship's officers. They had their own marine officers.

The initial corps of American marines had been raised in the Tun Tavern in Philadelphia. Robert Mullan, owner of the tavern, and Samuel

Nickolas were made Captains of Marines. Unlike the British Royal Marines, who served in bright red uniform coats, the American marines adopted a dark green uniform coat with white cuffs and facings like those of the British. Their small clothes—shirts, waistcoats, and breeches—were also white. They wore black leather neck-stocks, and their leather accouterments and cross-belts were white.

Packed into the two captured island vessels in an attempt at surprise, two and a half companies of marines and fifty sailors approached the harbor of New Providence. Although Hopkins' plans called for the fleet to remain over the horizon until the 200 marines landed, the commodore seriously misjudged his timing, and the fleet came barreling into the port immediately in the wake of the island vessels. Nonetheless, the marines stormed ashore on a nearby beach in their first amphibious landing and swept through the forts, which were abandoned after a nominal defense by the British garrison. This operation is recognized as the first undertaken by the marines as a distinct unit.[7]

The raid was a success limited only by the fact that the governor of New Providence had spirited 150 barrels of gunpowder out of the forts upon word of Hopkin's arrival in Grand Abaco. Seventeen large cannon (32s, 18s, and 12s) were taken as well as thousands of round shot and other ordnance supplies. Once the town was searched, the total number of cannon and mortars removed rose to 88 of various sizes. The marines also recovered twenty-four barrels of powder that remained in the forts. While lying in New Providence harbor, the fleet was rejoined by *Fly*, which had collided with *Hornet* in a storm. *Hornet*, damaged in the collision, had made for the South Carolina coast and later returned to Delaware Bay.

A FLEET ACTION

With island sickness ravaging his crews, Hopkins had no thought of holding the town of New Providence, and he ordered his captains to sail north to the Block Island Channel off Rhode Island. Here *Andrew Doria*, Capt. Nicholas Biddle, and *Fly* captured HM schooner *Hawke (14)*, and the Royal Navy bomb vessel *Bolton (8)*. Both were taken with little trouble. *Hawke* was the first Royal Navy warship captured by the Continental Navy. Shortly thereafter the British light frigate HMS *Glasgow (20)*, Capt. Tyringham Howe commanding, and its tender, (a sloop) were sighted. Ironically, the *Glasgow* was infamous as one of the warships that had bombarded the defenseless town of Bristol, and in true Royal Navy fashion Howe came barreling up ready for a fight. Although all seven Continental vessels cleared for action, no orders to engage came from Ezek Hopkins. In fact, not one order was issued by the commodore during the encounter until it ended.

The commodore's son, Capt. John B. Hopkins in *Cabot*, began the engagement. As *Cabot* and *Glasgow* came within pistol shot of one another, both ships opened with broadsides. It was immediately apparent that *Cabot's* 6 pounders were no match for the 9 pounders aboard *Glasgow*, and as *Cabot* sheered away, it was hit with a devastating broadside that wounded Captain Hopkins. Capt. Nicholas Biddle in *Andrew Doria* was forced away from the battle in order to keep from colliding with *Cabot* as it disengaged. The flagship, *Alfred*, commanded by Abraham Whipple now joined the fray with its 20-9 pounders. Lt. John Paul Jones, serving as first officer, was below at his station on the gun-deck urging on his gunners. Suddenly the American flagship's wheel and tiller tackle were struck, and the vessel broached (turned sideways). In this condition it could be raked at will by the enemy.

However, Biddle brought *Andrew Doria* back into range of the British frigate, and *Columbus* was nearing—shifting Howe's attention to his own predicament. Having acquitted himself brilliantly so far, Howe decided that there was no future in taking on the entire Patriot fleet even if they were attacking one at a time. He broke off the action and fled using his stern chasers to ward off pursuit. *Columbus* had one last chance to rake the fleeing Britisher firing a broadside at his stern counter, but most of its shot went high through the rigging. After four hours of fighting and maneuvering, Commodore Hopkins signaled a recall. This was the only direction he gave to his captains during the action.

Five Americans had been killed and nine wounded. The British tender had been taken by the prize crew aboard *Hawke*. The *Glasgow* was later reported to have sustained a good deal of punishment including "considerably damaged in its hull, 10 shot through its mainmast, 52 through its mizzen stay sail, 110 through its main sail, 88 through its fore sail, had its spars carried away and its rigging shot to pieces." *Glasgow* lost one man killed and three wounded. Each of these had been hit by musketry from American marines serving as sharpshooters. Although it was remarkable that any ship could escape eight opponents, American naval gunnery had been notably ineffective in not crippling the vessel.[8]

A NAVAL COURT MARTIAL

The afterglow of success surrounding the first American naval expedition to the Bahamas quickly faded as the details of the *Glasgow* action came to light. Numerous questions were raised of how a single British warship could do so much damage to an entire fleet and make good its escape. Although no Continental ship had been lost and several prizes had been taken during the first cruise, Commodore Hopkins quickly became the target of widespread criticism.

Flag captain Abraham Whipple demanded and received a court martial that found him to have been ineffective due only to the damage to *Alfred's* steering and not from cowardice or incompetence. John B. Hopkins' wound and Biddle's obvious aggression during the action

protected them from any serious charges; and the remaining captains of
the fleet bore the criticism with quiet embarrassment. Captain Hazzard of
Providence, however, had made no attempt to join the *Glasgow* fight
seeming content to sail back and forth well out of range. Hazzard was
hauled before a court martial and found guilty of neglecting his duty. He
was cashiered, and John Paul Jones was promoted and given *Providence*
as his own command.

The details of Ezek Hopkins' demise as "commander-in-chief" of the
navy are complicated and unimportant, and it took some time for public
reaction against him to take hold. Ultimately, he was admonished by the
Naval Committee for taking an unauthorized initiative in attacking New
Providence. Politics and recriminations regarding the *Glasgow* fight
among Hopkins' officers had prevented the fleet from putting to sea
again, and Hopkins was censured by Congress for their lack of activity.
Finally on January 2, 1778, Congress decided that it had "no further
occasion for the service of Ezek Hopkins, Esquire" and it resolved that he
"be dismissed from the service of the United States." The remainder of
his career as an American Patriot was marked by antagonism, hostility,
and alienation.[9]

Signals for the Continental Fleet by Day: A Sampling

For sailing: The flagship will loose the foretopsail, and sheet it home
For weighing and coming to sail: Loose all the topsails and sheet them home
For the fleet to anchor: Clew up the mainsail, and hoist a welt in the ensign
For seeing a strange vessel: Hoist the ensign, and lower and hoist it as many
times as you see vessels, allowing two minutes between each time
For chasing: For the whole fleet to chase, a red pendant at the foretopmast
head
To give over the chase: A white pendant at the foretopmast head
To fall into a line abreast: A red pendant at the mizzen peak
To fall into a line ahead: A white pendant at the mizzen peak
To speak to the commander: A welt in the ensign; and if in distress, accompa-
nied with two guns
Any vessel discovering a superior enemy shall fire four guns, and every vessel
in the fleet will answer with two guns
—Ezek Hopkins, February 17, 1776

Meanwhile other Continental vessels were active both singly and in
small groups. In April 1776, Capt. John Barry, commanding the Continental brig *Lexington (16)*, captured HM sloop-of-war *Edward (14)* in a
sharp one-on-one encounter off the Virginia Capes. Here was a classic
sea battle between equally matched opponents, and Barry's victory was
received with great rejoicing. In June 1776, Capt. Lambert Wickes,

Reprisal (16), and Barry, *Lexington (16)*, rescued the American privateer, *Nancy* that was filled with ammunition and military stores from the Caribbean destined for the Patriot army massing in New York. The *Nancy* was being hounded by a mixed group of Royal Navy and Loyalist vessels when Wickes and Barry interceded. Under cover of a fog the severely damaged privateer was purposely run aground at Cape May, New Jersey, unloaded, and set afire by its crew. Its magazine exploded in the growing darkness just as a boarding party from the British vessels reached it. The bodies of eleven British sailors and officers were found washed up on the beach the next morning.

In July 1776, *Reprisal (16)*, (Lambert Wickes), fought a desperate but indecisive engagement with HM sloop-of-war *Shark (16)* within sight of the West Indian island of Martinique. The French citizens on the shore created a party-like atmosphere as they watched the first ship-to-ship engagement of the Continental Navy in foreign waters. When the *Reprisal* returned to the mainland filled with military stores, *Independence (10)* (John Young), took its place on station at Martinique. Also in July, *Sachem (10)* (James Robinson) captured a heavily armed British privateer off the Virginia Capes that was brought into the Delaware with great pomp and ceremony.

In May 1777, the Continental vessels *Reprisal*, (Lambert Wickes), and *Lexington*, (Henry Johnson), joined by the privateer *Dolphin* (Samuel Nicholson), formed a small squadron in the Irish Sea that took eighteen prizes in a month—fourteen of these in just five days. The operations of this small squadron caused a great deal of consternation in Britain and Ireland, and the Royal Navy sent out a number of frigates and smaller vessels to intercept the Americans. In September Johnson was forced to surrender *Lexington (16)* to Lt. John Bazely in HMS *Alert (10)* after a three-and-one-half-hour pounding match. Although overmatched in terms of guns, the disciplined Jack-tars on *Alert* served their larger caliber weapons more efficiently than the American crew. Bazely was thereafter promoted post-captain.

During early 1778 the Continental vessels were hounded from the sea by Royal Navy escort ships and privateer hunters; but beginning in 1779 the Continental cruisers experienced their most successful period of operation in terms of prize money. Taking advantage of the disorder created by the French alliance, Capt. Gustavus Conyngham in the cutter *Revenge (14)* took sixty prizes in European and Caribbean waters in just eighteen months. Conyngham was able to frequent friendly Spain ports for the first time during this period for refits, provisions, and ammunition, and he could use both Spanish and French ports to secure and libel his prizes. This reduced the likelihood of recapture. Meanwhile, three American warships in a squadron with Abraham Whipple as commodore, made off with eleven prizes near Newfoundland and captured an armed escort ship having 22 guns. The prizes were brought into Boston to the sounds of great celebration. Finally, in 1779 Commodore John Paul Jones in *Bonhomme Richard (42)* successfully defeated *Serapis (44)*, Capt. Richard Pearson, in one of the most famous single ship encounters in naval history. The Continental Navy captured several million dollars' worth of shipping during 1779, and it had fought its most notable sea encounter. Yet it was also in 1779 that the Patriots and the Continental Navy experienced their greatest defeat at Penobscot Bay in Maine.

FATEFUL ENDINGS

Whether the Continental Navy successfully fulfilled the goals and objectives that the American Congress had in mind when it was created is a matter of debate. The eight warships, converted from merchantmen, that made up America's first Continental fleet each had a tragic ending. *Cabot* was captured by HMS *Milford (32)* in March 1777, and *Alfred* was captured exactly one year later by HMS *Ariadne (20)* and HMS *Ceres (14)*. *Andrew Doria, Fly, Wasp,* and *Hornet* were either burned or blown up by their crews in the Delaware River in 1777 to prevent their capture. *Columbus* was chased aground at Point Judith, Rhode Island and burned by its crew in April 1778. The last of the eight, *Providence,* America's most successful vessel of war with forty victories, was blown up by its crew in Penobscot Bay in 1779 in the aftermath of a failed attack on Castine, Maine.

None of the new-built frigates authorized by the Congress in 1775 got to sea before 1777, and eight of the thirteen rendered no sea service whatsoever. Four were destroyed before they were completed, and four others were lost in the defense of Philadelphia. The remaining five gave good service, but none survived the war. A fourteenth ship, the 28-gun frigate *Bourbon,* building at Chatham, Connecticut, since 1777, was still incomplete when sold at the end of the war. The fifteenth and sixteenth frigates built in America, *Trumbull (28)* and *Confederacy (32),* were added to the active American fleet in 1779, and more will be said about them presently. *Deane (32), Queen of France (32),* and *Alliance (32),* all built in Europe, were also added to the Continental fleet.

In 1777 the Patriot frigate *Hancock (32),* possibly the handsomest ship of the original thirteen built in America, was captured and taken into the Royal Navy as the *Iris (32).* Because of its speed and good sailing qualities, the ship became a favorite posting for young British officers wishing to make their fortunes and reputations by snapping up prizes. In 1780 the ship fought a fierce but indecisive engagement with the heavier French frigate *Hermione (36).* The *Hermione-Iris (Hancock)* engagement was one of the most celebrated single ship slugging matches in naval history. At the time the *Iris* was under the command of Capt. James Hawker, who as a lieutenant during the 1760s had so annoyed American colonials.

In 1778 the original frigate *Randolph (32)* blew up during an engagement with HMS *Yarmouth (64)*. The British vessel survived the explosion. There was a single American survivor picked from the water two days later who claimed that his captain, Nicholas Biddle, had the better of his opponent in the unequal fight and was going to demand his surrender just as the powder magazine detonated. Biddle's death was a great loss to America. The British also captured the frigates *Virginia (32)* and *Raleigh (32)* in 1778.

The French alliance allowed several Continental vessels to get to sea simultaneously. Briefly in late 1778 and early 1779 *Deane (32)*, *Queen of France (32)*, *Warren (32)*, *Boston (24)*, *Alliance (32)*, and *Ranger (18)* were free to serve together, but the *Warren* and two smaller Continental vessels were lost at Penobscot Bay. Proposals for combined operations between the American vessels and the French fleet under Adm. Comte Jean Baptiste D'Estaing were met with lukewarm enthusiasm on the part of the French.

The year 1780 began with only four Continental frigates in American waters, the rest being lost during the futile defense of Charleston. *Confederacy* and *Trumbull* were lost while convoying a group of merchant vessels off the Delaware Capes in 1781. It was the *Iris* (former *Hancock*) that chased and captured the Continental frigate *Trumbull (28)*. Later that same year, *Iris* was captured by the French squadron in the West Indies and bought into the Royal Marine. The *Hancock* was blown up in Toulon Harbor in 1793 during the French Revolution—the last surviving member of the Continental Navy then afloat.[10]

The final insult to the Continental Navy was the disappearance of the new-built sloop-of-war *Saratoga (18)* with all hands in 1781. The loss was probably the result of a storm at sea somewhere east of Martinique. One historian of the naval war has written, "By mid-1781 the Continental Navy was capable of little more than running errands and raiding commerce for the remainder of the war."[11]

FEEDING THE NAVY

Every officer and each man serving on board a vessel in the service of the Continental Navy was provided a daily proportion of provisions as expressed in the following weekly table approved by the Congress in October 1776. Officers, as in the British service, might supplement their daily allowance from their own purse or forego the daily allowance in lieu of a cash payment. Even though ship's provisions often lacked fresh fruit and vegetables, American sailors seem to have had enough food in terms of caloric intake. Seamen were given half a pint of rum per man every day, and a discretionary allowance when on extra duty and in time of engagement. A pint and half of vinegar for six men per week was allowed to help deter scurvy, but most American seamen touched land often enough to receive the necessary fresh provisions to prevent the disease. This was a fortuitous circumstance as the true cause of scurvy (a vitamin C deficiency) was unknown at the time. The disease was often wrongly attributed to the consumption of too much salt beef and salt pork.

Weekly Allowance of Provisions for One Seaman	
Sunday	1 lb. ship's bread, 1 lb. salt beef, and 1 lb. potatoes or turnips
Monday	1 lb. ship's bread, 1 lb. salt pork, ½ pint peas, and 4 oz. cheese
Tuesday	1 lb. ship's bread, 1 lb. salt beef, 1 lb. potatoes or turnips, and pudding
Wednesday	1 lb. ship's bread, 2 oz. butter, 4 oz. cheese, and ½ pint rice
Thursday	1 lb. ship's bread, 1 lb. salt pork, and ½ pint peas
Friday	1 lb. ship's bread, 1 lb. salt beef, 1 lb. potatoes or turnips, and pudding
Saturday	1 lb. ship's bread, 1 lb. salt pork, ½ pint peas, and 4 oz. cheese

HEALTH CARE

Congress also tried to establish a uniform method by which surgeons and surgeon's mates would be assigned to the vessels of the navy to insure the health of the crews. A ship up to 44 guns was to have a single surgeon and two mates; up to 35 guns a single surgeon and one mate; a vessel of 20 guns one surgeon; and smaller vessels only a single surgeon's mate. The surgeons were usually chosen by the ship's captain, and there was no board of certification as there was in the Royal Navy to determine their competence or the training of their assistants. Nonetheless, the Director-General of the army medical corps was empowered to appoint from the army four surgeons, twenty surgeon's mates, one apothecary, one matron, a clerk, and two medical storekeepers for the use of the navy. One nurse was allowed for every ten sailors in hospital, and many of these were female volunteers.

The Congress was unfortunate in its choice of Directors-General, however. The first was Dr. Benjamin Church, who turned out to be a British spy. The second was Dr. John Morgan, whose personality was so grating that he lasted in the job a mere three months. The third was Dr. William Shippen, who ran the service well enough for three years, but resigned over a scandal involving the sale of medical supplies. Finally, in 1780, the job went to Dr. John Cochran of Philadelphia, a competent physician who kept the position until the end of the war.

There was little that a surgeon could do aboard ship other than to curtail dysentery and scurvy. Not knowing the cause of either ailment, the best he could do for individual cases was to distinguish prolonged fevers, rashes, and bellyaches from possible epidemics that might spread throughout the crew. They might fumigate the vessel by burning pans of raw sulfur below decks or certify the need to boil out the water casks. Bleeding, the setting of broken bones, the extraction of bullets and splinters after battle, and the amputation of limbs were a surgeon's stock and trade. Certain medical procedures involving wounds to the head, brain, lungs, and bowels were just barely possible. All these were done without anesthesia of any kind beyond the stupor brought on by drinking large quantities of undiluted rum. The surgeon usually performed his operations during battle on the orlop deck or the first deck below the waterline. Most patients died of infection even though the surgeons and mates tried to lance or drain serious wounds daily.[12]

WAGES

In addition to shares of prize money, each man in the Continental service received a regular monthly wage in Continental dollars according to the following table that was devised by the Congress in 1776.

Monthly Wages in the Continental Navy, 1776	
Captain, 32 dollars	Lieutenant, 20 dollars
Master, 20 dollars	Master's mate, 15 dollars
Boatswain, 15 dollars	Boatswain's mate, 9½ dollars
Gunner, 15 dollars	Gunner's mate, 10⅔ dollars
Surgeon, 21⅓ dollars	Surgeon's mate, 13⅓ dollars
Carpenter, 15 dollars	Carpenter's mate, 10⅔ dollars
Cooper, 15 dollars	Captain's clerk, 15 dollars
Steward, 13⅓ dollars	Chaplain, 20 dollars
Able seamen, 6⅔ dollars	
Captain of marines, 26⅔ dollars	Lieutenant of marines, 18 dollars
Sergeant of marines, 8 dollars	Corporal of marines, 7⅓ dollars
Private of marines, 6⅔ dollars	Fifer or drummer, 7⅓ dollars

Warships

If your ship has but heels and sails remarkably fast you may take
liberties with the enemy.

—Robert Morris, The Marine Committee[1]

A SHIPBUILDING HERITAGE

The wooden warships of the Royal Navy that fought in the American
Revolution were all but indistinguishable from those used in the Seven
Years War. British shipwrights of the eighteenth century were of a conservative turn of mind and were content to provide ships that were
soundly built.[2] Whereas the French were constantly effecting minor
improvements in their ships-of-the-line and frigates, the mantle of leadership in marine design had actually passed to the Americans, particularly
those on the New England coast. By mid-century the Americans had
become the master commercial windship builders of the world, and this
same excellence lent itself to the design of their warships.

The ships built in the colonies were generally limited in size, but some
approached 1,000 tons. In 1742 alone at least forty vessels of between
400 and 600 tons burden were built on the Maine coast alone. The famous Baltimore clipper type, first built in the Chesapeake Bay area about
the 1750, came to be used as a basis for shipbuilding wherever speed was
paramount as in privateers, slavers, or smugglers. Elias Hasket Derby of

Salem is generally credited with developing a new type of vessel in 1776 designed for the naval service that could fight off a British sloop-of-war and still be swift enough to run from larger ships. His work led to an entirely new class of topsail schooner that was copied by American ship-builders throughout the war. Finally, Joshua Humphreys, noted for his work during the early nineteenth century, may have designed many of the best vessels of war produced during the revolution.[3]

The waterfront of an eighteenth century seaport town, even a small one, was a virtual forest of masts, yards, ropes, and pulleys. The wooden sailing ship was the largest and most complex mechanical system in the eighteenth-century world. Naval and merchant vessels were referred to largely with deference to their employment. Merchant vessels were cate-gorized by their rigging (as in a ship, brig, or sloop) while naval vessels were largely referred to by the number of gundecks or the available arma-ment on board as in *Alfred (20-9 pounders)*, that is, 20 cannon firing balls weighing 9 pounds. There is virtually no universally accepted system for recording this information, but the meaning of each notation is usu-ally clear from the context of the discussion.[4]

The accumulated variations in hull types, arrangements of masts and yards, sail types, and the rope riggings that controlled them determined the identification of the many types of sailing vessels.[5] Nonetheless, many sailing types defy general classification simply because of their limited use in a specific locality or trade. As Charles Nordhoff, a life-long mariner writing in 1884, pointed out, nautical descriptions of the parts of any particular vessel "will apply, with some slight variations, to all others, ships of the line, and frigates."[6]

The foundation of the vessel, the watertight container, which carried the crew, cargo, and cannon, was the *hull*. The hull needed to provide a stable platform from which the sails could be set and the vessel con-trolled. The design of a merchantman's hull provided primarily for buoy-ancy and cargo space; that of a warship for protection and for the ability to mount and to sustain the stress of large guns; and that of a smuggler or a privateer for speed. Balance and stability were added by stowing stones, bricks, or coal in the lowest portions of the hull to counteract the pressure of the wind on the sails and the weight of the cannon above the waterline.

Hulls of this period had a semi-circular cross section with rather blunt bows and sterns. The steepness of the angle of rise from the keel to the waterline was known as deadrise. The hull's resistance to being pushed sideways through the water by the wind was known as weatherliness. A hull that was weatherly exhibited very little leeway, or sideways move-ment, when pressed from abeam. American ship designers turned to the more pointed bows and "V" shaped cross sections having greater deadrise in an attempt to design speed and weatherliness into their vessels.

The wooden warship of the eighteenth century was the most complicated piece of machinery of its time. Powered by sails, defended by muzzle-loading cannon, and manned by several hundred seamen, marines, and officers, it was a formidable adversary. The example above is a ship-rigged frigate of about 28 guns.

The hull planking was supported by a framework of stout ribs attached to a heavy beam known as the keel. The keel was not perfectly flat having a very slight symmetrical curve at the ends somewhat like the runners of a rocking chair. Fittingly this characteristic of the keel was called rocker, and it helped the hull move through the water somewhat. The sheer was a measure of the longitudinal curvature of the deck, gunwales, and lines of the hull. The Continental frigate *Confederacy (32)* had one oddity for a large vessel of the period—the keel was rockered asymmetrically forward toward the bow. The shipbuilder's reason for employing this characteristic is a subject of debate among historical researchers, but the vessel was described by those who sailed in it as "very fast" and "well built."[7]

The wood most preferred for the keel was elm since it best resisted rotting due to continuous immersion in seawater. The ribs and skeleton of a vessel were usually formed from red oak although the American variety of white oak was ultimately found to be a superior building material.[8] When the British needed large numbers of vessels quickly, pitch pine or fir was used extensively. Fir-built vessels had a shorter life expectancy than those fashioned of oak, but they built faster because the softness of the resinous wood allowed it to be formed more easily.[9] Wood for use in marine construction was chosen for its natural shape in the tree. When they had grown to sufficient size these trees would be cut down and rough-hewn square. When the timbers arrived at the shipyard they were stored in open-air sheds for about a year to season. During construction they were fastened together by the use of mortise and tenon joints held fast by oak trunnels that were driven through predrilled holes to act as large wooden pins. In a well-designed joint, the trunnels carried very little stress acting only to hold the pieces in place. Experts at marine joinery were highly esteemed for their specific skills. Nonetheless, oceangoing vessels were constantly being rocked and twisted by the dynamic action of waves, even in calm or moderate seas, and the trunnels quickly loosened or wore. In the worst cases, they rotted or actually fell out.

With the keel laid and the ribs and skeleton in place the vessel was left for another season before the planking was added if possible. It was at this point that the construction of the generally smaller merchant vessels diverged from that of warships. Merchant vessels, more lightly ribbed than warships, usually had a single layer of planking. A warship—stoutly ribbed to withstand the pounding of an opponent's guns and the weight and stress of its own—had two layers of planking attached to the frame, one on the inside and one on the outside. This often gave the hull a thickness of over a foot. Oceangoing vessels were built with planks that met flush at their edges, providing a smooth, solid surface both above and in the water. The spaces between the planks were filled by driving in a fibrous caulking mixed with tar known as oakum and by coating the entirety with paint. Planking took a long time, and the work was grueling. Plankers were the highest-paid men in the shipyard.[10]

In the last quarter of the eighteenth century the bottoms of many vessels were being sheathed in copper to prevent the buildup of weeds and barnacles as well as the damage done in tropical waters by shipworms. The copper made a typical warship about 20 percent faster, but it produced a corrosion of the underwater iron fittings (electrolytic action) that was little understood at the time. The problem was eliminated by a painstaking application of a lacquered, watertight paper seal between the wooden hull and the copper sheathing. Although a few vessels were done earlier, the British did not begin to systematically copper their vessels of war until 1778; yet by 1782 virtually every active vessel of war in the Royal Navy had a copper bottom. The Americans did not have the metallurgical and technical resources to copper all of their ships, but some were sheathed in France or Holland.[11]

The size of the hull was determined by its cargo capacity. The hold was measured by a formula that approximated the number of large wooden "tun" containers, or their equivalent (33 cubic feet each), that could be stowed therein. Coasting vessels might have a capacity of 60 to 70 tons (note the change in spelling) while warships might range from 300 to 800 tons. Really large vessels weighed more than 1,000 tons. The distribution of the overall weight of the vessel and its cargo or guns was extremely important to a vessel's sailing qualities and safety. One cannon firing an 18-pound ball could weight more than 2,000 pounds. The center of gravity (the point at which all of the vessel's mass seemed to work) had to be directly over the keel when the ship sat upright in quiet water. The heaviest guns were placed as far down in the vessel as possible. This lowered the center of gravity and helped to stabilize the ship.[12]

The buoyancy of the hull was provided by the difference between its weight and the weight of water it displaced when afloat. The buoyant force acted on the hull at its center of buoyancy. When the ship was upright this point was designed to be in line with the keel and the center of gravity, which is also the fixed center of roll, pitch, and yaw. When the vessel was in motion, the center of buoyancy moved about as the ship

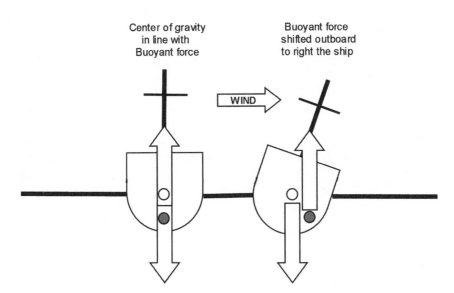

In this diagram of a vessel viewed from the stern, the white dot represents the center of gravity with its downward force, and the dark dot the point on which the upward buoyant force acts. These two forces must always be equal or the vessel will sink. The diagram is not to scale, and the center of gravity is unrealistically placed at the waterline for the purpose of simplification.

took different attitudes in the water. When heeled over on its side (roll) under the pressure of the wind, for instance, the center of buoyancy began to shift toward the outboard side (the part deepest in the water). As more of the windward side of the vessel was exposed, the buoyant force moved further in the direction of the tilt, tending to push the ship upright again from beneath. However, a number of factors acted against this natural tendency of the vessel to right itself. These included the blast of the wind on the exposed hull and sails and the shifting of any weights inside the vessel toward the roll. The inflow of water into the hull—especially the water that might come in through open gunports on the lower decks—was particularly dangerous.

Within the hull of a warship there was a common arrangement of decks. On the spar or weather deck (that which was open to the sky) the space between the bows and the foremast was called the forecastle. The space between the foremast and the mainmast was the waist, and that from the mainmast to the stern was the quarter deck. Behind the mizzen mast was the captain's day cabin. All around the upper deck were bulwarks between which were shuttered gunports that allowed cannon to fire outward. Attached to the bulwarks were rectangular casings called hammock nettings in which the seamen and midshipmen could deposit their canvas hammocks.

Most men-of-war did not carry a full tier of guns on the spar deck, the waist being open to the sky with gangways on each side. The deck below the spar deck was the main deck. This and the one below, called the lower-gundeck or berth-deck, had full tiers of gunports and guns. Between and among these guns the men ate and slept. The upper gunports could be left open for ventilation. The lower gunports were opened only in calm seas and for battle. Next below the lower gundeck was the orlop-deck, the first without gun ports cut in the hull, and a place of refuge for the wounded in battle. The aftermost part of the orlop reached "quite into the bottom of the vessel" and had an enormous space for storing dry provisions. Below the orlop was the hold. Forward and aft in the hold were the powder magazines. The rest of the hold was used to store provisions (in barrels), chains and cables, and the shot-lockers that held the cannonballs and other projectiles. In the aft-most part of the hold was the spirits-room, holding the rum and liquor, and guarded day and night by a sentry. Set between the beams that supported the tiers of the hold were the water tanks "fit nicely to the shape of the ship throughout" from which the drinking water for daily consumption was pumped. It was important to keep the water tanks in balance because the weight of water moving about in them could adversely affect the sailing qualities of the vessel.[13]

There were two basic types of sails: square and fore-and-aft, and the need to arrange these sails appropriately dictated the rig of the vessel. Riggers were professionals who used their expertise to find the most efficient and appropriate combination of sails and spars for each vessel depending on its intended use. The captain of a vessel, or the sailing master, often made decisions and modifications to its rig depending on his own preferences. Many vessels sailed particularly well with the wind coming from one relative direction, from the "port quarter" for instance. This was known as the vessel's best point of sailing, a very important characteristic if fleeing from a pursuer or trying to overtake an enemy.

Square sails (actually trapezoidal in shape) were set and carried on a variety of wooden poles known as masts and yards, and were best suited to a following wind coming from the stern. Although efficient in propelling a large vessel, the square sails were labor intensive, requiring a large number of men to set, furl, or trim them. Fore and aft sails generally required fewer hands, and rigs of three and four sided sails were common. The plane of the fore and aft sail generally ran with the long axis of the vessel much like the sails of a modern day-sailer. They sacrificed some efficiency in a following wind for the ability to sail better "into" or "slightly off" the wind. The angle of attack of such sails rarely passed fifty degrees. Sails of the revolutionary era had significantly less "belly" than those of earlier times; and square sails, in particular, had a greater vertical hoist in proportion to their horizontal spread than later types.

The term *mast* was applied to those vertical structures from which were swiveled horizontal timbers such as yards, booms, or gaffs used to support the sails. A ship was a three-masted vessel fitted with square sails on all of its masts. The three masts were named (from bow to stern) the fore, the main, and the mizzen. The mizzen mast was added behind the center of gravity to balance the effect of the wind on the fore mast. The term "mizzen" derives from an Arabic term, *misan*, which means "balance." Added to the vertical spars that served as masts was the bowsprit, a nearly horizontal timber protruding from the front of the vessel.

In the eighteenth century naval vessels had grown so large vertically that the main mast, made in sections, might have four or five separate parts with as many sails set from them. The lowest sections of the masts (or lower mast) were the heaviest pieces of lumber on the vessel, and they were set through the decks to rest firmly on the keelson at the bottom of the hull. Lower masts were sometimes bundled, or pieced together, from smaller diameter wood held together by giant metal bands. These "made masts," commonly used on French naval vessels, provided a solution to the scarcity of large diameter trees from the forests of the Baltic States or North America when supplies were interdicted in times of war, but they tended to fail suddenly. In the eighteenth century large masts shipped from New England forests in America to English shipyards were 36 inches in diameter and 36 yards long. The last one-piece masts to arrive in Britain from North America did so just as word of the battle at Bunker Hill reached London.

Each section of the mast was named for the yard and sail that were suspended from it. The lower mast carried a lower yard fixed horizontally to the mast by trusses that allowed it to be swiveled from side to side. From the lower yard hung a large sail called a course or mainsail. The topmast carried the topsail yards and the topsails. The topgallant mast similarly carried the topgallant yards and the topgallants. It was possible to name all the sails and yards arranged vertically by beginning at the deck as: courses, topsails, topgallants, or royals. By adding the horizontal placement of the mast along the deck to the sail name a particular piece of the rigging could be specified. At the junction of the lower mast and the topmast was a platform known as a top. Between the topsail mast and the topgallant mast were a set of cross trees. These structures helped to disperse the strain placed on the shrouds and stays of the rigging that held the masts upright. On naval vessels the tops were used as fighting platforms for marines and sharpshooters. A small hull could be "over sparred" by having too many yards aloft or by having spars and masts that were too thick and lacking in appropriate resiliency. Instead of being driven forward, these over sparred vessels tended to slip sideways (leeway) or behave stiffly with their bows driving into the sea.[14]

English and American colonial records suggest that the bulk of waterborne transportation in the eighteenth century was carried by a wide variety of vessels largely judged by the rigging aloft. A ship had a fore, main, and mizzen mast all of which were fitted with square sails. Sometimes a fore and aft sail was fitted directly behind the mizzen course to help in sailing into the wind. Vessels equipped with two or more masts rigged with fore and aft sails only were known as schooners. Many other types were known by local names that had developed with little regard to a fixed maritime vocabulary or were indiscriminately classified as sloops, shallops, brigs, and topsail schooners.[15]

Large sailing vessels were equipped with an amazing quantity of rope divided into an almost bewildering web of shrouds, stays, lifts, sheets, braces, halyards, and lines. There may have been three miles of rope on a small ship, and a 100-gun warship of the eighteenth century might have thirty miles of rope rigging.[16] All rope rigging was divided into two general types: standing rigging and running rigging. Standing rigging, like the shrouds and stays, was that which supported the masts and yards. Running rigging was passed through blocks and pulleys in order to adjust the position of the sails relative to the wind.[17]

Shipbuilding was a major industry in the American colonies from the time that settlement had become firmly established, but the industry was largely confined to the production of small commercial craft used in the coasting and fishing trades. The technical problems raised by the need to "fight a ship" efficiently were much harder for ship designers to resolve than the trade needs of most merchant vessels. The weight of the armament and the inherent requirements created by firing large guns proved to be the most troublesome aspect of warship development. The weight of the sails and rigging added to the mass of projectiles in the shot lockers, the weight of hundreds of seamen, and that of the provisions needed to keep them alive (especially the drinking water), made the production of a seaworthy fighting platform exceedingly difficult for shipbuilders. In order to resolve these problems "compromises were made in dimensions and proportions, which soon became national characteristics of their men-of-war." [18]

American naval shipbuilding can be traced back to 1690 when a warship (*Falkland*) was built for the Royal Navy at Portsmouth, New Hampshire. This was a fairly large ship; and, though the details are missing from the historical record, a few others of its kind were seemingly built over the next one hundred years. Yet naval shipbuilding was a specialized trade, and a dockyard apprentice was unlikely to gain sufficient experience in designing and building vessels of war without working in a government shipyard for some time.

No plans have been found that represent a colonial-built vessel of war prior to 1745. It seems certain from the surviving plans after that date,

Building a ship, even a small one like this 44-gun frigate, was a major undertaking requiring careful planning, plentiful materials, and exacting execution. The names of the individual craftsmen who produced America's first warships have largely been lost to history.

however, that a 24-gun Royal Navy frigate named *Boston* was built in that city by Benjamin Hallowell and launched in 1747 or 1748. In addition, a 44-gun warship named *America*, probably the largest warship built in the colonies before the Revolution, came off the ways at Portsmouth, New Hampshire in 1749. It is also certain that from 1755 to 1771 the British Admiralty built a number of vessels of war for operations on the Great Lakes or on Lake Champlain using colonial craftspersons. The largest of these was 84 feet at the keel, and due to the fact that they were to operate in lakes, each was very shallow in draft (or shoal). In the same period there are records of three warships (schooner rigged) being built on the Atlantic seacoast. Two were built on plans supplied by the Admiralty, but one, *Marble Head* was built to an all-American design in New York in 1767.

Colonial shipyards should have been little different from those in Britain. At this period in the development of shipbuilding as a profession, there were no great steam-powered cutting and lifting machines. Although water-powered sawmills were sometimes employed, all other woodworking was done with hand tools or treadle and spring-pole lathes. The hand tools needed to build warships were no different from those used to build merchantmen. Saw gangs were hired to "rip" planking at the saw pits with giant two-man saws, and timbers were formed with an adz and a broadax. Caulking gangs used mallets and fantail chisels to drive the oakum between the seams, and woodworkers forming the railings, hatchways, doors, appointments, and figureheads used hammers, chisels, augers, planes, and gouges similar to those used by shipwrights into the early twentieth century.

WAR FLEETS

Absolute numbers of warships maintained by each nation during the American war are difficult to determine. Even though there are copious records that may be consulted, annual estimates and monthly reports often conflict. This has much to do with the readiness of vessels to actually go to sea on a particular date as compared to those in dry dock, being refitted, having their bottoms scraped, or in some other state of temporary disrepair. Some lists include all vessels while others differentiate among those "In Commission," "Building" (under construction), or "In Ordinary" (naval vessels in reserve with only a minimal staff to maintain them). No navy, regardless of the excellence of its organization or the dedication of its mangers, had all its ships in good condition or available for service simultaneously. During the Seven Years War the Royal Navy maintained three-quarters of its ships at sea or ready for sea. This proportion was probably near the maximum figure feasible for any length of time in European waters. It has been said that it took three warships in a fleet to maintain one on the North American or West Indian Station: one on station, one being refitted, and the third either going to or coming from England. This concept helps to explain the importance of the British naval base at Halifax with its repair facilities, dockyard, and storehouses.

The Royal Navy entered the American Revolution in 1775 with approximately 250 vessels of war of all types and ended it in 1783 with slightly less than 500. This two-fold increase can be attributed in part to the production of a large number of smaller craft (sloops-of-war, cutters, and tenders) thought to be better suited to operation in North American coastal waters than larger ships. The increase in capital ships (ships-of-the-line and frigates) seems to have been about 50 percent from about 200 in 1775 to about 300 at the end of the war.

A Swedish source limited to five year estimates sets the British fleet in the 1775–1780 period at 117 ships-of-the-line and 111 cruisers (frigates and sloops-of-war), while it records that the Bourbon allies had in commission 129 ships-of-the-line and 92 cruisers, respectively. The French had taken great pains to bolster their alliance with their Bourbon cousin, Spain, which provided almost half of the vessels in each class. The source ignores small vessels of war like cutters and tenders.[19] A British source describes the Royal Navy fleet at the end of 1778 as having in commission 79 three-decked ships-of-the-line, 96 frigates and two-decked ships, and 140 smaller vessels. This source, using Admiralty records compiled in 1794, states that only 73 of the three deckers were in good repair. All but 7 of the First, Second, and Third Rate warships in the British fleet were maintained in home waters. Half of the available frigates, corvettes, and cutters were assigned to convoy duty or to searching out privateers. Approximately 60 percent of these were assigned to American rather than European waters.[20]

According to a contemporary French source, at the peak of the naval war in 1781 the total number of warships comprising the British fleet was 311, but this included a large number of corvettes and hastily built sloops-of-war throwing relatively little weight of metal and excluded the small cutters or tenders. The same source sets the French fleet at 211 warships of all rates and sizes and the Spanish 144 of slightly inferior but acceptable quality. The addition of Holland to the alliance in late 1780 added 26 ships-of-the-line and 40 frigates to the allied lists. It could be argued, though, that the Dutch as an enemy were less troublesome to Britain than they were as a neutral providing naval stores and carrying war materials for both the French and Americans.[21]

A further cautionary note is necessary with regard to these estimates. Published and unpublished navy lists from the period vary widely. The British, for example, eliminated warships under 100 tons from the designation of "frigate" on their lists in the middle of the period because they considered them too small to warrant the designation. Further, they often took major warships that were considered too old and redeployed them as troopships or hospital ships without documenting the changes on all duplicate records. The Admiralty was also fond of publishing lists padded with fictitious vessels of varying sizes for the purposes of propaganda and misinformation. Nonetheless, the estimates referenced above, while individually divergent as to the breakdown of numbers and types, all seem to show that the British and Allied fleets of 1778 were approximately equal in strength, at least on paper.[22]

RATES

Taken collectively, understanding the importance of the number and type of vessels used in naval warfare is a daunting task. However, the British developed a general system for classifying their warships by "Rate." The rating was First through Sixth. This was determined by the number of long guns (cannon only) officially carried aboard. Because each gun required a given minimum of space to operate, the number of guns generally reflected the size of the warship. Yet one naval authority believes that, because the Rate System was vague, the term "rate" had fallen into disuse by 1750 except in a few official documents and builders' plans to be replaced by the "gun-number" as in 44-gun ship or 28-gun frigate. If this is so for the American war, the rate system was certainly brought back into use during the Napoleonic Wars some decades later.[23]

Many captains added guns to the rated number, or they altered the size of the guns somewhat without respect to their number. This had to be done with great care in order to maintain the trim and buoyancy of the vessel. A vessel firing guns that were too big for its structure was in danger of shaking itself to pieces before its time. Nonetheless, two 20-gun warships might have drastically different compliments of weapons; for instance: 12-6 pounders and 8-4 pounders as compared to 4-9 pounders, 10-6 pounders, and 6-4 pounders. Making a certain determination of a vessel's armament from anecdotal sources is difficult for historians especially because this characteristic changed from time to time on the same vessel according the whims of its captain.

Ships capable of holding position in a line of battle (ships-of-the-line) were either First, Second, or Third Rates. First and Second Rates had three gundecks. Third Rates had two. First Rates carried in excess of 100 guns, Second Rates 90 to 98, and Third Rates 80, 74, or 64. The Third Rate "74" was the most common line-of-battle warship in 18th century European navies.

The most famous wooden ship-of-the-line was HMS *Victory* a 100-gun First Rater built in 1765. Built at the beginning of ten years of peace, *Victory* did not fight in a battle until 1778 (off the island of Ushant on July 27). The man-of-war is preserved as an example of its class at the Portsmouth Naval Dockyard, England. About 186 feet long, 52 feet at

The period illustration of a First Rate man-of-war above was meant to show the plan of the spars and rope rigging (up to thirty miles of it) that was used on a major warship. Nonetheless, it can give the reader a general impression of the size and power of a 100-gun three-decker. Such a vessel was the equivalent of many land-based fortresses.

the beam, 20 feet in the hold, with 32 sails and 27 miles of rope rigging, *Victory* carried 32 pounders, 18 pounders, and 9 pounders in the American Revolutionary period. Large men-of-war like *Victory* were used to fight the French and Spanish allies. The ships-of-the-line that were stationed off the American coast to deal with rebel frigates and privateers were the smaller Third Raters of the *Yarmouth, Augusta,* or *Raisonable* class of 64 guns. HMS *Boyne (70), Somerset (68),* and *Asia (64)* were all on American station in January 1775. Each Third Rater carried a nominal compliment of 480 to 520 sailors and marines.[24]

HMS *Somerset* was referenced by Henry Wadsworth Longfellow in his epic poem "Paul Revere's Ride," and Adm. Samuel Graves noted immediately after the retreat to Concord, "The vicinity of that formidable ship to Charlestown so intimidated its inhabitants that they reluctantly suffered the King's troops to come in and pass over to Boston, who would

have otherwise undoubtedly attacked." *Somerset* grounded on the back of
Cape Cod on November 2, 1778, during a very cold and stormy northeast gale. The ship was a complete loss; thirty seamen were drowned; and
300 of the crew of 450 were taken prisoner.[25]

A good deal is known about *Somerset* because its plans and records
have survived from 1746 when the warship's keel was laid down at Chatham dockyards. By 1751 at least five other vessels of this 1,400-ton class
were subsequently built to these same specifications: *Oxford, Swiftsure,
Grafton, Northumberland*, and *Buckingham*. The length of the gundeck
was approximately 160 feet and the beam 45 feet. A common distribution of its normal compliment of sixty-four guns was 26-32 pounders,
26-18 pounders, and 12-9 pounders. *Somerset* had at least 4 additional
cannon added to its armament beyond its nominal gun number. To build
a ship of this size took 2,000 trees, many of which had been planted
two generations prior to the plans for the ship being executed. In 1752
Somerset was completed at a cost of almost £50,000. Following eleven
years of service that included the Seven Years War, the ship was rebuilt at
a cost of £21,000, and from 1763 to 1778 an additional £38,000 were
spent in refits and coppering its bottom.

Fourth Rates were 50-gun vessels usually built with two decks. In the
early eighteenth century, Fourth Rates would have been intimidating
adversaries, but in the 1770s they were simply under-gunned, too small
and weakly armed to serve in the line. They tended to be posted in northern waters (like the Baltic Sea), on colonial stations (like America), or on
convoy duty where they could expect to face ships of equal or inferior
firepower. Except that they sailed poorly, such vessels were formidable
opponents for smaller enemy frigates. Each carried a compliment of
about 300 men. Many Fourth Rates were razed (cut down) as they grew
older to create more weatherly one deckers of 40 to 44 guns.

During the eighteenth century the term *frigate* appears to have become
a synonym for a fast vessel of war. Fifth and Sixth Rates were commonly
designated as frigates, and they were single-decked and ship-rigged with
three masts. Those frigates with between 32 and 44 guns were Fifth
Rates, those with 20 to 28 guns were Sixth Rates. The latter class were
remarkably quick (up to 13 knots) and weatherly making them excellent
at scouting and harassing merchantmen. They often had row-ports
between the guns and could be propelled by sweeps (large oars) when
necessary such as in getting in and out of port or nosing into inlets and
tidal streams to root out smugglers or privateers. The French term
corvette was often applied to frigates of 20 guns or less.

In 1756, under the supervision of Sir Thomas Slade, chief naval designer for the Admiralty, a plan was produced for a "sharp hulled frigate"
of 32 guns, which generally followed the pattern of previous British warships but diverged significantly in hull design from other models. Four of

these frigates were almost identical: *Southampton, Vestal, Minerva,* and *Diana.* In 1757 four more of the 32-gun class were built with slightly sharper features: *Alarm, Niger, Eolas,* and *Stag.*[26] Beginning in 1757 a new class of 36-gun Fifth Rate frigates of about 750 tons had been established along the lines of a captured French one decker. Although these were only four feet longer than the *Alarm* class of 32 guns, "they were constructed with every possible attention to their being swift sailers." The few that were built "were regarded with an admiration bordering almost on enthusiasm, so that the command of them was coveted as highly as that of the most powerful and complete ships in the British service."[27]

Two-decked Fifth Rates mounting 44 guns were considered by some British sea officers "the worst vessels which at any time composed any part of the British navy." Among these were the frigates *Roebuck, Diomede, Rainbow,* and *Serapis* (famed for its fight with *Bonhomme Richard*). The only practical way to make effective use of so many large weapons on a short vessel was to place some of them on the higher deck. However, this adversely affected the ship's pitch and roll characteristics. These determined to a great extent whether a ship would take on water in foul weather or suffer excess strain on its structure in combat. Such ships were uncomfortable, and their crews were often weary of the unnecessary buffeting they endured. All vessels at sea suffered to some extent from the swell of the ocean, but the ideal warship would roll from side to side slowly and easily, and pitch smoothly from bow to stern without jerking when parting the waves. Experience with the "manifold defects" of these two-decked frigates, including poor handling to windward and a tendency to founder (capsize) in bad weather, proved sufficient to abolish them by the end of the century.[28]

Soon after the outbreak of the rebellion more than forty frigates were deployed on the American station. Of these, *Phoenix (44), Roebuck (44), Milford (32), Liverpool (28), Lively (20), Fowey (20),* and *Rose (20)* proved particularly bothersome to the American rebels. Their names appear repeatedly in the historical record of the war. Each frigate carried between 160 and 130 men depending on its size. In 1778 records show eighteen Fifth Rates and twenty-three Sixth Rates in service in North America, with seven Sixth Rates sent to protect the rich sugar islands of the Caribbean.[29]

There were also many unrated vessels—tenders, cutters, bombs, schooners, and sloops. Among these was the Sloop-of-War, a particular class of vessels carrying less than 20 guns technically differentiated from the ship-rigged corvette by having only two masts instead of three. Nonetheless, some naval authorities consider any vessel of war with all its guns on a single deck a sloop-of-war. Built to serve in shoal water and to move under the auxiliary power of oars, the sloop-of-war was still a stoutly built war vessel. The rigging of the sloop-of-war class as square sail brigs was just coming into fashion in the 1770s. The hull type of the British sloop-of-war as a class was designed along the lines of a particularly fast sailing two-masted prize (*Amazon*) taken from the French in 1745, but the design was not strictly followed in all members of the class produced in the period.[30]

The two-masted brig HM sloop-of-war *Druid (14)* was typical of the class. Among the vessels of the *Druid* class used during the Revolution were *Ceres* and *Allegiance*. The Royal Navy contained smaller sloops-of-war like the *Racehorse (10)* and larger ones like *Weasel (16)*, *Albany (18)*, or *Jason (20)*. There were also a number of 14-gun brig-rigged vessels of war having shorter, thinner, and deeper dimensions like *Active* and *Trepassy*, a few larger 20-gun brigs of the *Sandwich* class, and several smaller 10-gun brigs of the *Egmont* class.[31]

During the period there were never more than twenty-three vessels specifically designated as sloops-of-war on the Royal Navy lists at one time, and all of this type seem to have been built in the 1770s and 1780s in response to the American War of Independence. At least three were on North American Station as early as January 1775: *Tamer (14)*, *Kingfisher (16)*, and *Swan (16)*. One of the most menacing of this class was *Hope (16)*, which aggressively patrolled the waters of Massachusetts Bay during 1776. Each sloop-of-war carried cannon of 6 to 9 pounds and about 100 men. They were formidable opponents for lightly built privateers and armed merchant vessels.

While a Third Rate warship like a 74 might take two to four years to build, a sloop-of-war could be built of oak in as little as five to nine months—in pitch pine or fir in as little as sixty days! Of course the average life of such a war vessel was less than ten years. Moreover, the construction of sloops-of-war could be let out to private shipyards leaving the Royal Navy dockyards free to work on larger vessels. The Admiralty hoped that these inexpensive vessels could suppress American trade and privateering while preventing military supplies from reaching the North American continent. The type soon became an essential and ubiquitous part of the Royal Navy delivering supplies, attacking coastal forts and batteries, and getting into the harbors and estuaries to pry out the enemy.

One-masted vessels had fallen out of favor with the British Admiralty between 1730 and 1760, and they did not reappear in the navy lists until the cutter was introduced in the mid-1770s for use along the inshore coastline. Cutters and schooners were an important part of the navy. The cutter with its light hull and flush deck was differentiated from a sloop by a long bow sprit fitted to reef in the jib sail.[32] A half dozen of these, considered by some to be the *Gaspee* class, were purchased from colonial sources in 1764 at the request of Admiral Colvill. Yet it was not until 1775 that the Admiralty decided to build additional cutters of its own design. In the interim the captains of men-of-war on the American station sometimes purchased small tenders from their own pockets. The little craft improved the effectiveness of the larger warships somewhat by making seizures in creeks and shallows that were credited to the parent vessel.[33]

The practice of purchasing tenders seems to have been quite common. However, the existence of these privately financed war craft wrecks havoc on the already chaotic historical record of seizures. Documents often report captors as "the tender" of this or that ship, while the parent vessel was elsewhere. For example Capt. Hyde Parker of the frigate HMS *Boston* made eight captures in Virginia waters through the agency of his small tender, and the captains of two frigates, HMS *Fowey* and HMS *Lively*, combined to man a single small vessel with similar results in New England waters. Many tenders were commanded by very junior officers who were expected to show good seamanship and tactical initiative.

Among the unrated vessels were gunboats and row galleys, both single and double masted, which were capable of independent movement with long sweeps (oars) even without wind for their sails. Although the galleys were very much larger than the gunboats with as many as sixteen sweeps to a side and with two or three men on each sweep they could move along for a time at three or four knots in a calm. In addition there were gun-brigs with two masts; bomb vessels commonly rigged as ketches with a recessed main mast, which allowed mortars to fire shells with high arcing trajectories; and fireships—derelicts converted to carry fire into the mass of moored enemy shipping in an anchorage.[34]

Schooners were based on a two-masted American merchant design of the same name. They were usually captured, purchased, or hired by the Royal Navy and re-rigged to meet its particular purposes. They were commonly armed with between 4 and 8 very light cannon (2, 3 or 4 pounders) and swivel guns. Schooners were used in much the same way as cutters, but their larger holds might also allow them to act as fleet tenders, carrying extra provisions and supplies for a group of larger vessels with which they traveled in consort.[35]

Large vessels carried a compliment of small craft aboard variously described as longboats, jolly boats, gigs, or launches. Boats were often used to ferry passengers, members of the crew, and supplies back and forth from the shore or between other vessels. They were referred to by many names and came in a variety of sizes. Many could "step a mast," but most relied on oars.[36]

THE AMERICAN FRIGATES

At the same time that they were deploying converted merchant vessels as warships, the members of Congress were planning the construction of thirteen frigates to be built from the keel up in what proved to be an

overly optimistic time of just three months. Five frigates of 32 guns, five
of 28 guns, and three of 24 guns were authorized. Approved in 1775
Randolph (32) was the first new frigate to sail the ocean (February 1777)
that was American-built from keel to gun truck.

Much is known of *Randolph* as the plans and specifications have survived the ship. About 135 feet long and 34 feet in beam, *Randolph*, built
in Philadelphia, was of almost 700 tons' burden. Another warship of the
same class and dimensions was built at Portsmouth, New Hampshire.
This was *Raleigh (32)*, completed and at sea by the fall of 1777. Other
members of this class of large frigates were *Warren, Hancock,* and
Washington. The 28-gun *Providence* was of 630 tons, 126 feet long,
and 34 feet in beam. This middle class frigate was also at sea by the fall of
1777 having been built in Rhode Island. The 28-gun frigates included
Congress, Virginia, Trumbull, and *Effingham.* The lightest of the American
frigates were about 500 tons' burden having 115 feet in length and 32 feet
in beam. Of the three members of this class (*Delaware, Montgomery,* and
Boston) only *Boston* saw the sea, and it had the longest career under
American command of any of the original thirteen frigates, cruising from
1777 to 1780. It is important to note, however, that not one of these vessels remained in the American fleet at war's end.

Political considerations decided many of the details of this naval construction program. The building contracts were spread among seven
states having considerable shipbuilding facilities. As things turned out,
only the frigates built in smaller and less significant colonial ports were
able to actually reach the sea under Continental colors. British operations
prevented the others from making their escape. The capture of New York
City at the entrance to the Hudson River; the seizure of Philadelphia and
closing of the lower Delaware River; and the invasion of the Chesapeake
caused the capture or destruction of six of the planned frigates: *Virginia,
Delaware, Washington, Effingham, Montgomery,* and *Congress.*

The single exception was *Randolph* (Captain Nicholas Biddle, commanding), which escaped the icy Delaware by nosing out passed Point
Henlopen in a February snowstorm. The British sentinels posted at the
mouth of the bay had been driven off their station by the foul weather.

Inspectors were appointed to keep tabs on the work of building the
frigates as it proceeded. Among the inspectors were some shipbuilders,
some ship captains, and some political hacks who knew nothing of shipbuilding. In New Hampshire, Thomas Thompson was made inspector;
in Massachusetts, John Avery and John Odin; in Rhode Island, Daniel
Tillinghast; in Connecticut, Barnabas Deane; in New York, Augustus
Lawrence and Samuel Tudor; in Maryland, Jesse Hollingsworth; and in
Pennsylvania, Robert Morris took over the task as Chairman of the
Marine Committee.

Among the shipbuilders given responsibility for the frigates were the Hackett family shipyards of Portsmouth, New Hampshire, Kittery, Maine and Salisbury, Massachusetts; Sylvester Bowers, shipbuilder of Providence, Rhode Island; Wharton and Humphreys Shipyards, Warwick Coates, shipbuilder, the brothers Manuel, Jehu, and Benjamin Eyre, shipbuilders, and Grice Shipyards all of Philadelphia; John Cotton, shipbuilder of Chatham, and J. Willets, shipbuilder of Norwich, both in Connecticut; Lancaster Burling, shipbuilder of Poughkeepsie, New York; John Greenleaf, Stephen Cross, and Ralph Cross of Greenleaf and Cross Shipyards of Newburyport in Massachusetts; and George Wells, shipbuilder of Fells Point, Maryland.

In addition James K. Hackett of Portsmouth built two ship-rigged sloops-of-war for the Continental Navy probably designed by his cousin and partner, William Hackett. The archetype of the sloop-of-war class for the American Navy was *Ranger (18)*. The other members of this 308-ton class were *Saratoga (18)* and the *General Gates (18)*. Other American vessels of war were the brigs *Reprisal (16)* and *Lexington (16)*, the cutter *Revenge (14)*, the sloops *Independence (10)* and *Sachem (10)*, and the tiny *Mosquito (4)*. Finally, the Hackett shipyards of New Hampshire produced *America (74)* the only ship-of-the-line to actually be completed in the colonies during the war. The 2,000-ton *America* was given to France in September 1782 to replace the French warship *Magnifique (74)*, which had been wrecked near Boston. *America*'s armament was designed to include a battery of 30-18 pounders, 32-12 pounders, and 12-9 pounders. The crew and marines were projected to be 626.[37]

Two more 74s were planned for building at Boston and Philadelphia, but they were never started due to the anticipated end of hostilities. A 28-gun frigate, *Bourbon*, was authorized by Congress in 1777, and the building project placed under the direction of John Cotton of Chatham, Connecticut. Although the region was never threatened by British forces, the frigate remained unfinished six years later when the war ended.

Joshua Humphreys may have designed many of the best vessels of war produced during the revolution, but he also designed and built the sloop-of-war *Saratoga (18)*, which was plagued by repeated flaws in its material structure, was struck by lightning on three occasions while sitting at anchor, and apparently foundered with a loss of all hands within seven months of being commissioned. In each of these circumstances some argument can be made to deflect fault from Humphreys' design. The entire Continental Navy suffered from a shortage of appropriate materials during the war, and the mainmast of *Saratoga* was fitted with a grounding cable after the third lightning strike that should have directed the electric charge into the water at the keel. The ship probably encountered a sudden tropical depression that caused its demise somewhere east of

Cape François in the West Indies in March 1781. There were no survivors, and the wreck of the vessel has not been found.

The credit given Humphreys as designer of the new Continental frigates has long been a matter of controversy because of his groundbreaking work in designing the *Constitution* class frigates of the Federalist Era navy. It is known with certainty that Humphreys appeared before Congress on December 13, 1775, with "the plans of several men-of-war." One authority proclaims that the plans "were not drawn by Joshua Humphreys" because he "was a very poor draftsman," and the plans that have survived "are the work of a good draftsman."[38] Nonetheless, the designs could have been envisioned by Humphreys and executed on paper by a talented, but unidentified associate. Based on the totality of his work, it remains highly likely that Humphreys personally designed the vessels that are commonly associated with his firm.[39]

Only three flush-deck warships are known to have been built during the Revolution and none have been definitely attributed to Humphreys. The privateer *Mohawk (36)* built in Salem, Massachusetts, in 1779, was one of these. The main battery was composed of 18-6 pounders on the gun deck, and the flush spar deck was fitted for 18 smaller cannon, which seems to look forward somewhat in terms of design to Humphreys' later plans for flush two-deck frigates carrying between 36 and 44 guns of the *Constitution* class ("Old Ironsides") made famous during the War of 1812. Lost under the command of Capt. John Carnes to a slightly larger British vessel, *Mohawk* was taken into the Royal Navy and its lines and measurements were taken at Deptford Dockyard, England, in 1783. The vessel had an original copper bottom and was considered a good, fast sailer.

It is highly probable that Congress established the size and the rates of the ships to be built without involving itself in details; but the Marine Committee, at least, appears to have "arranged for the designs and to have approved several of them when completed."[40] It is also possible that only the vessels laid down in Pennsylvania and Maryland were built according to the official plans with the others having been endowed with small, but meaningful, deviations from the official plans envisioned by their builders.[41] Colonial shipbuilding styles exhibited many regional differences with New York builders favoring one detail and Philadelphia builders favoring some other. These would mostly entail minor modifications of well-defined methods of ship design and construction.[42]

Only one official draft of the 32-gun American frigate class has survived, and a single plan of a 28-gun type was made by the British after its capture. No plan of the lines of the 24-gun type has been found, but the dimensions of several vessels of this class were recorded by the British after their capture showing the measurements "as built." The new American warships were noted as being very seaworthy, and they could outrun anything that they could not outfight. Judging from the specifications, the American vessels were longer in the keel than those of a similar class in the Royal Navy; more lightly built in terms of frame spacing; had a greater deadrise (angle of rise from the keel); and had somewhat less freeboard and depth of hold. It is known today that many of these characteristics tend to make a hull more speedy through the water. *Hancock*, one of the 32-gun frigates built in Massachusetts, was captured and purchased into the Royal Navy. A British officer described it as "the finest and fastest frigate in the world."[43]

Robert Morris, chairman of the Marine Committee, wrote of his faith in the new frigates to Nicholas Biddle, commander of *Randolph*. "I must observe that there are no cruising ships an overmatch for you except two-deckers. . . . Therefore you have only to avoid two-deckers or engaging [an enemy] when there is more than one in sight. . . . Any of their other single ships you need not fear. . . . If the *Randolph* has but heels [and] sails remarkably fast you may take liberties with them." Once he had worked out the rigging and learned its best sailing points, Biddle found the new frigate "the very best vessel for sailing that [he] ever knew."[44]

A careful consideration of the plans taken from captured vessels by the British Admiralty show *Hancock* to be a handsome ship with extensive ornamentation at the bow and a large rattlesnake carved on its stern. An inventory of *Virginia*, of the 28-gun class, noted a figurehead of an Indian warrior. *Randolph* also seems to have had a figurehead of some sort. It is safe to assume that decorative applications like these, common to vessels of the period, would not have been omitted from ships of the national navy. Since carvings could be done separately while the vessels was being built, no delay would be found in producing such ornaments.

Among the materials purchased for the ships were several pigments to be added to linseed oil to make paint. These included white lead, yellow ocher, red oxide, and something called Spanish brown. Black oil paint, tar, and clear wood varnish were also supplied in large quantities. This information allows the historian to make assumptions about what the frigates looked like. Furthermore, there is a great deal of information about the appearance of the American warships based on eyewitness descriptions, particularly those of British spies and Loyalist informers. Hulls below the waterline were usually painted black and the sides of most vessels were usually yellow with black moldings or narrow black stripes. Alternately, some vessels were wholly black with red, white, or yellow stripes in very narrow horizontal bands. The carved work was done in colors suitable to the subject. The decks were oiled and the bulwarks done in red or brown. Nettings, weather clothes, and standing rigging were usually tarred black. The gun trucks were painted red or brown, the tubes black, and the tompions (muzzle plugs) red or yellow.[45]

8

Cannon and Powder

Cannon lend dignity to what might otherwise be a vulgar brawl.
                                        —Frederick the Great

Only thunderbolts can be preferred to cannon.
                                        —Napoleon Bonaparte

NAVAL GUNNERY

In an engagement between two vessels of roughly equal firepower the opposing commanders would use their judgment of speed and distance to close to within the range of their guns. This could be a considerable distance, as the maximum range of naval guns could be well over a mile. However, the practical range of cannon in the eighteenth century was usually no more than a few "cable lengths" (about 200 yards each), and fighting ranges may have been as close as a "pistol shot" (under 50 yards).[1]

As the distance between the contestants closed, each commander would attempt to maneuver his vessel so as to bring the largest number of guns to bear as possible upon his opponent while simultaneously avoiding those of the enemy. Modern vessels equipped with gun turrets can sweep through most of a 360-degree circle, taking aim at almost any target without changing the orientation of the vessel itself. However, the smooth-bore cannon of an eighteenth-century sailing ship were mounted on wooden trucks, and the great weight of the guns allowed little lateral sweep. Yet some side-to-side aiming could be accomplished by the brute power of men using handspikes. Because the guns could be aimed only a few degrees forward or aft through the gun ports, one of the skills needed in a fight was the ability to place the ship in positions that allowed the gun crews a shot at the enemy.

The greatest concentration of guns resided along the sides of the vessel and combined to produce the broadside—a nearly simultaneous firing of the main battery of guns perpendicular to the long axis of the ship. The guns recoiled from the ship's side automatically when fired, and the muzzle usually came to rest just inside the railing of the ship where reloading could be done behind the safety of the ship's side. A great breeching rope was used to keep the gun from flying across the deck uncontrollably, and a block and tackle was used to run out the gun, pulling the muzzle forward again before firing. The effectiveness of the broadside had been proven over two hundred years of almost constant warfare at sea. They could be devastating even if they did not damage the hull of the ship below the waterline—blowing out great holes in the masts, overturning cannon, producing flesh-piercing splinters, and killing the gun crews and seamen directly.

British gunners of the period generally aimed for the area between the water and the railing of the ship in an attempt to strike the hull where the damage to the guns and crew would be maximized. Expert gunners could "skip" a cannonball along the water's surface like a stone to hit their target at great distances. A good gun crew could fire one broadside every five minutes, and an excellently trained crew might fire one every three minutes for short periods. To the modern mind—familiar with rapid-fire weapons—this is a very slow rate of fire; but it must be remembered that an engagement might unfold over many hours, or days, as the antagonists drifted along under shortened sail at 2 or 3 knots.

French gunners, who were considered less expert in their trade than the British even though they received formal training in gunnery, generally aimed for the masts and rigging of their enemy. Since naval cannon could not be elevated much above seven degrees, they tended to fire on the uproll of the ship to send their shot high in the air. A well-aimed solid shot could take down a mast while chain shot and bar shot were designed so that they tore away the sheets and stays like rotating sickles as they flew through the air. Damage to these supporting structures was more important than simply poking holes in the sailcloth. Grape and canister (clusters and cans of smaller projectiles) were more commonly used for the purpose of killing the crew rather than for damaging the ship. All of the navies of the eighteenth century used similar ordnance.

In the late 1770s Sir Charles Douglas, Flag Captain to Admiral Rodney, suggested several improvements in naval gunnery practices. He changed the cartridge-casings holding the gun charges from silk to cotton flannel to prevent static discharge, utilized steel springs to absorb some of the recoil of the cannon, and introduced the flint and steel gun lock to replace the slow match. Douglas' improvements were officially approved by the Admiralty in 1781. They were first used by the West Indian Squadron in the Battle of the Saintes in 1782 where more men were killed in the French flagship alone than in the entire British fleet.[2]

CANNON

While shot of smaller caliber could take down a yard or damage a mast, experience showed that cannon firing any shot smaller than 12 pounds did very little damage to the timbers of a man-of-war, and 12-, 18-, 24-, and 32-pound projectiles were commonly used in various warships. Frigates rarely carried any guns larger than 18 pounders in their main battery. The lightest guns generally carried on men-of-war (4, 6, and 9 pounders) were placed on the highest decks above the waterline to work upon the enemy's rigging and crew. The 32 pounders, which were the most effective in terms of penetration and destruction wrought, were almost always restricted to the lowest deck. After 1779, improved understanding of weapons technology made large caliber weapons of smaller overall weight possible and changed the traditional distribution of large caliber weapons somewhat. The 32 pound carronades, with their large bore and short muzzle, were adopted by the British in 1779 for use in close-range slugging matches like at the Battle of the Saintes in 1782 where they shattered the French flagship, *Ville de Paris*, into a ruin.[3]

Iron was the basic metal for all cannon, as well as for pistols, muskets, swords, pikes, and broading axes as well as cannonballs, grapeshot, and other projectiles. It was also needed to make a large number of items aboard ship including fittings and implements for serving the guns; chains and fasteners for gun carriages and for the rigging; hinges for doors, hatch covers, and chests; barrel hoops for storing provisions; bolts, screws, and reinforcements of all types; and even cast-iron ingots to serve as ballast in the lowest depths of the hold. Anchors alone required massive amounts of iron, and it was no small loss when a captain cut loose his anchor in an emergency (cut his cables) or lost one to the inevitable consequences of operations at sea.

Although the British had prohibited the establishment of mills for the slitting, rolling, plating, and forging of iron by the Iron Act of 1750, Americans had developed a large number of iron mines, bloomeries, and ironworks for the production of unworked pig iron. America produced one-seventh of all the world's iron in 1775. A line of furnaces and ironworks stretched from South Carolina to New Hampshire. The relatively secure Hudson Highlands Region from Danbury, Connecticut, in the east

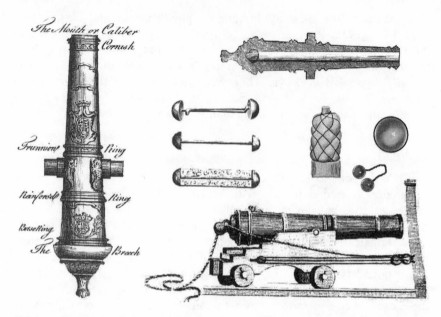

Shipboard cannon of the period were all muzzleloaders. Prepared bags of gunpowder (cartridges) were put in the cannon and rammed down toward the breech. Loose powder could be used in an emergency, but it was dangerous and inconvenient. A cloth wadding was rammed down over the powder charge to "seal" the barrel before the projectile was introduced. Period cannon fired solid spherical balls of iron, grape shot attached to a wooden sabot, and several types of bar or chain shot.

through Pompton, New Jersey, in the west was noted for its iron ore, and throughout the war the iron furnaces and foundries located there were vastly important to the rebels. The Ringwood Furnace and Charlottenburg Furnace in New Jersey, and the Deane Furnace near West Point were all important. The Brown brothers of Stirling, New York (Ringwood) cast 3,000 small iron cannon, mortars, and swivel guns for the Patriots during the war.

There was a large furnace at Hopewell in Pennsylvania some miles from the American encampment at Valley Forge, and another at Cornwall a dozen miles north of Lancaster that cast guns for the ships building in Philadelphia. The ore barges used by the furnaces north of Trenton on the Delaware River furnished the "Durham boats" for Washington's crossing in 1776. Another larger foundry was at the Batso Furnace in the pine barrens of southern New Jersey. Here iron ore blooms formed through a biological process in the shallow waters of the local marshes and wetlands. Unlike the majority of other iron furnaces where ore was cut from the bedrock, hard rock mining was unnecessary at Batso because the local marsh ore could be literally scooped up from the muddy mineral-rich bottom from rowboats and light barges.

The Salisbury Furnace located in interior Connecticut was the most important iron working facility in America because of its size and relatively secure location. While it made many smaller pieces of artillery, it dominated the production of large cannon, had a shot tower for making of projectiles, and machinery for making hand grenades. At the outbreak of the rebellion, the Salisbury works were owned by Richard Smith, a lukewarm Loyalist who initially fled to England and then returned to Connecticut to claim his property. In the meantime, the colony confiscated the furnace for the good of the public and placed Col. Joshua Porter in charge. The local sources of ore and firewood were abundant, and the Salisbury foundrymen, like most others in the period, avoided mineral coal by using pure charcoal produced in the forests. This made the operation of the works more secure from interruption than would otherwise have been the case.

A great deal is known about the Salisbury works from the many documents that have survived the war. These lend a transparency to the operation that is of unusual benefit for historians. Lemeul Bryant was hired as cannon founder, and David Carver, Zebulon White, and David Oldman were retained as cannon mold makers. The furnaces required a great number of additional workers including pattern makers, banksmen (who properly "charged" the furnace), woodcutters, charcoal makers, limestone miners, and teamsters. It was found that with each firing of the great iron furnaces a good deal of their insides was somewhat eaten away requiring that their linings be resurfaced periodically. Consequently, a whole company of smiths, brickmakers, masons, quarrymen, and carpenters was kept on hand to maintain the plant and other parts of the facility such as the giant water-powered bellows that provided the blast. These men served the patriotic cause of independence just as surely as any soldier who carried a musket, fired a cannon, or swung a sword.[4]

The process of casting large metal objects was called founding. Some items like anchors, cooking kettles, and round shot could be used with some minor internal flaws, but the guns had to be perfect if they were not to fail catastrophically when fired. Although brass (actually bronze) ordnance was considered preferable to that made of iron due to weight considerations, the domestic production of brass or bronze guns by the Patriots proved difficult because most failed to stand "proof." In proofing the piece, it was intentionally overloaded with powder and double shot to disclose any unseen flaws. Although French cannon founders preferred bronze, iron pieces were easier to cast correctly. Moreover there were many iron founders in American experienced in casting pots, kettles, stove plates, and other household items. Nonetheless, because the British had never allowed the colonies to produce cannon, experienced cannon founders were difficult to find.

Cornwall Furnace was owned by the active Patriot brothers Peter and Curttis Grubb. They hired Morgan Busteed, an experienced brass bell founder who first attempted to cast a large iron cannon at Cornwall in April 1776; but it was not until August that Busteed produced a gun that would pass proof. Thus frustrated, Congress sent Capt. Daniel Joy, an experienced iron founder originally from England, to assist Busteed. In September, the two men produced a second 12 pounder that withstood proof although it was thought to be too heavy. All the American foundries cast iron cannon on the French pattern, which was slightly longer than the British and "double fortified," having a thicker wall than the standard. Congress thereafter directed Col. Jedediah Elderkin to make inquiries in Europe concerning the best means of founding guns, of boring their barrels, and of turning their trunions. Elderkin was able to contact a number of founders who provided additional expertise. Nonetheless, of forty-two 12-pound ship's cannon that were cast at the Cornwall furnace, all but twenty-four failed proof, attesting to the continued difficulty of the process. Captain Joy remained at Cornwall until 1780 supervising the production of 8- and 10-inch explosive shells, and 12-, 18-, and 24-pound cannonballs for the war effort.[5]

The largest iron cannon cast at Salisbury before the revolution were 18 pounders. The size was dictated by the amount of molten metal that could be produced in one pour. The process was not continuous, and preparing the furnace for a pour could take many weeks. Salisbury works could produce only enough metal for two 18 pounders per pour, but by 1778 the facilities were improved to allow for the casting of 32 pounders. When all the guns to arm *Alliance* and *Confederacy* were ordered from Connecticut, the furnace could not deliver, and the contract was transferred to a works in Massachusetts, which also failed to deliver. This caused a delay in the deployment of both ships. In service *Alliance* carried 28-12 pounders and 8-9 pounders, while *Confederacy* carried 28-12 pounders and 8-6 pounders.[6]

Some of the furnaces, secure because they were located inland, found it difficult to transport the enormously heavy naval guns to the coast. Private contractors with horses and wagons were busy supplying provisions to the war effort, and Congress was forced to approve the immediate impressment of appropriate transportation. This damaged public relations somewhat with the local farmers and teamsters. Salisbury's position on a navigable river was a great advantage not shared by many other furnaces. Hundreds of cannon and shot made at Salisbury found their way down the Connecticut River by barge to the towns along Long Island Sound where they were fitted to warships and privateers.[7]

Swivel guns were far less standardized than naval cannon, and they ranged from heavy muskets set in wood stocks to small all-metal cannon supported by an oar-lock style mounting set in the rail of the vessel or on a vertical timber. Because they were never very secure in their mountings, swivels rarely fired more than one pound of shot, usually loose balls or langrage (a mixture of shot, pebbles, broken glass, etc). The use of langrage was considered a violation of the accepted rules of warfare worthy of only pirates and smugglers. Many swivels appeared like miniature cannon while others had "monkey tail" handles curved much like a skeletal pistol grip. The barrels were commonly between 28 and 36 inches long with a bore between 1 and 2 inches. In January 1777 the Salisbury Furnace was ordered to cast a ton of swivel shot (and 200 hand grenades) for a single ship (*Oliver Cromwell, 18*) attesting to the huge quantities required to supply an entire fleet.

There seems to have been an adequate underground stock of small caliber artillery pieces for purchase by privateers when the war began.[8] Furthermore, as late as 1779, Capt. Stephen Betts of Norwalk, Connecticut, was able to quickly secure six small ship's cannon for the defense of

The swivel gun, seen here fixed to the railing of the replica Continental vessel *Providence*, was an awesome man killer when loaded with musketballs, grape shot, or langrage. Too heavy to be handheld and too small to damage the timbers of a ship, the swivel gun was used as an antipersonnel weapon, clearing the decks of an enemy vessel like a giant shotgun. They were also effective in repelling boarders.

the town against British raiders at the Battle of the Rocks. The redcoats and Loyalists under Maj. Gen. William Tryon "simply could not dislodge the small group of patriots" who had positioned the guns among the rocky crags that jutted up twenty to thirty feet from the rolling farmland of the town.[9]

The committee of safety in New York accumulated almost 300 cannon in an artillery park (depot) on Valentine Hill in the Bronx in 1776. Many of these were "small, old, and mounted on wooden garrison trucks," but they were still considered serviceable. The records of the New York Conspiracy Committee show that the cannon in the depot were the target of a nighttime sabotage by Loyalists who spiked the touch holes, and jammed large cobbles into the muzzles. Several suspects were arrested but no hard evidence of their guilt was forthcoming.[10]

John Glover and Ephraim Bowen experienced a great deal of trouble securing guns for Washington's fleet in 1775. Even when they could locate some, the owners demanded steep prices or made outrageous provisions for their rental. Glover wrote to one man, "Doubtless you will remember when I received your guns, it was agreed that if they should be lost, I was to see you paid four [hundred] pounds for the pair."[11] One of Bowen's first considerations was acquiring cannon suitable to the sea service. Many of Washington's vessels were too old or structurally too weak to absorb the strain of large cannon being fired upon their decks. Capt. William Coit thought his command so unfit in this regard that he noted, "If obliged to fire both guns of a side at a time, it would split her [*Harrison*] open from her gunwale to her keelson." His guns were mere 3 pounders, thought to be as ineffective as popguns against a ship's timbers.

There were a large number of small cannon (2, 3, and 4 pounders) in private hands in New England at the early stage of the war before the privateers bought them all up. Bowen's first acquisition was an assortment of 3 pounders, mortars, and swivels, but these were so varied in size, age, and quality that he initially was loathe to use them. Yet, due to a growing scarcity he was forced to install some of these weapons on *Harrison*. Of these Captain Coit said with great sarcasm, "[The] 4 three pounders [were] brought into this country by Lords Saye and Seal, to Sayebrook when they first came [in the seventeenth century]. A pair of coehorns that Noah had in the Ark; [and] . . . six swivels, the first that were ever landed at Plymouth, and never fired once."[12]

Bowen's next stop was at Simeon Potter's chandlery in Bristol. He owned 10-4 pounders and 10 swivel guns, and his waterfront shop also served the needs of mariners for ironwork, sails, hooks, lines, nails, clothing (called slops), axes, knives, swords, lead and iron shot, and gunpowder in kegs. Bowen found that Potter was not going to allow his own economic prosperity to suffer because of the patriotism of his neighbors. He refused flatly to lend or lease any weapons, and he proposed a price of $1,000 for four of the carriage guns excluding the swivels. When it became known that the governor of Rhode Island had offered the fleet 10-4 pounders, Bowen bargained Potter down to $700. By making a cash payment in pounds sterling (£220) he was able to include the swivels, gun implements for loading, and 200 rounds of shot. Bowen was also able to acquire 6-6 pounders for *Washington* from a separate source. A survey of these 6 pounders by a British naval officer shortly after the brig's capture, however, found "the guns and carriages totally unserviceable" and "not fit for war."[13]

Naval guns came attached to short, stocky trucks with thick wooden wheels made of elm or beech wood that allowed them to be run in and out of the gunports without damaging the decks. These were not notably different from garrison carriages except that the naval guns had wooden wheels instead of the common ironbound ones found in fortress pieces. The cannon tube rested between the sides of the frame on vertical members called transoms. The height of the side pieces on the trucks depended

This is part of the main battery of the replica Continental sloop-of-war *Providence*. It was composed of 4 pounders mounted on wooden naval carriages called trucks. The gunports are closed. The actual vessel carried a total of 10 to 12 cannon, and swivel guns in proportion, during its career, depending largely on the whims of its skipper.

on the height of the portholes in the ships from the deck. This was a simple but essential detail. The gun needed to be mounted in a rest position
that caused the muzzle to "touch above the port-hole, in order that it
may not push the shutter open when the ship rolls in stormy weather."[14]

Naval cannon were best deployed in the offensive mode against both
naval and shore targets. Since their weight was carried by the buoyancy
of the ship, the very largest guns that the structure of a warship could
support were thought best.[15] Contemporary sources note that artillery
tubes fitted for ships before 1780 generally had longer barrels than field-
pieces of the same caliber that accompanied the infantry on the battlefield. Terms like "long three's" or "short six pounders" are found in a
number of period sources. They refer to the barrel length rather than the
range of the weapon.[16] A recognized documentary source from the period, A Treatise of Artillery (1780), suggests, "Field pieces or battalion
guns should be short and light, in order to be able to advance or retreat
as fast as the army.... For these reasons we make in our new construction the length of light field pieces 14 diameters of their shot, the ship
guns 15 of those diameters."[17]

GUNPOWDER

The Patriots used all of the gunpowder available to the colonies before
the war in driving the British from Boston (April 1775–March 1776).
When Washington arrived at the Patriot works surrounding Boston, he
was so struck by the lack of gunpowder that he did not utter a word for
half an hour. He wrote to Congress, "We are so exceedingly destitute [of
gunpowder] that our artillery will be of little use."[18] On Christmas Day
1775, he reported, "Our want of powder is inconceivable. A daily waste
and no supply administers a gloomy prospect." Three weeks later the
entire rebellion hinged on the paper cartridges in the men's ammunition
pouches and the fixed ammunition stored in the limber chests of the artillery.[19] Edmund Burke, well known as a voice of moderation in Parliament, wrote to a friend, "The greatest difficulty the Provincials labour
under is the want of gunpowder. Habituated as they have always been to
supplies from abroad of every thing—they have not been as diligent in
establishing manufactures of military stores as their situation necessarily
requires."[20]

Washington's immediate problem with respect to powder was partially
solved by the timely capture of the British store ship, Nancy loaded with
ordnance supplies and 100 barrels of powder. Also, numerous privately
consigned cargoes of gunpowder began to arrive from France and from
the Dutch West Indies, yet by early 1776 all the gunpowder that had been
imported since the beginning of hostilities had also been dispersed among
the many Committees of Safety in the other colonies. Congress consigned

ten tons of this to Washington, and smaller quantities were brought in by agents of the individual colonies. With sufficient powder in New England to answer their immediate purpose, Congress stopped any transfers of powder to Boston from other colonies lest it fall into British hands.[21]

The Dutch West Indian island of St. Eustatius was a veritable warehouse of arms and gunpowder for the Americans throughout most of the war. Its main street was lined with storehouses, and its wharves were stacked with barrels and crates. At any one time a dozen American vessels might be riding at anchor in the harbor waiting to take on shipments of war material. The Royal Navy kept a discrete patrol in the neutral waters around the island, and American skippers waited for the proper alignment of wind and tide to make a desperate run for the open ocean. One of the great failures of the Royal Navy was their inability to cut off these shipments of war material.

The Congress took steps to secure a reliable supply of gunpowder adequate for pursuing its ends. A group of New York merchants secretly chartered a pair of swift ships, loaded them with good American wheat, and sent them out to Europe to return with gunpowder and other war material. The scheme recognized that the value of good American produce was more enduring than the untested worth of the new Continental dollar. The Patriots also began to receive powder, ordnance, muskets, and flints through the services of Hortalez and Company, a front for the French government. Hundreds of barrels of powder and other munitions were delivered to New York by the French just prior to the British invasion in July 1776.

Secret shipments of gunpowder and arms continued during the early war years, but there was always some shortage. Nonetheless, the only American battle loss directly attributable to a shortage of gunpowder was at Breed's Hill. The formal alliance with France in 1778 almost completely eliminated any severe shortages among American land and naval forces and also provided much needed uniforms, blankets, and kit. Nonetheless, as late as July 1780, the failure of a single shipment of gunpowder from France so distressed Washington that he wrote that it "ensured the continuance of the stalemate" between Britain and America.[22]

9

George Washington's Private Navy

> You are to proceed ... immediately on a cruise against such vessels as
> may be found on the high seas ... to or from Boston in the service of
> the ministerial army to take [and] seize all such vessels ... of which
> you have good reason to suspect are in such service.
> —Washington's Orders to his Sea Captains, 1775

BOSTON

George Washington provided the germ of the idea of a naval offensive in
1775 while sitting on Dorchester Heights overlooking an entire British
army virtually shut up in Boston by an estimated 10,000 colonial militiamen on the landward side. The fighting at Lexington and Concord on
April 19, 1775, had incensed the colonials and filled them with pride for
inflicting a crushing blow on the hated redcoat columns as they had
retreated back to the city. The ragtag farmers and shopkeepers quickly
organized themselves into a self-styled Army of Observation, and Congress appointed Washington its commander-in-chief.

Gen. Thomas Gage, the British army commander in Boston, clearly
had been overwhelmed by the circumstances surrounding the April
encounter. Yet most military commanders might find a base virtually

surrounded by water like Boston a comforting advantage in the face of so many of the enemy. Supported by the warships of Vice Adm. Samuel Graves, it would seem at first that control of the local waters insured the British both security and a practical lifeline by way of the sea. With secure sealanes the redcoats could be supplied with food, ammunition, firewood, and additional troops. Washington proposed to attack these supply lines, and thereby discomfort the redcoats in their own barracks.

Moreover, Boston harbor proved a disappointing base for the Royal Navy. It was shallow with approaches that were narrow and difficult for large warships to navigate (see Map 2). Even experienced naval officers found that they were constantly in danger of running their vessels aground on the awkwardly placed mudflats, sandbars, and rocky shoals. Local pilots, who generally sided with the rebels, could not be found or could not be forced to help. Because of the pattern of tidal channels, it was also difficult to anchor the ships in positions that favored the bombardment of the rebel entrenchments. Moreover, Graves' fleet had been battered during the New England winter, and January and February 1775 had left his warships "one cake of ice"—choking the blocks, freezing the tackle, and requiring repairs that the facilities of a colonial port were hard pressed to provide. The springtime insurrection, coming on the heels of the thaw, had forced Graves to suspend the normal schedule of refits and maintenance.[1]

In a letter to the *London Chronicle* (dated October 24, 1775) a Loyalist observer described how the personnel of the North American Squadron felt about Graves, "A good seaman and brave, and...very active, but somewhat severe, of few words, and rough in his manner."[2] However, the admiral was also a deliberate and unimaginative commander maintaining the bulk of his force at anchor and sending out only his least powerful warships to patrol the vast sealanes in ones and twos.[3] Moreover, Graves "entertained a mortal antipathy" toward Gage that the general returned in kind. Although the two British commanders "attempted to function with an outward decorum," neither was willing to appreciate the other's most pressing problems. Both men would be replaced before the year was out.[4]

Massachusetts Bay, the scene of these remarkable circumstances, is three hundred miles long and approximately fifty miles wide from Cape Ann on the north to the familiar horn of Cape Cod on the south (see Map 1). Except for that portion inside the horn, it is open to the sea. The mainland coastline of the bay is crenellated with many small harbors and coves, and all of it with the exception of Boston was in rebel hands. From Cape Cod to Nova Scotia the approaches to the bay covered more than four degrees of latitude and was more likely to be fogged in than any other place on the Patriot-held coastline. In the presence of British patrols and privateers, the fog bank was a great friend to rebel shipping. An incoming vessel finding an enemy cruiser in the bay could always make for a more easterly port such as Newburyport or Portsmouth with little chance of being detected. Harbors like Beverly, Salem, Marblehead, Gloucester, and Plymouth were dotted with scattered small islands and dangerous shoal water, but an American vessel familiar with the coast might safely make any one of them.

Oddly Admiral Graves had taken no steps to occupy or neutralize any of the larger coastal ports, which were also a threat to his own lines of supply and communications. He could easily have done so by stationing a major warship in the mouth of each. In May 1775 Lord Dunmore, Royal Governor of Virginia, suggested exactly such a plan in a letter to Graves. "Such a ship having so considerable a body of men aboard [approximately 130 to 480 sailors and marines]... would strike awe over the whole country, and a small post onshore under the protection of the guns of such a ship would maintain itself against all the efforts which are in the power of an undisciplined multitude to make." Dunmore also suggested that the ship's boats and other small craft could patrol about the mouths of the rivers to effectively prevent the "admission of arms and ammunition into the colony."[5]

Instead of following this advice, Graves set a few frigates and sloops to patrolling the whole expanse of Massachusetts Bay, while the bulk of his fleet lay idle like painted ships upon a canvas sea supposedly defending several thousand redcoats in a city almost totally surrounded by water and virtually immune from a successful ground attack. Nonetheless, Graves feared the Americans presence, and he "ordered the ships of war in the harbor to be secured with booms all around to prevent their being boarded and taken by rebel whaleboats."[6]

Among the ships set to patrol the bay was HMS *Cerberus (32)*, named for the mythological three-headed dog that guarded the gateway into the underworld. *Cerberus* had dropped anchor at Boston during May 1775 with three army officers on board including Gage's replacement. The choice of a ship of that particular name was not lost on the Americans, for all three British generals on board would figure prominently in the history of the land war. A London newspaper noted of their posting to America:

Behold the *Cerberus* the Atlantic plough.
Her precious cargo Burgoyne, Clinton, Howe.
Bow, wow, wow![7]

WASHINGTON'S MARBLEHEAD SKIPPERS

Colonial consciousness of the military value of prosecuting a war at sea was fueled largely by the necessity of procuring arms and gunpowder for the army. Washington envisioned an armed American vessel eluding the British patrols and intercepting some of the richly laden and weakly armed transports and supply ships that kept the redcoats functioning in the city. Such a cruiser might make "a fortunate capture of an ordnance ship [that] would give new life to the camp, and an immediate turn to the issue of this campaign."[8]

Washington's agents commissioned eight small, fast, and lightly armed vessels to sail from Marblehead, Beverly, and other nearby ports. Each vessel sailed under a white ensign bearing a green pine tree with the words "An Appeal to Heaven" inscribed below it. The general also commissioned a dozen sea officers to command these vessels, among them captains Nicholas Broughton, John Selman, William Coit, Sion Martindale, Winborn Adams, Samuel Tucker, Daniel Waters, John Ayres, William Burke, John Skimmer, John Mugford, and John Manly.[9] Some of these men were incompetent, some effective, and some heroic, but each was a pioneering member of America's first navy.

As a group, Washington's "Marblehead" captains captured fifty-five prizes. A number of these captures were important in that they changed the course of the early rebellion. This was particularly the case with the capture of the ordnance brig *Nancy*, the supply vessel *Concord*, and the troop transports *Anne, George, Lord Howe*, and *Annabella*. It was also reported in May 1776 that the armed ordnance vessel *Hope (6)* with 1,500 barrels of gunpowder and other warlike items aboard had been captured. The *Hope* alone was valued at more than £40,000. The *London Chronicle* reported somewhat erroneously that these vessels were all taken "within sight of the [British] fleet in Boston."[10]

It is almost impossible for historians to know with confidence how many vessels were being stopped at sea and either captured or released by the Americans. Because they feared prosecution as pirates if captured, none of Washington's skippers kept logs and few bothered to write after-action

Washington's Fleet of Schooners

Name	Guns	Type	Commander(s)
Hannah	4	4 pd.	Broughton
Hancock	6	4 pd.	Selman/Manly/Tucker
Franklin	6	unknown	Tucker/Mugford/Franklin
Harrison	6	4 pd.	Coit/Dyar
Washington	10	6 pd., 4 pd.	Martindale
Warren	4	4 pd.	W. Adams/Burke
Lee	6	4 pd., 2 pd.	Manly/Waters
Lynch	4	4 pd., 2 pd.	Ayres

reports except in the case of a remarkable capture.[11] In a large number of cases the documents used by the prize agents and courts in libeling vessels have been lost or destroyed leaving only anecdotal remarks or personal letters as sources of detailed information. Due to the nature of their business, newspaper reports of events are particularly redundant in their reporting of captures. Even the *Journals of the Continental Congress* are filled with inaccurate reports and mutually inconsistent accounts.[12]

Nonetheless, in a crisis, perception is often more important than reality, especially when the perception is founded on a kernel of truth. A British soldier, serving in Boston, wrote to the editor of a London paper, "We are now almost as much blocked up by sea as we have been for these eight months by land. ... There is nothing to prevent the rebels from taking every vessel bound for this port; for though there are twenty pennants flying in this harbour, I cannot find ... one vessel cruising in the bay." This was not completely accurate. There were a number of Royal Navy and Loyalist cruisers on patrol. Nonetheless, though he had no firsthand knowledge of the situation, the editor of London's *Public Adviser* noted, "By the last letters from America we are informed that the Provincials are very successful in their naval enterprises ... [and] some of our vessels [are] being almost daily taken under the eyes of our fleet."[13]

The many months it took for information to pass back and forth over the Atlantic created an impediment for British prosecution of the war. Intelligence gathered by spies and informants in America was often acted upon by the ministry in London when it was vastly out of date. Moreover, unsupported rumors transmitted by fast moving packets were often reported as facts by the British press. Lord Richard Howe sent to America to command the fleet found the situation on his arrival to be vastly different from that which had been described to him in England. Months later, English newspapers would inaccurately report Howe's death at sea near the Newfoundland Banks. Ambrose Serle, Howe's secretary, complained that the papers had "freely killed Lord Howe ... a trifling difference between the plot and the action of a lye!"[14]

The reality of the naval war off the coast of Massachusetts was not nearly so one-sided. Graves' patrols were remarkably vigilant given the onerous nature of their task, yet the Royal Navy captured only two of Washington's most active cruisers. The "David and Goliath" contest had its effect in that it served to document the continued activity of the rebels and the British inability to stop them.[15] A Loyalist refugee in London expressed his growing lack of confidence in Graves to a friend. "What excuse can be found for a British Admiral, who with 30 or 40 ships [*sic*] under his command suffers a garrison to starve though surrounded by plenty of every necessary within reach of his ships, who tamely and supinely looks on and sees fishing schooners, whale-boats and canoes riding triumphant under the muzzles of his guns, and carrying off every supply destined for their relief."[16]

Due to his failure to protect British supply transports, Samuel Graves was superseded by Rear Adm. Molyneaux Shuldham. Graves, a Vice Admiral of the White, was justifiably upset by the indignity of being displaced by a junior, and he stubbornly held on to the command for one month and then decided to winter in London. He later wrote in his own defense of his operations in the waters off Boston, "It is much to be lamented that [cargoes] of such consequence should be sent from England in a vessel destitute of arms even so to protect [itself] from a rowboat."[17]

In 1776 news reached the Americans of the sailing of forty troop ships from England carrying 5,000 redcoats to North America, and another fleet of thirty-three from Scotland with 3,000 Highlanders directed specifically for Boston. Some arrived safety at Halifax in Nova Scotia, and others joined the British fleet before it abandoned Boston Harbor.[18] Although seven small British men-of-war were sent out as escorts to stem the tide of captures, Shuldham was just as frustrated as Graves by the continuing success of the Americans in picking off stragglers. Within two months he was making the same complaints as his predecessor. "However numerous our cruisers may be or however attentive our officers to their duty, it has been found impossible to prevent some of our ordnance and other valuable stores, in small vessels, falling into the hands of the rebels." In further response to the ongoing problem, Shuldham suggested to the Admiralty that "all supplies to this country [should] be sent in armed vessels, I mean such as our old forty gun ships with only their upper tier of guns."[19]

THE FIRST AMERICAN CRUISER

Col. John Glover had leased his own schooner, *Hannah*, to the American army at $78 per month and had enlisted Nicholson Broughton to serve as captain of the 4-gun schooner. Broughton was aided in running the vessel by a professional sailing master and four seamen hired at the port of Beverly. A commercial sailing master in former times, he is recognized by some historians as the first American naval officer although all of his service was in the "army's navy." He was given a "crew" of soldiers drafted from a militia regiment to serve as boarders and marines. While the captain and most of the men were from the seaport town of Marblehead and familiar with sailing, the ad hoc nature of the entire enterprise surrounding the fitting out of the *Hannah* as a vessel of war suggests a general lack of appreciation for the true difficulties to be found in creating an effective American naval presence.

Col. Stephen Moylan, sent by Washington to advance the preparation of his cruisers, wrote, "You cannot conceive the difficulty, the trouble and the delay there is in procuring the thousand things necessary for one of these vessels ... I dare say one of them might be fitted in Philadelphia or New York in three days ... But here you must search all over Salem, Marblehead, Danvers and Beverly for every little thing is wanting." Moreover, Washington could expect little help from Congress since he had failed to inform them of his naval experiment—an oversight he did not correct until October 5, 1775, when two vessels carrying supplies to the British blundered into colonial hands. In writing Congress for instructions as to the disposition of the captured cargoes, Washington made his own naval activities known for the first time.[20]

The fifty-one-year-old Broughton was known as a steadfast adherent of the Continental Association, and he had taken a militant roll in routing out disaffected Loyalists in the name of the Patriot cause.[21] Unfortunately, Broughton proved to be insensible to the political realities of the rebellion. He was overly aggressive in attacking neutral and friendly shipping, tactless in raising the expectations for immediate payment of prize money among his crew, contentious when dealing with the general's agents, and disobedient in following the very specific instructions he had from Washington concerning the *Hannah*. Yet his greatest faults seem to have been that he could not contain his ardent hatred for those who were disaffected to the cause or to subordinate his own self-interest with respect to prize money for the good of the rebellion.

Broughton sailed from Beverly on the morning of September 5, 1775, with a compliment of forty militiamen poised to serve as gunners, boarders, or prize crews. The *Hannah* was fitted with a double brace of 4 pounders amidships and a handful of swivel guns positioned along the rails. Standing out into Massachusetts Bay, he immediately observed two patrolling sentinels, the British frigate *Lively (20)* and the sloop *Savage (8)*. Broughton, with only 4 small cannon, tacked away towards Cape Ann as the two warships pressed towards him. By skirting the rocky shoal waters near Cape Ann, he safely rounded the cape and went out of sight.

Lt. Hugh Bromedge,[22] in command of *Savage*, gave up the pursuit almost immediately, wisely foregoing a rapid chase through unfamiliar and dangerous coastal waters. The heavier *Lively*, commanded by Capt. Thomas Bishop, remained on patrol near the shore until dark. Next morning after spending a night lying off Cape Ann, Broughton regained the bay only to be chased into Gloucester by the ever-vigilant *Lively*. On the third morning of his cruise, Broughton was pleased to see a horizon empty of British warships, but he immediately sighted a fat merchant ship, the 260-ton *Unity*, ostensibly bound for Boston. Standing to windward but within easy cannon shot, he forced *Unity* to spill its wind and await an inspection of its documents and cargo by an American officer. The boarding officer, Lt. John Glover, Jr., found the vessel to be a prize only recently taken by the *Lively*. On board was a tiny prize crew of Jack-tars commanded by a midshipman. The original American crew were held prisoner below decks. The ship belonged to John Langdon, a well-known New Hampshire shipowner, shipbuilder, and Patriot leader.

Broughton has left no sound rationale for how he came to consider the *Unity* a fair prize rather than a recapture. There was a well-known distinction between the two categories in law that dated back to 1708. He escorted the vessel into Gloucester and then continued his cruise of the bay to no further avail. He returned to port that evening, deposited his British prisoners with the local Committee of Safety, and awaited a decision concerning the legitimacy of his prize from General Washington. In the absence of a properly convened admiralty court Washington would have to make a ruling as to the legitimacy of all prizes.

Unfortunately, during the delay Broughton seems to have inflated the expectations of his crew with regard to the immediate payment of their prize money. It seems reasonable to presume that he was trying to maintain the enthusiasm of his men, who had been chased back into port twice in three days, and were now sitting at anchor aboard a small, crowded vessel only yards from the shore with its inviting taverns, soft dry beds, and waterfront harlots. The captain refused to allow the crew shore leave, but he does not seem to have denied all these comforts to himself, retiring to shore each night.

Several days passed before Washington decided to return *Unity* to its owner with only the suggestion that a small reward be made to the officers of *Hannah* for its recapture. No bounty was suggested for the crew. Outraged members of the sloop's compliment, led by John Searle, confronted the captain demanding a part of the reward money. A scuffle followed in which the *Hannah*'s officers sided with Broughton and the remaining militiamen sided with Searle. The captain properly declared the proceedings a mutiny and ordered Searle and his companions arrested. However, the men were all armed, and they simply refused to be placed under arrest. The Gloucester Committee of Safety informed Washington of the mutiny by express, and he responded with a contingent of troops who disarmed the crew and marched them off to confinement at the army camp in Cambridge. All thirty-six militiamen were tried by courts martial and sentenced to various punishments, including floggings and fines, but only Searle was actually given the thirty-six stripes demanded by the court. The others were returned to their regiments never again to see duty at sea.

Washington bore Broughton's limitations as a sea officer with great patience focusing rather on the misbehavior of the soldiers, who he deemed "rascally privateers." This was unfortunate because the captain seems to have mistaken the general's consideration for license. A week later Broughton ventured out to sea with a new crew, which was again dragooned into service from the militia. Over the next ten days he never sailed further out to sea in the morning than he could retrace by nightfall. Each night he returned to his bed in Marblehead, and each morning he weighed anchor for a short cruise. Rather than aggressively patrolling the bay, he simply stopped such shipping as happened to cross his path.[23]

Finally word of Broughton's activities moved Admiral Graves to set Capt. John Collins the task of capturing or destroying the rebel pest. Collins commanded HM brig *Nautilus (16)*, which carried a standard crew of 100 sailors and Royal Marines. Broughton was north of Marblehead when he first encountered Collins, who crammed on all sail to cut off the American cruiser from its usual port. Broughton tacked and made for nearby Beverly hoping to elude *Nautilus* by running through the coastal shallows. This time the tactic and the tide turned against him as *Hannah* ground fast on a large shoal that crossed the mouth of the harbor. Entering the inlet in the slacking water, Collins understood that his heavier vessel (300 tons) could not go where a lighter vessel (78 tons) had failed to pass. Therefore, he anchored some distance from the *Hannah* and began a slow but steady bombardment of his intended victim and the nearby town of Beverly.

During these trials the tide continued to run out exposing a strip of land over which the crew of *Hannah* was able to escape to the nearby beach with all four of the vessel's cannon, its swivel guns, and ammunition to serve them. The Americans set up a pair of guns on the beach and then began a long-range cannonade of the British brig. It is impossible to know if the British captain was unaware of the danger posed to *Nautilus* by the outgoing tide; but the small margin of safe water beneath Collin's keel suddenly failed him. Both ships were now held fast aground until the rising tide might refloat them. Collins was now in grievous straits because the vengeful townspeople aroused by the British shot falling among their residences began to man their own substantial harbor defenses. They fired upon the *Nautilus* with cannon and muskets making several hits upon its hull but mostly putting holes in its sails and taking out parts of its rigging, freeboard, and woodwork. Worse still, Collins found that his vessel was careening (tilting on its side) as the tide continued to race out to sea. In this condition he could make only a poor defense because none of the guns in his main battery could be made to bear on his tormentors. Several hours later a rising tide allowed *Nautilus* to make a discrete retreat to Boston.

Collins' report on the damage done to his command during the encounter included one man seriously maimed and another who ultimately died of his wounds. Broughton's crew suffered no casualties, and the citizens of Beverly were all safe, although there was some damage to buildings around the center of town. The schooner *Hannah*, which had sustained very few hits from the enemy, had been grounded so hard by its own skipper that its ruptured keel was beyond repair. So ended the inglorious career of America's first cruiser.

THE CRUISE OF CAPTAINS BROUGHTON AND SELMAN

Once returned to Beverly, Broughton was given a new command, one of two "Grand Banks" schooners. The larger of the pair, owned by Thomas Grant and rechristened *Hancock*, was 72 tons; and the smaller, renamed *Franklin*, was 60 tons. *Hancock (6)* went to Broughton, while *Franklin (6)* was given to John Selman, also a militia captain. Each received a compliment of seventy militiamen before they sailed on October 22, 1775. This was the first naval operation to have the explicit approval of the Congress.

John Selman was only thirty-one years old, but Colonel Glover and everyone associated with him seemed to think him an able and experienced seaman. He may have been related to the owner of *Franklin*, Archibald Selman. Unfortunately the younger man may have fallen under the bad influence of Broughton with whom he was to sail in consort. *Franklin* and *Hancock* left port with orders to intercept a pair of British supply transports headed to Quebec. The brigs were said to be loaded with 6,000 stand of arms, powder, and ball and unescorted. The identity of the spy in London who forwarded the information of the sailing of these brigs has escaped absolute identification.

Notwithstanding their orders, Broughton and Selman failed to keep the rendezvous, waylaying and seizing a half dozen innocent fishing boats and merchant vessels instead. The Americans then made an amphibious attack on the quiet seacoast town of Charlottetown (Prince Edward Island). They ransacked the residences, took the civilian magistrate captive, and generally created a valueless, unnecessary, and embarrassing public relations incident among its peaceful citizens.

Washington was so exasperated by the obvious insubordination of his two sea officers that he resolved to remove both from command and send them back to the army. Initially, Selman and Broughton refused to return to duty with the army and resigned their commissions. However, both thought better of the matter later and finished the war as officers in the Essex County Militia (MA). Nonetheless, chance had unknowingly favored the American captains. The transports they had failed to intercept were escorted by the British frigate HMS *Lizard (28)*. The presence of the frigate was not the only information left out of the intelligence from London. The *Lizard* was also carrying £20,000 in coin to pay for the defense of Quebec and to set the Indians against the settlements on the frontier.

Both Broughton and Selman claimed later that all the eagerness they exhibited was due to their revolutionary spirit and their patriotic devotion to the cause. Historians might find some excuse for Selman in his youth and inexperience, but he also seems to have been bad-tempered, prone to towering rages, and hasty in his decisions. Selman never tired of defending his actions, and he even blamed his misfortunes on Washington in a letter to Eldridge Gerry in Congress. The general, according to Selman, had exhibited an unwarranted "coolness" to the seamen of Marblehead "who had undergone cold, nakedness and short allowance of provisions, with the giving up of everything sent home as a prize" solely in order that they might hinder the efforts of the enemy. However, the Marbleheaders who served at sea in 1775 also seem to have become "equally famous because of their scandalous ways, their notorious disregard for law and order, their brawling, their carousing and their unwillingness to accept any restraints whatsoever."[24]

CAPTAIN MARTINDALE

No one of Washington's skippers was more fastidious about outfitting his command than Sion Martindale. He not only demanded that the two-masted schooner *Washington* of 160 tons be rerigged as a square-sail brig and fitted with a new deckwork to support twelve 6-pound carriage guns and twenty swivels, but he also wanted a fifer, a drummer, and a surgeon assigned as part of his crew of seventy-five. The brig was the largest and best armed of the general's vessels of war.

Martindale was an experienced merchant seaman and sailing master from Rhode Island. He had aboard as sailing master Benjamin Wormwell, part owner of the schooner, who had sailed from Plymouth throughout his career. Wormwell's partner, George Erving, was a Loyalist whose share in the vessel had been confiscated by the Plymouth Committee of Safety when he fled to Boston. It may have been Wormwell who suggested the alteration of the rig to square sails.

Taken as a whole, Martindale seems to have harbored a desire to establish a genuine "naval" atmosphere aboard *Washington* similar to that found aboard Royal Navy warships. Moylan wrote, "Martindale is going upon too large a scale and has lost sight of the purpose behind fitting out his vessel."[25] Yet Martindale's crew was in constant turmoil and seemingly always on the verge of mutiny. The surgeon, Dr. John Manvide, noted that the militiamen refused to work the brig as sailors because they considered themselves soldiers. "They were willing to lend a hand to weigh anchor but...refused to do more." The crew was turned from this "wicked behavior" by a promise of one-third the prize money and several suits of warm clothes. Washington's agent, William Watson, suggested that the problem lay in the fact that the men had enlisted as soldiers, not as marines. This was a persistent problem among Washington's fleet.[26]

Washington "indulged" Martindale's requests but made it perfectly clear to all his agents that he did not intend his cruisers to take on British warships directly, only to raid their lightly armed supply ships and transports. His secretary, Joseph Reed, wrote of Martindale's demand for twelve guns, "There can be no occasion for such a number of guns, unless he means to go without powder for them as we cannot spare so much. . . . We think eight or at most ten 6 pounders quite sufficient with 10 or 12 swivels." Martindale was convinced to accept a main battery of 6-6 pounders and 4-4 pounders. Nonetheless, he amassed a bill of £1,000 in fitting, rigging, and clothing his command. This was twice the money spent on any other vessel in Washington's fleet.[27]

In December 1775, the *Washington* put to sea on its first voyage, and it was almost immediately run down off Cape Ann by HMS *Fowey (20)*. Outgunned two to one, Martindale wisely surrendered, but most Americans thought it odd that he did so without firing a shot. The American crew was taken prisoner to Halifax, where Martindale became noteworthy for the outlandish statements he issued periodically through the press.

CAPTAIN COIT

On October 25, 1775, William Coit and fifty volunteers from among the Connecticut militia arrived in Plymouth to take over the 60-ton schooner *Harrison*. Coit was described as having a soldierly bearing and a frank and jovial manner. He was just thirty-three and a law graduate of Yale, but he had had enough sea time to earn a master's certificate. He found the schooner dirty, weakly put together, and a dull sailer. The deck was so rotten that a hole was easily put through it with a handspike. The mainmast was "rotted off in the hounds," and the cabin was scarcely large enough to sleep five men spoon-fashion.[28]

Coit made for sea quickly because the autumn cruising season was coming to a close, and even the best of mariners viewed operations in the North Atlantic in winter with concern, if not trepidation. On October 26, the local harbor pilot serving aboard, Daniel Adams, put *Harrison* aground at Plymouth. This all but destroyed the vessel's ancient mainmast. On November 4, Coit again attempted to get sea, this time with a new mainmast. Once again the schooner became the victim of a shoal, but Coit was able to get it off in just a few hours and gain the bay.

At dawn the next day, *Harrison* was off Boston lighthouse where Coit stopped and captured two unarmed merchant vessels without firing a shot. Both contained provisions for the British troops in Boston. While the value of the prizes was not spectacular, the seizure of the cargo was of great consequence to the enemy who relied on their control of the sealanes in order to maintain their troops ashore. The cruiser's company was elated by the prospect of prize money, but quickly become indisposed to the idea of long cruises. Coit returned to Plymouth in just two days because his Connecticut men refused to stay at sea any longer. He therefore wisely asked permission, which was granted, to send the Connecticut militia back to camp and recruit a crew of genuine seamen from among the civilian population of Plymouth.

Because it was difficult to recruit sailors away from the highly profitable privateers that were fitting out in almost every port, it was not until late November 1775 that Coit could again make a cruise. Although he left in consort with Martindale in the *Washington*, the two cruisers soon separated because *Harrison* could not keep pace with the larger vessel. It was soon thereafter that the *Washington* was captured. Coit chose again to sail right up to Boston, and he closed on an armed transport anchored inside the lighthouse. His intended victim was the *Empress of Russia*, a brig commanded by Lt. John Bourmaster. The brig's commander observed Coit's approach and became alarmed when he saw the cannon protruding from *Harrison*'s open gunports. Demonstrating a good deal of foresight, Bourmaster ordered that the halyards and lines be cut before he abandoned the brig to boarding by the rebels. Consequently, Coit's prize crew found that they could not make off with the vessel, and they set fire to it instead.

All of these events were perfectly visible from the shore. Capt. Hyde Parker, Jr. of HMS *Phoenix (44)* and Capt. John Stanhope of the sloop *Raven (10)* had observed the incident from the anchorage. Parker immediately sent a half dozen longboats filled with Jack-tars and Royal Marines to retake the transport and put out the fire. Stanhope, cutting his anchor cable and getting the *Raven* under way, began a pursuit of *Harrison*, which lasted some three hours. Coit was able to maintain the upwind position thereby keeping out of the range of *Raven*'s guns. The chase was joined by two other Royal Navy vessels, *Mercury (20)* and *Nautilus (16)*, which sent a shower of grapeshot and other missiles in Coit's direction at every opportunity. The *Harrison* fled down the bay toward Cape Cod on a favorable but frustratingly intermittent wind. Once Coit resorted to using the long sweeps (oars) on board to open the distance with his pursuers. At nightfall, under a rising cover of sleet and snow, he ducked into Barnstable Harbor on Cape Cod.

For the next four days *Harrison* stayed in the harbor. On the fifth morning Coit again sailed forth and almost immediately stopped and boarded the *Thomas*, a merchant vessel owned by Richard Derby, a friend of the Revolution. Despite the protests of its master, Coit declared the vessel a prize and its cargo of wine contraband. He sent the *Thomas* under a prize crew into Plymouth after confiscating some of the wine for his own use. He then took a fishing schooner with four Loyalist harbor pilots aboard and escorted it into Plymouth. The arrest of the pilots was a severe blow to the operations of the Royal Navy. The long chase of *Harrison* to Barnstable against overwhelming odds was widely celebrated by the Americans. However, the unfortunate seizure of the *Thomas* and the fact that the incident came close upon similar events involving Broughton and Selman, convinced Washington to replace Coit as one of his skippers.

Thereafter Coit returned to Connecticut where he applied for and received command of the state cruiser *Oliver Cromwell (18)*. However, his performance fell far short of expectations, and eight months later he was again looking for employment afloat. In September 1777, he was given command of a 12-gun privateer, *America*, with which he made several valuable captures. In 1781 his wartime exploits ended when he was wounded and made prisoner. He survived the war, and in 1802 quietly passed away taking the laurels of his long chase down Massachusetts Bay in *Harrison* with him to his grave.

COMMODORE OF THE FLEET JOHN MANLY

The *Lee (6)* was a 74-ton schooner belonging to Thomas Stevens of Marblehead that was fitted out in October 1775. The first captain of *Lee*, John Manly, is often considered the second-in-command of the early Continental Navy. In November 1775, Manly made the first important capture of the naval war. He intercepted a lightly armed Royal Navy storeship that had become separated from its convoy. The *Nancy* disgorged a stockpile of valuable military stores.[29]

Immediately thereafter General Washington designated Manly "Commodore of the Fleet," an honor to the man and a signal to the other captains that good performance would bring reward. The winter of 1775–1776 offered an opportunity to reorganize Washington's fleet. The schooner *Lynch* was added to the flotilla under Capt. John Ayres. At the same time William Burke was commissioned to command the *Warren*, a 64-ton schooner chartered from John Twisden of Marblehead. Its crew and officers came from among the New Hampshire militia. Manly was given his choice of vessels, and he chose *Hancock*. The *Lee* reverted to the command of Waters and the *Franklin* to Tucker.

Since the taking of *Nancy*, Admiral Graves had assigned Lt. Christopher Mason of *Nautilus* the task of patrolling outside the Boston lighthouse. On January 22, Mason sited *Hancock*, but lost it in the fog. Later that day he escorted a convoy of several vessels into Boston Harbor. He then docked the *Nautilus* in order to take on provisions. After reporting to his superior, Mason spent the next three days provisioning, but Graves failed during that time to assign a duty vessel in *Nautilus'* place.

On the morning of January 25, 1776, *Hancock* was moving under shortened sail just off Boston lighthouse posing as a pilot vessel when it intercepted *Happy Return*, a provision ship from Britain. Manly sent a prize crew aboard and directed the captured vessel to Plymouth. He then waylaid the ship *Norfolk* in a similar manner. Just as his prizes safely cleared the bay, Manly was confronted by the Loyalist sloop *General Gage (8)* entering the approaches to Boston. George Sibles, master of the sloop, had noted the odd circumstance of two supply vessels veering away from Boston, and he vectored his own vessel to intercept and challenge *Hancock*.

The opponents approached carefully, but the first fire of each went high into the rigging. Nonetheless, an American gunner was killed instantly by a shot from the British 4 pounders into his chest. After several exchanges both vessels stood off, but Manly, being short of ammunition, wore ship and made for Plymouth on a favorable wind. Sibles, satisfied that the encounter would probably end as a draw, tacked for Boston. The exchange of fire could be seen clearly from the anchorage in Boston. Four 50-gun ships (*Preston, Chatham, Renown,* and *Centurion*), a frigate, *Lively (20)*, and a cutter, *Adventure (8)* made no attempt to interfere or to aid the Loyalist sloop. Mason in *Nautilus*, whose task it was to defend the harbor, never stirred from the wharf.

Four days later *Hancock* left Plymouth, and was working up the coast when its crew spotted a sail approaching from astern on a following wind. This was HM brig *Hope (14)* commanded by Lt. George Dawson. *Hope* had just arrived on station in the bay, and Dawson had immediately begun aggressively patrolling in search of the Americans. *Hancock* was already too far out to sea to return to the safety of Plymouth, and if Manly came about, the wind would be in his face. A three-hour chase ensued during which Manly found that he had no hope of shaking off the brig. He chose instead to ground his vessel on a sandbar near the town of Scituate about half way between Plymouth and Boston.

Late in the afternoon Dawson approached the stranded American schooner and anchored with the shore in range of his cannon. A back and forth fusillade broke the stillness of the growing darkness, and for the next four hours the two vessels of war traded cannon shot. It was estimated from the balls found on the beach after the night-long engagement that more than 400 rounds were fired making this the greatest cannonade between the Royal Navy and any of Washington's fleet. Dawson also sent in an attacking force in boats that tried to set the schooner afire, but the raiders were driven off with small arms and swivels. Shortly after this attempt, the Americans abandoned their vessel in favor of a more defensible shore position. Believing that *Hancock* was awash due to the grounding, Dawson sailed away at dawn claiming a victory. Nonetheless, two days later, *Hancock* sailed up to the Scituate wharf for repairs, and within the month Manly had slipped past the sentinels in the bay and was back in his home port of Beverly.

It is remarkable that American vessels so easily eluded the British patrols. In February no fewer than three Royal Navy vessels were on station outside the approaches to Beverly. HMS *Fowey*, Capt. George

The photograph above includes several typical small arms available to seamen when boarding enemy vessels or driving off attackers. From top to bottom: a .69 caliber blunderbuss, a .75 caliber sea service musket, a .63 caliber sea service pistol, and a cutlass with a brass knuckle guard. All the firearms used a flint and steel ignition system that was subject to failure in wet or stormy weather.

Montagu, and HM brig *Nautilus*, now commanded by Capt. John Collins, kept a close watch on the inlet, and *Hope* touched base with the blockaders periodically as it patrolled between Cape Ann and Plymouth. In February, Dawson in *Hope* lay off Plymouth Harbor when Washington's schooner *Harrison (6)*, with a newly appointed captain, Charles Dyar, made its way out in company with the *Yankee*, a Massachusetts' privateer, Corbin Barnes (master). Dawson closed on the two vessels quickly, chased them back into the harbor, and brought *Hope* well inside the approaches to the port with bow guns blazing. Had Barnes not turned to aid Dyar, *Harrison* would most certainly have been taken. For three hours the two American vessels exchanged fire with *Hope* within sight of the residents of the town. Dawson then disengaged with some small damage to his ship, not knowing that he had so damaged the aged *Harrison* as to put it out of commission forever.

In late February, Manly set out to the northeast in company with *Franklin* (Tucker) and *Lee* (Waters). All three vessels escaped detection, but bad weather forced them to anchor just offshore of Gloucester. On March 1, Washington's schooner *Lynch* (Ayres) passed within sight of HMS *Fowey*, which fired a few rounds from its 9 pounders in Ayres' general direction without chasing or doing any damage. The four American captains now planned a cruise in the Atlantic with Manly in overall command. This was one of the few times that more than two American vessels were able to operate together as an offensive squadron in North American waters.

The Officers and Vessels of Washington's Fleet after the Reorganization of February 1776

Hancock
- John Manly, Captain and Commodore
- Richard Stiles, 1st Lt.; Nicholas Olgilby, 2nd Lt.

Lee
- Daniel Waters, Captain
- William Kissick, 1st Lt.; John Gill, 2nd Lt.

Franklin
- Samuel Tucker, Captain
- Edward Phittiplace, 1st Lt.; Francis Salter, 2nd Lt.

Harrison
- Charles Dyar, Captain
- Thomas Dote, 1st Lt.; John Wigglesworth, 2nd Lt.

Lynch
- John Ayres, Captain
- John Roche, 1st Lt.; John Tiley, 2nd Lt.

Warren
- William Burke, Captain; no others listed

A dozen miles (six leagues) off Cape Ann, the squadron was intercepted by Dawson in the *Hope*, who recognized the *Hancock* as he approached. The astonished British commander made the rather reckless decision to take on all four American vessels at once. Whether this was due to his condescending attitude toward the rebels' abilities in general or possibly to a mistaken belief that Manly's three companions were prizes rather than vessels of war is uncertain. Nonetheless, Dawson bore down on the little group with all fourteen of his cannon protruding from their gunports primed and ready.

The Americans had a combined firepower of twenty-four small guns (16-4 pounders and 8-2 pounders), and they had the ability, if properly handled, to engage *Hope* on all sides raking the brig simultaneously from both stem and stern. The pugnacious Dawson opened the fight late in the afternoon, and continued a running duel with the Americans for almost an hour, covering in the interim several miles of open ocean. The stormy surface of the Atlantic kept Manly from maneuvering his squadron to best advantage, and he was unable to bring the British brig to heel due to the unfavorable winds. Ultimately Dawson disengaged after sustaining one man wounded, a shot through his hull, and some minor damage to his rigging. He immediately returned to Boston where he received the astonishing news that the British army expected at any moment to evacuate the city.

Consequently by March 10, 1776, there was not a single British vessel of war on patrol in Massachusetts Bay. Each one had been sought out by dispatch vessels and told to report to Boston for new instructions. Unaware of this turn of events, Manly's squadron continued to cruise the bay picking up scattered prizes like the supply ships *Susannah* and *Stakesby*, both of 300 tons. The *Susannah* was brought in safely, but the *Stakesby* ground on a shoal while approaching Gloucester. Manly was forced to abandon the crippled prize after unloading most of the cargo. The American squadron lay at Gloucester making repairs, which were delayed by a raging nor'easter that decimated the coast of Massachusetts for several days.

Meanwhile, Admiral Shuldham had replaced Graves as senior officer of the British Fleet in America. Informed by his captains that the rebel cruisers were out and about, Shuldham dispatched several ships to intercept them and to protect any stragglers from supply convoys broken by the storm. First out were HMS *Renown (50)* and HMS *Niger (32)*, then the frigates *Lively (20)* and *Fowey (20)*, and ultimately the ever aggressive *Hope*. Some days later *Hope* found the grounded *Stakesby* and burned it. Dawson, in *Hope*, then made for Cape Ann expecting to catch a rebel mouse out of its hole near Gloucester; but Manly's squadron eluded them all. Even as Shuldham was sending out his patrols, *Hancock* slipped to within easy sight of Boston, and Manly was contentedly watching as hundreds of dismayed Loyalists crowded the wharves trying to find a place aboard His Majesty's ships to Halifax or England.

In a final piece of bravado before the naval war in Massachusetts Bay wound down, Manly chased a British provision vessel within plain sight of the Royal Navy. The cutters *Savage (8)* and *Diligent (8)* cut loose from their moorings and chased *Hancock* all the way to Plymouth where the Patriot shore batteries forced an end to their pursuit. Manly sailed two days later with *Warren (4)*, Captain William Burke, in consort. Both *Hancock* and *Warren* had filled their ammunition lockers in anticipation of sustained action. *Warren* had four new 4 pounders installed aboard taken from the captured ship *Susannah*.

Commodore Manly now had five small vessels of war afloat simultaneously. The bulk of the Royal Navy warships had sailed from Boston, but Manly still had to deal with the balance of the British squadron. These were escorting more than sixty transports to Halifax filled with Loyalists escaping the wrath of the Patriot army ashore. *Franklin* and *Warren* set off toward Cape Ann to set an ambush for any lone vessels making toward Halifax, and *Hancock, Lee,* and *Lynch* nosed in close to Boston to maintain a clear view of British operations there. Unfortunately, *Franklin* and *Warren* were forced off their station by the attentive HMS *Milford (28)*, Capt. John Burr. *Warren* made its escape to seaward, but *Milford,* bow chasers blazing, followed *Franklin* right up to the port of Gloucester. Only the appearance of a sudden squall saved the American as Burr was driven back to sea empty-handed.

On the afternoon of March 27, 1776, Manly noted a parade of transports and armed vessels sailing from Boston. The 50-gun men-of-war *Chatham* and *Centurion* took station at the head and tail of the convoy, respectively, and the smaller British warships guarded the flanks, herding in stragglers like sheepdogs. Manly's squadron of three schooners followed at a safe distance to windward until they came in sight of Nova Scotia hoping to dash in and snap up stragglers, but none of the transports fell behind even though they sailed through a snow-spitting New England gale for two days. The ability of the officers of the Royal Navy to keep such a large number of sailing vessels on station within the convoy in heavy seas and poor visibility was remarkable and serves as a testament to their seamanship.

Reversing course on the first of April, a frustrated Manly brought his three cruisers back south and was rewarded almost immediately with a single straggler. This was the unarmed merchant brig *Elizabeth,* Peter Ramsey (master), that had been detained at Boston by several Loyalists, who had dallied to gather the last of the valuables belonging to the town's citizens. In addition to tons of valuable merchandise, there were on board sixty-three loyal civilians and a dozen redcoats, who fired a volley of musketry at *Hancock* before Ramsey surrendered. When examined in Portsmouth, the *Elizabeth* was found to be a very valuable prize financially, but it also disgorged twenty-two notorious Loyalist leaders who were jailed.

By early May, Manly had his entire squadron gathered together again at Beverly, but at this point his continued service as commodore became awkward. Washington had left Massachusetts to prepare the defenses at New York and had taken Reed, Bowen, and Glover with him. Consequently, Manly found that he had to report to Gen. Artemus Ward, who commanded of the Eastern Department of the Continental Army. Ward was easily frustrated by the delicacies of naval affairs, and he was generally impatient with anything concerning the disposition of prizes. The American crews and officers were particularly anxious to receive their wages and prize monies; but, while Ward was willing enough to authorize the payment of wages, he refused to distribute the prize shares to the men.

Manly was particularly dissatisfied because several months had passed with no payment since he had captured the ordnance vessel *Nancy*. Washington had attempted to get an evaluation of the vessel and its contents from Congress to no avail. The arms and powder had been confiscated and used by the army to drive the British from Boston, but Manly had not received a single dollar from his share. Moreover, the commodore could not guarantee the continued presence of all his seamen. The sailors signing on to privateers all along the New England coast were receiving their prize shares in good, hard coin, not promised Continental dollars made of paper. Meanwhile, dozens of other prizes had been libeled for auction, including the valuable *Elizabeth*, but nothing had been paid out to Washington's men. Informed of the growing dispute over prize money, Washington wrote to Ward ordering that the appropriate payments be made, but Ward refused claiming that he did not have the cash on hand and did not expect such sums soon.[30]

Washington was also frustrated by Ward's inability to get the schooners back to sea, and he correctly doubted Ward's dedication and diligence with regard to the naval war. He was shocked to learn that Manly had refused to undertake another cruise without a bigger ship, yet Ward would not let the commodore outfit any of the ships among several prizes riding at anchor for further cruising.

At this time Manly became aware that Congress had issued him a commission as a Continental naval officer with the rank of captain and that the Naval Committee had assigned him the frigate *Hancock (32)*. The report of his transfer to Continental service reached Beverly just as the disagreement with Ward over prize money came to a head. Manly's imminent departure had an immediate negative effect on Washington's cadre of sea officers. A series of resignations flew across Ward's desk. Seven officers, all lieutenants or masters, left the squadron in a single week seeking out places on the privateers fitting out in Salem. With these officers went most of the best seamen. By the time Manly took leave of the fleet and reported to Newburyport to oversee the building of his new command, Washington's tiny squadron was all but out of commission for lack of personnel to man the schooners. "Manly had served his time on Washington's schooners, and served well. Like most Patriots who went to sea, Manly's appetite for prize money surpassed his desire for fame. He earned both and collected [only] the latter."[31]

After a brief respite required by the fitting of his new frigate, Manly continued his naval service to America as a Continental sea officer. On June 27, 1777, Manly, commanding *Hancock (32)*, and Capt. Hector McNeil, commanding the frigate *Boston (24)*, were sailing in consort when they spied the Royal Navy frigate HMS *Fox (28)*. The Britisher, greatly outgunned by two ships, wisely took to his heels, but *Hancock* was much faster. The *Fox* was overtaken, captured, and a prize crew put aboard. This promised to be a signal victory for America. The three vessels continued to sail together until near darkness when they encountered HMS *Rainbow (44)*, commanded by Sir George Collier, and HM brig *Victor (18)*. Certainly Manly's frigates, even with a prize crew aboard *Fox*, had the advantage of the two British vessels in terms of guns. However, darkness prevented an immediate encounter, and the ships sailed on awaiting a sunrise engagement.

The next morning revealed, however, a third British sail that turned out to be HMS *Flora (32)*. The opposing sides were now more than evenly matched. Yet, while Manly was preparing his ship for a squadron attack, McNeil deserted him without warning by running off downwind. Knowing that *Hancock* and *Fox* were overmatched by the three British warships, Manly also attempted to flee. *Fox* was quickly retaken by *Flora*, but *Hancock* was not forced to surrender until the next morning after a long night's chase in light winds. McNeil in *Boston* escaped. Manly was made prisoner and after his exchange in April 1778, he was tried by the Marine Committee for the loss of his vessel and acquitted. McNeil, however, was dismissed from the Continental service for leaving formation and for failure to aid his comrades to the fullest of his ability.

Manly's return to service after his enforced absence found the Continental Navy bereft of an appropriate command. He therefore took a place as captain of the Massachusetts privateer *Cumberland (20)*. In December 1778 he was again captured, this time in the West Indies by HMS *Pomona (28)*, and he was jailed in British Barbados. In the swashbuckling fashion of a Hollywood movie, Manly arranged an escape for himself and some fellow prisoners, seized a British tender in the harbor from its night-watch, and returned safely to Boston in April 1779.

Thereafter, Manly's luck, if not his fighting spirit, turned. In June 1779 he dismasted his next command, the privateer *Jason (18)*, near the Isle of Shoals off Portsmouth, New Hampshire, and he lost a man to the sea in the grounding. Immediately after refitting the *Jason*, Manly took two British privateers in brief but sharp fights off Sandy Hook near New York. These were *Hazzard (18)* from Liverpool and *Adventurer (18)* from Glasgow. In September 1779, he was taken prisoner a third time, this time by HMS *Surprise (28)*, Capt. Robert Linzee, after a two hour nighttime fight.

Manly was sent to England's Mill Prison where he was harshly treated as one of America's most notorious naval captains. Although he tried to escape three times, he only gained his release through one of the prisoner exchanges arranged by Benjamin Franklin from France. Once in France he accepted a second Continental command, the frigate *Hague (32)* (formerly *Deane*), which he ground fast on a reef near the French Island of Guadalupe in the Caribbean. Here for two days with the reef affording him some semblance of protection he fought off four separate attacks by passing British warships, including that of a three decker. Having floated off with a spring tide, Manly finally escaped through the shallows. He made for Boston where he paid off his crew for the final time in May 1783.

During the war a tavern song was altered in favor of John Manly and the other American seamen serving in privateers who defied the British North American Squadron at sea:

> Then rouse up, all our Heroes, give MANLY now a cheer,
> Here's Health to hardy Sons of Mars who go in Privateers...
> They talk of Sixty Ships, Lads, to scourge our free-born Land,
> If they send out Six Hundred we'll bravely them withstand...
> Then rouse up all my Hearties, give Sailor Lads a Cheer,
> Brave MANLY... and [all] those Tars who go in Privateers.[32]

CAPTAIN ADAMS

Of all Washington's skippers Winborn Adams of Rhode Island was among the most parsimonious and most dedicated to his duty. Given the schooner *Warren (4)* in October 1775, Adams made for sea without costing the Continental Congress a penny of extra expense. He rejected the offer of extra sails, a refurbished cabin, and four new guns. In 1774 Adams had taken part in the seizure of gunpowder from Fort William and Mary at Portsmouth as a captain of militia. The forty-five-year-old Adams received his sea captain's commission through the influence of Brigadier Gen. John Sullivan, but he had a wide experience at sea having served as a sailing master for most of his adult career.

On November 1, Adams took an unnamed lumber sloop as prize and sent it into Portsmouth, but the vessel was released four weeks later as belonging to a friend of the Revolution. About November 25, Adams captured a merchantman from Nova Scotia, *Rainbow*, filled with turnips and potatoes for Boston. Being low on his own provisions, and plagued with an old and unreliable suite of sails, he decided to escort the prize into port. Here news of the *Rainbow*'s capture was almost lost in the excitement that surrounded Manly's capture of the *Nancy*. Yet, prize money was prize money, and invigorated by his success, Adams and his crew quickly made their way again into the increasingly wintry sea.

Of all Washington's captains, Adams seems to have been the most dedicated to prolonged winter cruises. However, his almost continuous bouts with foul weather placed a great strain on his vessel and his crew. Fifty volunteers quickly dwindled to thirty due to sickness, and after two of his crewmen died at sea in mid-December, he finally admitted that he should return to port for a refit. Here he replaced his sails and his 4 pounders, which had proven unsafe to fire. Although Washington ordered that Adams be given anything that he wanted for the *Warren*, the skipper accepted only twenty volunteers from the New Hampshire militia to fill out his compliment.

On Christmas Eve 1775, Adams sailed south toward Boston. On this cruise he recaptured the 70-ton sloop *Sally*, a prize of the British frigate HMS *Niger (32)*. He and his crew ultimately received one third part of the value of this recapture as a reward from the owners. Unfortunately, New Year's Eve (December 31, 1775) spelled the end of most of the enlistments among the *Warren's* crew and among the troops of the Army of Observation as well. Adams was simply unable to recruit a new group of sailors from among the civilian population with a finger-numbing winter upon them. At this time the entire Revolution was in danger of collapsing as the colonials dissolved back into the countryside to sit by their own warm firesides for the winter. The cold discouraged even the dedicated Adams. He returned to Cambridge, rejoined his militia regiment, and ended his naval career. By war's end he had risen to the rank of lieutenant colonel. Adams had given his best effort to Washington's little fleet—possibly the greatest effort for the least reward of all the general's skippers.

CAPTAIN TUCKER

Born in Marblehead, Massachusetts, in 1747, Samuel Tucker was another of Washington's successful and dedicated captains. A veteran seamen, he had shipped in the British man-of-war *King George* at age eleven as a ship's boy. By age twenty-one he had gained his master's certificate and served as captain of his own vessel in the merchant service. Tucker was in England when word of the Revolution reached there, and he narrowly escaped death on the voyage to America during a violent and dangerous storm at sea. Robert Morris recommended him to Washington as a potential naval commander.

In January 1776 Washington commissioned Tucker to command the schooner *Franklin (6)*. While cruising in *Franklin* in consort with Capt. Daniel Waters in *Lee (6)*, Tucker captured the 300-ton brig *Henry and Ester* and the sloop *Rainbow*. In March 1776 he helped Manly to capture the 300-ton ship *Susannah* and then took command of *Hancock* when Manly was chosen for the Continental Navy. Tucker was thereafter considered the commodore of Washington's small fleet, and he made several important captures while commanding *Hancock (6)*, including two British supply brigs.

When Washington's fleet was dissolved in fall 1777, Tucker was given command of the Continental frigate *Boston (24)*. As part of his first cruise in *Boston*, he took John Adams to France as a representative of Congress, and he also captured five legitimate prizes on his way back to America. He next cruised as commodore in consort with *Confederacy*

(36) in spring 1779 and in company with *Deane (32)* that summer. Several Loyalist privateers were taken by this squadron, including the heavily armed ship *Viper.*

Tucker then defeated HM sloop-of-war *Thorn (16)* in a violent ship-to-ship engagement. The capture was a great public relations boon to the Americans because very few Royal Navy vessels had fallen to the rebels since the French had entered the war. Tucker then sailed to South Carolina to join the American squadron poised to defend Charleston, and he lost *Boston* and his own freedom when the city surrendered in May 1780. Tucker was quickly exchanged, and he thereafter assumed command of *Thorn*, which had been taken into Continental service. After making several captures in the Bay of St. Lawrence, Tucker was again captured this time by HMS *Hind.* He gave his parole and stayed out of action ashore for the remainder of the war. At the time of his death in 1833 he was the highest ranking American officer of either the army or the navy to have survived the Revolution.[33]

LT. JAMES MUGFORD, HERO OF THE REVOLUTION

When Tucker took command of *Hancock*, his first lieutenant, James Mugford, was given command of *Franklin*. This "leap-frog" reorganization was quite common in eighteenth-century navies. Ironically, Mugford was never made a full captain, serving as master and commander of the *Franklin* with the rank of lieutenant.

On May 17, 1776, Mugford captured the Royal Navy ordnance ship *Hope* that was loaded with military stores including entrenching tools, blankets, and 75 tons of gunpowder. He then ran the *Franklin* and its newly acquired prize through an ineffective British blockade and tied up to the Boston wharf. The Jack-tars and officers of the Royal Navy were "intolerably vexed and chagrined" by Mugford's cavalier attitude and obvious distain for their presence. Two days later, Mugford in *Franklin*, in company with Captain Cunningham of the small privateer *Lady Washington*, passed through the channels in the harbor to exit the bay, once again tweaking the nose of the British warships stationed offshore.[34]

However, it was late in the day and the tide was going out. *Franklin* ran aground, its bow sticking fast on a mudflat dangerously close to the British sentinels on station off Boston. Cunningham wisely anchored *Lady Washington* nearby in the growing darkest. Both skippers prepared for a possible night attack from the nearby HMS *Renown (50)* and two other men-of-war. It was not surprising, therefore, that the rebel crews were armed and keeping a keen lookout when a number of small boats, claiming to be friends from Boston, approached between nine and ten o'clock that night. The rouse was immediately identified as a "cutting out" operation launched by the British.

Mugford, on *Franklin*, was the first to warn off the boats, and when they continued to approach he fired his pistol into them. This was followed by all his officers and armed men, twenty-one in total, discharging their weapons into the inky darkness. Cutting his own anchor cable to allow the *Franklin* to pivot on the mudflat, Mugford brought his broadside and swivels to bear upon the open boats, and his crew discharged loads of grape shot in their direction. Before they could reload, the British Jack-tars and Royal Marines were ranging alongside attacking the American crew with small arms fire and boarding pikes. They were met with a strong defense using swords, pikes, and boarding axes. The result was a giant brawl with almost 200 British seaman trying to gain the deck from unstable boats and two dozen American seamen hacking down on them from the railings. The number of boats was reported to be up to a dozen, of which at least two were destroyed by the cannon fire. The *Franklin*'s crew did great execution among the attackers.

At the same time, a half dozen boats with 100 men had tried to board the *Lady Washington*, which had on board only seven Americans. The privateer's crew was equally successful in driving off its attackers. Cunningham gave the British such a warm reception with his swivel guns and pikes that they soon relented after suffering considerable loss. No American was lost on either vessel excepting Mugford, killed by a pike [35] thrust through his body. Dozens of British were reported killed. A partisan newspaper account noted that one American sailor was positive of killing nine of the enemy singlehandedly.

The report of General Ward, the overall American commander in Boston at the time, generally agrees with the anecdotal accounts, and his remains the official after-action report of the engagement.

Captain Mugford was very fiercely attacked by twelve or thirteen boats full of men, but he and his men exerted themselves with remarkable bravery, beat off the enemy, sunk several of their boats, and killed a number of their men; it is supposed they lost sixty or seventy. The intrepid Captain Mugford fell a little before the enemy left his schooner; he was ran through [*sic*] with a lance while he was cutting off the hands of the pirates as they attempted to board him, and it was said that with his own hands he cut off five pairs of theirs.... The *Lady Washington* ... was attacked by five boats, which were supposed to contain near or quite a hundred men; but after repeated efforts to board her they were beaten off by the intrepidity and exertions of the little company, who gloriously defended the *Lady* against the brutal ravishers of liberty.[36]

Mugford was a great loss to the American naval effort. He seems to have served with distinction as an inferior officer under Captain Tucker, and he had exhibited great potential as an independent commander. The entire Marblehead regiment of the army marched home to perform military honors at his burial. Mugford was the only one of Washington's skippers to die while in his service.[37]

MISCELLANEOUS OFFICERS

Not much is known about those captains of Washington's fleet that joined near the end of its period of operation. The vessels of Washington's navy continued to cruise in Massachusetts Bay throughout the whole of 1776. Capt. John Skimmer was assigned to take command of *Franklin*. He and Tucker, in *Hancock*, were joined in their patrols by the sloops *Lee*, Capt. Daniel Waters, *Warren*, Capt. William Burke, and *Lynch*, Capt. John Ayres.

In September 1776 HMS *Milford* (Burr) and HMS *Liverpool (28)* (Capt. Henry Bellew) captured the *Warren* making it the second, and last of Washington's fleet to fall to the Royal Navy. *Liverpool* had just deposited a pair of prizes at Halifax and was returning to sea when the lookouts spied the rebel schooner sailing on a strong easterly wind. Captain Bellew set all the sail his frigate would carry in an attempt to close on the schooner before it could make an escape. Captain Burke in *Warren* ran right into the oncoming path of HMS *Milford*, which was approaching from the opposite direction with several prizes under its lee. When *Warren* struck, Bellew hurried a boat over to the schooner in an attempt to claim the entire prize for *Liverpool*. However, British Admiralty law said that any vessel in sight of a prize when it was made deserved an equal share.

Waters appears to have turned over command of the *Lee* to John Skimmer some time before summer 1777. He and John Ayres are among a list of Revolutionary sea officers that was compiled in 1794 from the *Miscellaneous Naval Papers of the Library of Congress* (dated March 18, 1794). A previous list had been given out by the Board of Admiralty in September 1781 (*Papers of the Continental Congress, 37, 473*), which was based on a register of known officers acknowledged as being incomplete at that date. Waters seems to have received a captain's commission in the Continental service in March 1777, but there is no such evidence available for Ayres although he is thought to have continued in the Continental service.

Skimmer and Tucker, in *Franklin* and *Hancock* respectively, ranged the New England coast from Cape Cod to Maine all winter, capturing in December 1776 a brig filled with winter clothing that was much needed by the army. In August 1777 Skimmer was placed in command of the *Lee* for the purpose of making a cruise to Europe with dispatches for the American agents there. While bound from Gibraltar to Boston, he captured a British merchant brigantine, *Industrious Bee*, which had been built in 1764 in England. The Navy Board at Boston considered the prize vessel a likely candidate for conversion to a vessel of war and purchased it for the Continental Navy. Renamed the *General Gates*, the brigantine was fitted with 18 guns and placed under the command of Skimmer.

Skimmer sailed in *General Gates* on May 24, 1778, in consort with the privateer *Hawke*. He planned to cruise the Newfoundland banks. Here he captured the ship *Jenny*, and the brigantines *Thomas* and *Nancy*. In August the *General Gates* and the *Hawke* parted company. Skimmer then captured the sloop *Polly* to which he transferred a prize crew. The next day Skimmer sighted the brigantine *Montagu*, a Loyalist privateer. The privateer's commander, Captain Nelson, defended his vessel with unusual vigor. An engagement of epic proportions took place over the next five hours.

Nelson expended every bit of his ball and shot and resorted to firing odd pieces of iron from his guns including knives, crowbars, and pieces of chain in an attempt to disable the American's rigging. About three hours into the fight a double-headed bar shot fired by the *General Gates* passed through the captain's day cabin of *Montagu* and lodged among the smashed woodwork and furniture. Nelson retrieved the foot-long device and fired it back at the Americans from one of his own guns. The bar shot struck a swivel gun on the quarterdeck of *General Gates* and split in two parts. One of these struck and instantly killed Skimmer. Two hours later Nelson surrendered to Skimmer's lieutenant, William Dennis.

Dennis brought all three vessels to Boston where *Polly* and *Montagu* were declared fair prizes. The *General Gates* continued in service in Nova Scotian waters and in the West Indies until April 1779, when it returned to Boston so battered by weather and hard use that its crew despaired of reaching port. During this time it captured the schooners *Friendship* and *General Leslie* and the brigs *Arctic* and *Union*. Its last mission before being sold in June 1779 was as a convoy ship for prisoners of war exchanged by the British in New York.

SUMMARY

In 1775 Washington's skippers legitimately captured a total of twenty-five vessels, and in 1776 they netted another twenty-two. All of the schooners stayed clear of New York after July 1776 because the British invasion fleet had arrived there. *Hancock* and *Franklin* cruised the Virginia Capes; *Lynch* returned to Boston after a short and unproductive cruise of Massachusetts Bay; and *Warren* and *Lee* sailed near Nova Scotia until the *Warren* was captured. As each of the vessels returned to New England they were sold. When the *Lee* was decommissioned in fall 1777, it was the last of the eight schooners fitted out by the general's agents.

The operations of this small squadron were hampered by the continued presence in the bay of British frigates and two or three smaller Royal

Navy vessels, particularly *Fowey (20)*, *Hope (14)*, *Nautilus (16)*, *Liverpool (28)*, and *Milford (32)*. The misadventures of many of Washington's skippers suggest major flaws in the system used to determine their qualifications as naval officers. Others proved dedicated and capable. A competent sea officer or captain needed to possess good tactical skills, a detailed knowledge of his intended area of operation, a consistent and fair manner with his men, and a good idea of the best sailing qualities of his vessel. Misunderstandings, accidents at sea, and adverse winds or tides often had undue influence on the outcome of any cruise, and they were understood to be a normal part of the course of nautical events. By comparison to these, the inevitable squabbles over prize money and misinterpreted orders were trivial considerations.

10

The Invasion of New York

The whole bay was full of shipping as ever it could be. I declare
I thought all London Afloat.
—an American in New York, summer 1776[1]

DEFENDING NEW YORK

New York was one of the finest natural harbors in the world. Nestled
between Staten Island and Sandy Hook, Lower New York Bay was a
decent anchorage for wooden sailing ships, and the approach to the
outer anchorage was straight forward and easily executed. The Upper
Bay was practically landlocked with the exceptions of outlets up the
Hudson River or the passage to Long Island Sound appropriately called
Hell's Gate (see Map 3). The natural channel to the sea between the
Lower and Upper Bays, called the Narrows (one of many places sharing
the same descriptive name), was up to 100 feet deep and three-quarters
of a mile wide between Long Island and Staten Island except at the harbor bar, where there was barely 50 feet of water depending on the tide.
Crossing the bar could be tricky and more than one experienced captain
grounded his ship in the attempt.

Second only to Philadelphia in terms of its volume of trade, New York
town, the city on the Island of Manhattan, had been the home of British
military headquarters in North America since the Seven Years War. It was

not uncommon for New Yorkers to see Royal Navy warships riding at anchor in the harbor. Until the outbreak of the recent political difficulties, these vessels had been viewed by the residents as gratifying symbols of economic security, personal protection, social stability, and imperial grandeur. Growing discontent with the regulation of the empire in the decade before the Revolution had changed all that for many New Yorkers.[2]

In 1774 supporters of the Sons of Liberty and the Continental Association had held their own "tea party" on a New York wharf, and by early 1775 they had formalized their own inspections of incoming cargoes to New York, turning away merchant vessels that carried British manufactures and luxury items under the very noses of the British cutters and warships stationed in the bay. One merchant captain, having been intimidated by the mob to leave the wharf, returned with his vessel under the escort of HM sloop-of-war *Kingfisher (16)*. However, he was so severely accosted by the mob when he came ashore that he immediately set sail for another port without unloading his cargo. The inability of a British warship to protect a subject of the empire from an "American" mob in a British colonial port spoke volumes to anyone with the ears to hear concerning the health of the Anglo-American relationship.[3]

When news of the fighting at Lexington and Concord reached New York most of the Sons of Liberty arose in anger. They seized two small vessels loaded with provisions belonging the British army and emptied them. They then broke into the city arsenal, took 600 stand of muskets, and seized part of the provincial gunpowder supply. New York's Royal Governor, William Tyron, along with Oliver DeLancey, and other prominent royalists began to fear the insurgent mobs and removed themselves to the *Duchess of Gordon*, a British merchant ship anchored in the East River. Only *Kingfisher* seems to have been on patrol in the harbor during these demonstrations. On May 26, 1775, HMS *Asia (64)* arrived in the harbor under the command of Capt. George Vandeput. In an effort to manifest a continuing royal authority, Admiral Graves had posted the third rater to New York to bolster the support of loyal New Yorkers. *Asia* was joined shortly thereafter by the frigate HMS *Phoenix* (44), HM sloop-of-war *Viper* (14), and HM cutter *Savage* (8). These vessels posted themselves prominently around the harbor in a show of force.

Simple military logic demanded that the rebels concede control of the local waters to the Royal Navy. Yet it was politically impossible for the Americans to give up the city without a struggle, and they refused to do so continuing their military take-over of the shore positions under the very guns of the Royal Navy. Throughout summer 1775 the rebels made steady progress on their trenches, redoubts, and gun-batteries, but they could hardly fortify the entire shoreline. Except in a few places with steep banks, most of Manhattan's perimeter was within practical range of naval cannon or assailable by amphibious landings.

This was made abundantly clear in August 1775. British sailors patrolling the harbor in a small armed boat sent out by Captain Vandeput discovered that the Americans were removing the guns and munitions in the Royal battery at the tip of Manhattan. The sailors fired a warning shot to signal Asia, which was anchored some 1,000 yards away near Murray's wharf at the foot of Wall Street. The Americans, from Col. John Lamb's Artillery Company, believing they were being attacked, fired at the patrol boat and killed one man. The Asia responded to the rebel fire by loosing a broadside of cannonballs and grapeshot in the direction of the city.

Very little damage was done by Asia, and no resident of the city was killed or hurt. Nonetheless, the residents were immediately reminded of the fearful bombardment visited on the town of Falmouth, New Hampshire, in 1775, and the similar bombardments of Bristol, Stonington, New Bedford, Beverly, Gloucester, and a half dozen other towns. An English supporter of the rebellion in London wrote to a Patriot friend in New York, "I expect your city will be laid in ashes." The uncontested presence of British warships in the harbor was evidence enough of the residents' helplessness. Another contemporary observer noted that the bombardment by Asia "threw the whole city into such a tumult as it never knew before, [the people] moving away their effects. All that day and all night were their carts going, boats loading, and women and children crying, and distressed voice heard in the roads in the dead of night." It was estimated that one-third of the population of 25,000 chose to leave the city rather than to continue to live under the frowning guns of Asia and the other warships.[4]

The Loyalists among the city's residents were buoyed by the show of force. There were many loyal New Yorkers drawn from those elements of colonial society considered politically to be Tories. Among these were the colonial office-holders, whose own incomes and those of their relations and friends depended on the continuance of the old order. Others were loyal from habit. George III was their rightful king. Still others were loyal simply because their families, friends, and neighbors were loyal. Nonetheless, even the most loyal American well understood that cannon often failed to discriminate between friend and foe, especially if fired randomly into a group of dwellings.

In February 1776, the hated Asia ran aground at the foot of Broad Street, and the Americans immediately began to drag cannon on to the docks with the intention of firing on the vessel while it was stranded. However, the tide turned before a single shot was fired, and Asia, Phoenix, the Duchess of Gordon, and two British prizes moved their anchorage to Bedloe's Island (Liberty Island) out of range of the rebel's Manhattan battery. Thereafter the ships regularly changed their moorings in an effort to outwit Patriot schemes being hatched ashore.

In March 1776, Washington became aware of intelligence about a small squadron of Royal Navy vessels setting out from Boston for New York, and he sent a courier with an appropriate warning. The squadron included two warships, two bomb vessels, and several troop transports with their attendant marines. One of these, HMS *Mercury (28)*, carried British Gen. Sir Henry Clinton and his staff. The people of New York, especially the Loyalists, were anxious to see the fleet of warships, transports, and ancillary vessels as it sailed into the harbor. Congressman Andrew Allen noted, "When Mr. Clinton arrived I fully expected that hostilities would immediately have commenced."[5]

Initially, Washington also feared a preemptive strike at New York City, but he quickly realized that Clinton's force was too small to affect rebel control of the city. For his part, Clinton merely closeted himself briefly with Governor Tyron and the other Loyalist leaders aboard *Duchess of Gordon*, watered his ships at the springs on Staten Island, and then sailed away to the south with his entire force. The Americans were stunned at his departure not knowing that he was actually destined to attack Charleston. Immediately thereafter the rebels posted a guard over the watering point on Staten Island closing it to use by the Royal Navy.[6]

GATHERING STORM

In April 1776, the Patriots in New York were briefly unnerved by an unexpected occurrence. All the vessels of the British flotilla had abandoned their regular stations in the Inner Harbor. Some made sail out to sea while others passed through the narrows and anchored near Sandy Hook. The departure of these warships marks the end of the provincial control of New York by the fractious colonial legislature and the beginning of American military rule by the Continental Army. Thereafter, the fate of the city was placed in the hands of the American generals, and "several other gentlemen of distinction." Committees of Safety became local governing boards, and sub-committees like the Conspiracy Committee were set up to rout out Loyalist sympathizers, disaffected Patriots, and genuine saboteurs.[7]

The British abandonment of New York Harbor allowed most of the Patriot army from New England to enter the city by water unchallenged. John Sullivan's six regiments and Nathaniel Greene's Rhode Island men came by boat through Long Island Sound. Other soldiers arrived by foot from the west on the New Jersey shore of the Hudson and from the north to the mainland Bronx, but most were deployed to the various fortifications that ringed the harbor through the services of untold numbers of ferries, barges, and flatboats. These dispositions could not have been made under the guns of the Royal Navy. Moreover, two secret shipments of French gunpowder, arms, and artillery arrived in the city by sea during this period. These included enough artillery and ammunition to bring the American stockpile up to several hundred pieces, some of which were quite large, and they afforded the rebels for the first time a vast quantity of small arms ammunition (more than one million rounds or about fifty cartridges per man) without which the six-month-long defense of the city would have been impossible.

Upon his arrival in New York City, Washington again attempted through his agents to assemble a small fleet to control the local waters, especially the passage up the Hudson River to the north. These included the sloop *General Schuyler* (Lt. Joseph Divison) that was purchased from New York; the sloop *General Mifflin* and the row galley *Lady Washington (10, including one 32-pound bow gun)* that were owned by the local committee of safety; and the row galleys *Washington* and *Spitfire* that came from Rhode Island under command of Commodore John Grimes. Mixed in with these were the schooner *General Putnam (16)* and the sloop *Montgomery (14)* belonging to the New York State Navy, the row galleys *Hester, Shark,* and *Whiting,* and a score or more of other small armed vessels whose ownership and armament remain undetermined. Washington also received aid from the citizens of the state of Connecticut, who patrolled the sound in dozens of armed whaleboats and a handful of small warships.[8]

Prior to the arrival of the British invasion fleet in July 1776, the larger New York craft—*Schuyler, Putnam,* and *Montgomery*—cruised in the coastal waters of New Jersey and Long Island with some success, recapturing several British prizes. Washington suggested to New York's Special Committee for Maritime Affairs that it would be helpful if these vessels stayed in the harbor or in the local rivers on patrol. The New Yorkers were flustered by this request as they were looking forward to a return on their investment in the vessels in the form of prize money. In response, Washington suggested that he purchase *General Schuyler,* which was characterized as "too small for successful privateering,"[9] and he wrangled control of *General Putnam* by pleading for it as a loan. *Washington* and *Spitfire* had been placed in service in Narragansett Bay in 1775 by the Rhode Island General Assembly. Before leaving for New York they recaptured the American brigantine *Georgia Packet* and the sloop *Speedwell* from under the very guns of HMS *Scarborough (20)* and brought them safely into Narragansett Bay. They slipped into New York's Upper Bay on August 1, 1776, just in time for the British invasion of Long Island.[10]

INVASION FLEET

In early June 1776, several British warships reappeared taking post at critical navigational junctions around the city. HMS *Chatham (50)* came in and took post at the narrows of Long Island Sound, and the hated HMS *Asia (64)* returned to its old stomping grounds at the narrows near Gravesend. HMS *Niger (32)* anchored at the eastern entrance to Hell's Gate at Whitestone and HM schooner *Halifax (10)* stood sentinel at Throg's Neck near the mouth of Westchester Creek. General William Howe kept to his cabin in the frigate HMS *Greyhound (20)* in the Lower Bay with a group of transports exhibiting no obvious desire to land any troops. The *Greyhound* and its consorts just sat at anchor in the bay ominously waiting.

Intelligence concerning the sailing of a British fleet from Halifax to New York consisting of 130 warships and transports was reported to Washington by an American privateer. No one in North America had ever seen such a number of vessels. If true, this fleet posed an unimaginable threat to rebel control of the region. As the main body of vessels began to appear on June 29, the reason for General Howe's inactivity aboard *Greyhound* quickly became clear. As the ships anchored in two's and three's in the Lower Bay near Sandy Hook, the terrible might that the Crown had brought to bear on America increased to overwhelming proportions. One astonished New Yorker noted, "I . . . spied as I peeped out the Bay something resembling a wood of pine trees . . . . The whole bay was full of shipping as ever it could be. I declare I thought all London Afloat."[11]

Yet to the wonderment of all observers, the number of arriving vessels continued to grow throughout the early summer. Adm. Lord Augustus Howe, naval commander of the armada, arrived in late July in his flagship, HMS *Eagle (64)*. Ambrose Serle, Howe's naval secretary, noted, "Nothing could exceed the joy that appeared throughout the fleet and army upon our arrival. We were saluted by all the ships of war in the harbor, by the cheers of the sailors all along the ships, and by those of the soldiers on the shore. A finer scene could not be exhibited, both of country, ships, and men."[12]

The stream of British vessels seemed unending. On August 1, Admiral Parker in the battered HMS *Bristol (50)* returned to the anchorage with nine warships and thirty-five transports recalled from the failed attack on Charleston. A short while later twelve more transports filled with troops and artillery from Scotland appeared. Finally, Commodore William Hotham in HMS *Preston (50)* arrived with fifteen men-of-war and eighty-five transports filled with redcoats and the first 8,000 Hessian troops to reach America. If reports of 130 ships had posed a threat, the effect of 400 was overwhelming. The British land force had swelled to more than 24,000 men. Additionally, there were thousands of sailors available for duty on the five ships-of-the-line and four dozen frigates— almost one third of the entire Royal Navy establishment. Each warship was a self-contained fortress armed with scores of naval cannon.[13]

"This morning," wrote Serle on August 12, "as soon as it was light, we were gladdened with the sight of the grand fleet in the offing. The joy of the navy and the army was almost like that of a victory ... So large a fleet made a fine appearance ... with the sails crowded, colors flying, [and] guns saluting." It is not certain what response this spectacle may have stirred in the hearts of the hundreds of spectators that lined the wharves and rooftops of the city. A number of Loyalist leaders, avoiding the rebel patrols near the shore, made their way out in small boats and canoes to the *Asia*, which was most conveniently placed to receive them.[14] For the proponents of liberty, rebellion, and independence amazement must have been tempered by extreme apprehension. A shocked American officer wrote, "You would be surprised if you was here to see what a mighty fleet of ships our enemies have got; they lie down against Staten Island, more than a mile in length from East to West, and so thick and close together...that you can't see through."[15]

The American plan for the defense of New York, conceived by General Charles Lee and approved by Washington, was to keep the British artillery off the heights of Brooklyn that overlooked Manhattan from Long Island. To aid the guns on Brooklyn Heights, batteries facing Long Island and bearing on the East River were established within the city. To prevent the men-of-war from taking position in the East River, Gen. Israel Putnam had seized Governor's Island and fortified it. The tiny island, properly garrisoned and aided by some floating batteries, had the potential of keeping the Royal Navy out of the strategic passage between Manhattan and Brooklyn. Putnam also built an artillery battery at Red Hook, a knob of land projecting into the harbor adjacent to the Brooklyn lines. Armed whaleboats and other small vessels constantly patrolled the waters between the islands and batteries.[16]

Lee's defensive plan envisioned a contest for the city itself confined to the southern tip of Manhattan, not a battle on the open plains of Brooklyn. All the streets leading to the Hudson on the west were barricaded and several redoubts and two strong forts were built one on either bank overlooking the river. A series of redoubts were built to defend the Kingsbridge crossing on the northern end of Manhattan. Fortifications were also built on the heights in the Bronx at Fordham and Morrisania overlooking the Harlem River from the mainland. Lee's main batteries, aimed at the East River to prevent ships from entering, neglected to defend against an amphibious attack on Long Island. Inexplicably, Washington chose to deploy his army in large detachments spread among the geographical features of the bay and separated from each other by unfordable bodies of water. One historian of the campaign noted, "To scatter the American forces from Kingsbridge to Flatlands, with a great river intervening, was to invite disaster."[17] The largest segment of American troops, 7,000 men from among the army's best regiments, was posted on Brooklyn Heights with their backs to Manhattan across the East River.

Admiral Howe initially attempted to position his frigates in the East River as both Lee and Putnam had predicted, but the admiral's purpose was to shell the rebels in Brooklyn, not those in Manhattan. Fortunately for the Americans the winds remained unfavorable for the Royal Navy during most of the summer. Had the frigates been able to take the Americans in the rear the course of the war might have been unalterably changed in favor of the British. Although he knew of a possible fault in his strategic planning, Washington seems to have continued to believe in his ability to keep the waterways between the divisions of his army open to passage, and he funneled additional forces into an all but obvious trap in Brooklyn even after the British had made their initial landings on Long Island.[18]

THE WILL OF NATURE

Once it had massed in the Lower Bay the British fleet prepared for landings on nearby Staten Island where camps could be created to house the troops and relieve their long confinement aboard ship. The winds and waters of Lower New York Bay, however, continued to be treacherous, perverse, and stubbornly defiant, reaping a great defensive benefit for the Americans. A number of the British transports became confused by the changing pattern of tides and threatened to run afoul of one another. Some were driven dangerously close to Gravesend and were forced to anchor to keep from grounding. These became the targets of incessant American rifle fire, but only a single battery posted at the ferry station between Brooklyn and Staten Island was able to bring its artillery to bear. If more cannon had been placed within range of the harbor bar and Gravesend Bay, the British might have faced as grim a result as that at Charleston.

There is no question that the American plan of defense in summer 1776 was overly optimistic and strategically flawed. Its limitations were obvious at the time. Col. William Douglas wrote to his wife, "It will be in vain for us to expect to keep the shipping out of the North River [Hudson] unless we can fortify at the narrows." Douglas understood that, given the difficulty in passing over the bar from the Lower Bay, the best defense against the British fleet would have been to keep it out of the Upper Bay altogether. Moreover, New York Harbor was filled with unseen natural obstacles, and the narrow passages between Manhattan, Long Island, Staten Island, and the mainland were a rabbit warren of intricate turns, menacing rocks, and deadly tidal races. These navigational features proved to be of great advantage to the Americans, but there is some question as to whether they were an active part of American strategic thinking or simply an accident of geography that worked in their favor.[19]

The difficulty of safely navigating the bar was demonstrated by Adm. Sir George Collier, commanding HMS *Rainbow (44)*, when he grounded his vessel on the bar near Gravesend. Collier faulted the local pilot, a Loyalist, for being unskillful in doing his job. A modern historian points out quite correctly that "Britain's most competent naval officers, of whom Collier was one, were entirely dependent on the goodwill and the abilities of local pilots." The need for the British to find competent pilots from among the local population applied to any American port, unfamiliar to the Royal Navy.[20]

Gen. Sir Henry Clinton suggested a landing at Spuyten Duyvil where the Harlem River joined the Hudson. The posting of even a small warship here would have compromised Washington's escape route from Manhattan over the Kingsbridge to the mainland. However, Spuyten Duyvil, or the Devil's Mouth, had been aptly named by the Dutch in the seventeenth century. Its swirling waters, narrow confines, and cross-currents were all but impossible to navigate safely, and an anchored vessel would be imperiled by the rocky shores if it tried to maintain its position among the strong eddies and tidal countercurrents. Moreover, the heights over the creek were fortified (Cox Hill Fort) requiring a near suicidal attempt to pass in the face of an entrenched enemy.

On the other end of the passage between Manhattan and the Bronx was the more famous Hell's Gate where the Harlem River joined the East River. In 1779 HMS *Hussar (28)* proved that the remarkable danger of these waters was not overstated. While carrying almost £2 million in gold coins for the army payroll on Long Island, Capt. Charles Pole, believing he knew the waters, attempted the navigation of the Hell's Gate against the advice of his pilot. Just before reaching Montressor's (Randall's) Island the ship was swept onto Pot Rock and sank in 16 fathoms of water. The money was not recovered, and it remains the object of treasure hunters to this day.

By way of contrast the Hudson River had water and width enough for large warships up to the falls near Troy more than one hundred miles inland, making it possible for the British to land in Westchester behind the rebel army and trap it on Manhattan had they so chosen. This strategy was also suggested by Clinton, but rejected by the Howes. Nonetheless, the lower Hudson is a tidal estuary. This made progress very difficult for sailing craft, and most vessels anchored when the tide was ill and sailed only when it was favorable. The Tappan Sea (or Zee from the Dutch), which flanks Westchester County on the west, was more than three miles wide at the point where the banks of the river opened out from the Hudson Highlands. The entire British fleet could have anchored there with plenty of room to tack back and forth against the wind if need be.

Yet Tappan was not the perfect anchorage, and it had steep, heavily wooded banks that would have made amphibious landings difficult. Moreover, at the narrow point of the river upstream of Tappan were the "horse races" named for the daily cycle of tidal waters that affect the estuary. The races could be formidable obstacles to the navigation of the river in either direction, but they were not particularly dangerous except in late autumn or when the river was otherwise carrying an unusual amount of runoff. Later in the season large ice flows and whole sheets of ice made winter navigation of the river all but impossible for wooden ships. A contemporary observer noted of the winter of 1779–1780, "The North River was wholly frozen over and the East River had an astonishing quantity of floating ice. As, in spite of this, many people ventured out in boats, sad accidents happened almost daily ... on account of the ice." During this same winter the Americans were able to roll cannon from New Jersey across to Staten Island on the frozen surface of the Arthurskill with no fear of the ice failing beneath them.[21]

A MID-RIVER ENCOUNTER

During the first week of July 1776 the Americans celebrated the declaration of their independence with bonfires, illuminations, and cannon firings in the city that were clearly visible from the decks of the ships of the Royal Navy and encampments on Staten Island. However, the Patriots were almost immediately given a rude awakening regarding the forts and other obstacles they had built to defend the passage of the Hudson River. HMS *Rose (20)*, HMS *Phoenix (44)*, and their tenders sailed between two of the rebel strongholds straddling the lower Hudson River at Fort Washington (New York) and Fort Constitution (Fort Lee, New Jersey). A Jack-tar on the *Phoenix* climbed to the main topgallant yard and sat there straddling the giant spar throughout the entire engagement in a show of the utmost contempt for American marksmanship.[22]

Nonetheless, the passage of the ships was hardly a routine matter. The plunging cannon fire from the lofty banks of the river was continuous. Capt. James Wallace of *Rose* noted in his journal, "They shot away our starboard fore shroud, fore tackle pendant, fore lift, fore topsail clew lines, spritsail and main topsail braces, one 18 pound shot in the head of our fore mast, one through the pinnace [a boat], several through the sails and some in the hull.... Number of guns not known, weight of metal from 12 to 32 pounder." The warships returned the fire with spirit, especially on the Manhattan side. The balls from the two frigates passed through the residences in the main part of the city and just missed Trinity Episcopal Church at Broadway and Church Street. This caused a sudden and overwhelming rush of frightened residents to abandon whole parts of Manhattan in anticipation of a general bombardment by the entire fleet that never came.[23]

Washington's tiny American squadron actively operated on the river between Dobb's Ferry and Poughkeepsie, where two Continental frigates were being built. The same stretch of water was patrolled by *Rose*, *Phoenix*, the 14-gun schooner *Tryal*, and two small-armed tenders, *Charlotte* and *Shuldham*. Throughout the remainder of July the opposing vessels were seemingly content to make their way up and down the river on the tide appearing at Haverstraw, Sing-Sing (Ossining), and Tarrytown. The British warships seemed indifferent to the fire of the American batteries ranged along the banks of the river.

On the afternoon of August 3, 1776, Washington's little flotilla, recently reinforced by the row galleys from Rhode Island, engaged the enemy in the river for almost two hours before retiring with four killed, two badly wounded, and about a dozen other injuries. Lt. Colonel Benjamin Tupper was in command of the operation. He wrote, "[M]y flag being hoisted on board of *Washington*, I came up with the [British] ships and attacked.... The *Phoenix* fired the first gun, which was returned by the *Lady Washington*, whose shot went thro' the *Phoenix*. Upon my

The Patriot plan to control the passage of the Hudson River by fortifying the New York and New Jersey banks looked good on paper, but it was overly optimistic in reality. The fire from Fort Washington (right) and Fort Lee (left), while intense, proved unable to stop the passage of a Royal Navy squadron led by HMS *Phoenix*.

orders the *Lady Washington* put about to form a line; the tide was such that the *Washington* and *Spitfire* were exposed to the broadsides of the ships for 1/2 of an hour without suffering much damage. We engaged them an hour and a half, and then we thought to retreat to Dobb's Ferry."[24]

A second American account of the operation says that there were six galleys in the attacking force. Although the writer identified only three, the others may have been the row galleys *Hester, Shark,* and *Whiting.* "The *Spitfire* advanced to the assistance of *Washington* and behaved well." The galleys suffered a good deal of damage. *Washington* had its bow gun knocked away, some of its oars destroyed, and its hull holed above the waterline. *Lady Washington* was said to have had its 32-pound bow gun "split down the barrel seven inches." The *Spitfire* took several shots just below the railings and through the rigging.[25]

A British account reports six attackers composed of schooners and row galleys. "We began and kept up a constant fire at them for two hours, at which time they row'd away down river and came to an anchor in sight of us."[26] The *Phoenix* was hulled only twice, but the British vessels did not chase the Americans in their retreat because of the narrowness of the river and the shifting wind.

Thousands of spectators viewed the engagement from windows and rooftops as the vessels "played smartly" upon one another. The Reverend Pastor Shewkirk noted, "The smoke of the firing drew over like a cloud, and the air was filled with the smell of powder." Yet this was risky business for the onlookers. A few civilians ashore were wounded by stray shot, but none were killed. A 9-pound ball passed through the "Old German Church" on Broadway. Another entered a house through an open bedroom window, pierced the wall just above the head of a bedstead, crossed a staircase, and came to reside in a room on the opposite side of the building.[27]

FIRESHIPS ON THE HUDSON

On August 16 the same British vessels were anchored off Philipse Manor near Tarrytown. Just before midnight the Americans launched a fireship attack—one of the most feared tactics that could be used against an enemy fleet in a crowded anchorage. Fireships were disposable relics filled with combustible materials and explosives, which scattered the flaming debris in a wide circle around the vessels. The object of the attack was to set fire to the enemy vessels before the crews could cut their anchor cables, set sail, and move out of danger. The first American fireship hit the tender *Charlotte* and both vessels burned to the waterline. All the crew of the tender got off safely. A second attacker narrowly missed the *Rose,* which cut its cable to get clear. The fireship then crashed bows-on into the larger *Phoenix*. It took twenty minutes for the crew of the frigate to tow off the blazing hulk and control the fires. The next morning the British flotilla abandoned its post and retreated downriver to Staten Island in the bay. While passing the American shore batteries the vessels once again came under significant but ineffective fire. Only the active interposition of Washington's flotilla had prevented the British from taking control of the Hudson River waterway.

A BRITISH D-DAY

On the same day that their warships quit the Hudson River, the British began to embark their invasion troops from the camps on Staten Island in which they had been living. It took several days to get the 15,000 troops aboard the transports that would take them across the narrows to Gravesend Bay where a wide, level, and sandy plain invited a major amphibious landing. At dawn on August 22, *Rainbow*, *Phoenix*, *Rose*, and *Greyhound* anchored on springs near the beach aiming their broadsides to cover the landings. The bomb vessels *Carcass* and *Thunder*, equipped with high arcing mortars, took station near the shoals within range to pitch explosive shells into any American advance from their forward entrenchments on Gowanus Heights. The landings were made in seventy-five flat-bottomed boats that delivered 4,000 invasion troops in each wave. The landings lasted for three hours. The only Americans to dispute these landings were a handful of Pennsylvania riflemen of Col. Edward Hand's regiment.

Thus began the Battle of Brooklyn, the largest battle of the entire Revolutionary War in terms of the number of troops and naval vessels involved. Close to 30,000 men fought over the next few days on the western end of Long Island. Ambrose Serle, Admiral Howe's secretary, noted, "The disembarkation of... troops upon a fine beach, their forming [into companies and regiments] upon the adjacent plain... exhibited one of the finest and most picturesque scenes that the imagination can fancy or the eye behold." On August 25 more than 4,300 Hessians were landed in a separate operation, making the invasion force on Long Island a remarkable 20,000 men.[28]

Washington, noting that the winds remained unfavorable for the British fleet, brought over almost 2,500 reinforcements from Manhattan under cover of his row galleys. Washington now had almost 10,000 troops on Long Island; but, although outnumbered two to one, he was nonetheless somewhat relieved in not having been cut off from the mainland by a landing in force on the Hudson above Manhattan. The escape routes to the mainland by way of Kingsbridge remained open to Westchester as well as to Connecticut. For several days the armies in Brooklyn stared at one another, and small parties skirmished in the woods. Washington's officers and advisors were confident of holding the heights of Brooklyn against repeated frontal assaults in the same fashion that the militia had held the entrenchments at Breed's (Bunker) Hill in 1775.[29]

The loss to the redcoats on Breed's Hill—1,100 killed and wounded—had been almost incomprehensible. That the British generals had chosen to make repeated onslaughts of this nature on entrenched Patriot positions was an indication of the low regard in which they held Americans as military opponents at that time. However, the British staff showed that they had learned to respect American marksmanship when confronting rebel entrenchments. In fact every major operation launched by the British against rebel entrenchments during the New York campaign contained a significant flanking movement, several of which were carried out with the aid of the Royal Navy.

On the morning of August 27, 1776, after a long night march to the east of the American entrenchments, more than 10,000 British and Hessian troops suddenly fell upon the left flank of the rebel lines pouring through Jamaica Pass and rolling up the American defenses from east to west. American Col. Samuel Miles noted, "To my mortification I saw the main body of the enemy in full march between me and our lines." The fleeing defenders set off a chain reaction of fear among their comrades. The rout did not end until all the Americans on Long Island not yet dead or captured resided on Brooklyn Heights. A British officer noted, "Thus repulsed on every quarter, they appear to have been easy prey.... It requires better troops than even the Virginia [sic] riflemen ... when they know their retreat is cut off."[30]

The American army was now pinned against the East River and faced by more than twice its number in its front. Two of its generals (Sullivan and Stirling) were prisoners, and its espirit de corps was at low ebb. The day had been a stunning success for British arms undoing almost all of Washington's plans in a single maneuver.[31] A British officer noted the vigor with which the Hessians in particular came to grips with Patriot troops, "It was a fine sight to see with what alacrity they dispatched the rebels with their bayonets after we surrounded them so that they could not resist."[32]

AMERICAN DUNKIRK

Intelligence received from Gen. William Heath suggested that a group of Royal Navy warships had passed down the length of Long Island Sound from the east and were poised to post themselves in the East River to make a retreat to Manhattan impossible. Although the intelligence proved faulty, Gen. Alexander McDougall correctly warned that if even a single frigate was able to work its way into the channel, it could sever Washington's communications with Manhattan and the mainland.

Washington quickly appreciated that his army was facing imminent disaster if it stayed where it was. The river crossing to Manhattan was a mile wide behind the American army, and Washington had only ten flatboats at Fulton's Ferry with which to transfer troops.

The commander-in-chief called a council of war on August 29 to discuss a retreat to Manhattan where he could escape the Royal forces in his front and get out from under the threat of the guns of the British warships. A unanimous resolution to that effect was passed late in the day, and a massive amphibious operation in the face of the enemy on land and sea was scheduled for the next night. Orders were immediately issued to requisition every flat-bottomed boat or barge thought capable of transporting troops, artillery, and equipment. The 14th Massachusetts Regiment composed of mariners from Marblehead and commanded by Colonel John Glover was chosen to carry out the operation.

All summer the Royal Navy warships had watched as Washington funneled troops back and forth across the river, and they had become accustomed to a good deal of activity between Manhattan and Brooklyn. The battery at Fort Stirling near the ferry would keep the British warships from becoming too inquisitive, and the row galleys of Washington's flotilla would screen the activity. It was planned that the New York vessels would return to their positions in the Hudson after the operation in order to maintain communications between New England and the southern colonies, but the Rhode Island vessels would move east to patrol Long Island Sound before making their way home.

At about seven o'clock in the evening, the Marbleheaders arrived at the ferry point. An hour later the first American troops from the lines arriving at the embarkation point were loaded in silence under the watchful eye of Washington himself and ferried over to the relative safety of lower Manhattan. The tide was initially running with the loaded barges and boats, but the same wind that had kept Admiral Howe's warships out of the East River, now worked against the Americans as it threatened to sweep the flatboats out of the channel to the southwest and into the waiting hands of the British fleet. Fortunately, at midnight the wind shifted somewhat enabling the mariners to sail to Manhattan while loaded and to row only on the return trip when empty. The opportunity to enter the East River that this change in wind finally offered the Royal Navy seems to have been missed by the captains of the British frigates.

As the transfer continued Washington's most reliable troops spread out filling the every-increasing vacancies in the rebel lines in an effort to conceal the movement to the embarkation point. At sunrise the last of these Americans were afforded the benevolence of a thick fog that concealed their departure. No operation could have had better luck. Every man, save a few too severely wounded to be moved and a handful of deserters, was extracted from Brooklyn without the slightest notice by the British on land or sea. The army now abandoned the city to be deployed in very strong positions on Harlem Heights. One of the last Patriot officers to exit Long Island, Benjamin Tallmadge wrote, "In the history of warfare I do not recollect a more fortunate retreat." Washington noted, "Providence—or some good honest fellow, has done more for us than we were disposed to do for ourselves." Admiral Collier, commander of HMS *Rainbow*, has left a different analysis. "How this has happened is surprising, for had our troops followed them close up, they must have thrown down their arms and surrendered; or had our ships attacked the batteries, which we [had] been in constant expectation of being ordered to do, not a man could have escaped." Nonetheless, the Battle of Brooklyn Heights was the first great victory of British combined arms in the Revolution, and it generally erased the embarrassment of the Crown forces over their failures at Boston and Charleston.[33]

AMPHIBIOUS OPERATIONS

The British and Americans shared a history of successful landings during the French Wars of the first half of the eighteenth century. They had successfully landed ground forces from transports by boat—most notably the colonials at Louisburg in 1745 and the redcoats at Quebec in 1759. Although Washington's escape from Long Island is always noted as remarkable, general histories of the Revolutionary War tend to understate the ubiquitous character of the amphibious operation as a tactic in an extended theater of war almost devoid of bridges and with few adequate roads.

Amphibious landings, particularly in the face of an entrenched enemy, were among the most difficult military maneuvers to carry off successfully in the eighteenth century, and they remain equally complicated today. Even without the threat of enemy fire, the simple loading, transfer, and unloading of troops at sea while avoiding surf, tide, and currents was challenging. Troops often landed without their officers or artillery support, with wet ammunition and missing weapons, or in the wrong place or in the wrong order to quickly implement tactical operations. The first boatloads of troops were always the most vulnerable to enemy counterattacks, and were usually closely supported by the cannon of the navy.

During the weeks that followed the landings at Gravesend, Admiral Howe's fleet would successfully participate in a half dozen or more significant waterborne operations in an attempt to out-maneuver the rebel army. The first and most successful of these was at Kip's Bay on the east side of Manhattan Island. Chronologically there were also major landings on the island outposts in the East River; at Throg's (Frog's) Neck near Westchester Creek in the Bronx; at Pell's Neck at Hutchinson Creek near the eighteenth-century town of Eastchester; at Fort Washington overlooking the

Hudson River; and at Fort Lee atop the towering Palisades in New Jersey. Washington's army also performed a number of amphibious operations during this period of the war besides the remarkable retreat from Brooklyn. It crossed the Hudson River to reach New Jersey after the Battle of White Plains; it crossed the Delaware into Pennsylvania to escape apprehension by Cornwallis and Howe; and it finally recrossed the ice-filled Delaware to attack the Hessians at Trenton, New Jersey, on Christmas Day 1776. Washington's amphibious retreat from Brooklyn and his crossing of the Delaware at Trenton were among the most pivotal events of the war.

General Howe decided to make the Kip's Bay landing in the lower third of Manhattan rather than falling directly on the flank of Washington's more northerly position on Harlem Heights because the narrowness of the island at that point allowed the navy to directly support both the landings and the advance inland. The frigates *Phoenix (44)*, *Roebuck (44)*, *Orpheus (32)*, *Carrysfort (28)*, and *Rose (20)* anchored on springs in the East River opposite Kip's Bay forming an end to end cordon with a combined broadside of more than 80 cannon to cover the landing of 4,000 troops. At the same time Howe sent a man-of-war and two frigates up the Hudson as a diversion. A deafening bombardment by the naval cannon of these vessels signaled the start of the invasion of Manhattan. In the face of the advancing Crown forces, the Patriot militia stationed at Kip's Bay immediately scattered in one of the worst episodes of panic in American military history, and a frustrated Washington came within a long pistol shot of being captured on the field. Those Americans who reached their strong entrenchments on Harlem Heights were fortunate that day.

With the British wishing to avoid a frontal assault and consolidate their hold on the local waterways, the two sides settled in and stared at each other. Governor's Island, Ryker's Island, Montressor's Island, and any of the small bare rocks in the East River that could support a battery of artillery or an infantry outpost were occupied by the Crown forces. In many cases the redcoats simply turned the Americans out of their own fortifications. Montressor's Island was located at the confluence of the Harlem and East Rivers, and as a military post it was particularly well placed to pose a threat to the rebel positions at Fordham Heights and Morrisania on the Bronx mainland. The American commanders determined that a nighttime amphibious operation should be mounted to retake Montressor's and thereby deny free passage of the rivers to the Royal Navy. Col. Michael Jackson was given the command of three barges and 180 men to make the night attack. The first barge was well in advance of the others and made a solitary landfall. Unfortunately, these Americans were observed, and Jackson and his sixty men received a warm welcome. Fourteen were killed and several captured before they could retreat. The uncoordinated attack was an abject failure.[34]

While the British occupied most of the rebel outposts in the harbor with little trouble, General Howe found that he could not drive the Americans from their main entrenchments on Harlem Heights, a naturally strong position well out of range of the navy's guns.[35] Frustrated in his attempts to directly confront the Americans, and having learned from prisoners and deserters that the rebels were planning to abandon the position in favor of one on the mainland (White Plains), General Howe decided to cut off their escape route over Kingsbridge. Admiral Howe agreed to attempt a landing in the Bronx at Throg's Neck to the east by way of the dangerous Hell's Gate. On October 12 General Howe left a portion of his forces in the American front on Manhattan to make a diversion, and he embarked 14,000 invasion troops, including all of his 8,000 Hessians, on more than eighty transports escorted by nine warships. General Howe wrote, "I determined to get upon their principal communication with Connecticut, with a view to forcing them to quit the strongholds in the neighborhood of Kingsbridge, and, if possible, to bring them to action."[36]

Just as the fleet began to sail into the Hell's Gate it was surrounded by a thick fog that obscured its route. To any navy other than the Royal Navy, or any admiral other than "Black Dick" Howe, the obstacles would have seemed insurmountable, but, as Clinton reported, "The Admiral, who was present, persisted notwithstanding ... every hazard, and by his own excellent management and that of his officers the whole got through." The entire contingent managed the deadly passage with only the loss of one artillery barge, a few men, and three 6 pounders; but the local pilots were amazed by the ease with which the warships and transports successfully negotiated the passage.[37]

While the morning fog had initially concealed the movement, the tactic quickly became apparent to the Americans, who had no doubt that its ultimate goal was to cut off their retreat. Fortunately, General Heath had posted small detachments of Americans along the Bronx coastline in anticipation of just such a move. Washington wrote, "I have reason to believe that the greatest part of their army has moved upwards [East], or is about to do it, pursuing their original plan of getting in our rear and cutting off our communications with the country [mainland]."[38]

Notwithstanding the success of negotiating the passage of Hell's Gate, Throg's Neck proved a poor choice for a landing. Only after the redcoats had formed their lines of march ashore did they find out that the neck was actually separated from the mainland by a wide salt marsh. A single wooden bridge and a tidal ford were the only routes off the neck. General Heath posted about two dozen American riflemen from Hand's regiment to dispute these crossing. The bridge planking was removed as soon as the frigates and barges filled with troops were seen. Howe found the advance of several thousand troops hampered by a score of Pennsylvanians well placed behind temporary barricades and in a local mill building. Due to their lack of knowledge concerning the natural topography of Throg's Neck, the British had made their first tactical blunder of the campaign. An American observer noted, "Had they pushed their imaginations to discover a worst place [to land], they could not have succeeded better." Yet, the British operation and the threat that it posed moved Washington to reconsider remaining on Manhattan any longer, and he immediately put plans into operation to remove the entire rebel army to White Plains.[39]

As part of Washington's plan for a retreat Colonel Glover was sent to Pelham Bay in the Bronx with a brigade of four Massachusetts regiments to head off any of Howe's troops on Throg's Neck that might force their way along the shore road to the east. Meanwhile, Howe reembarked 3,000 of his men under Sir Henry Clinton and Charles Lord Cornwallis and sent them to make a secondary landing at Pell's Point three miles further to the northeast of Throg's Neck at the mouth of the Hutchinson River. Fortunately, Glover spotted the amphibious force entering the tidal marshes at the mouth of the river (actually a marsh-filled shallow creek) from a hilltop near the eighteenth-century village of Eastchester in the Bronx. He reported, "I saw a number of ships in the sound underway [and] in a very short time saw the boats upwards of two hundred sail, all manned and formed in four grand divisions." To amass such a great number of small craft, Howe must have stripped much of the fleet of its boats and launches.[40]

Initially taken by surprise, Glover had not gone half the distance to the shore when his own advanced party encountered the British advanced guard moving inland. While the two spearheads exchanged skirmish fire, Glover deployed his men on ground that was "strong and defensible, being full of stone fences, both along the road and across the adjacent fields." Glover held his own regiment of Marbleheaders and three small artillery pieces on a hillside across the creek from the invaders. Fortunately for the Americans, a British frigate that was dispatched to provide covering fire for the attacking troops ran aground on the extensive mudflats out of range and bearing of Glover's positions.[41]

By placing his men behind stone walls and instructing each successive unit to hold the enemy in check as long as possible before falling back to a similar position in their rear, Glover showed an instinctive understanding of the best characteristics of the American soldier, who fought with great tenacity from cover but wavered when standing in an open field. The encounter lasted from late morning until dusk, and Glover reported that the American withdrawal was made "with the greatest reluctance" and with "as much good order and regularity as ever they marched off a public parade."[42] Meanwhile, Washington's troops were given precious time to reach White Plains without further molestation. The final attempt to pin the rebel army in Manhattan had been foiled.[43]

In the hope of retaining control of the lower Hudson, Washington left behind a significant number of troops in Fort Washington (3,000 men) and Fort Lee (5,000 men). Unfortunately, the American planners were mistaken with regard to the strength of these positions. The attack on Fort Washington on November 15 was carried out by Hessian troops under Col. Johann Rall, who would lose his life in a few weeks while commanding at Trenton. Additional simultaneous thrusts by British troops against the Patriot outposts included an amphibious crossing of the Harlem River and a bombardment of rebel positions by HMS *Pearl (32)* from the Hudson. The British victory at Fort Washington was stupendous: 2,800 prisoners with muskets, 146 pieces of artillery, and almost all of the Patriots' reserve ammunition.

Four days later General Cornwallis embarked 4,000 men in flatboats to cross the Hudson to the New Jersey side. In an orderly and precise amphibious operation, these troops landed to the north of Fort Lee, scaled the nearly vertical palisades that lined the western bank of the

This period illustration of Cornwallis' landing at the base of the palisades on the west bank (New Jersey side) of the Hudson River evidences the orderliness, regulation, and technique that characterized the amphibious operations of the Royal Navy.

river, and drove south along the cliff tops. Fortunately for the rebels, this amphibious operation was observed from the clifftops, and the troops at Fort Lee were warned in just enough time to abandon their entrenchments and flee into New Jersey. However, they retreated without their stock of provisions, without their wagons, and without their severely wounded. Hundreds of the latter were left to the mercy of the enemy, and the majority died while confined in New York prisons.

The defeats suffered by the Patriots in the New York in 1776 should have ended the war, but it did not. The campaign was a series of crucial engagements each fraught with strategic significance, and it serves as a prominent example of American and British tactical thinking.[44] The rebels evidenced their respect for the power of warships throughout their planning for New York's defense. When driven from Brooklyn, they quickly reestablished their lines in strong positions on Harlem Heights, on Fordham Heights, and in the interior mainland well out of the range of naval guns. By so doing they largely eliminated the tactical advantage of the British navy, if not its strategic value. Meanwhile the Royal Navy had shown its versatility by maneuvering in dangerous waters, by safely transporting landing troops throughout the theater of operations, and by providing supporting fire for its troops.

SUBMARINE WARFARE

The New York Campaign cannot be left without mention of David Bushnell, an inventor from Connecticut, who is generally given credit for the invention of the first attack submarine. Bushnell and Phineas Pratt, a fellow student at Yale, had conceived of an underwater bomb with a time-delayed flintlock detonator that might be attached to the bottom of an anchored warship by means of a hand-powered underwater vehicle— the *American Turtle*.

The one-man-powered *Turtle* had a screw propeller and had undergone extensive trials in the waters of the Connecticut River off Old Saybrook under the command of Ezra Bushnell, the inventor's brother. The submarine—it really just skimmed under the surface of the water—was tested for maneuverability and submergibility, and it worked as it had been envisioned. However, Ezra Bushnell died of unrelated causes before the submarine could be deployed.

Transported by water in another vessel to New York in August, the *Turtle* was launched into the Upper Harbor on the night of September 6–7, 1776. Its intended target was HMS *Eagle*, Howe's flagship, moored near Bedloe Island. The pilot was Ezra Lee, a capable but less practiced pilot than Bushnell. *Turtle* made its way undetected to the stern of *Eagle* where Lee tried to implant the underwater bomb under the hull by driving a connecting screw into the rudder post. However, it is supposed that

Lee' auger struck some of the metal strapping and refused to penetrate. After a second unsuccessful attempt he was detected by the British lookouts and chased by the guard boats. The bomb was nonetheless released into the water, and it ripped the night with a fearful explosion some minutes later. Unfortunately, the explosion was some distance away from any of the enemy shipping in the harbor. Nonetheless, the British recognized the threat that *Turtle* posed and set additional guard boats to patrol among the fleet. The *Turtle* never attempted to repeat its attack. It was left behind when the Americans abandoned the New York waterfront, and was scuttled by the British after it was seized. A series of floating bombs based on a similar timed fuse principle was used in 1777 against British warships in the Delaware River. Called the Battle of the Kegs, the attack proved equally ineffective.[45]

Whaleboat Warriors
and Bateaux Battalions

It is much to be lamented that [cargoes] of such consequence should be sent from England in a vessel destitute of arms even so to protect [itself] from a rowboat.
—Rear Adm. Molyneaux Shuldham, RN

These nocturnal movements of the whaleboats about the harbor, and the knowledge of there being some hundreds of them, capable of carrying from 10 to 16 men each, with ease, began to cause some apprehension in the large men of war, particularly in those stationed some distance from the town.
—Vice Adm. Samuel Graves, RN

THE SMALL-BOAT NAVY

Handicapped by their lack of warships in 1775, the Americans adapted many different types of civilian watercraft to their war effort especially with regard to their amphibious operations in coastal waters and the need to transport troops across rivers and bays. These included a large number of sloops and schooners used in the coasting trade; harbor vessels such as scows, ferries, barges, and lighters; and many simpler boats such as skiffs, whaleboats, bateaux, gondolas, flatboats, and canoes. There were also references in orders and letters to types that were known in their day as pirogues, pettiaugers, shallops, smacks, and wherries, many of which were accompanied by conflicting descriptions of their appearance. Some contemporary observers seem to have recognized the various types of watercraft in use and correctly matched them to their proper names, but others seem to have used terms indiscriminately making no attempt to distinguish between the various flat-bottomed craft and the sharp-keeled vessels. Resolving the nomenclature is further frustrated by the common practice of naming each type according to the favored nicknames assigned by local mariners, such as Albany Boats, Durham Boats, or Pinkies.

During the American war a considerable number of small vessels were used for tactical purposes. For instance, Gen. John Sullivan required twenty-three vessels of various types and sizes to move his Rhode Island troops to New York in 1776. During the retreat from Brooklyn, Gen. Hugh Hughes was required to impress any craft available along the waterfront that was capable of carrying Patriot troops. A surviving American army return from 1781 details thirty-one vessels used to move 4,150 men across the Hudson River, including four flatboats, four schooners, and twenty-three sloops. Furthermore, while encamped on Staten Island, the British are said to have built seventy-five flat-bottomed landing craft in preparation for the landings on Long Island. Of the British vessels we have no definite description, but they were estimated to have had a capacity of about fifty men each.[1]

WHALEBOATS

In 1772 American colonials had their first recorded success in whaleboats when they attacked and destroyed *Gaspee* in Narragansett Bay. A large number of independent whaleboat raids were made by the Americans thereafter. Almost all were combined operations accomplished with the aid of militia or Continental troops. The waters of Matawan Creek and Raritan Bay in New Jersey, Chesapeake Bay, Massachusetts Bay, and Long Island Sound abound in these miniature vessels of war. Whaleboats were among the smallest vessels of war deployed by the Americans in the Revolution. Like the patrol boats of more recent wars—PTs and PBRs for instance—these wooden watercraft formed a "mosquito fleet" used to annoy Britain's outposts, threaten their communications, and menace the Royal Navy itself. Although the whaleboat commanders kept no logs or other regular records to document their escapades, the diaries and letters of those who served in them attest to their effectiveness and activity.[2]

Whaleboats seem to have been as common in Revolutionary America as minivans are today in suburbia. In New England whaling was a major industry, and once established it affected the lives of many people. Young men were eager to serve on the whaling ships each with their dozen boats. New York's Long Island also had large commercial whaling ports at Sag Harbor, East Hampton, and Southampton. A score of whaleships called the Hudson River home. Whalers also sailed regularly from ports like Mystic, New London, and Stonington in Connecticut, as well as from many coves on the Long Island Sound. Massachusetts hosted a number of ports that supported whalers, particularly Gloucester, New Bedford, and Edgartown (on Martha's Vineyard). In 1775 the island community of Nantucket alone was home to more than 150 whaleships.

Americans were the best whaleboat men in the world, yet the Revolution, while it lasted, put a virtual halt to commercial whaling. There is no doubt that many of the whaleboats used in the Revolution were dragooned into service from the owners of an inactive whaling fleet, but it is equally true that many were borrowed, purchased, or built for the purpose of warfare. In November 1775 the provincial congress of Massachusetts resolved that "Mr. Lemeul Williams ... transport in the cheapest manner from Dartmouth to Newport, the remainder of the Whaleboats purchased and left there ... 16th September last, and that he be directed to deliver them to Governor Cooke [of Rhode Island]." One year later an additional sixty "armed whaleboats" were sent to Rhode Island.[3]

Whaleboats as a type were sharp-keeled, double-ended, and made of long thin boards, usually three quarters of an inch thick cedar or other appropriate wood, in lapstreak fashion with one board slightly overlapping the next. Although up to 40 feet long they were easy to build, lightweight, and generally stable in the water. Whaleboats were designed to function in the turbulence of ocean waters; bays, sounds, and rivers posed no navigational problem for them. They had between eight and twelve oars that varied from 6 to 10 feet in length, and either a detachable rudder or a steering oar at the stern. They usually came with a one-piece mast and a lug sail for moving before the wind; but they were not spectacular performers under sail, allowing a lot of leeway when the wind was abeam.

Whaleboats had a maximum speed of 3 to 4 knots when rowed by a full crew, but the resistance of the water rose dramatically at the upper end of this range. Modern tests show that the amount of effort needed to raise the speed of the boat to 4 knots was twice that needed to maintain 3 knots. When occupied by only two persons, both rowing, speeds of 4 to 6 knots might be accomplished for short intervals. A particular account from the period noted a trip of 75 miles made by a flotilla of nine fully manned boats in just 24 hours, and not one boat fell behind the grueling pace. The restriction on speed seems to have been associated with the ratio of the number of men rowing versus the deadweight in the boat. Large whaleboats were capable of carrying two dozen persons or their equivalent weight in material, guns, or livestock.

The whaleboat was uniquely well-suited to amphibious operations because it could be moved quickly and quietly. With the mast stepped down, it had a minimal profile when approaching land or other vessels, and if painted a dark color it could be almost undetectable at a short distance at night. Each boat could carry a reasonable force in terms of the number of men, and many were fitted with a single small cannon or swivel guns. When working in concert with a number of other boats they could bring a respectable force to bear on the enemy. Moreover, due to their light weight, the boats could be carried across short distances on land by the crew, leaving and re-entering the water with little fuss. This characteristic of whaleboats was of particular benefit when raids were being made in shallow waters or where spits of land crossed the most direct path of attack or retreat. Because they were sharp-ended, they handled better than blunt-ended boats of similar size through the surf.

It took only six days after the battle of Lexington for the local Committee of Safety to order that all the available whaleboats in Massachusetts Bay be concentrated around Boston. During the weeks that followed more than one hundred whaleboats streamed forth from time to time to attack the British in the harbor. Groups of rebels landed on the larger islands and began herding the cattle and sheep toward the shore where they were loaded into the largest of the whaleboats and taken to the mainland. More than 400 animals were removed in a single operation. On subsequent nights the hay and forage were set afire, and the lighthouse and other navigational aids in Boston Harbor were destroyed. On May 27, 1775, a group of whaleboats had a signal victory when they struck and burned the Royal Navy schooner *Diana*.

In New York on January 23, 1776, American Gen. William Alexander (Lord Stirling) loaded four whaleboats with picked troops and captured the British supply transport *Blue Mountain Valley* (John Dempster, master) in the harbor. It was brought as a prize to Elizabeth, New Jersey. There are few details available about this operation, but Congress voted Lord Stirling its thanks for the apparent success and lack of bloodshed. During July and August 1776 Adam Hyler and William Marriner of New Brunswick, New Jersey, so annoyed the British fleet anchored in New York Bay that an armed force of redcoats was sent inland to destroy their boats, which were kept on the Raritan River. Nonetheless, whaleboat parties led by both men continued to patrol the waters between Staten Island and Egg Harbor, New Jersey, compelling Loyalist fishermen and coasting vessels to ransom their craft or be brought in as a prize. One night Hyler with two armed boats captured an unwary British corvette anchored in Coney Island Bay without firing a shot. He then removed the crew and set the vessel afire, not knowing that it contained $40,000 in gold coins.

In 1777, R. J. Meigs organized a raid on Sag Harbor, New York, on the eastern end of Long Island. He recruited about 230 men in

Few British vessels were safe from a concerted attack by the Patriots in their whaleboats. The attack on the shipping in Peconic Bay, pictured here, was one of the most successful of these raids with a dozen British vessels destroyed, the town burned, and ninety captives taken from among the Loyalist population.

whaleboats at New Haven, Connecticut, and on the afternoon of May 23 the whaleboats rowed across the sound. They were then carried several miles overland to Peconic Bay and again launched in preparation for a midnight attack on the shipping in the harbor. The attackers, divided into five separate units, were able to get within 200 yards of the British before being detected. Although the enemy ships opened fire upon them, the raiders captured the port with relative ease. Twelve enemy vessels were destroyed along with a considerable stock of provisions. Six British were killed and ninety (mostly Loyalist militia and civilians) were taken by boat to Connecticut as prisoners. None of the attackers was lost in the operation.[4]

Also in 1777 William Marriner and John Schenck of New Jersey combined to raid the western end of Long Island not far from the New Utrecht ferry where many wealthy Loyalists had country homes. Marriner had a list of prominent Loyalist leaders that he hoped to kidnap including the mayor of New York, David Matthews (who had escaped from confinement in 1776), and the president of the Chamber of Commerce, Theophylact Bache. The raiders divided into four groups. Bache and another Loyalist, Miles Sherbrook, were taken—the latter hiding in his woodshed with his breeches in his hands. Ironically, the raiders were also able to free American Capt. Alexander Gordon, who had been held prisoner in one of the homes since the fall of Fort Washington. The Loyalist prisoners were ultimately exchanged for captive Patriot leaders.

Marriner also led a series of raids on British shipping in the lower harbor of New York. When a group of small craft anchored in the protective cove behind Sandy Hook, he descended upon them with a fleet of whaleboats capturing three sloops and an armed schooner. Finding it impossible to bring the sloops out, he grounded them and set them afire. However, he escaped with the schooner and its cargo. From this operation alone each man in the raiding party realized $1,000 in prize money.

Finally, Marriner with nine compatriots in a single whaleboat dropped silently down the Raritan River on the night of April 18, 1781. He brought his boat with muffled oarlocks under the stern counter of the rebel privateer *Blacksnake (8)*, a prize recently brought in by a British crew. Within seconds he had seized and disarmed the lone sentry, locked the prize crew below decks, cut the anchor cable, and set the fore courses. The brig glided silently passed a nearby Royal Navy three-decker without raising an alarm. On the next morning Marriner found himself at sea in command of a small, but formidable, vessel of war. He then used his apparently bottomless well of bravado—he had only nine men with him—to take the lightly armed British schooner *Morning Star* from its captain, Richard Campbell, after a brief but bloody confrontation on its deck against a crew of thirty. Marriner ran both vessels through the Cranberry Inlet to Tom's River, New Jersey, where they were condemned and sold.

A number of whaleboat raids were planned by Washington's chief of intelligence, Benjamin Tallmadge. In September 1779 Tallmadge assembled fifty dismounted dragoons, twenty-eight Continental infantrymen, and about fifty whaleboatmen at Shippan Point near Stamford, Connecticut. Their objective was the Loyalist refugee camp at Lloyd's Neck eight miles across the sound. These Loyalists had been waging their own whaleboat war by raiding along the Connecticut coastline, kidnapping Patriot leaders, and seizing rebel shipping. Militia Gen. Benjamin Silliman was their most notable victim. Their camp on Long Island was composed of two houses and several temporary huts very near the edge of the water. Tallmadge left the Connecticut shore at eight o'clock at night and landed two hours later. His men carried both houses by force of arms, but failed to completely surround a village of temporary huts. The first musket fire alerted most of the Loyalists who fled into the brush and set up a desultory defensive fire. Tallmadge burned the Loyalists' boats and returned to Connecticut without loss.[5]

In November 1780 Tallmadge again planned an expedition across the sound, this time against a mid-island forage depot at Coram and an ocean-side Loyalist outpost at the Smith House in Mastic optimistically called Fort St. George. The depot was reportedly unfortified, but the fort consisted of two houses and a redoubt connected by a lightly timbered palisade and a ditch in a triangular configuration. A detachment of forty dismounted dragoons and forty whaleboatmen set out from the town of Fairfield, Connecticut, in the growing darkness of November 21. Aided by favorable winds the party landed near the present location of Port Jefferson on the north shore of Long Island. Here they were stopped by a gathering storm whose winds and freezing rain were so fierce that the raiders had to take shelter under their overturned boats on the beach. Avoiding detection throughout the night Tallmadge left twenty men to guard the boats and commandeered several horses. A small party of mounted men made for Coram where they burned 300 tons of hay at the forage depot. The loss of the hay was significant because it deprived the local farmers and carters the free use of their own horses and oxen for hauling produce and grain to the British garrisons in the city of New York during the following winter.

Tallmadge divided the remainder of his party into three units with specific tasks during the attack on Fort St. George. The first was led by Caleb Brewster, who was to destroy any obstructions while the other units attacked and surrounded the houses. The attack went as planned with the raiders taking the redoubt and reducing the fire from the houses within ten minutes. The entire garrison was taken prisoner save seven killed or badly wounded. Only one raider was wounded. The party then burned the fort and a supply vessel anchored at a small dock nearby the house. A considerable quantity of ammunition was also destroyed because it could not be carried. The raiders and their prisoners then returned to their waiting boats and arrived safely in Connecticut the following night (November 23).[6]

In autumn 1781 Tallmadge planned a final raid on Lloyd's Neck where the Loyalists had finally erected a substantial fortification known as Fort Slongo (Salonga). This attack was led by Maj. Lemuel Trescott. Leaving from Shippan Point, the dismounted dragoons, militia, and whaleboatmen landed at four in the morning of October 3 and quickly overran the enemy works. Among the prisoners were two captains, one lieutenant, and eighteen rank and file. The Loyalists also lost their regimental colors, a bronze 3 pounder, and a great quantity of ammunition. There were no American losses save one man with a minor wound.[7]

In October 1781, New Jersey's Adam Hyler, seemingly quiescent for several years, suddenly burst into activity. In the next eleven months he carved for himself a place in naval history as an unparalleled leader of whaleboat warriors. Hyler led a flotilla of whaleboats down the Raritan River to South Amboy. In company with them was a small-armed sloop christened *Revenge* towing behind some additional boats. Hyler's target

was a group of five vessels (two lightly armed) guarded by a British warship and a shore battery. All of the enemy aboard and ashore seemed to
be sleeping, even those on the guardship. In fact, unknown to the raiders,
the merchant vessels at least were riding at anchor with no one on board.
Hyler divided his men. One group would take the three merchant vessels;
one the smaller armed vessel; and his own, with *Revenge*, the larger
armed vessel. The silent attack made resistance futile, and all five vessels
were taken quickly. Cargo, guns, and naval stores were unceremoniously
dumped into *Revenge* and the towed boats as the merchantmen were set
afire. The shore battery finally detected something amiss and the bark of
its cannon (fortunately too far away to be effective) roused the entire anchorage. Finally, the cannon of the guardship spoke, but the *Revenge* was
already making for the sea with its whaleboats tagging along behind on
tow ropes. After the success of this operation Hyler moved on to successfully command a privateer; but he was injured in an accident in early
September 1782 and died of infectious complications shortly thereafter.

   In 1781 and 1782 Capt. Caleb Brewster was particularly active in his
own whaleboat war. In 1781 he captured an armed sloop and its crew on
Long Island Sound; and on December 7, 1782, he took part in a major
encounter with a contingent of Loyalist whaleboats known as the "boats
fight." American shore lookouts spotted several boatloads of Loyalists
proceeding down the sound. Brewster put out from Fairfield with his
men to intercept them. He forced his own whaleboats into the center of
the enemy flotilla. The vicious hand-to-hand conflict that ensued injured
or killed every man involved. Brewster received a rifle ball through the
shoulder. Two Loyalist boats were captured and the rest escaped to Long
Island. The "boats fight" was the bloodiest of all the whaleboat operations during the war. In March 1783, Brewster and his men returned to
the sound to capture the British armed vessel *Fox* by boarding as it lay at
anchor in the sound. This was the last whaleboat operation of the war.

   Partly in response to these activities and others like them, the British
mounted several amphibious raids of their own with the help of the
Royal Navy. In April 1777 the redcoats, commanded by William Tryon,
landed unopposed at Compo Beach near Westport, Connecticut, and
marched inland to raid the towns of Bethel, Ridgefield, and Danbury.
The American supply depot at Danbury was burned with a great loss of
valuable blankets, preserved meat, and flour. While trying to impede the
British return to their ships, Continental Gen. David Wooster was killed,
and Col. Benedict Arnold assumed command of the local troops. The
British retreat was accomplished only with considerable loss of life.

   One historian has called William Tryon "the evil genius of the royal
cause in America" because of his many successes in prosecuting the Loyalist raids on Patriot strongholds. Once the governor of North Carolina,
Tryon was assigned the task of governing New York just in time to face

the beginnings of the insurrection. He proved invaluable as the military leader of the Loyalist resistance in New York and Connecticut. Tryon operated with a force of more than 2,000 Loyalists encamped on Long Island near Flushing, Queens. He also organized a stronghold on the north shore near Glen Cove and from there launched amphibious raids across the sound into Connecticut.[8]

The 1777 raid was followed in July 1779 by a larger affair employing more than eighteen warships and 2,000 Loyalist soldiers. It targeted the towns of East Haven, New Haven, West Haven, Fairfield, and Norwalk. The landing at Calf Pasture Beach in Norwalk was the largest amphibious operation mounted by Loyalist forces during the entire Revolutionary War. Described in British records as a nest of privateers, Norwalk alone housed more than sixty whaleboats. Two new-built privateer brigs were on the ways at the Raymond Brothers shipyards when the Loyalists attacked and burned much of the town. Norwalk, with its protective archipelago of small sandy islands and shallow waters, had served as an American vice admiralty court for small prizes taken on the sound, a fact that has almost escaped historians because all the court records were burned during the 1779 raid along with eighty-eight homes, dozens of barns, and a church.

THE LAKE CHAMPLAIN FLEET

On the morning of September 25, 1780, Maj. Gen. Benedict Arnold climbed aboard the British warship *Vulture* in the Hudson River below West Point. One of America's most fervent Patriots had turned traitor. *Vulture* had been drifting up and down on the tide since the previous night when Maj. John Andre, Adjutant to the British commander in New York, had gone ashore for a secret meeting with the post's commandant. Arnold's plan to turn over West Point to the British had been uncovered. Inasmuch as he ultimately abandoned the Patriot cause in such a dishonorable fashion, Arnold has been justly placed on the trash heap of infamy, but there is little doubt that prior to his treason he was one of America's best tactical commanders. At Ticonderoga, Quebec, Valcour Island, Ridgefield, and Saratoga he proved that he was an able fighter. Rising from provincial colonel, to brigadier, to major general of the Continental Army, Arnold appears at all the important junctures in the record of the Revolutionary War, and at critical moments in battle he intercedes with the proper stratagem to turn the trick on the British. His disaffection was as overwhelming as it was unexpected.

After his treason was discovered, Arnold returned to the war as a British major general of provincial forces, and he continued his successes on the battlefield against his former comrades in New England and Virginia. Ironically, it was Arnold that led the British raid on his home state of

Connecticut in 1781. During the burning of New London a massacre of American troops took place at Fort Griswold some distance up the Thames River very near the present day U.S. Coast Guard Academy. Arnold was not in immediate command of the troops accused of the outrage. Described by one biographer as being simultaneously "the luminescent hero and the serpentine villain," Arnold was nonetheless noted by all the troops that served under him as a "fighting general and a bloody fellow."[9]

It is possible that Arnold's most important roll in the war was as "Admiral" of the American fleet on Lake Champlain in 1776. Having failed to take Quebec in April 1775 and having received a wound, Arnold was briefly posted as military governor of American-held Montreal. Forced to abandon the city in May 1776 because of the arrival in the St. Lawrence River of a British fleet with an army under Gen. Sir Guy Carleton, Arnold retreated to Ticonderoga, New York, during the summer. His strategy was to defend the Lake Champlain-Lake George invasion route from Canada to Central New York.

Throughout the French and Indian Wars, control of this region had been heavily contested by the French and the British (with a heavy reliance on American colonial troops). Although the objective was control of the water passage between Canada and Albany, the struggle had generally been a contest of forts and outposts. The 40-mile radius centered on Lake George may have been the most heavily fortified area in all of North America containing six major forts and outposts. In a fashion typical of his capricious military style and unpredictable character, Arnold chose to make his defense of the region afloat. Once again, like Washington's little flotilla in Massachusetts Bay, Arnold's lake navy would be largely the "Army's Navy."[10]

At nearby Skenesboro (Whitehall, New York), Arnold was able to amass hundreds of shipbuilders, carpenters, and blacksmiths to build or recondition a fleet of seventeen armed vessels, including seven gondolas, five row galleys, three schooners, a cutter, and a sloop. Skenesboro, at the southern end of a long finger-like extension of Lake Champlain, had a water-powered sawmill and a small boat-building facility used to repair lake barges. Skilled carpenters and joiners were lured away from the coastal cities by promises of exorbitant wages to be paid in hard coin, and the British presence in New York during the summer and fall of 1776 also helped to divert some shipbuilding manpower to the lake region. It is remarkable, nonetheless, that Arnold was able to create such a vast "shipbuilding" operation in the heart of the American wilderness.

Moreover, ambiguities in the chain of command in the region plagued the early organization of the lake fleet. In March 1776, Congress promoted Gen. John Thomas to command the Canadian Department of the Army. According to the organizational chart, Arnold as governor of

Montreal was his subordinate. Thomas' appointment brought him into direct conflict with Philip Schuyler, head of the Middle Department in Albany, where both commanders chose to place their headquarters. Orders issued by Thomas were declared invalid by Schuyler because they originated within his department geographically. Schuyler was also at odds over precedence and authority with General Horatio Gates, who disliked Arnold intensely. Nonetheless, Arnold was able to get the supplies, armament, and support he needed at a time when the remainder of the American army was poised to defend New York City.

Several derelict castoffs or provisions vessels were captured from the British during the initial occupation of the lake region by the American militia in 1775. Arnold had them refitted for the lake fleet. These were *Enterprise (12)*, sloop; *Royal Savage (12)*, schooner; *Revenge (8)*, schooner; *Liberty (8)*, schooner; and *Lee (6)*, cutter. He also had built at Skenesboro the gondolas *New Haven (3)*; *Providence (3)*; *Boston (3)*; *Spitfire (3)*; *Philadelphia (3)*; *Connecticut (3)*; *Jersey (3)*; and *New York (3)*; as well as the galleys *Trumbull (8)*; *Congress (8)*; *Washington (8)*; and *Gates (8)*.

The crews of the refitted sailing vessels varied between thirty-five and fifty men, depending on the number needed to handle the sails. All the new-built vessels were flat-bottomed, or nearly so, and could be rowed, sailed, or poled through the shallows. Arnold may have designed some of the vessels himself. The gondolas, in particular, may have been based on the design of the cargo barges with high curved bows and lateen mainsails that regularly plied Lake Champlain in peacetime. Each gondola had a crew of forty-five; and each galley had a crew of eighty. The wood used to construct the fleet was new-cut and unseasoned resulting in a great deal of leaking, but a heavy coat of pitch made most of the new vessels moderately watertight. They were between 50 and 72 feet long and 15 and 20 feet wide. The guns were ranged in size between 18 pounders and 2 pounders. Each gondola had a 12-pound bow gun and a pair of 9s amidships. The larger galleys were generally armed with two 18s, two 12s, two 9s, and four 4s. Each vessel had a set of giant 14-foot sweeps to serve as oars and a mast, or pair of masts, deploying simple sails that could be handled by their generally inexperienced crews.[11]

General Carleton, the overall commander of British forces on Lake Champlain had no shortage of skilled manpower to build boats or man his fleet. He simply tapped the resources of the Royal Navy anchored in the St. Lawrence River. While the strategic control of the fleet on the lake resided with Carleton, the immediate operational commander was Thomas Pringle, a senior captain in the Royal Navy who usually gets too little credit for his part in the operations that were to follow. Ship's carpenters from the fleet first dismantled and then reconstructed several small warships at Fort Saint Jean (St. John's) at the northern outlet of the lake under the supervision of Lt. John Schank of the Royal Navy and Lt. William Twiss of the army engineers. These vessels had been brought from the St. Lawrence River through the rapids of the Richelieu River. When the water grew too shallow they were dragged in pieces overland. The British fleet included two schooners, *Maria (14)* and *Carleton (12)*, a gundalow, *Loyal Consort (7)*, and twenty-eight gunboats each armed with a bow gun. Twenty-eight open longboats filled with troops and a score of canoes filled with Indians were added to the invasion force. As an amazing afterthought, Carleton had an entire ship, HM sloop-of-war *Inflexible (18)*, painstakingly brought over from the St. Lawrence to the lake. Although it delayed the British departure by four weeks, the 80-foot-long *Inflexible* with its 18-12 pounders outclassed every vessel in Arnold's force. Meanwhile construction of a radeau named *Thunderer (12)* was completed. The 91-foot-long *Thunderer* with 6-24 pounders, 6-12 pounders, and 2 howitzers threw enough metal to take on the American fleet by itself. In August 1776 Carleton finally sailed up the lake (south) in search of Arnold's fleet, which he hoped to destroy so that British troops could use the waterway to invade central New York that autumn.

It was not until October that Arnold realized that the British fleet was searching him out in such strength, but he was as optimistic as ever. He carefully placed fifteen of his vessels in a shallow defensive crescent at the north end of an inlet formed by Valcour Island and the shore of the lake. The galley *Gates (8)* was left incomplete at Skenesboro, and the schooner *Liberty (8)* was detached to other duty. The northernmost entrance to the inlet was too shallow and too narrow for navigation. As Carleton passed the island on the morning of October 11 he unknowingly went well beyond Arnold's position. The American *Royal Savage (12)* and the row galleys led by Arnold in *Congress (8)* moved toward the center of the inlet from behind to lure the British into the rebel field of fire and then withdrew to the defensive crescent. Attacked by the Americans from the rear, the British fleet was forced to reverse course and entered the inlet in one's and two's against the wind while under heavy fire. *Thunderer* (Lt. George Scott) and *Maria* (Lt. John Starke), having overshot the island by two miles to the leeward, never managed to claw their way into the first day's battle. The flagship *Inflexible*, commanded by Schank, was able to engage only after several hours. The battle then spread to the rest of the fleet and was characterized by an almost continuous cannonade.

Lt. James. R. Dacres, commanding the schooner *Carleton*, was the first to come within range of the Americans. Dacres anchored with a spring on his cable within range of the Americans and fired again and again doing great damage to the hastily constructed American fleet. A lucky shot from the rebels parted the spring, however, leaving the schooner

Fleet Lists for the Battle of Valcour Island, October 11–13, 1776

American Fleet			British Fleet		
Gen. Benedict Arnold			Gen. Sir Guy Carleton[a]		
Name	Crew	Commander	Name	Crew	Commander
Royal Savage (12)	50	Hawley	Inflexible (18)	120	Shank
Revenge (8)	35	Seamon	Maria (14)	120	Starke
Liberty (8)	35	Premier	Carleton (12)	45	Dacres
Enterprise (12)	50	Dickenson	Thunderer (12)	35	Scott
Lee (6)	45	Davis	Loyal Convert (7)	35	Longcroft
Congress (8)	80	J. Arnold	3 gunboats (1-24)	—	unknown
Trumbull (8)	80	Warner	6 gunboats (1-18)	—	unknown
Washington (8)	80	Thatcher	8 gunboats (1-12)	—	unknown
Gates (8)[b]	80	Chapel	11 gunboats (1-9)	—	unknown
New Haven (3)	45	Mansfield	1 longboat (1-4)	—	unknown
Providence (3)	45	Simmons	3 longboats (1-2)	—	unknown
Boston (3)	45	Summer	24 longboats	—	unknown
Spitfire (3)	45	Ulmer	(none)		
Philadelphia (3)	45	Rue			
Connecticut (3)	45	Grant			
Jersey (3)	45	Grimes			
New York (3)	45	Reed			

Notes:
[a] The naval commander was Capt. Thomas Pringle.
[b] This vessel was not deployed.

swinging on its anchor and open to an unremitting raking fire. Within minutes Dacres was knocked unconscious by a flying piece of woodwork, and all the senior officers were wounded. During this episode a nineteen-year-old midshipman, Edward Pellew, climbed out on the Carleton's bowsprit under rebel fire to kick the jibsail over into the wind so that the vessel could fall away from the American line. Pellew, one of the best known names from the age of fighting sail, went on to become a celebrated frigate captain and admiral (Admiral Lord Exmouth) during the Napoleonic Wars. Momentarily in command, he was able in this instance to save the schooner from destruction. Dacres also lived to hoist his own admiral's pennant.

On its return to the defensive crescent the Royal Savage ground on the tip of the island and was abandoned by the Americans when it became the common target of a number of British gunboats. These mounted a single bow gun and were manned by crews of twenty. Although one of the British gunboats was blown up, they generally stayed about 700 yards from the Americans in order to avoid being sprayed by grape shot. Nonetheless, the Patriots were being knocked to pieces. The gondola *Philadelphia* sank at its mooring. The British set the abandoned rebel schooner afire as night fell to keep it from being retaken, and Indians in the woods and on the island began a promiscuous fire at the Americans who were silhouetted against the glow of the fire. As the flames subsided in the gathering darkness a fortuitous fog settled on the scene of battle, and the firing ceased. Arnold decided to abandon his position by slipping silently through the British fleet in the night.[12]

Guy Carleton was initially startled by the sudden disappearance of the Americans, but Arnold's fleet, damaged beyond repair during the previous day's fighting, had moved a mere eight miles up the lake to Schuyler's Island. Pursued by *Inflexible, Carleton,* and *Maria,* several American vessels grounded themselves on the lakeshore, surrendered, or fought until they were so shattered that they could fight no more. Most of Arnold's fleet was burned or destroyed during the second day of fighting. Five were burned in Ferris Bay (Arnold's Bay, Panton, Vermont) by their own crews. The small group of vessels that escaped up the lake retreated to Fort Ticonderoga after destroying the American post at Crown Point on October 13. Of 700 Americans who began the battle, 80 were killed or wounded, and more than 100 were taken prisoner. A great number were initially listed as missing because their bodies were unceremoniously dropped into the lake during the night. Others lost their way in the woods trying to reach the American lines. British casualties were fewer than forty men including eight dead and eight wounded on *Carleton* from the first day of fighting.

While the Battle at Valcour Island was not a tactical victory for the Americans, it proved to be an immensely important strategic one. General Carleton, faced with an early onset of winter conditions in the northeastern woods and greatly delayed in his invasion timetable, was forced to return to Canada and put off further operations on the lake until the following year. This gave the Americans much-needed breathing space to recover from their loss of New York City and their retreat across New Jersey during 1776. Carleton's remarkable caution in waiting four weeks for the arrival of *Inflexible* may have cost him the campaign. Nonetheless, he was knighted for his victory in the wilderness.

The next time a British army traversed Lake Champlain it was led by Gen. John Burgoyne, who was forced to surrender his army at Saratoga almost exactly one year after the lake battle at Valcour. Naval historian, Alfred Thayer Mahan, has noted, "The little navy on Lake Champlain was wiped out, but never had any force, large or small, lived to better purpose or died more gloriously. That the Americans were strong enough to impose the capitulation of Saratoga was due to the valuable year of delay secured to them by their little navy on Lake Champlain, created by the indomitable energy, and handled with the indomitable courage of the traitor, Benedict Arnold."[13]

THE BOAT DEPARTMENT

As early as 1775 the Quartermaster General (QMG) of the American Army of Observation appropriated £50 per month for the repair of boats as part of his expense accounts. During the New York Campaign of 1776 the Quartermaster's Department also established a policy of engaging privately owned boats whenever possible and of constructing and maintaining government owned vessels only when absolutely necessary. The tonnage of the hired vessels was recorded and the rate of payment (about one shilling per ton per day) was noted, but no other details about these arrangements are extent.

In June 1776, Washington ordered Deputy Quartermaster General (DQMG) Hugh Hughes to build six row galleys for deployment in the Hudson River, and Hughes ordered the appropriate materials from New Jersey. No example of the contracts for these materials or of the plans for the galleys has been found, but it can be assumed that they looked somewhat like those fashioned for the Lake Champlain fleet. Flat-bottomed, 53 feet long, and about 16 feet wide, each galley had one mast for sails and was supplied with 14-foot-long oars known as sweeps. Shipbuilder Benjamin Eyre was engaged to construct the galleys as well as a number of small craft called bateaux. Washington wished to string the bateaux together into a floating bridge by building a causeway over them. He wrote to William Duer to provide six anchors and anchor cables to fix the floating boats in the waters of the Harlem River between Manhattan and the Bronx. Such floating bridges (pontoon bridges today) were commonly used during the war, and steps were taken to build and maintain boats specifically for this purpose.

The difficulty posed by crossing rivers and bays when moving large armies about the American countryside should not be lightly dismissed. The British had been content to establish their colonies on the more easily accessible Atlantic coastal plain seemingly hemmed in by the Appalachian Mountains. The mountains had become a boundary between the settlements and the wilderness interior, but there were several significant water routes through the mountains into the interior. The Hudson River was the only one that was navigable to large ships for any significant distance. The Delaware, the Susquehanna, the Potomac, and others were open to small boats, barges, and, of course, canoes allowing for the generally free movement of trade goods and produce by water. Yet, in the absence of modern bridge building technology, all the major waterways into the interior also impeded movement across the direction of their flow specifically from north to south or vice versa. For this reason the British chose to use their naval supremacy to move their troops from colony to colony by sea.

The Americans were not so fortunate in the control of their own waterways. In December 1776 Washington had undisputed control of the Delaware River only because he had commandeered all the available boats on both sides of the river. This kept the British from advancing on his tattered army in Pennsylvania and allowed him to prosecute the attacks on Trenton and Princeton. The British made a great effort to take control of Delaware Bay in the weeks before they invaded Philadelphia reducing the Patriot positions on Mud Island and attacking Fort Mifflin through the use of naval bombardment. Nonetheless, it is important to realize the significance of the fact that the Americans were able to maintain local control of crossings at places in the interior similar to Dobb's Ferry or West Point on the Hudson. These allowed the Americans to move troops and supplies through the colonies by land to counter similar moves by the British at sea.

In the absence of bridges, there were a large number of public ferries that connected important roads in the colonies. The public ferries were privately owned and many had monopolies at specific crossings over major waterways particularly over the great bays that indented the shoreline of the middle states (New York, Delaware, and Chesapeake). Some ferrymen, exercising their rights, required full rates to be paid for each soldier, wagon, horse, and cannon that was transported even if the trip was made in army vessels. Others, being more patriotic, let the American army cross at half price. Nowhere did the army cross for free. For this reason the Quartermaster's Department maintained a separate fund in its budget for paying ferry rates.

When Nathaniel Greene became QMG in 1778, he immediately took steps to set up an organized effort to supply boats for the Army by establishing an agency known as the Boat Department separate from the shipbuilding projects proposed by Congress. He choose Benjamin Eyre as the department's first Superintendent of Naval Business. Eyre was a professional shipbuilder, but by 1779 he had set up a system of boat building that included a number of maritime craftspersons that were employed by the department. From May 1778 to May 1779 the Boat Department completed four schooners, seventeen Durham boats, and a score of scows, flatboats, bateaux, and rowboats. Yet production was hampered by a lack of boards and planking, which had to be gleaned from the surrounding woodlands. The QMG also established a group of men, kept close at hand, who were used to handling boats to help during crossings. Nathan Beach of Pennsylvania was one of these. He noted that in June 1779 he had entered the Boat Department as a steersman, the boats having been built in Dauphin County specifically for Gen. John Sullivan's expedition against the Iroquois in central New York. Called Continental Boats by Beach, these were made specifically for the purpose of transporting baggage and provisions by water for an army on the march.

The common bateaux was a vessel favored by fur traders and built with pine boards, which were relatively short-lived when compared to oak or cedar and altogether unsuitable to the rough services to which they were exposed during army maneuvers. In spring 1781 there were almost 200 government vessels (mostly bateaux) in storage on the Hudson and Mohawk Rivers. In winter it was customary to lay up small boats in order to preserve them for the next year, and in spring each would be inspected and repaired if needed. Of those inspected in 1781 only eighteen were in good condition, nonetheless it was thought that the rest could be brought up to usable condition with minor repairs. Among these, besides bateaux, were listed barges, scows, skiffs, flat-bottomed boats, whaleboats, gunboats, sloops, pettiaugers, and a single schooner. The variety in the documentation attests to the wide array of vessels used by the Army.

The Boat Department employed 17 shipwrights in the yards at Philadelphia, 65 at Fort Pitt, and a combined total of 125 along the Connecticut and Potomac Rivers. The average worker was paid about $12 a day for a six-day work week, foremen a few dollars more. These wages were equivalent to that paid by commercial shipbuilders but considered exorbitant by some members of Congress. A further number of woodworkers, caulkers, and riggers were kept busy under Nehemiah Hubbard (DQMG) at Middletown on the Connecticut River, under Udny Hay on the Hudson at West Point, and under Morgan Lewis in the Northern Department.[14]

Hubbard constructed sixteen scows in Connecticut in a single month and wrote that his men could build one scow a day for ten days if the local sawmills could provide 30,000 feet of planking in the same time. Lewis repaired sixteen bateaux and built forty more in a fortnight. He authorized the building of 100 more from the stocks of material available in the Northern Department. He expected that this might take between twenty and thirty days. Tar and pitch were also scarce, but it was the lack of the fibrous caulking called oakum and nails, especially small nails, that threatened to impede the production of boats. More than 1,600 pounds of 8-penny nails and 2,200 pounds of 10-penny nails were needed by the Northern Department alone. Hay reported that 193 bateaux had been completed but that the quantities of boards used for this purpose had hampered the concurrent need to construct barracks and supply wagons.

When Timothy Pickering became QMG in 1780, he disbanded the Boat Department as being too expensive, but he assured Washington that sufficient watercraft for the needs of the army could be borrowed from the French fleet, or by impressment around Baltimore or the other ports on the Chesapeake. Pickering also directed that all the small craft in the Delaware Bay be collected. When the French and American armies crossed the Hudson at Haverstraw in August 1781 in order to make an undetected march on Virginia, thirty flatboats were used to ferry 6,000 troops in groups of 40 men each. Pickering noted that 2,000 Americans had been taken across with their artillery and baggage in just twenty hours. According to a sub-lieutenant of the French army, however, the passage of their 4,000 men over the 2-mile-plus water course beginning the next day was long and tedious (sixty hours), but without accident thanks to the skill of the American ferrymen. Similar, but less impressive feats were accomplished when the allied armies crossed the Delaware and several smaller water obstacles in order to invest Yorktown.

Invoking Poseidon

"If I told you that there's heartbreak and shipwreck in store, would you trade away immortality?" Odysseus answered, "Yes . . . I'd gladly endure what the sea deals out."

—Homer's *Odyssey*, Book V

The coasts of England have been insulted by the Yankees!

—a London newspaper, 1778

JOHN PAUL JONES

Born in Scotland in 1747, John Paul Jones is the best known single-ship commander to have served in the Continental Navy. His name is synonymous with American naval heroism. Having broken British maritime law by executing a mutineer without trial while in the merchant service, John Paul quickly vanished from sight and changed his name by tacking on "Jones." There is also evidence that before the Revolution he made his living as a smuggler in North Carolina. When the war began Jones was able to use the patronage of several influential colonial shipowners to receive a commission in the Continental Navy.

Jones was initially made the first lieutenant of the flagship, *Alfred*. Having survived the political storm that surrounded Commodore Hopkins' fiasco in the action against *Glasgow*, Jones was given command of *Providence (12)*. He quickly proceeded on a series of independent

cruises taking sixteen prizes in short order. Although *Providence* mounted
only a dozen 4 pounders and some swivel guns, Jones found the vessel
fast and maneuverable, and he later wrote that its crew was the best he
ever commanded. These initial successes cemented his reputation.[1]

After leaving *Providence* Jones traveled to France in a new command,
the American sloop-of-war, *Ranger (18)*. Armed with 4 pounders, he ravaged the Channel and the Irish Sea. Palpable fear overtook the British
public when Jones attacked the home of Lord Selkirk on the west coast
of Britain, stole his silver plate, and burned several vessels in the nearby
port of Whitehaven. The alarm was sounded all along the coast, and several British cruisers were sent in pursuit of Jones, "the Yankee pirate."
One of these was the *Drake (22)*, a sloop-of-war built in an American
shipyard in Philadelphia before the war.[2]

Ranger and *Drake* encountered one another an hour before sunset on
April 24, 1778, in the Belfast Lough near Waterford. Jones, with his yards
set back, waited for the *Drake (22)* to approach. *Ranger* showed no
colors—a privilege of naval protocol justified so long as the flag was
shown before first fire. The British vessel sent a junior officer in a boat to
check *Ranger*'s papers. He was immediately taken as a prisoner of war.
Lt. George Burdon, commanding *Drake*, raised the red British naval ensign and was approaching *Ranger*'s stern when Jones broke out the American colors, yawed, and opened a broadside. Although his officer had been
captured, Burdon was seemingly caught unawares by the opening salvo,
and he allowed Jones to suddenly cross his bows raking him from stem to
stern. Wanting a prize, Jones stood off, blasting *Drake*'s rigging with chain
and bar shot to dismast it and peppering the deck with grape to keep the
Jack-tars from making repairs. "The English ship was badly maneuvered,
fired its broadsides all at once, which occasioned it to heel very much
from its antagonist, and by which means it received many of the American
shot between wind and water, which occasioned it to leak badly; and in
some measure...shortened the action."[3]

Burdon was mortally wounded in the first minutes of the battle.
Drake's first lieutenant and forty-two of the crew were also killed or
wounded, which may help to explain the awkward progress of the British
in the action. Within an hour their vessel became unmanageable, and the
remaining crew wisely surrendered. A great propaganda triumph, *Drake*
was the first Royal Navy warship taken by an American in British waters.
The victory was all the more important because the two opponents were
so equally matched, the *Drake* having "guns of the same caliber as those
aboard the *Ranger*." Jones lost only three killed and five wounded, and
he sent his first officer, Lt. Thomas Simpson, to take over the prize,
which was sold in France.[4]

Jones disliked Simpson, a political appointee, and found fault with his
handling of the *Drake* on the return cruise to France. In fact, Jones placed

Simpson under arrest for insubordination. Jones also found himself at odds with a large segment of his own crew over the distribution of prize money, bad treatment, and his charges against Simpson (who was generally well-liked). Seventy-seven sailors and twenty-eight warrant and petty officers complained to the American commissioners in Paris that Jones was arbitrary, bad tempered, and insufferable. Supported only by Benjamin Franklin, who promised him command of a new powerful frigate building in Holland, Jones dropped his charges against Simpson, who sailed away in command of *Ranger* while Jones awaited his new command.[5]

The frigate promised by Franklin never materialized, but late in 1778 a ship was found that could serve Jones' purpose. The *Duc de Duras* was a tired East Indiaman of 900 tons built in 1766. Like others of this armed merchant type, the ship was sturdy, but ponderous and slow. It was armed with 6-9 pounders on its upper deck, 28-12 pounders on its main gun-deck, and 6 ancient 18-pound garrison guns mounted so close to the waterline that they could not be run out in any weather other than a flat calm. Jones handpicked his officers and personally approved the 380 men that served aboard, many of whom were British deserters or former prisoners of war (Americans looking for a berth after exchange). Before sailing Jones renamed the ship *Bonhomme Richard*.

Serving as the commodore of a small squadron including *Bonhomme Richard (40)*, the corvette *Pallas (26)*, the brig *Vengeance (12)*, the small cutter *Cerf [Stag] (18)*, and the American-built frigate *Alliance (36)*, Jones sailed into the Atlantic from France. The agreement among Commodore Jones, captain of the *Bonhomme Richard*; Pierre Landais, captain of the *Alliance*; Denis Nicolas Cottineau, captain of the *Pallas*; Joseph Varage, captain of the *Cerf*; and Philippe Nicolas Ricot, captain of the *Vengeance* was based on American Maritime Law, but it was agreed that any disputes among the captains would be regulated by the minister of the French Marine and Benjamin Franklin acting jointly. This was because all the captains save Jones were French. Captain Landais was also an honorary citizen of Massachusetts. Each of Jones' companion vessels, excepting *Alliance*, was outfitted and maintained by France, and all sailed under American commissions issued by Benjamin Franklin.

On September 23, 1779, Jones sighted a large number of sail off Flamborough Head, England. These were forty-one supply ships under the protection of the frigate HMS *Serapis (50)* and HM sloop-of-war *Countess of Scarborough (22)*. *Serapis* was a fast, new frigate rated at 44 guns, but Capt. Richard Pearson had added to the British frigate's armament (20-18s, 20-9s, and 10-6s) bringing the gun count to 50. As the wind was light it took more than three hours for Jones' squadron to make its approach to the supply fleet. *Pallas* made for the *Countess of Scarborough*, engaged, and quickly made it a prize. *Vengeance* and *Cerf* inexplicably took no part in the action, and *Alliance*, though initially making to engage

The battle between *Bonhomme Richard* and HMS *Serapis* was one of the classic single-ship engagements of the age of fighting sail. Both vessels were battered wrecks by the end of the battle, and the casualties were among the highest experienced in any such action during the war.

Serapis, sheered off at the last moment. With darkness falling *Bonhomme Richard* and *Serapis* maneuvered for advantage.

With its first fire two of the ancient 18 pounders on *Bonhomme Richard* blew up, killing most of the lower gundeck crews and blowing a hole in the main gun-deck above. Fortunately Richard Dale, Jones' first lieutenant in charge of the main battery was unharmed. Lt. Edmund Stack was in the main top with a file of French Marine sharpshooters, and Midshipmen Nathaniel Fanning and Robert Coram were similarly placed in the fore and mizzen tops, respectively, with armed members of the crew. The two vessels entangled, and with his guns unable to bear, Jones attempted to board *Serapis*. He was driven back. At this point in the action, Pearson, feeling that he had demonstrated his superior firepower and tactics, called out to Jones, "Has your ship struck?" From the deck of the *Bonhomme Richard* came the reply, "I have not yet begun to fight!"[6]

Bonhomme Richard backed off, and the two antagonists were again broadside to broadside. Now the pounding match began, ball for ball and broadside for broadside. The ships again became entangled, and grapples were thrown and made fast. Sharpshooters in the American fighting tops began clearing the British deck. Suddenly *Alliance* came out of the growing darkness, and the Americans gave a cheer supposing that

Captain Landais would put his vessel along *Serapis'* unengaged side. To their horror, Landais swung the other way and let go a broadside into *Bonhomme Richard.* He then put about and put another into its bow. Jones was astonished at the actions of his subordinate who many have mistaken him for the enemy in the dark.

With the *Bonhomme Richard* sinking under him, Jones was once again asked to surrender. "No, sir, I haven't as yet thought of it, but I'm determined to make you strike." At about this time, seaman William Hamilton, who had been fighting in the tops, inched his way out onto a yard arm with a basket of grenades determined to drop one into the open hatches of *Serapis.* After several tries, a grenade fell through, exploding among a pile of loose cartridges on the British gundeck. A terrible roar followed the exploding ammunition as the flames passed from pile to pile among the gun emplacements. About twenty men were killed and many more were terribly burned. During the action the British also had attempted to blow up their opponent transferring "upwards of one hundred and eighteen pound cartridges" onto the shattered lower gundeck of the American through their own unused gunports, but they had failed to strike with dispatch.[7] When a final British attempt to board Jones' ship failed, Pearson struck his own colors. Anxious that *Alliance* might return, Pearson later wrote that further battle seemed "in vain and in short impracticable from [a] situation... with the least prospect of success."[8]

One of the most bitter and famous ship-to-ship actions in naval history was over. It had lasted for close to four hours. Jones lost 150 killed and wounded; Pearson had 120 casualties. A survivor noted the shocking sight, "the mangled carcasses of the dead aboard our ship; especially between decks, where the bloody scene was enough to appall the stoutest heart. To see the dead lying in heaps—to hear the groans of the wounded and dying—the entrails of the dead scattered promiscuously around, the blood over one's shoes."[9]

Although *Countess of Scarborough* was made a prize by *Pallas,* not one of the Baltic supply fleet had been taken. This failure was remarkable as *Vengeance* and *Cerf* had remained totally unengaged. The *Bonhomme Richard* was a total loss. No amount of effort could save it. When Jones transferred his command to *Serapis,* he found his prize a leaking wreck also. Only with the efforts of both surviving crews did the ship make harbor in the Texel, Holland.

Captain Pearson later faced a court martial before the British Admiralty for losing two warships in a single action, but the safety of the convoy and the number of enemies ranged against *Serapis* saved him from reprimand. He was later knighted, causing Jones to remark, "Let me fight him again... and I'll make him a lord!" Jones was immediately raised to the status of a legend in America. His victories stood in sharp contrast to the failures of the rest of the Continental Navy.[10]

NATHANIEL FANNING

The longest and most detailed eyewitness account of the *Bonhomme Richard-Serapis* fight was written by Nathaniel Fanning. The American midshipman was in charge of one of the tops during the fight. In his account Fanning also described the life of an American sea officer and privateer serving in France. Although he was Jones' personal secretary aboard *Bonhomme Richard*, his anecdotes concerning Jones' personality were very unflattering and uncomplimentary. Fanning credited the commodore with only two positive qualities—personal courage and good seamanship.

Born in Stonington, Connecticut, Nathaniel Fanning and his eldest brother Edmund (a Continental Navy lieutenant and journalist in his own right) witnessed the bombard of their town by HMS *Rose* in 1775. Immediately thereafter the twenty-year-old Nathaniel asked for and received permission from his father, Gilbert to cruise upon privateers against the British. The Fannings should rank high in the hierarchy of American naval families. As far as can be determined, all eight of Gilbert Fanning's sons served at sea during the Revolution.

Nathaniel's third cruise on the privateer *Angelica (18)* in May 1778 was his début as a sea officer. Because of his experience, Capt. William Denison appointed him prizemaster. While not a commissioned officer, in this capacity Fanning could take command of a captured vessel and sail or fight it into a friendly port with a small prize crew. While on *Angelica*, however, he was taken captive by the frigate *Andromeda (28)*, which was carrying Gen. William Howe who had been called home to England. Although the American officers were given the freedom of the deck, Fanning and the crewmen were cruelly confined in the hold. Nonetheless, the prisoners managed to break through the floorboards of their cell and steal both food and wine throughout the trip from Howe's own private pantry, which was nearby, without detection.

Arriving in England in June 1778, the crew of *Angelica* was deposited along with other captive American sailors at Forton Prison. Fanning wrote of his confinement, "I lived truly very miserably, not having any more provisions and small beer during the twenty-four hours than would serve for one meal. . . . This however our good friends, the English, even thought too much for rebels." Yet conditions at Forton were superior to those experienced by other Americans held aboard prison hulks in New York where scores of men died daily from disease, privation, and exposure.[11]

The little bit of money that Fanning had with him allowed him to purchase information and some small comforts, and those sympathetic to the prisoners' plight among the English population took up subscriptions for them that amounted to several hundred pounds. These funds were distributed by Reverend Thomas Wren, a Unitarian minister of whom Fanning wrote with great respect. The prisoners set up and staffed a school among themselves where "reading, writing, arithmetic, and navigation" were taught. Fanning took lessons in French from the officers of that country who were held captive with him. Notwithstanding these small privileges, the prison was surrounded by high walls that were guarded by armed men and fierce dogs; and a bounty of £5 was offered for any person capturing an escaped prisoner, dead or alive. Fanning quickly gave up any idea of escape and smuggled out a letter to David Hartley, a noted humanitarian and pro-American parliamentarian, in an effort to affect his exchange. After little more than a year of confinement, Fanning and 119 other sailors were exchanged as part of one of Franklin's prisoner cartels.[12]

Arriving in Nantes in June 1781 penniless and ragged, Fanning was surprised to receive a small purse of gold coins ostensibly from the citizens of France to help tide him over until he could find employment. The money actually came from the coffers of the French king. After a short period of rehabilitation in France, Fanning was offered a place as a midshipman and commodore's secretary under John Paul Jones aboard *Bonhomme Richard*. Although he worked closely with the commodore preparing the ship for departure, Fanning found Jones difficult, with a personality that blew hot and cold. Jones was, according to Fanning, five feet, five inches tall with sandy reddish hair, and he exhibited a quick and nervous temperament. He treated his officers "with a good deal of respect in some particulars, and in others with a degree of severity." The two men seem to have had a falling out over some accidental damage done to a piece of navigational equipment during which incident Fanning felt himself poorly used by the commodore. Nonetheless, Jones' dynamic and self-assured character as a commander of other men remained evident even to Fanning's critical eye.[13]

The *Bonhomme Richard* sailed from L'Orient on August 14, 1779. During the *Serapis* fight in September, Fanning was in the fighting tops. In the first hour of fighting most of the men in his charge were killed or badly wounded; but Fanning descended to the deck and took a fresh party aloft. With these men he cleared the *Serapis'* tops of defenders and crossed with a small party from yardarm to yardarm until they were directly above the deck of the British ship. From here his men launched grenades and other missiles upon the British crew below. One of these grenades proved the deciding factor in ending the conflict.

After returning to France, Jones credited Fanning's leadership as being a prominent factor in obtaining the victory over *Serapis*, and the commodore recommended Fanning's promotion to lieutenant. Nonetheless, Fanning found Jones so insufferable that he politely refused any new place among his officers, opting instead for a chance to command his own privateer. Yet more than dissatisfaction and disenchantment influenced Fanning to remain in France as a privateer.

The enemy had shifted its land war to the American South since the alliance. Savannah and Charleston had fallen. Gen. Benjamin Lincoln had surrendered an army of 5,000 Patriots, and Gen. Horatio Gates had been badly beaten at Camden, South Carolina. A few months of active campaigning below the Mason-Dixon Line had regained for British arms all the prestige lost at Saratoga by General Burgoyne. It seemed more important now than ever that the Royal Navy's attention be diverted from the western Atlantic. American strategy, formulated largely by Franklin, dictated that British shipping in European waters be imperiled in order to fan the fire of public resentment against the further prosecution of the war. The pressing need for bolder action against British merchant shipping in the Channel and Irish Sea led to an increased deployment of privateers—one of which was now offered to Fanning.

Because he was not a French citizen, Fanning was urged to take a position as second-in-command of the French privateer *Count de Guichen*, a sturdy lugger armed with 14-3 pounders. The nominal commander was Capt. Pierre Anthon, but it was understood that Fanning was to make the operational decisions. Although Anthon and Fanning seem to have gotten along quite well, Fanning applied for French citizenship so that he might in future take full command of the vessel. The officers and crew of French privateers received no wages, but were commonly advanced sums of money that were deducted from any prize shares. The captain received the equivalent in French gold and silver coins of £45, the second-in-command £35, and the lieutenants £25; the gunners, boatswains, carpenters, and sailing masters, £15 each; the able seamen £10, the marines £5, and ordinary seamen £5 each. If no prizes were taken the crew kept these sums in payment for their trouble. Otherwise they would share in the prize money as they would have in an American vessel.[14]

On March 23, 1781, *Count de Guichen* sailed from Morlaix, a fine anchorage straddling the Channel northeast of Brest. In a single morning, Fanning boarded and ransomed four small British merchantmen. The captains of these vessels were forced to sign notes valued at £300 apiece and to hand over a hostage to insure that the notes would be honored when presented to British banking concerns in Europe. If the captains refused, their vessels would be sunk. This procedure was not uncommon when the value of a vessel and its cargo was not worth the risk of sending it into port under a prize crew. Nonetheless, Franklin disliked the practice of ransoming vessels because he was looking to amass British prisoners in France that might be exchanged for American sailors held in England.

On the following day Fanning encountered a British privateer fitted out as a light frigate. Although the frigate was of greater size and weight of metal, its captain initially avoided battle with the *Count de Guichen*. The ever-aggressive Fanning, whose lugger was the faster of the two combatants, quickly closed the distance. Still out of range the frigate yawed and fired a ragged broadside in Fanning's direction, and then made sail downwind. Twice more the British captain tried this tactic, but the balls splashed harmlessly far short of the lugger and the grape shot passed noisily high overhead. Fanning ultimately came within range and, running the lugger under the stern counter of his prey, he raked the frigate from stern to stem. He then passed across the enemy's bow and raked it in reverse. As Fanning's men were preparing to board, cutlasses and pistols in hand, the British captain suddenly surrendered. The vessel was valued at £40,000 when libeled and sold at auction in France. Fanning received half the captain's normal share because of his arrangement with Anthon.

In April 1781, Fanning and Anthon again made sail into the Channel. Their success was immediate and remarkable. In just a few days more than £50,000 in ransom notes had been accumulated. Unfortunately, Fanning's good luck suddenly ended. The *Count de Guichen* was run down by the British frigate *Aurora (28)*, and both Fanning and Anthon were made prisoners. Remarkably, Anthon was able to retain possession of the original ransom notes (which he stuffed into his pockets) by offering his captors fake notes that he and Fanning had prepared for just such an occasion. When the two officers were exchanged six weeks later, the real notes were presented for collection at Morlaix.

Fanning, now flush with cash, determined to travel home to Stonington, Connecticut, aboard a French merchant vessel by way of the West Indies. Unfortunately, the ship on which he was traveling was wrecked in a storm west of the Isle of Bass just off the French coast. Fanning lost all of his possessions including a cachet of gold coins that represented more than a year's worth of prize money. Forced ashore in France for a second time without a penny to his name, he signed on again with Anthon aboard the privateering cutter *Eclipse (18)*. Armed with 6 pounders and rigged fore and aft, the English-built *Eclipse* proved that it could outrun any vessel it could not outfight, and its command would prove the making of Fanning's reputation.

Sailing in December 1781 from Dunkirk, the cutter alternated between chasing merchantmen and running from British frigates. In January *Eclipse* took a rich merchantman loaded with textiles destined for St. Kitts in the West Indies. A prize crew successfully brought the vessel into Brest. This capture was followed by nine days of fierce storms in the Channel. Fanning was sure that *Eclipse* would founder, but the desperate exertions of the crew brought the battered cutter into Dunkirk in one piece. Nonetheless, with all the damage sustained at sea, the vessel was laid up for several months of refitting.

During this period the French owners of *Eclipse* offered its sole command to Fanning, who immediately accepted and moved among the polyglot unemployed sailors ashore in France to recruit a new crew. Fanning was far more aggressive than Anthon, whose cautious instincts led him to attack only when a positive outcome was assured. Fanning was always willing to fight for a prize. With this in mind he recruited almost three dozen "naked men" to serve as boarders. "The[se] were Maltese, Genoese, Turks, and Algerians. They were large, stout, brawny, well made men, and delighted in boarding an enemy. Upon these occasions they striped themselves naked, excepting a thin pair of draws, and used no weapons but a long knife or dirk, which were secured in their girdles around their waists."[15]

During this period of inactivity engendered by the refit, Fanning also proposed to sail in a cross-Channel packet to Dover, disembark in England, and collect in person some of the ransom notes written on banks in London. This was remarkably audacious. Arming himself with a purse containing counterfeit coins, Fanning sewed the ransoms into his cloths. This was fortunate as he was robbed of his purse by highwaymen on the way from Dover to London by coach. For three weeks he moved about London undetected as an enemy officer. His business completed, he returned to France and to *Eclipse* without further incident.

Franklin then requested that Fanning return again to England as a special, secret courier with peace proposals from the American commissioners to sympathetic members of Parliament. He was to deliver the messages to Lord Shelburne and Lord Stormont. These men, while not friends of the Revolution, were influential at court and political opponents of Lord North. Stormont, in particular, was in charge of all allied prisoners held in Britain and had been in formal contact with Franklin in that regard for some time. The messages delivered, Fanning was required by their lordships to wait in London for a reply. He spent the intervening period visiting the local coffeehouses and taverns, attending Drury Lane Theater and the Haymarket Opera, and visiting the Tower of London and a waxworks museum. Within four weeks he had returned to France with a cachet of sealed diplomatic letters for the American commissioners.

Meanwhile, the refit of *Eclipse* was finally nearing completion. Fanning, with the possibility of future deception in mind, had it painted exactly like a Royal Navy cutter, and he ordered dark blue uniforms lined in white and cut in the British fashion for his deck officers.[16] The uniforms of French naval officers resembled the dark blue coats and coatees of some of their Army regiments, and dark blue breeches and black boots were worn at almost all levels of command at sea. The French uniform coats were lined in red unlike those of the British, which were lined in white. The Continental Congress initially ordered that the waistcoats, breeches, and linings of American naval uniforms be done in red also. These were all changed to white mostly through the badgering of the Naval Committee by John Paul Jones. Officers of all three navies wore white small clothes, stockings, and breeches, with black buckled shoes with their blue dress uniform coats. Common sailors in this period had no recognized uniform dress. They wore a wide variety of clothing similar to that of working mariners in the fishing and shipping trades.[17]

In June 1782 Fanning left Dunkirk for a cruise in the North Sea with 110 men aboard and provisions enough to circumnavigate the British Isles. Disguising the *Eclipse* as HM cutter *Surprise* in order to further frustrate detection by the Royal Navy, Fanning took on the personal pseudonym of Capt. John Dyon, identifying himself as such when he dropped anchor at the Orkney Islands. However, he found himself blockaded in the harbor by two armed British ships. If he attempted to leave in daylight, his identity would certainly be challenged. The bold commander, therefore, abandoned his disguise and sent two officers and a dozen seamen ashore with a brazen demand on the town for a ransom note of £50,000. He would bombard the town if they refused in order "in some measure [to] retaliate for the depredations of some of the commanders of the British ships of war upon the coasts of the United States." The outraged townspeople drove the shore party back to the water's edge where they were lucky to get a boat back to *Eclipse*. Several cannon from the *Eclipse* "loaded with grape, round, and canister shot" were discharged in the direction of the crowd. That evening, with the help of a local pilot who was bribed with £5, Fanning carefully negotiated the dangerous shoals at the harbor entrance and made a "miraculous" escape in the dark from the two ships on watch outside.[18]

Continuing his cruise, Fanning sent in a number of small prizes and forced other captains to sign ransoms. Four English sloops were taken in a single evening's work. Three were sunk and the fourth was sent into France with all the prisoners aboard. This was greatly appreciated by Franklin; nonetheless, Fanning as a commander of a French vessel was entitled to a crown per head from the French government for each live prisoner he sent in. Off the northern coast of Ireland, *Eclipse* fell in with two British frigates. While maneuvering to run away, Fanning caused the cutter to spring its mainmast, but even with shortened sail he was able to keep to windward. Fanning then did the unexpected by reversing course, flying down before the wind, and splitting his two pursuers. As he passed between the frigates each fired a broadside that caused a good deal of damage on deck but allowed *Eclipse* to run freely into the open sea. The frigates soon gave up the chase. While several of his men had been wounded during this episode, none had been killed or were likely to die.

Thereafter, Fanning was rewarded by the capture of *Lovely Lass (24)*, an armed British merchantman. Fanning quickly maneuvered his cutter under the privateer's stern, fired a broadside, and boarded with an overwhelming force. The butcher's list attests to the violence of the hand-to-hand combat. Of the boarders two were killed and seven wounded, while the British vessel lost ten killed and eleven wounded including two boys. The *Lovely Lass* was of 560 tons burden and carried a valuable cargo of typical West Indian produce, sugar, and rum. Fanning then put into L'Orient for a quick repair to his mainmast.

In August, *Eclipse* was again cruising in a large triangular area formed by the Lizard at the southern tip of Cornwall, the Isle of Wight, and the Cherbourg Peninsula near Normandy. These were dangerous waters for the cutter, but Fanning took two prizes within site of twenty-eight British men-of-war anchored in Torbay on August 10. Making good his escape Fanning captured an English sloop into which he placed 195 British prisoners after taking their written oaths that each would have an American held in England exchanged for them.

The next morning, August 11, Fanning found himself chased by three British warships. The closest of these, HMS *Jupiter (50)*, ran down on *Eclipse* and demanded that the cutter identify itself. Fanning responded that he was Capt. John Dyon of HM cutter *Surprise*. The commanding officer of *Jupiter*, momentarily unsure because *Eclipse* had the look of a King's cutter, put a boat in the water with a boarding party to check its papers. Fanning waited patiently while the boat pulled in his direction. When it was almost abreast of the cutter and masking *Jupiter*'s broadside somewhat, Fanning quickly made sail in an attempt to outrun the heavier warship.

A long pursuit ensued. Hour after hour the two vessels sped across the Channel with nothing to indicate a change in the interval between them. To his dismay Fanning found that *Eclipse* was running directly into the path of an entire British fleet sailing before him toward France. *Eclipse* was caught between a hammer and an anvil with nowhere to run. In a gesture of total insolence, Fanning broke out a set of British colors and set his course for the space between two lumbering 74s. As he approached to within hailing distance, he was challenged by one of the three-deckers, and he answered that he was John Dyon in the British cutter, *Surprise*. Throughout its approach the *Eclipse* held its course, maintained its set of sail, and passed right through the center of the British line to leeward. Only after he was through did one of the three-deckers attempt a ranging shot.

The *Jupiter*, however, had maintained the chase and, by cranking on additional sail, was closing rapidly as night began to fall. The British captain, having failed to trap Fanning among the fleet, fired his bow chasers several times trying to hole the cutter or take down a mast or piece of rigging. Thirteen men aboard *Eclipse* were wounded by this fire during the night including Fanning who received a "wound in the leg, and another in the forehead, by a splinter" that knocked him down to the deck and stunned him for several minutes. At dawn a favorable shift in the wind left the *Jupiter* to leeward, and its commander reluctantly reversed course toward the British fleet. *Eclipse* had escaped, and later that morning was rewarded with a fine British collier, which was brought into France as a prize loaded with coal, and a small sloop in ballast, which was sent to England with ninety-four prisoners after they had given their certificates.

Finally, *Eclipse* overtook a 600-ton troop transport, *Lord Howe (24)*, which besides a crew of 87 had aboard 110 infantrymen belonging to an English regiment. Although outnumbered almost three to one, Fanning laid the cutter alongside and loosed his boarders upon its decks. He reported, "The fact was, that in this instance, as well as in several others of a similar kind, the courage of the Englishmen failed them at the moment they saw a crowd of naked men leaping on board them, or suspended in the air, ready to drop down upon their heads." A fierce hand-to-hand battle ensued in which 46 percent of all those involved were killed or wounded. The British lost two officers and twenty-one soldiers killed among the land forces; two petty officers, seventeen seamen, and three boys killed among the crew; and thirty-eight officers, seamen, and soldiers wounded. *Eclipse* had three petty officers, ten seamen, five marines, and two boys killed; and twenty-two others of all ranks wounded. The capture of *Lord Howe* proved to be Fanning's last major operation of the war.[19]

The stories surrounding *Eclipse* and Fanning preceded them into L'Orient, where he briefly basked in popular adulation. He had taken fifty-two enemy vessels and hundreds of prisoners, had ransomed scores more, and had proven his ability as a privateering captain within sight of the enemy's coast. The Royal Navy was particularly incensed by the way "Captain John Dyon" had twisted its tail. Yet in September 1783 the peace was signed in Paris, and Fanning's career as a privateer and swashbuckling leader of men came to a sudden end. He wrote, "In consequence of the news of peace, an embargo was immediately laid upon all privateers." Fanning had earned more than £12,000 since his escape from shipwreck, and he was received in his hometown of Stonington as a great naval hero after the war.

In 1804 during the war with the Algerian pirates, Fanning returned to the naval service as a commissioned officer in the United States Navy (lieutenant). He was given command of *Gunboat Number 1* in Charleston Harbor where he was stricken with yellow fever and died shortly thereafter—a sad ending for such an audacious fellow.

13

The French Alliance

France, like a vulture, is hovering over the British Empire, hungrily watching the prey that she is openly waiting the right moment to pounce upon.
—William Pitt, Earl of Chatham, speaking to Parliament in 1775[1]

THE ALLIANCE

The colonists had been successful in importing their own stock of gunpowder and arms before the outbreak of hostilities; but all of this and most of the domestic stockpiles were used in the initial encounters of the war, especially during the victory at Boston, which used all the gunpowder imported into Massachusetts up to that time. Thereafter without a considerable navy of its own it was inconceivable that the Americans could overcome Britain without the help at sea of some established foreign power. From a practical point of view the likely candidates for such an alliance were limited to Holland, Spain, and France. All of these had been repeated foes of the British in the previous century. Nonetheless, from the very beginning of the war France was the prime target of American diplomacy.

The victory of the Patriots at Saratoga, New York, in late 1777 has traditionally been cited as the impetus needed to establish an alliance with France in 1778. However, the French Council of State had faced the

necessity of entering the war on the side of the Americans from the opening of hostilities in Boston. Through overt and clandestine efforts, Charles
Gravier Vergennes, French Minister of State, planned to weaken Britain
economically through the loss of its colonies and to reestablish the
balance of power in Europe that had been lost in the Seven Years War.
Initially, he had hoped to sustain the American war effort solely with
military supplies and money. In 1776 he secretly arranged for the rebels
to receive aid through the services of Hortalez, Rodriquez, and Company,
a front for the French government managed by the playwright
Beaumarchais.[2]

Fearing that a compromise Anglo-American peace was in the offing in
late 1777 and mistrusting the assertions of the American commissioners
in Paris to the contrary, Vergennes sought a sufficient reason to actively
enter the war in 1778. In February 1778 Capt. John Paul Jones commanding *Ranger* entered Quiberon Bay on the coast of France with word
of the successful conclusion of the battle of Saratoga the previous fall. As
Ranger sailed into the roadstead at sunset, the French warships anchored
there let go with a salute of nine guns officially recognizing a ship of the
American Republic. Upon hearing of the salute, Britain protested to
France, sending a sternly worded ultimatum that the French ministers
rejected at their first opportunity. Only in this manner can the victory of
the Americans over the British at Saratoga be said to have actually
insured the active participation of the French.

During the first half of 1778, before France officially entered the war,
well over 150 French merchant vessels were seized by the British for carrying contraband to America. Records kept in the French archives list 134
merchant vessels taken at sea and 21 others seized in British ports, particularly in the Caribbean. French shippers complained about the losses, but
the British claimed that each vessel was in violation of neutrality for carrying contraband as recognized under international maritime law.

A private company—the largest trading firm in France, Basmarein and
Raimbaux—had increased its investment in the American cause in terms
of general merchandise sent to the Patriots for the purposes of trading in
tobacco and grain. The profit potential of these exchanges attracted
investors in Basmarein and Raimbaux from all over the kingdom.
Unfortunately, almost half the seizures by the Royal Navy belonged to
Basmarein and Raimbaux. Moreover, other French companies were also
affected by the British depredations. The largest of these secondary companies was Sabatier Fils and Despres, merchants from Nantes, who
traded heavily in textiles with the Americans. The merchant community
of France, especially those men with strong ties to the throne, were anxious lest their American ventures go amiss and force them to forgo an opportunity for a great deal of profit, and they demanded the protection of
the Royal Marine for their vessels.[3]

However, the simple seizure of merchant shipping that was, in fact, carrying weapons and gunpowder to the rebels, was not considered a grave enough matter to convince the French people that they should enter the war. Although the Anglo-Americans had been partners with the French in smuggling molasses from the West Indies, they had also been archenemies of French interests in Canada, the Great Lakes, and the trans-Appalachian West for more than a century. Americans had been consistently and vocally anti-Catholic and anti-French, and convincing the French population to go to war on their behalf was going to be difficult.

In April 1778, the French government responded to the pleas of its shippers by creating convoys of French merchant shipping to America. The Royal Marine escorted these convoys forty leagues (about 80 miles) out from the coast of France and met them forty leagues before they entered the Leeward Islands of the Caribbean. In anticipation of an alliance, France also dispatched a war fleet under Admiral D'Estaing from the Mediterranean to America, and when the frigate *Belle-Poule* was fired upon by the British in June 1778, Vergennes seized upon the incident to declare a war on Britain that he had previously positioned his country to fight. The unwarranted attack on *Belle-Poule*, and the anti-British reaction of the French population to it, had served Vergennes' political purposes well.[4]

The Minister of State's immediate problem thereafter was to design a war strategy that would assist the Patriots, preserve French possessions in the Western Hemisphere, and possibly strip off a few rich British outposts in the Indian Ocean as well. Nonetheless, his principal objective was to restore the balance of economic and political power lost to Britain in the previous war. He attempted to attract Spain into the alliance because it could be of great potential help to France at sea. Vergennes claimed that French ships alone could "dominate the English Channel [and] force Britain to choose between peace and general bankruptcy." Although Spain was a secondary naval power, it had enough warships to function as a distraction in the Caribbean, the South Atlantic, and the Mediterranean particularly at the islands of Gibraltar and Minorca. With the British Royal Navy thus overextended, the French ships-of-the-line could crush the scattered British squadrons in detail—something they never before had been able to do.[5]

A PURELY MARITIME WAR

Naval historian Alfred Thayer Mahan has said of the war in 1778 between Great Britain and the House of Bourbon (France and Spain) that "it stands by itself in one respect [as] a purely maritime war." Notwithstanding the several thousand French and Spanish infantrymen sent to North America, there was between the European powers an approximate equality on the high seas that had not been achieved since the seventeenth century and would not be seen again even into modern times. With the exception of the Spanish effort to retake Gibraltar, not only did the allied Bourbon kingdoms carefully refrain from land battles on the European Continent, but they actively sought out major naval encounters in the Atlantic, the Caribbean, and the Indian Ocean.[6]

This aggressiveness at sea was uncharacteristic of the French Royal Marine in particular, and it may have signified the French perception of weakness on the part of the British Royal Navy. In the years after the Seven Years War, the British ruling classes became indifferent to the needs of the Royal Navy. Having won an empire and having humiliated their traditional enemies, they seemed to have misunderstood the perils that continued to exist. The failure to maintain the Royal Navy in fighting trim was to have devastating consequences. Many of the British vessels that fought in the Seven Years War were to enter the American Revolution as over-aged derelicts.

By contrast the French continued building warships with greater resolve during the interwar years. These vessels were among the swiftest warships in the world. Moreover, Spain had built or refitted most of its ships-of-the-line in the same period. The British viewed this build-up with a certain amount of disquietude while squandering the advantage they had gained in the Seven Years War. Much of the Royal Navy had been systematically sold off by 1775, and its lackluster building program suffered from a severe shortage of seasoned timber made worse by the loss of the great stands of oak and pine in North America and by the neutral stance taken by the Baltic nations and Russia. Nonetheless, by 1778 the British and Bourbon naval forces were essentially equal.[7]

French entrance into the war transformed it from a ground engagement in the mid-Atlantic states to a multi-ocean naval war. The French alliance, and that of Spain and finally Holland, forced the British to "severely modify [their] strategy for suppressing the American rebellion."[8] Initially, the British planned to destroy the Patriot army by crushing the rebellion in its urban centers, such as in New York in 1776 or in Philadelphia in 1777; but this strategy failed mainly because the rebel armies were able to melt into the unrestricted colonial hinterland. The plan to split off New England from the other colonies by attacking along the Lake Champlain–Lake George channel from Canada had been tried twice in this war and several times in the previous century with equal lack of success. Alternately, the British planned to wear down American resistance by detaching mobile forces from its urban bases, particularly New York and Charleston, to run down the scattered bands of Patriots. This strategy proved to be seriously deficient, especially in view of the need to detach additional forces to counter the French potential of invading the undermanned and economically important British possessions in the West Indies.

The British also failed to exploit a number of tactical opportunities offered to them by concentrating on countering French strategy rather than taking the naval initiative. The British navy missed over a dozen strategic opportunities by ignoring the realities of naval operations—repeatedly obtaining a meaningless naval superiority in autumn in Europe and in summer in the Caribbean when adverse weather, particularly the hurricanes of the West Indies, made French incursions unlikely.[9] "For such strategic ineptitude the British could have no excuse."[10]

The general French strategy for their part in the naval war was good, especially their ability to obtain a tactical superiority for Admiral de Grasse's 1781 Chesapeake campaign. The French used their ships to pour troops into the islands of the West Indies while the Spanish concentrated on reinforcing their settlements in Louisiana and West Florida. French troops were also dispatched to India, Minorca, Gibraltar, Senegal, Dutch Guyana, Pensacola, and Hudson Bay.

The first action by French troops in direct support of the Patriots was at the siege of Savannah in the fall of 1779, but this operation ended in abject failure and the withdrawal of the French fleet. Meanwhile the arrival in New England of a land army of 6,000 troops under Gen. Jean Baptiste Comte de Rochambeau in 1780 had little immediate effect on the course of the war beyond supplying the Patriots with badly needed artillery and muskets. The French troops themselves would not become significant on the battlefield until 1781. Nonetheless, their presence in New England confined British movements in and around New York and deprived the Royal Navy of the important harbor at Newport, Rhode Island.

While the lack of deep water over the narrows at New York made it a less-than-ideal harbor for naval vessels that needed to come and go with regularity, the approach to Newport through Narragansett Bay was more convenient, and the bay formed the most defensible harbor on the Atlantic coast. The obvious importance of Rhode Island as a naval base had led to its occupation by the British in December 1776. Commodore Peter Parker, leading an invasion force composed of several warships and transports containing hundreds of troops, had used his naval guns to support the landings on the central island of Newport from flatboats identical to those used in the landings in New York some months earlier. The British North American Squadron made the bay its headquarters for almost three years. The base had been held against the combined attacks of Admiral d'Estaing and American ground forces under Gen. John Sullivan in 1778, but it was suddenly made available, without opposition, to the French navy in 1780. In July the French troops landed at Newport as easily as they would have in France.[11]

The British abandonment of Rhode Island was probably a tactical error, but the strategic situation seemed grave at the time. British Adm. Sir Mariot Arbuthnot had reached his headquarters at New York at the same time as the French fleet of Rear Adm. Charles Arsac de Ternay, which was carrying the troops under Rochambeau. Arbuthnot found his ships short of stores and short of men; and many had fouled bottoms that had passed their usual time for a major overhaul. Arbuthnot, new to the North American Station, could not image a positive result culminating from a sea battle with de Ternay. Simply put, he allowed himself to be worried into abandoning Newport. Gen. Sir Henry Clinton, General Howe's replacement as army commander, played no small part in this decision by hastily withdrawing British troops from Rhode Island to "defend" New York.

Once at anchor in Newport, the French found the Patriots so depleted by five years of war that they could not contemplate a new campaign in concert with their army. Rochambeau, described as "the soul of patience and diplomacy," placed himself under Washington's command, and the two men quietly planned a joint operation for 1781 to draw General Clinton from his stronghold in New York. However, American Gen. Nathaniel Greene had unexpectedly bled the British army in the colonial south under Lord Cornwallis to the point that it needed to receive supplies and reinforcements from the sea. As Cornwallis abandoned the Carolinas and moved to Yorktown in Virginia, Rochambeau and Washington deftly moved their men south from New England without alerting the British in New York. This movement of land forces, with all of its attendant river crossings and extended marches over almost 1,000 miles, was one of the most momentous events of the war. The allies were thereby allowed to besiege Cornwallis with his back against the sea at Yorktown and set the stage for one of the most decisive naval operations in history.

In 1781, a British squadron was based in New York under Vice Adm. Lord Thomas Graves. Thomas Graves (not to be confused with Samuel Graves who had commanded in Boston) had served in the West Indies from 1778 under Vice Adm. John Byron, whose bad luck had earned him the nickname "Foul-weather Jack." Byron had left England in 1778 to join Howe's fleet in New York and had his fleet scattered by such severe gales that the ships had proven unfit for service. Byron then attempted to join Admiral Howe in the Caribbean and was again attacked by violent winds and storms forcing a series of essential repairs. Graves had shared Byron's misfortunes, and he had also served under the equally unfortunate Hardy as a junior flag officer in the Channel during 1779. In 1780 his own star rose somewhat when the squadron he brought to America was on station as Charleston fell to British arms, and in 1781 he had reinforced a hard-pressed Arbuthnot in an indecisive action off the Virginia Capes.

This made Graves the likely choice to take over command of the North American Squadron when Arbuthnot suddenly returned to Britain in poor health during summer 1781. From New York, Graves kept a cautious eye on a small squadron of eight French warships under de Ternay based in

Rhode Island. The more numerous British warships on station were more than a match for the French, who were essentially bottled-up in the harbor. However, Graves, although an able sea officer, lacked the flexibility and ingenuity of a good naval strategist. A perennial second-in-command, he tended to follow orders cautiously and deliberately. It was quite by chance, therefore, that a mediocre admiral like Graves was left to deal with the problem of rescuing Cornwallis and the British army in Virginia.

When Charles Cornwallis entered Yorktown in 1781 he was confident that he had completed the most dangerous part of his present military operation. Although he was surprised to find himself besieged to landward by a major Franco-American army, he had a reasonable expectation that he would be relieved on the York River side of his position by Graves' fleet of nineteen warships, which sailed from New York as soon as the redcoats' predicament was made known to him. Yet Graves was seemingly unaware that a French fleet of twenty-six ships-of-the-line campaigning in the Caribbean under Admiral de Grasse had stolen a march on the Royal Navy's West Indian Squadron under Adm. Sir George Rodney and had run North into the coastal waters off Virginia unchallenged.

There was no excuse for Rodney's ineptitude in this regard. Early in 1781 he seems to have become infatuated with patrolling near St. Eustatius, a Dutch island possession that was a major source of war material for the Americans. He captured the island in February, and exulted in the rich booty that flowed from the warehouses of the former neutral possession. Rodney was of the old sea-hawk school of British naval operations, and he was unwilling to limit his share of prize money by stationing himself away from such rich hunting grounds. He had divided his squadron between the Dutch island and Martinique, where the French usually concentrated their forces. Rodney's subordinate, Adm. Samuel Hood, was ordered to watch the French base, but he had been left too weak by the scattered nature of the British dispositions to bring de Grasse to battle when the French fleet appeared there in April. Hood later noted, "Never was a squadron so unmeaningfully stationed." De Grasse thereafter spent several months avoiding the West Indian Squadron while concentrating every available French vessel and soldier that he could find in the Caribbean at Cape Francois in San Domingo. From there he had suddenly driven north to Virginia leaving the distracted British commanders ignorant of his movements. Admiral de Grasse's 1781 offensive operations at this juncture have been called "the most important and most perfectly executed naval campaign of the age of sail."[12]

While Rodney frantically tried to locate de Grasse's fleet in the Caribbean his health failed, and he turned the bulk of his command over to Hood who immediately made for New York. Here he joined with Graves and was serving under him when the station commander sailed to relieve Cornwallis in Virginia. Here they found twenty-seven French warships

The French Navy of the American Revolution was generally fortunate in its sea officers. Chief among these were (left to right) Captain Isaac Jean de la Clocheterie whose action in *Belle-Poule* began the war for France; Admiral Francois de Grasse whose efforts won independence for America; Admiral Charles Henri d'Estaing whose reserve saved the British Squadron in New York; and Admiral Saint Tropez de Suffern whose doggedness almost won India for the French.

and 3,000 marines quietly sailing for the undefended mouth of Chesapeake Bay (see Map 6).

The immediate relief of Cornwallis was impossible under these circumstances. Noting that the French were "in no sort of battle-order" and had not yet affected their occupation of the bay, Graves cautiously edged his well-formed battle line down upon the French fleet. De Grasse moved away from the bay close-hauled to the wind to take up the challenge. What followed was little more than a long-range cannonade. Having engaged less than half of Graves' line and having battered its rigging in typical French fashion, de Grasse cleverly outmaneuvered the British admiral, sailed back into the mouth of the bay, and dropped anchor in a strong defensive crescent. Joined by Commodore Charles Destouches and the French Rhode Island squadron that had slipped into the mouth of the bay in the interim, de Grasse's fleet now numbered thirty-four ships-of-the-line and assorted smaller vessels.[13]

Graves later claimed that there had been confusion over signals between himself and Hood's division of the fleet that had allowed the French to maneuver freely during the battle. There is no doubt the Graves had adopted Adm. Richard Kempenfelt's numeric code for signally while Hood's ships may have been using the older system based on the Fighting and Sailing Instructions issued as a standard folio of signals by the Admiralty in 1757. Yet these signals had been revised for the American station in 1778 by Admiral Howe. Moreover, it seems extraordinary that Hood's ships would have sailed in consort with those of Graves for more than two weeks at sea without agreeing on a common code or at least noting the need to do so.

Regardless of the cause of the failure, after the engagement Graves was left at sea with a substantially inferior fleet and several battered warships, one leaking badly. Although Hood later maintained that Graves could have slipped into the bay behind the French defensive line, the maneuver would have required unprecedented audacity on the part of the commander not to mention a reliance on the tactical instincts of each of his captains. Graves was not the man for such desperate measures, especially in what appeared at the time to be a minor setback. Surely Cornwallis, with 6,000 men in good order in a fortified position, could hold out until a second relief effort from the sea could be pieced together.

There was really nothing immediate for Graves to do but to return to his base at New York and marshal his forces. Here he was joined by a substantial reinforcement including twenty-five ships-of-the-line recently arrived under Rear Admiral Digby. Given an unprecedented opportunity in the form of forty-four men-of-war and several 50-gun ships, Graves set sail once again for Virginia in mid-October to dislodge or destroy the French fleet. However, on the same day that the British fleet cleared Sandy Hook, New York, Cornwallis surrendered, thinking (mistakenly) that he had been abandoned. Graves received news of the capitulation at sea from a dispatch boat several days after the fact, and he turned about to defend New York, which he was certain would be the next point of attack. Ironically, after the surrender of Cornwallis De Grasse quickly lost interest in mainland operations preferring to return to the West Indies and make an attempt on some of the sugar islands remaining in British hands. This move was in complete concordance with French strategy and war aims.

The loss of 6,000 land troops in a secondary theater of what had become a worldwide conflict at sea was not an irretrievable catastrophe for the British. It is interesting to ponder that had Graves pursued De Grasse immediately he might have caught the inferior French fleet and rendered it impotent, thereby wiping out the effect of Yorktown. His decision, instead, to retake a defensive posture in New York was of greater consequence. It allowed the brief control over the Chesapeake Bay exercised by the French in September 1781 to become the decisive event of the American Revolution. By most standards the Battle of the Chesapeake, one of the most decisive sea operations in history, had been a somewhat boring affair. Graves had lost no engagement. No ships had been taken on either side, few cannonballs had flown, and only one vessel had been severely damaged. Yet Graves' inability to bring the French fleet to heel had lost America.[14]

The American war was virtually over, at least from the American point of view. Yet, it was not immediately evident that the wider war was over. Rochambeau's French troops went into winter quarters in Williamsburg, Virginia. General Washington stayed in Philadelphia during the winter of 1781–1782. The American forces in Virginia were broken up with some units being detached to Greene's command in the Carolinas and others being sent to the Hudson Highlands to watch over the British in New York. There were still 30,000 redcoats in North America, and the majority were recalled to New York. The British focus on retaining New York may have been their Achilles' heel, and they would not abandon it until 1783.

The global naval war also continued until 1783. In August 1781 a combined French, Spanish, and Dutch fleet of forty-nine ships-of-the-line, mostly Spanish, drove the British Channel Fleet of thirty ships under Admiral Darby into Torbay on the English coast. In December 1781 Admiral Kempenfelt with twelve ships-of-the-line sighted a French convoy of transports and supply ships escorted by Admiral de Guichen with nineteen warships. Kempenfelt dispersed the entire convoy taking seventeen prizes from among the transports and driving the French warships back to Brest. This was an important face-saving victory for the British navy. Ironically Kempenfelt, "an officer [of] high professional abilities" who had devised a numerary signal code for the Royal Navy in 1778 was killed in the accidental sinking of HMS *Royal George* in August 1782. His work on signals was a complete revolution of method that allowed admirals to relay most orders directly to their captains.[15]

Meanwhile French Adm. Saint Tropez de Suffern was annoying Adm. Sir Edward Hughes in the Indian Ocean. Although the naval war in the East Indies is often considered a footnote to the American Revolution, the British and French fleets stationed there fought no fewer than five major sea battles off the coast of India from December 1780 to June 1783 (Mangalore, Provedien, Negapatam, Trincomalee, and Cuddalore; see Map 5). All these actions were indecisive except the first and the last. At Mangalore in 1780, with the help of the Bombay Marine of the East India Company, Hughes defeated and drove from the war Hyder Ali, the Nabob of Mysore, a powerful ally of France in the Indian Ocean; and in 1783 at Cuddalore Suffern attacked the British so fiercely that he left Hughes' fleet largely incapacitated. All of India lay open at Suffern's feet after Cuddalore, and he was just about to claim the entire subcontinent for France, when word came that the war was over. Had the war lasted one more year the history of the India during the nineteenth century might have been considerably different.

The naval war also continued in the Caribbean (see Map 4). Hood, with twenty-two ships-of-the-line tried to bag de Grasse's fleet of twenty-six ships anchored in the British-held harbor of Basseterre on the island of St. Kitts. De Grasse had laid siege to the British fortifications on the island. Brimstone Fort on St. Kitts (the Gibraltar of the Caribbean) was a formidable stone edifice built upon an ancient volcanic outcrop overlooking the blue Caribbean with the Dutch island of St. Eustatius visible in the hazy distance.[16] Hood planned to slip in behind the French in the semicircular anchorage to relieve the island garrison. However, de Grasse marshaled his fleet on January 26, 1782, and attacked Hood twice in a single protracted engagement at sea once again inflicting a good deal of damage to British rigging. Once again the British manning the island garrison surrendered before the full weight of the Royal Navy could be brought to bear, and Hood was forced by de Grasse's superior numbers to seek shelter in the gathering darkness of the Caribbean. He subsequently rejoined Rodney's squadron of twelve battleships.

In early 1782 the British fleet under Rodney, reinforced to thirty-six ships-of-the-line, sought out and found the French fleet. Admiral de Grasse had concentrated thirty warships near the island of Guadeloupe in the eastern Caribbean. On April 12 they faced off for what was to be the most desperate fleet action of the American war, the Battle of the Saintes (or Saints), named in reference to the many small islands nearby named for religious figures. During the opening phases of the encounter de Grasse was somewhat hampered in his maneuvers by a string of 150 transports carrying troops for a planned expedition against Jamaica. These he sent off to safety before committing himself to an engagement.

The two battle fleets met on opposing courses for a passing encounter, but the changing winds threw many of the French warships into confusion. This allowed Rodney to cut through de Grasse's line doubling and raking many of the French ships over the next two hours of heavy fighting. The French drew off leaving four men-of-war behind including de Grasse's heavily damaged flagship, *Ville d' Paris (104)*, and the admiral, who surrendered himself to Hood on HMS *Barfleur (90)*. More than three hundred dead were found aboard the French flagship alone. This was more than the butcher's bill for the entire British fleet. The surviving French warships, twenty-six in all, reassembled at San Domingo under the Marquis Louis de Vaudreuil, but the naval war in the Caribbean as well as that in all the western Atlantic was essentially at an end.[17]

The momentum of the successful allied war effort since 1781 led to an increasing likelihood of the revolution coming to a speedy conclusion. This placed Vergennes under some stress to extricate France from the

An artist's concept of the Battles of the Saintes picturing the encounter of the French flagship *Ville d'Paris* (left) and the British man-of-war *Barfleur* (right). The battle victory saved the sagging reputation of the British Royal Navy.

conflict with its war aims fulfilled just as events were turning against him. The peace negotiations being held in Paris increasingly centered on Spanish, rather than French war aims; and unilateral operations by the Spanish were muddying the diplomatic waters. Vergennes urged better allied coordination to avoid a bad peace, but he became convinced that the situation would deteriorate if the war continued.[18]

Ultimately, Vergennes found his policies being undermined by the unpredictable consequences of Anglo-American politics, which he had enormous difficulty understanding. As the war wound down Vergennes was also hampered by a fear that the Americans would agree to any peace proposition that explicitly or implicitly recognized their independence without regard to allied war aims. He wrote to Benjamin Franklin, who served on the peace treaty committee:

I am at a loss, Sir, to explain your conduct and that of your colleagues on this occasion. You have concluded your preliminary articles without any communication between us, although the instructions from Congress prescribe that nothing shall be done without the participation of the [French] King. You are about to hold out a certain hope of peace to America without informing yourself on the state of the negotiation on our part.[19]

Franklin penned an apology to the French foreign minister two days later that included a good deal of diplomatic deference, but very little in the way of substance on this issue, "It is not possible for any one to be more sensible than I of what I and every American owe to the [French] King for the many and great benefits and favors he has bestowed upon us." The Americans would uphold their commitments under the alliance until 1793 thereafter abandoning the French monarchy, but allying themselves with Napoleon during the War of 1812.[20]

Although Britain was at its lowest point in terms of naval power as it entered 1781, it emerged from the final campaigns of the American Revolution with its sea power largely intact and its prestige on the mend. The Royal Navy had solidified its hold on Gibraltar, and the victory at the Saintes was sufficiently decisive to re-establish the Royal Navy's supremacy on the oceans and insure the return of its island possessions and its coastal trading posts in India at the peace talks. Nonetheless, the improvement in British naval fortunes came too late to change the outcome of the war with respect to America. In September 1782 a preliminary peace was reached among all parties. The major consequence of this was the recognition of American independence in January 1783.

The British had almost 30,000 troops garrisoned in the United States until 1783. About mid-November 1782 the first division of British troops took transports in New York and headed to Halifax. Nathaniel Fanning saw them pass by while aboard a French warship near Nantucket Shoals. Four days later, he recorded what he saw in New York Harbor.

[We] passed the British fleet of men-of-war, and transports [anchored near Staten Island], wearing a French ensign and pendant, and came to anchor in the East River, opposite the city. ... A boat from the British Admiral's ship [Admiral Digby] came along side of our ship, with a lieutenant in her ... [who asked the French captain] how he dared to wear his pendant, when he saw an Admiral's flag flying below. The French captain replied, that he had nothing to do with the British Admiral; he knew nothing about him, nor did he care anything about him; his business was with the American commander-in-chief in New York [George Washington].[21]

The Royal Navy lieutenant returned some time later with two boats filled with armed men to repeat the British admiral's demand that the pendant be taken down in deference to his rank. Accordingly, the French commander formed a file of marines on his deck at the gangway. The Frenchman said to the lieutenant, "Very well, haul it down, if that is your orders." When the British Jack-tars and their officer came up the gangway, the French marines aimed their muskets directly at them in a most menacing manner, and "they skulked into their boats again" and "returned from whence they came, and the French ship continued to wear its pendant."[22]

France's participation in the American war proved tragic for the French Crown. Vergennes had sought and won a war, which unfortunately failed "to bring about the rapprochement he sought, and which raised dangers from within the [French] monarchy far greater than those which threatened it from without."[23] Unwittingly the foreign minister had helped to prepare a financial and political crisis that was to lead France into its own revolution in less than a decade. Nonetheless, Vergennes poses an impressive figure in the history of American independence. He successfully combined a "consistency of ends with a flexibility of means" in his support of the Americans. However, he unwisely risked France's own empire by fighting such a damaging and costly war simply to reduce Britain to parity in the balance of European politics. Nonetheless, there is no question that he had provided America with the support absolutely necessary to achieve its goal of independence.[24]

14

Prisoners of War

It is better to be slain in battle, than to be taken prisoner by British
brutes, whose tender mercies are cruelties.
> —a Patriot held prisoner in New York City[1]

POWs

There is no question that the Patriots held prisoner by the British in
America suffered terribly, and that their treatment may have violated the
accepted standards of treatment for war prisoners in the eighteenth century.
The worst abuses seem to have been suffered by the 3,000 Patriots captured
during the British invasion of New York in 1776. Instead of being confined
by civil authorities, they were placed under the jurisdiction of the military,
which was poorly equipped and ill-disposed to deal with them humanely. It
is equally certain that the Patriots held many persons suspected of being
Loyalists in equally unbearable conditions. Many American Tories died in
Old Newgate Prison, a copper mine in Connecticut that was used to house
prominent Loyalist prisoners. The mine was cold and damp year round.
The floors were tilted and the ceilings in many place prevented the captives
from standing erect. Moreover, black Americans (runaway slaves) found
serving with the Crown forces in the south when captured were customarily
sent to the lead mines of Virginia as laborers or were sold to the West Indies
by the Americans. Many blacks volunteered to serve with the troops of

Virginia's Royal Governor John Lord Dunmore or on the ships of the Royal Navy. Most of these blacks were abandoned by the British when they evacuated Norfolk, and many simply disappeared into the mists of history.

Historians know a great deal about the prison abuses experienced by the Patriots from the diaries and journals of the prisoners themselves. A number of these were published in the nineteenth century to document the first person accounts of the Revolution as the aging generation of Patriots was dying off. However, many of the accounts were written from memory by aged persons several decades after the fact. Joseph Plumb Martin, for instance, is widely quoted by historians, but he was ninety-three years old when he wrote his memoirs of the war. It must also be remembered that all the accounts generated at the time were unchallenged and largely anecdotal in nature. Moreover, they were accompanied by no useful analysis at the time of their publication.

The American captives of 1776 were housed in various buildings in and about the city of New York, including several non-conforming churches, a number of poorly ventilated warehouses, and two sugar refineries. With a large portion of the city's buildings lost during the Great Fire of 1776, the first group of captives all but exhausted the available space that might be used for prisons. The overflow from further operations and captures at sea was placed on mastless prison hulks in Wallabout Bay near the Flushing section of Queens. This was where the worst conditions could be found.[2] These men, especially those on the prison hulk HMS *Jersey*, complained regularly about the amount of their rations and their being kept below decks for extended periods. They also complained of a lack of firewood, clothing, and blankets in winter; of severe discipline and the demand that they maintain complete silence; of overcrowding; of exposure to diseases, including smallpox; and of inadequate ventilation caused by being closed down in the holds of ships or shut into buildings with few or no windows. Moreover, they were apparently open to constant abuse by their guards who played frightful pranks on their charges and woke them in the dead of night simply to disrupt their sleep.[3]

Contemporary sources note that the British claimed that the conditions were the same afforded to Scottish prisoners held during the revolt of 1746 and that American rebels should expect no more. Every American was aware that the Scots had been terribly brutalized, maltreated, or summarily executed. Therefore, the Patriots threatened retaliation in kind upon British soldiers held captive in consequence of any mistreatment received by American prisoners. Washington, himself, warned that he would not hesitate to treat the British prisoners in America with as much severity as his own countrymen received; and Franklin wrote, "We are determined to treat such prisoners precisely as our countrymen are treated in England; to give them the same allowance of provisions and accommodations, and no other."[4]

After the Saratoga Convention of 1778, the treatment of Patriots held prisoner both in America and in England became "less susceptible" to abuses. The Crown retreated from its earliest draconian policies as an immediate consequence of Burgoyne's surrender into American hands of an army of 5,000 men. Since the British refused to exchange soldiers for sailors, Burgoyne's men, both redcoats and Hessian, were moved about the colonies in a group in an attempt to secure them without repatriation. They were thereafter known as the Convention Army. Congress and the American commissioners in Paris used them as pawns in a political game surrounding the recognition of American sovereignty. We know a great deal about their sufferings from the journal of Baroness Von Reidisel, wife of the Hessian commander who went into captivity with her husband rather than be parted from him. Burgoyne had been permitted to travel to England under parole, but General Von Reidisel and Maj. Gen. William Phillips were held until exchanged for American Gen. Benjamin Lincoln, who was captured with 5,000 men at Charleston in May 1780.[5]

THE RIGHTS OF PRISONERS

Prisoners of war were entitled, by common practice between European nations, to certain rights and immunities. The peculiarities of eighteenth century protocols regarding prisoners proved to be complex, however. The rules applicable to the handling of war prisoners, unlike those of modern times, had simply not yet been "precisely defined or uniformly enforced."[6] As Edmund Burke declared in a session of Parliament dealing with the question of the status of American prisoners, "How difficult it is to apply these juridical ideas to our present case."[7] Although efforts to limit the brutality of war by the acceptance of conventions had been growing in the eighteenth century, the existing protocols remained fragile and could be violated without malice through insufficient care or simple misunderstanding.[8] It may be that the established conventions were earnestly applied, even in the face of rhetoric to the contrary.

However, there is evidence that certain protocols, at least with respect to sailors, had been codified. Published in 1763, *Traites' des prises qui se font sur Mer,* a French treatise detailing the protocols regarding prisoners taken at sea, was cited by American diplomats in their letters of protest to the British several times. In April 1777, Benjamin Franklin, Silas Deane, and Arthur Lee referred to them in a letter drafted to Lord Stormont, then British Ambassador to France. The letter asked that his lordship alleviate the sufferings of the prisoners according to "the rules established, and generally observed by civilized nations."[9]

By common usage between sovereign nations, certain privileges had come to be expected with respect to prisoners. In most conflicts prisoners of war proved only a minor annoyance. Soldiers and sailors could expect to save their lives by begging quarter and surrendering their arms to their captors in battle. The wounded could expect humane care. Captives commonly spent only a short time in prison and officers were allowed limited freedom to remain unconfined under their parole, or word of honor. Since it was uneconomical for either side in a conflict to expend the resources needed to maintain and guard even a small number of prisoners for any length of time, captives were usually quickly exchanged by means of a formal arrangement known as a cartel. Such cartels normally applied to all ranks and were accomplished by exchanging men of equal rank, or by exchanging a man of superior rank for several of inferior rank following a previously negotiated scheme.

However, American prisoners of war were both an embarrassment and a quandary to the British Crown. Since Britain did not recognize the existence of the American states as a sovereign nation, but, rather as absolute subjects of the king, they could not officially hold Patriots as prisoners of war. "Traitors were not afforded the protection owed under the international war code to soldiers and subjects of recognized governments."[10] In the early days of the war, the British resolved this difficulty to their own satisfaction by simply holding the Patriots illegally. This was a direct violation of the habeas corpus provisions of the British constitution, under which some Patriot prisoners in the West Indies, claiming the ancient rights of Englishmen, brought suit in court in 1775 and actually affected their release. This difficulty was overcome in 1776 by the temporary suspension of habeas corpus by Parliament, allowing the prisoners to be held on probable cause for treason. Although this raised a storm of protest among those ministers to Parliament friendly to America, the suspension of habeas corpus was renewed in 1777, and captured Patriots were thereafter held "at the pleasure of the King" under a bill of attainder.[11]

The Howe brothers, in their alternate role as peace commissioners in America, were seemingly open to exchanging prisoners man for man and officer for officer, as they would have with France, Spain, or any other European government. However, British diplomats dealing with prisoners maintained a steadfast refusal to sanction the exchange of seamen for land troops. It was thought in London that this would particularly hobble the operations of the American navy, and particularly the privateers, who were causing the British the greatest anxiety. The status of naval captives remained largely unresolved until 1781.

NEGOTIATIONS

To their credit, the brothers Howe repeatedly corresponded with the Patriots during the 1776 campaign and met with congressional delegates to discuss the disposition of prisoners. General Howe and his brother, the admiral, extended offers of universal pardons to the Americans in exchange for reconciliation as early as July 1776, but the Congressional representatives at the meetings rejected their repeated entreaties.[12] In what may have been a crucial decision in establishing the status of American prisoners, General Howe relented with respect to pardons and arranged for the release of both Gen. John Sullivan and Gen. William Alexander (Lord Stirling) in November 1776. The offer to exchange two high ranking rebels, one of whom was a member of the Irish peerage whose father had been a Jacobite in the Scottish Rebellion of 1745, was an extremely sensitive issue. Lord George Germain, the colonial secretary, was sharply critical of the Howe brothers for their liberality during this period.[13]

As the campaign wore on, Admiral Howe became disgusted with these meetings because the Americans insisted on discussing only prisoner exchanges rather than reconciliation. Ultimately, General Howe presided at these conferences alone, always trying to bring the discussions back to the topic of pardons and political compromise. He was met with an unvarying negative response. Washington aptly expressed the American position: "Those who have committed no crime, need no pardon."[14]

In light of the devastating defeat of the Patriots in New York in 1776, General Howe may have expected a different response. Therefore, throughout the winter of 1776–1777 he patiently awaited the collapse of the rebel cause in the wake of his successful campaign through New Jersey. The collapse never occurred largely because of the American victories at Trenton and Princeton. Howe's guarded campaign against the Patriots and the repeated attempts at reconciliation by both Howe brothers were a marked departure from the violent, brutal, and unrelenting prosecution of the Scottish rebels in 1746, which was characterized by a general lack of restraint on the part of the government.

General Howe did little to change the immediate situation of the bulk of the prisoners. He may have believed that the war would soon end, and the problem would resolve itself. It was not until after the British defeat at Saratoga that it became clear that the war was going to last longer than previously expected.[15] Edmund Burke expressed the moderate Whig view in Parliament, "Though rebellion is declared ... modes of coercion have been adopted, [that] have much more resemblance to a sort of qualified hostility towards an independent power than the punishment of rebellious subjects.... The government against which a claim of liberty is tantamount to high treason is a government to which submission is equivalent to slavery."[16]

Howe was replaced by Henry Clinton in New York in May 1778, thereby freeing him of some responsibility for the fate of the prisoners housed there after that date. Even if Howe was not directly responsible for the conditions in which the captives were confined, some of the subordinates he appointed were particularly loathsome fellows. Joshua Loring, the commissioner of prisoners in New York and the husband of Howe's mistress, admitted starving to death 300 men by appropriating part of their rations. Loring's provost marshal, William Cunningham, swore in a deathbed confession, "I shudder at the murders I have been accessory to, both with and without orders from the government, especially while in New York, during which time there were more than 2,000 prisoners starved in the different churches, by stopping their rations, which I sold." The misdeeds testified to by these men are consistent with other contemporary evidence as to their nature and scope.[17]

The most infamous of atrocities regarding prisoners committed during the Revolution can be laid at the feet of small groups of Loyalist and Patriot partisans many of whom were acting out of private or family grievances. In one area of New Jersey alone there were five illegitimate executions of prisoners performed by just two feuding families. British regulars also sometimes strayed from a scrupulous adherence to the prisoner of war policies of their commanders, but it seems certain that at least the Hessians were encouraged by their British commanders to give no quarter on the battlefield. The battle of Brooklyn Heights (New York) and the raids at Paoli (Pennsylvania) and Tappan (New York) were most notable in this regard. Although few Patriots were subsequently killed after surrender, many more lost their lives due to prolonged confinement as POWs.

A survivor of the prison hulks estimated that 1,500 Americans died in the first year of their confinement in New York. It must be remembered, however, that in their headlong retreat into New Jersey, the Patriots left behind those men so seriously hurt that they could not be removed. Although British records indicate the allocation of hospital staff to prison facilities, the large number of wounded and sick Patriots taken in the New York Campaign may account for the higher rate of mortality in the first year of their confinement.[18]

Prison conditions in England, while not comfortable, were much better than those experienced in the colonies. With minor exceptions (notably Ethan Allen) those prisoners held in England were all seamen, and it is interesting to suggest an association between the rate of survival of these men and their youth, hardiness, and experience in dealing with deprivation at sea. The available data does not allow us to make such a connection, however, regardless of how tempting it appears. Nonetheless, while half of the Americans confined on prison ships in New York may have died, fewer than 11 percent of naval prisoners held in England succumbed during their confinement. This was a lower rate of mortality than that experienced by soldiers in winter encampments at Valley Forge or Morristown where mortality among the troops reached 20 percent. Forton Prison in England, where most American sailors were held, had been built during the reign of Queen Anne as a hospital, and unlike a prison hulk it was dry, if not warm, and had an open area in which the prisoners were able to exercise and avoid the close environment of their cells periodically.

15

Epilogue

[Admiral de Grasse's 1781 offensive was] the most important and
most perfectly executed naval campaign of the age of sail.
—Johnathan R. Dull, naval historian

THE AGE OF FIGHTING SAIL

The American Revolution can safely be viewed as part of a single prolonged naval conflict covering a period of about a century and a quarter
beginning with the Glorious Revolution in 1688 and ending with the
British victory at Trafalgar in 1805 during the Napoleonic Wars. This
was a period in which the armed merchantmen of the age of trade were
replaced by genuine warships whose task was to control the sealanes. As
the naval tactics of the period changed gradually and the shipbuilding
technology and effectiveness of naval gunnery changed very little, consideration of the naval tactics used by either side during this period can be
viewed as a simple evolution in strategy and implementation. The American Revolution was a watershed during this period with improved windship designs, new technologies in terms of cannon, improved gunpowder
and communications, and innovative tactics. Many of the naval advances
available during the classic sea battles of the Napoleonic Wars were
pioneered during the American War for Independence.[1]

In 1775 it was inconceivable that the Anglo-American colonies could have overcome the overwhelming military superiority of Great Britain. Yet the belligerent Patriots seemed certain that they could defeat the British army that they so despised. On the other hand, the one great fear shared by all Americans was that they would not be able to overcome the presence of the Royal Navy. In fact, this was a reasonable apprehension. The Americans never proved capable of defeating any of the large British warships. With few exceptions they took on only the least fearsome of British vessels such as tenders, cutters, and sloops-of-war. The smallest of these vessels carried only swivel guns and light cannon. The largest carried between 14 and 16 cannon, formidable against lightly built privateers and smugglers but too few and of insufficient weight to take on American frigates. This may be why the *Bonhomme Richard–Serapis* fight, a battle between 40-gun-plus frigates, stands out in American naval history.

The ministers in London, and the Howes in America, predicted in late 1776 that the Americans would request the help of France in their rush to independency, but they likewise thought that the French would find the crumbling rebel army a poor investment. William Howe incorrectly suggested that the French would be wary of entering a war they would surely lose. As one historian of Parliamentary affairs has noted, "With fears that France would now exploit British distress, the discussions at Whitehall [the ministry offices] were about how to wear down American resolve by blockade and battery of the coastline where it was populated enough to make a difference."[2] Yet American victories at Trenton, Princeton, and Saratoga sabotaged their predictions and blunted their warnings. French entrance into the war transformed it from a ground engagement in the colonies into a multi-ocean naval war. The conflict at sea, so neatly focused at its beginning on blockading the New England coastline, quickly blurred to include the Channel, the Mediterranean, the Indian Ocean, and particularly the Caribbean. Britain was forced therefore to "severely modify [its] strategy for suppressing the American rebellion."[3]

Inasmuch as the French briefly took command of the seas from the Royal Navy during the American war, their general strategy can be considered appropriate and successful. This was especially true in that they were able to obtain a tactical superiority for Admiral de Grasse's 1781 Chesapeake campaign.[4] The British focus on preserving their stranglehold on New York proved to be the fault in their strategic plan. These results point out one of the great principles of naval warfare—being stronger than your enemy at the right time and place.[5]

Although far stronger than it needed to be to overwhelm the Americans, the Royal Navy was simply unprepared to match her European rivals. The entry of the French alone expanded the scope of the conflict. When Spain joined the allies in 1779, it brought an overwhelming advantage in ships-of-the-line, which was again increased by the entrance of Holland into the war in 1781. However, the Spanish were interested in little beyond the recovery of Gibraltar and Minorca, and the Dutch entered too late to make more than a minor contribution.

The French minister, Vergennes, had urged better Allied coordination to avoid a bad peace, but he was seemingly unaware of an obvious fault in his reasoning. While there was no doubt that the Americans could not have forced their separation from Britain without foreign aid, they were still more closely tied to Britain by cultural, religious, and economic similarities than they were to France, Spain, or Holland. The Americans, for their part, remained faithful to their allies until the preliminary peace had been signed. Nonetheless, they would gradually drift away from France during the decade after the war.[6]

The American war created great social and political dissention in Britain. In 1780, in particular, anti-war sentiment in England was the seed for violent anti-government riots—somehow inexplicably linking the war in America with anti-Catholic, anti-corruption, anti-taxes, and anti-French sentiments. Known as the Gordon Riots for their firebrand leader, Lord George Gordon, it seems certain that the disorders became disconnected from their root causes as they spread. Peers and ministers of government were mauled and bruised, their clothing torn from them, their carriages overturned, and their servants assaulted as they watched. Lord Sandwich was hounded from his coach and forced to take refuge in a coffeehouse while the wheels were smashed and the glass panels shattered. Charles Dickens would describe the extent of the disorders in *Barnaby Rudge* (1841) from documents and interviews with survivors, and Horace Walpole noted at the time that the North government did not know how to respond to it.

The riots and the bad war news from America rocked the government of Frederick Lord North. In March 1782 North, who had held office since 1770, conceded that his government was over. North was replaced as prime minister by the Marquis of Rockingham, a moderate with respect to the American problem whose price for forming a coalition government was American independence and the removal of his political enemies from office. Among those removed from office was Lord Sandwich. Rockingham also brought back to the Admiralty a number of seasoned naval officers who had avoided command under Sandwich's administration. Chief among these was "Black Dick" Howe, who consented to take command of the home fleet. Howe immediately set sail for Gibraltar with thirty-four ships-of-the-line and a substantial number of provision ships in order to relieve the British garrison there for a third time during the course of the war. This operation cemented the British hold on the "sentry-box" of the Mediterranean and kept it off the peace talk table in Paris.

Meanwhile, the newly appointed First Lord of the Admiralty, Augustus Keppel, succumbed to political pressure to replace Adm. George Rodney in the West Indies with Adm. Sir Hugh Pigot. Keppel was embarrassed, however, when word of Rodney's victory at the Saintes belatedly arrived in England. Thereafter, Rodney's ire was quelled by a lordship and a large pension for life. The victory at the Saintes also won an Irish peerage for Samuel Hood. Pigot and Hood spent the remaining months of the war chasing the French fleet about the Caribbean.[7]

The terms of the Treaty of Paris that was signed in January 1783 hardly reflected the allies' performance during the war. The American Navy was essentially driven from the seas by Britain, yet America gained its freedom. Spain had done very little to further the allied cause, yet Spain regained Minorca and was given Louisiana as a gift from the French for its support. The French Royal Marine had gained control of the seas and beaten the British Royal Navy for the first time in a century, yet France failed to gain much in the peace other than bragging rights and a single sugar island (Tobago). Moreover, French participation in the American Revolution ultimately proved tragic, helping as it certainly did to prepare a financial and political crisis that was to lead France into its own revolution in less than a decade.[8]

January 1783 usually marks the end of the American Revolution, but the British continued to hold New York City until the spring. At least 100,000 Loyalists fled to England or Canada during the course of the Revolution, but many waited until the last minute to take ship with the redcoats from New York hoping in vain for a positive turn in British fortunes. One historian has noted, "The formation of the Tory or Loyalist party in the American Revolution; its persecution by the Whigs during a long and fratricidal war, and the banishment or death ... of these most conservative and respectable Americans is a tragedy but rarely paralleled in the history of the world." Ironically, the scene in New York harbor in 1783 was much like that reported by John Manly in 1776 when the British had first abandoned Boston.[9]

Appendix 1: Important Vessels and Commanders Belonging to the North American Squadron during the Enforcement Crisis, 1764–1767

Adm. Alexander Lord Colvill	Squadron Commander; HMS *Romney*
Capt. Archibald Kennedy	Squadron Vice Commander; HMS *Coventry*
Capt. Walter Sterling	HMS *Rainbow*
Capt. Richard Smith	HMS *Squirrell*
Capt. Thomas Bishop	HMS *Fortune*
Capt. Charles Antrobus	HMS *Maidstone*
Capt. Henry St. John	HMS *Guarland*
Capt. Robert Fanshaw	HMS *Speedwell*
Capt. Charles Leslie	HMS *Cygnet* (1764–1766)
Capt. Philip Durell	HMS *Cygnet* (1766–1767)
Capt. Joseph Deane	HMS *Mermaid*
Capt. Jeremiah Morgan	HMS *Viper* (1764)
Capt. Jacob Lobb	HMS *Viper* (1765)
Capt. John Brown	HM brig *Hawke*
Capt. Jeremiah Morgan	HM sloop *Hornet*
Lt. (Capt.) James Hawker	HM sloop *Sardoine*
Lt. Constantine J. Phipps	HM sloop *Diligence*
Lt. Henry Mowat	HM sloop *Canceaux*
Lt. John Lewis Gidoin	HM sloop *Jamaica*

Lt. Thomas Allen	HM cutter *Gaspee*
Lt. Robert Dugdale	HM cutter *Magdalen*
Lt. Thomas Hill	HM cutter *St. John*
Lt. Thomas Laugharne	HM cutter *Chaleur*

Appendix 2: Disposition of the Royal Navy on the North American Station, January 1775

Ship	Guns	Men	Station
Boyne	70	520	Boston
Somerset	68	520	Boston
Asia	64	480	Boston
Preston	50	300	Boston
Mercury	20	130	Boston
Glasgow	20	130	Boston
Tartar	28	160	Halifax
Rose	20	130	Rhode Island
Swan	16	100	Rhode Island
Hope	6	30	Rhode Island
Fowey	20	130	Virginia
Lively	20	130	Salem
Scarborough	20	130	New Hampshire
Canceaux	8	45	New Hampshire
Kingfisher	16	100	New York
Tamer	14	100	South Carolina
Cruizer	8	60	North Carolina
Savage	8	60	East Florida

Ship	Guns	Men	Station
St. John	6	30	East Florida
Magdalene	6	30	Philadelphia
Halifax	6	30	Maine
Diligent	6	30	Maine
Gaspee	6	30	Maine
Diana	6	30	unassigned

Source: Jack Coggins, *Ships and Seamen of the American Revolution: Vessels, Crews, Weapons, Gear, Naval Tactics, and Actions of the War for Independence* (Harrisburg, PA: Stackpole Books, 1969), p. 2.

Appendix 3: 1794 Admiralty List of Vessels of War in Service or Built before 1783

Name	Guns	Type	Year Listed	Notes
Atlas	98	Ship	1782	
Albion	74	Ship	1763	
Alcide	74	Ship	1779	
Alexander	74	Ship	1773	
Alfred	74	Ship	1778	
Arrogant	74	Ship	1761	
Africa	64	Ship	1781	
Agememnon	64	Ship	1781	
America	64	Ship	1777	
Anson	64	Ship	1743	
Argonaut	64	Ship	1782	
Asia	64	Ship	1764	Fired on New York, 1776
Adamant	50	Ship	1779	
Assistance	50	Ship	1781	
Acteon	44	Frigate	1779	
Argo	44	Frigate	1781	

Name	Guns	Type	Year Listed	Notes
Assurance	44	Frigate	1780	
Arethusa	38	Frigate	1781	
L'aigle	36	Frigate	1782	
Actaceon	32	Frigate	1776	Charleston
Active	32	Frigate	1776	Charleston
Aeolus	32	Frigate	1758	
L'aimable	32	Frigate	1782	
Alarm	32	Frigate	1758	
Amazon	32	Frigate	1773	
Amphion	32	Frigate	1780	
Andromache	32	Frigate	1781	
Astrea	32	Frigate	1781	
Andromeda	28	Frigate	1777	Brought Howe home
Aurora	28	Frigate	1777	
Active	20	Sloop-of-war	1776	
Ariadne	20	Sloop-of-war	1776	
Albany	18	Sloop-of-war	1776	
Ariel	16	Sloop	1779	
Alligence	14	Sloop	1776	
Atlanta	14	Sloop	1776	
Alecto	12	Sloop	1779	
Aetna	8	Cutter	1781	
Adventure	8	Cutter	1775	NAS
Brittania	100	Ship	1762	
Barfeur	98	Ship	1768	
Blenheim	90	Ship	1761	
Bedford	74	Ship	1775	
Bellona	74	Ship	1760	
Berwick	74	Ship	1779	
Bombay Castle	74	Ship	1782	
Boyne	70	Ship	1775	NAS
Belliqueux	64	Ship	1780	
Bienfaisant	64	Ship	1759	

Name	Guns	Type	Year Listed	Notes
Bristol	50	Ship	1775	Charleston
Belle Poule	36	Frigate	1778	French built
Boston	32	Frigate	1762	
Bristol	32	Frigate	1776	
Boreas	28	Frigate	1774	
Brilliant	28	Frigate	1779	
Bonetta	16	Sloop	1779	
Bulldog	14	Sloop	1782	
Brazen	14	Cutter	1781	
Beaver	14	Sloop	1775	NAS
Bolton	8	Bomb vessel	1776	NAS
Cambridge	80	Ship	1750	
Canada	74	Ship	1766	
Conqueror	74	Ship	1775	
Courageux	74	Ship	1761	
Cumberland	74	Ship	1774	
Chicester	74	Ship	1753	
Le Caton	64	Ship	1782	French built
Crown	64	Ship	1782	
Centurion	50	Ship	1774	NAS
Chatham	50	Ship	1758	NAS
Cerberus	32	Frigate	1775	NAS
Ceres	32	Frigate	1781	
Cleopatra	32	Frigate	1780	
Carysfort	28	Frigate	1767	
Cyclops	28	Frigate	1779	
Champion	24	Frigate	1779	
Camel	24	Sloop	1782	Storeship
Camilla	20	Sloop-of-war	1776	
Cygnet	18	Sloop-of-war	1776	
Ceres	14	Sloop-of-war	1776	
Childers	14	Sloop-of-war	1778	
Crane	14	Sloop	1776	NAS guardship
Cockatrice	14	Cutter	1782	

Name	Guns	Type	Year Listed	Notes
Carcass	8	Bomb vessel	1776	NAS
Catherine	8	Yacht	1720	
Chatham	8	Yacht	1741	
Duke	98	Ship	1777	
Defence	74	Ship	1763	
Diadem	64	Ship	1782	
Diomede	44	Frigate	1781	
Dolphin	44	Frigate	1781	
Daedalas	32	Frigate	1780	
Diana	32	Frigate	1776	
Daphne	20	Sloop-of-war	1776	
Druid	14	Sloop-of-war	1776	
Dorset	10	Yacht	1753	
Dromedary	24	Sloop	1779	Storeship
Drake	14	Sloop-of-war	1779	
Dependence	14	Sloop	1776	NAS guardship
Diligent	8	Cutter	1775	NAS
Edgar	74	Ship	1773	
Egmont	74	Ship	1766	
Elizabeth	74	Ship	1768	
Eagle	64	Ship	1777	
Essex	64	Ship	1763	
Europe	64	Ship	1769	
Europa	50	Ship	1782	
Expedition	44	Frigate	1781	
Experiment	44	Frigate	1776	Charleston
Eolas	32	Frigate	1776	
Enterprise	28	Frigate	1774	
Edward	14	Sloop-of-war	1775	
Egmont	10	Sloop	1776	
Expedition	10	Cutter	1775	
Formidable	98	Ship	1777	
Fame	74	Ship	1759	
Fortitude	74	Ship	1780	

Name	Guns	Type	Year Listed	Notes
Fortunee	40	Frigate	1779	Prison ship
Flora	32	Frigate	1780	
Fox	32	Frigate	1780	
Fox	28	Frigate	1777	
Fowey	20	Frigate	1775	NAS
Friendship	18	Sloop-of-war	1776	Charleston
Fairy	16	Sloop	1778	
Fly	16	Sloop	1776	
Fortune	16	Sloop	1778	
Falcon	14	Sloop	1782	
Gibraltar	80	Ship	1780	
Ganges	74	Ship	1782	
Goliath	74	Ship	1781	
Grafton	74	Ship	1771	
Grampus	50	Ship	1782	
Grana	28	Frigate	1781	
Glasgow	20	Frigate	1776	NAS
Greyhound	20	Frigate	1776	NAS
Hector	74	Ship	1779	
Hero	74	Ship	1753	Prison ship
Hebe	38	Frigate	1782	French built
Hermione	32	Frigate	1782	
Hussar	28	Ship	1776	NAS
Hind	?	?	1780	NAS
Hawke	14	Sloop	1775	
Helena	14	Sloop	1778	
Hope	14	Sloop	1775	NAS
Halifax	10	Sloop	1776	NAS
Invincible	74	Ship	1765	
Irresistable	74	Ship	1782	
Inflexible	64	Ship	1780	Storeship
Intrepid	64	Ship	1770	
Isis	50	Ship	1774	
Iphigenia	32	Frigate	1780	

Name	Guns	Type	Year Listed	Notes
Iris	32	Frigate	1782	Hancock
Inspector	16	Sloop	1782	
Incendiary	14	Frigate	1782	
Jupiter	50	Ship	1778	
Juno	32	Frigate	1780	
Jason	18	Sloop	1776	
Kings Fisher	18	Sloop	1782	
Kingfisher	16	Sloop	1775	NAS
Kite	14	Cutter	1778	
London	98	Ship	1766	
Lion	64	Ship	1777	
Leander	50	Ship	1780	
Latona	38	Frigate	1781	
Lowestoffe	32	Frigate	1762	
Liverpool	28	Frigate	1776	NAS
Lizard	28	Frigate	1775	NAS
Lively	20	Frigate	1775	NAS
Liberty	16	Cutter	1779	
Magnificent	74	Ship	1766	
Malborough	74	Ship	1767	
Monarch	74	Ship	1765	
Montagu	74	Ship	1779	
Magnanime	64	Ship	1780	
Modeste	64	Ship	1759	French built
Monmouth	64	Ship	1773	
Medway	60	Ship	1755	
Minerva	38	Frigate	1780	
Magiciene	32	Frigate	1781	French built
Milford	32	Frigate	1776	NAS
Minerva	32	Frigate	1776	
Maidstone	28	Frigate	1758	
Medea	28	Frigate	1778	
Mercury	28	Frigate	1776	NAS
Myrmidon	20	Frigate	1780	Supply ship

Name	Guns	Type	Year Listed	Notes
Merlin	20	Sloop	1777	
Megaera	14	Sloop	1782	Fireship
Mutine	14	Cutter	1778	
Mary	10	Yacht	1723	
Medina	10	Yacht	1771	
Margaretta	4	Cutter	1775	NAS
Namur	90	Ship	1756	
Nonsuch	64	Ship	1774	
La Nymphe	36	Frigate	1780	French built
Niger	32	Frigate	1759	NAS
Nemesis	28	Frigate	1780	
Narcisus	20	Frigate	1781	
Nautilus	16	Sloop	1775	NAS
Nimble	14	Cutter	1781	
Orpheus	32	Frigate	1780	
Orestes	18	Sloop	1781	
Otter	14	Sloop	1782	
Prince George	98	Ship	1772	
Princess Royal	98	Ship	1773	
Le Pegase	74	Ship	1782	
Polyphemus	64	Ship	1782	
Prothee	64	Ship	1780	French built
Prudent	64	Ship	1768	
Prince Edward	60	Ship	1781	
Portland	50	Ship	1770	
Preston	50	Ship	1775	NAS
Princess Caro-line	50	Ship	1781	
Phaeton	38	Frigate	1782	
La Prudente	38	Frigate	1779	French built
Perseverance	36	Frigate	1781	
Pearl	32	Frigate	1762	NAS
Pegasus	28	Frigate	1779	
Pomona	28	Frigate	1778	NAS

Name	Guns	Type	Year Listed	Notes
Proserpine	28	Frigate	1777	
Porcupine	24	Frigate	1779	
Prosperity	22	Sloop	1782	Stores vessel
Perseus	20	Sloop-of-war	1776	
Pluto	14	Cutter	1782	
Pilote	14	Cutter	1778	
Portsmouth	8	Yacht	1755	
Princess Augusta	8	Yacht	1710	
Queen	98	Ship	1769	
Quebec	32	Frigate	1781	
Royal William	84	Ship	1719	
Resolution	74	Ship	1770	
Robust	74	Ship	1764	
Royal Oak	74	Ship	1769	
Russell	74	Ship	1764	
Raisonable	64	Ship	1768	
Repulse	64	Ship	1780	
Ruby	64	Ship	1775	
Rippon	60	Ship	1758	NAS
Renown	50	Ship	1774	NAS
Romney	50	Ship	1762	NAS
Rainbow	44	Frigate	1761	NAS
Resistance	44	Frigate	1782	
Roebuck	44	Frigate	1774	Fired on New York, 1776
Resource	28	Frigate	1778	
Rose	20	Frigate	1775	NAS
Resolution	14	Cutter	1779	
Racehorse	10	Sloop	1776	
Royal Charlotte	10	Yacht	1749	
Sandwich	98	Ship	1759	Guardship
Suffolk	74	Ship	1765	
Sultan	74	Ship	1775	

Name	Guns	Type	Year Listed	Notes
St. Albans	64	Ship	1764	
Sampson	64	Ship	1781	
Sceptre	64	Ship	1781	
Scipio	64	Ship	1782	
Standard	64	Ship	1782	
Salisbury	50	Ship	1769	
Serapis	44	Frigate	1779	
Santa Leocadia	36	Frigate	1781	Spanish built
Santa Margarita	36	Frigate	1779	Spanish built
Southhampton	32	Frigate	1757	
Stag	32	Frigate	1776	
Success	32	Frigate	1781	
Syren	32	Frigate	1776	Charleston
Sybil	28	Frigate	1779	
Solebay	28	Frigate	1776	Charleston
Surprise	28	Frigate	1779	
Sandwich	20	Sloop-of-war	1776	
Scarborough	20	Sloop-of-war	1776	
Sphynx	20	Sloop-of-war	1775	Charleston
Savage	16	Sloop	1778	
Scourge	16	Sloop	1779	
Shark	16	Sloop	1780	
Swallow	16	Sloop	1781	
Swan	16	Sloop	1767	NAS
Sea Flower	16	Cutter	1782	
Scour	14	Sloop	1781	
Senegal	14	Sloop	1775	NAS
Speedy	14	Sloop	1782	
Spitfire	14	Frigate	1782	
Speedwell	14	Cutter	1780	
Sprightly	14	Cutter	1778	
Sultana	14	Cutter	1780	
Spider	12	Cutter	1782	French built
Savage	8	Cutter	1775	NAS

Name	Guns	Type	Year Listed	Notes
Triumph	74	Ship	1764	
Trident	64	Ship	1768	
Trusty	50	Ship	1782	
Thetis	38	Frigate	1782	
Thalis	36	Frigate	1782	
Tartar	28	Frigate	1756	NAS, 1776
Triton	28	Frigate	1773	
Trepassy	20	Sloop-of-war	1776	
Termagent	18	Sloop	1781	Spanish built
Thorn	16	Sloop	1776	NAS
Trimmer	16	Sloop	1782	French built
Tamer	14	Sloop	1775	NAS
Tisiphone	12	Sloop	1781	
Tryal	12	Cutter	1781	
Terror	8	Bomb vessel	1779	
Thunder	8	Bomb vessel	1776	Charleston
Union	90	Ship	1756	Hospital ship
Ulysses	44	Frigate	1779	
Unicorn	32	Frigate	1776	
Victory	100	Ship	1765	
Valiant	74	Ship	1759	
Vengeance	74	Ship	1774	
Volcano	64	Ship	1776	New York Guardship
Vigilant	64	Ship	1774	
Venus	32	Frigate	1758	
Vestal	32	Frigate	1776	
Vestal	28	Frigate	1779	
Victor	18	Sloop-of-war	1777	
Vulture	14	Sloop	1776	Stores vessel
Viper	14	Sloop	1780	
Vesuvius	8	Bomb vessel	1776	
Warrior	74	Ship	1781	
Warspite	74	Ship	1758	

Name	Guns	Type	Year Listed	Notes
Warwick	50	Ship	1767	
Winchelsea	32	Frigate	1764	
Wasp	16	Sloop	1782	
Weasel	16	Sloop	1776	
William & *Mary*	8	Yacht	1694	
Yarmouth	64	Ship	1754	
Zebra	16	Sloop	1780	

Maps

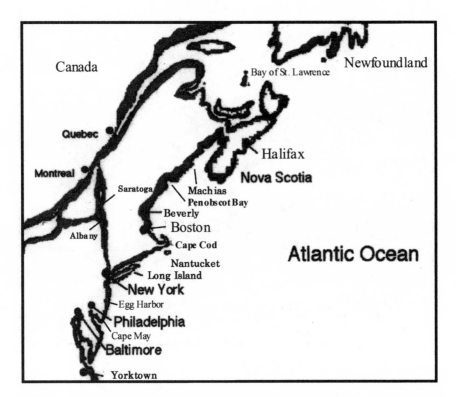

Map 1. The Atlantic Coast from the Virginia Capes to the Gulf of St. Lawrence.

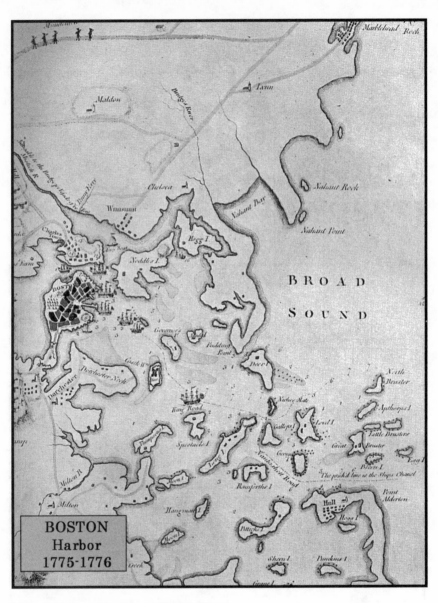

Map 2. Boston Harbor in 1775–1776.

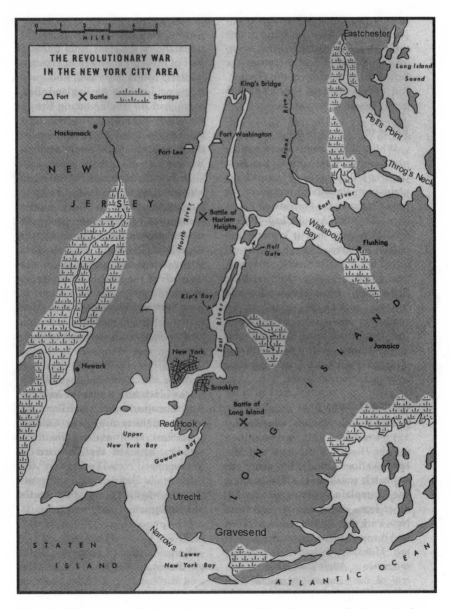

Map 3. This map of the region surrounding the city of New York in 1776 is from an early-twentieth-century textbook.

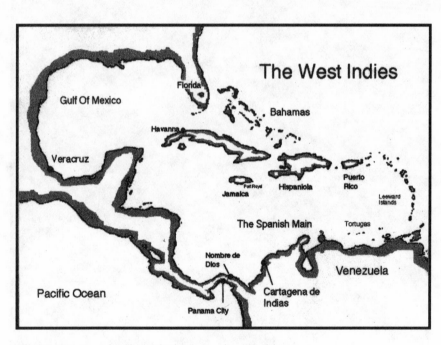

Map 4. Major islands and places in the Caribbean.

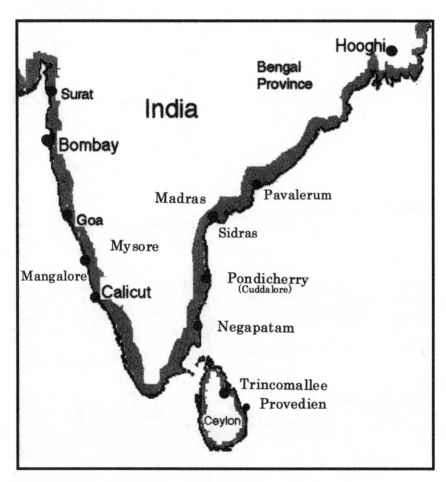

Map 5. Scenes of major naval battles.

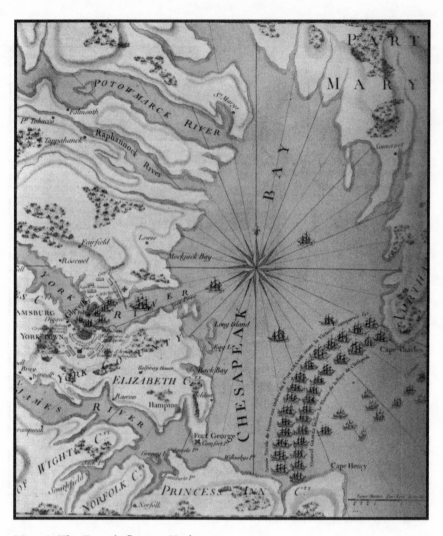

Map 6. The French fleet at Yorktown.

Notes

INTRODUCTION

1. See Dorothy Denneen Volo and James M. Volo, *Daily Life during the American Revolution* (Westport, CT: Greenwood Press, 2003); and Dorothy Denneen Volo and James M. Volo, *Daily Life in the Age of Sail* (Westport, CT: Greenwood Press, 2002).

2. Marjorie Hubbell Gibson, *HMS* Somerset, *1746–1778: The Life and Times of an Eighteenth-Century British Man-o'-War and Her Impact on North America* (Cotuit, MA: Abbey Gate House, 1992), 2.

3. Thomas Jefferson Wertenbaker, *Father Knickerbocker Rebels: New York City during the Revolution* (New York: Charles Scribner's Sons, 1948), 82.

4. Neil R. Stout, *The Royal Navy in America, 1760–1775* (Annapolis, MD: Naval Institute Press, 1973), 138.

5. Oliver M. Dickerson, *The Navigation Acts and the American Revolution* (New York: A. S. Barnes, 1963), 172–83, 295–300.

6. The "Child Independence" quotation is from Richard B. Morris, *The American Revolution Reconsidered* (Westport, CT: Greenwood Press, 1979), 17.

7. The term "cruise" was first applied in written records to the commerce-raiding voyages of private warships in 1651, and naval warships were first referred to as "cruisers" in written records in 1679.

8. Francis R. Stark, *The Abolition of Privateering and the Declaration of Paris* (New York: Columbia University Press, 1897), 121.

9. See William Bell Clark, *Ben Franklin's Navy: A Naval Epic of the American Revolution* (Westport, CT: Greenwood Press, 1969).

10. Arthur Bowler, *Logistics and the Failure of the British Army in America, 1775–1783* (Princeton: Princeton University Press, 1975), 53. Also see Robert W. Neeser, ed., *The Dispatches of Molyneux Shuldham, Vice Admiral of the Blue and Commander in Chief of His Britannic Majesty's Ships in North America: January–July 1776* (New York: Naval Society Publications, 1913).

11. See Richard Buel, Jr., *In Irons: Britain's Naval Supremacy and the American Revolutionary Economy* (New Haven: Yale University Press, 1998), 46–47.

12. Richard Buel, Jr., 113.

CHAPTER 1

1. Quoted in Neil R. Stout, *The Royal Navy in America, 1760–1775* (Annapolis, MD: Naval Institute Press, 1973), 82–83.

2. Quoted by Nathaniel Fanning, *The Memoirs of Nathaniel Fanning, an Officer of the American Navy, 1778–1783* (Bowie, MD: Heritage Books, 2003), 101.

3. John J. McCusker and Russell R. Menard, *The Economy of British America, 1607–1789* (Chapel Hill: University of North Carolina Press, 1991), 82.

4. Carroll Storrs Alden and Allan Westcott, *The United States Navy: A History* (New York: J. B. Lippincott, 1945), 5–6.

5. Simon Schama, *A History of Britain,* vol. 2, *The Wars of the British, 1603–1776* (New York: Hyperion, 2001), 409.

6. Simon Schama, 409.

7. Neil R. Stout, 44; see also the pioneering study of the enforcement crisis by Oliver M. Dickerson, *The Navigation Acts and the American Revolution* (New York: A. S. Barnes, 1963).

8. Neil R. Stout, 29.

9. Neil R. Stout, 53.

10. Samuel Eliot Morison, *Sources and Documents Illustrating the American Revolution, 1764–1788, and the Formation of the Federal Constitution* (New York: Oxford University Press, 1965), 77.

11. It should be noted that these expenses could be recovered from the officer making the seizure through the mechanism of a civil lawsuit for damages.

12. Neil R. Stout, 63.

13. Stanley Weintraub, *Iron Tears: America's Battle for Freedom, Britain's Quagmire, 1775–1783* (New York: Free Press, 2005), 4.

14. Reported by Neil R. Stout, 86.

15. Colvill was succeeded in 1767 by Joseph Deane (1766), Archibald Kennedy (1766–1767), Samuel Hood (1767–1770), James Gambier (1770–1771), John Montagu (1771–1774), and Samuel Graves (1774–1775). With the outbreak of war Graves was succeeded by Molyneux Shuldham (1775–1776), Richard Howe (1776–1778), James Gambier (1778–1779), Mariot Arbuthnot (1779–1781), Thomas Graves (1781), Samuel Hood (1781–1782).

16. Paul A. Gilje, *Liberty on the Waterfront: American Maritime Culture in the Age of Revolution* (Philadelphia: University of Pennsylvania Press, 2004), 99.

17. Paul A. Gilje, 99.

18. HMS *Coventry* was so chronically short of hands that it rarely left its anchorage, thereby limiting its effectiveness.

19. Quoted in Neil R. Stout, 82–83.
20. Quoted in Neil R. Stout, 80.
21. Neil R. Stout, 84.
22. Reported in Neil R. Stout, 70.
23. Neil R. Stout, 49.
24. James Truslow Adams and Charles Garrett Vannest, *The Record of America* (New York: Charles Scribner's Sons, 1935), 83.
25. In Dedham, Massachusetts, in 1765, on a petition to the government every man signed with his signature rather than using a mark attesting to the widespread literacy of the population.
26. James Truslow Adams and Charles Garrett Vannest, 111.
27. Quoting British Secretary of State Conway in a letter to General Gage dated December 15, 1765, found in Neil R. Stout, 99.
28. See Thomas Jefferson Wertenbaker, *Father Knickerbocker Rebels* (New York: Charles Scribner's Sons, 1948).
29. Roger Champagne, "The Military Association of the Sons of Liberty," *Narratives of the Revolution in New York* (New York: The New York Historical Society, 1975), 1–11.
30. Samuel Eliot Morison, 17.
31. Neil R. Stout, 103–4.
32. Charles A. Beard and Mary R. Beard, *The Rise of American Civilization* (New York: Macmillan, 1927), 216; also see John C. Millar, *Origins of the American Revolution* (Boston: Little, Brown, 1943), 244–46.
33. James Truslow Adams and Charles Garrett Vannest, 250.
34. Samuel Eliot Morison, 78.
35. Samuel Eliot Morison, 79.
36. Robert Carse, *The Seafarers: A History of Maritime America, 1620–1820* (New York: Harper & Row, 1964), 156.
37. Oliver M. Dickerson, 298.
38. Mark Kurlansky, *Cod: A Biography of the Fish that Changed the World* (New York: Penguin Books, 1997), 94.
39. Neil R. Stout, 30.
40. John C. Millar, 266–67. Richardson was arrested and found guilty of murder. He was pardoned by the king after spending two years in jail.
41. John C. Millar, 261.
42. John C. Millar, 261.
43. See Dorothy Denneen Volo and James M. Volo, *Daily Life in the Age of Sail* (Westport, CT: Greenwood Press, 2002), 266–67.
44. The expectation that the navy would not fire on colonial cities proved otherwise false. *Asia* opened a broadside on New York City in 1776, and a number of coastal towns underwent naval bombardment from Royal Navy warships during the course of the war. See Neil R. Stout, 117.
45. John C. Millar, 294–95.
46. Paul A. Gilje, 99.
47. A diary entry of December 29, 1772, quoted in Neil R. Stout, 155.
48. Quoted in Neil R. Stout, 155.
49. Quoted in Neil R. Stout, 141.

50. The spelling of the name of this vessel is given in various sources as *Gaspe'* and *Gaspee*. There was in 1775 a warship on station in Maine named *Gaspee* armed with six guns and a crew of thirty men, but this was not the cutter that was commanded by Lt. Dudingston in 1772. As *Gaspee* was the more common spelling of the name, the author has decided to use it.

51. John C. Millar, 267.

52. Claude Halstead Van Tyne, *The Loyalists in the American Revolution* (Ganesvoort, NY: Corner House Historical Publications, 1999), 11–12.

53. Claude Halstead Van Tyne, 23.

54. Claude Halstead Van Tyne, 23.

55. Besides Neil R. Stout and Oliver M. Dickerson, already cited, there were substantial studies by Edward Channing, "The American Board of Commissioner of the Customs," *Massachusetts Historical Society Proceedings*, 43 (1909–1910), 477–90; and Dora Mae Clark, "American Board of Custom." *American Historical Review*, 45 (1939–1940), 777–806.

56. Richard Buel, Jr., *In Irons: Britain's Naval Supremacy and the American Revolutionary Economy* (New Haven: Yale University Press, 1998), 32.

57. Neil R. Stout, v.

CHAPTER 2

1. Quoted in Theodore Roscoe and Fred Freeman, *Picture History of the U.S. Navy: From Old Navy to New, 1776–1897* (New York: Charles Scribner's Sons, 1956), 33–34.

2. Quoted in Theodore Roscoe and Fred Freeman, 33–34.

3. A spring is a rope placed on the anchor cable and run to the opposite quarter of the vessel. This creates a triangle of two ropes and the length of the ship. By hauling on the spring and shortening or lengthening one side of the triangle the broadside of the vessel can be turned in the desired direction relative to the fixed anchor.

4. Evidence given at the time conflicts as to the nature of the vessels involved. The cargo vessels may have been sloops, schooners, or one of each. *Unity* is described as a sloop after its conversion to a vessel of war. Two eyewitnesses, Jabez Cobb and Nathaniel Gregory, describe the *Margaretta* as a "schooner," while other evidence suggests it was a sloop-rigged cutter or tender. See William Bell Clark (ed.), *Naval Documents of the American Revolution*, Vol. 1 (Washington: U.S. Government Printing Office, 1964), 655 and 757.

5. In this case the author has decided to defer to the competent scholarship of John Fitzhugh Millar, *Early American Ships* (Williamsburg, VA: Thirteen Colonies Press, 1986), 157.

6. The unidentified British vessel was under command of Captain Loftres. See William Bell Clark, *Naval Documents*, 1122–23.

7. William Bell Clark, *George Washington's Navy: Being an Account of His Excellency's Fleet in New England Waters* (Baton Rouge: Louisiana State University Press, 1960), 63.

8. Quoted in Nathan Miller, *Sea of Glory: A Naval History of the American Revolution* (Annapolis, MD: Naval Institute Press, 1974), 28n. Thomas Graves'

career continued unabated, and he served as a commander under Nelson at the Battle of Copenhagen.

9. Quoted in Nathan Miller, 38.

10. See William Bell Clark, *George Washington's Navy.*

11. Nathan Miller, 72.

12. William Bell Clark, *George Washington's Navy*, 62–63.

13. The *London Chronicle*, December 30–January 2, 1776, as reported by William Bell Clark, *George Washington's Navy* , 61.

14. Arthur Bowler, *Logistics and the Failure of the British Army in America, 1775–1783* (Princeton: Princeton University Press, 1975), 53. Also see Robert W. Neeser ed., *The Dispatches of Molyneux Shuldham, Vice Admiral of the Blue and Commander in Chief of His Britannic Majesty's Ships in North America: January–July 1776* (New York: Naval Society Publications, 1913).

15. Gardner W. Allen, *A Naval History of the American Revolution*, Vol. I (Williamstown, MA: Corner House, 1970), 83–84.

16. Quoted in Stanley Weintraub, *Iron Tears: America's Battle for Freedom, Britain's Quagmire, 1775–1783* (New York: Free Press, 2005), 43.

17. Howard I. Chapelle, *The History of the American Sailing Navy: The Ships and Their Development* (New York: W. W. Norton, 1949), 53.

18. Howard I. Chapelle, 87.

19. Howard I. Chapelle, 87.

20. Francis R. Stark, *The Abolition of Privateering and the Declaration of Paris* (New York: Columbia University Press, 1897), 121.

21. Samuel W. Bryant, *The Sea and the States* (New York: Thomas Y. Crowell, 1967), 86.

22. Gerald S. Graham, *The Royal Navy in the War of American Independence* (London: Her Majesty's Stationery Office, 1976), 7–8.

23. Nathan Miller, 260.

24. Robert Carse, *The Seafarers: A History of Maritime America, 1620–1820* (New York: Harper & Row, 1964), 181.

25. Robert Carse, 175.

26. See James M. Volo, "The War at Sea," *Living History Journal* (January, 1987). Also see William Bell Clark, *Ben Franklin's Privateers: A Naval Epic of the American Revolution* (Westport, CT: Greenwood Press, 1969).

27. Nathan Miller, 261.

28. Robert Carse, 177.

29. Sometimes called the *Andrea Doria* in honor of the Italian freedom fighter.

30. Barbara W. Tuchman, *The First Salute: A View of the American Revolution* (New York: Alfred A. Knopf, 1988), 4–6.

CHAPTER 3

1. Gardner W. Allen, *A Naval History of the American Revolution*, Vol. I (Williamstown, MA: Corner House, 1970), 22.

2. Peter Force, ed., *American Archives* (Washington, DC: Self-published, 1840), 1354.

3. The Library of Congress lists nearly 1,700 known privateers and letters of marque carrying 15,000 guns and crewed by 59,000 seamen.

4. Samuel W. Bryant, *The Sea and the States* (New York: Thomas Y. Crowell, 1967), 86.

5. For more specific information on the vessels belonging to the state navies, see Chapters 1 and 2 in Paul H. Silverstone, *The Sailing Navy, 1775–1885* (Annapolis, MD: Naval Institute Press, 2001); and John Fitzhugh Millar, *Early American Ships* (Williamsburg, VA: Thirteen Colonies Press, 1986). The author has deferred to the expertise of these authorities in all cases where contradictory information seems to be available.

6. Paul H. Silverstone, 15

7. Richard Buel, Jr., *In Irons: Britain's Naval Supremacy and the American Revolutionary Economy* (New Haven: Yale University Press, 1998), 67–68. Near Charleston the soundings were more than 140 miles to the east.

8. John Fitzhugh Millar, 190–91.

9. See Paul H. Silverstone, 15; and John Fitzhugh Millar, 77.

10. Gardner W. Allen, 22.

11. Gardner W. Allen, 33.

12. George Athan Billias, *General John Glover and His Marblehead Mariners* (New York: Henry Holt, 1960), 29.

13. Chester A. Hearn, *George Washington's Schooners: The First American Navy* (Annapolis, MD: Naval Institute Press, 1995), 29.

14. See the Pilgrim Society Archives at http://www.pilgrimhall.org/sailingoff.htm.

15. Nathan Miller, *Sea of Glory: A Naval History of the American Revolution* (Charleston, SC: Nautical and Aviation Publishing, 1974), 49.

16. Nathan Miller, 46.

17. See Dorothy Denneen Volo and James M. Volo, *Daily Life during the American Revolution* (Westport, CT: Greenwood Press, 2003), 133–34.

18. Gardner W. Allen, 14.

19. Michael Lewis, *The History of the British Navy* (Fairlawn, NJ: Essential Books, 1959), 77–80.

20. Dorothy Denneen Volo and James M. Volo, *Daily Life in the Age of Sail* (Westport, CT: Greenwood Press, 2002), 103.

21. Gerald S. Graham, *The Royal Navy in the War of American Independence* (London: Her Majesty's Stationery Office, 1976), 5.

22. Stanley Weintraub, *Iron Tears: America's Battle for Freedom, Britain's Quagmire, 1775–1783* (New York: Free Press, 2005), 150.

23. Michael Lewis, 140–41.

24. Stanley Weintraub, 6.

25. Quoted in Gerald S. Graham, 22.

26. Nathan Miller, 331.

27. Gardner W. Allen, 57–58.

28. Thomas Jefferson Wertenbaker, *Father Knickerbocker Rebels* (New York: Charles Scribner's Sons, 1948), 163.

29. Maurice Ashley, *Louis XIV and the Greatness of France* (New York: Collier, 1962) 37–38.

30. Fred Anderson, *Crucible of War: The Seven Years' War and the Fate of Empire in British North America, 1754–1766* (New York: Alfred A. Knopf, 2000), 383.

31. Nathan Miller, 326.

32. Gerald S. Graham, 4.

CHAPTER 4

1. Gardner W. Allen, *A Naval History of the American Revolution*, Vol. I (Williamstown, MA: Corner House, 1970) 6.

2. Alfred Thayer Mahan, *The Influence of Sea Power Upon History, 1660–1783* (New York: Dover, 1987), 89.

3. Richard M. Ketcham, ed., *The American Heritage Book of the Revolution* (New York: American Heritage, 1958) 134. See also Theodore Roscoe and Fred Freeman, *Picture History of the U. S. Navy. From Old Navy to New, 1776–1897* (New York: Charles Scribner's Sons, 1956) 88–89.

4. Nathan Miller, *Sea of Glory: A Naval History of the American Revolution* (Charleston, SC: Nautical and Aviation Publishing, 1974), 226.

5. Gardner W. Allen, *Mahan on Naval Warfare: Selected from the Writings of Rear Admiral Alfred Thayer Mahan* (Boston: Little, Brown, 1919), 50.

6. William Bell Clark, *Captain Dauntless: The Story of Nicholas Biddle of the Continental Navy* (Baton Rouge: Louisiana State University Press, 1953), 71–72.

7. G. J. Marcus, *The Formative Years: A Naval History of England* (Boston: Little, Brown, 1961), 429.

8. Alfred Thayer Mahan, 80.

9. Quoted in Stanley Weintraub, *Iron Tears: America's Battle for Freedom, Britain's Quagmire, 1775–1783* (New York: Free Press, 2005), 164.

10. Gardner W. Allen, *A Naval History*, 19.

11. Nathan Miller, 330.

12. Quoted in Stanley Weintraub, 157.

13. Quoted in N. A. M. Rodger, *The Command of the Ocean: A Naval History of Britain, 1649–1815* (New York: W. W. Norton, 2004), 335.

14. Quoted in Stanley Weintraub, 201.

15. Nathan Miller, 345.

16. Stanley Weintraub, 105.

17. See Russell F. Weigley, *The Age of Battles: The Quest for Decisive Warfare from Breitenfeld to Waterloo* (Bloomington: Indiana University Press, 1991).

18. Nathan Miller, 134.

19. John Creswell, *British Admirals of the Eighteenth Century: Tactics in Battle* (Hamden, CT: Archon Books, 1972), 48. Also see Alfred Thayer Mahan, *The Influence of Sea Power Upon History, 1660–1783* (New York: Dover, 1987), 259.

20. See Ulane Bonnel, *The French Navy and the American War of Independence* (New York: Ambassade de France Service de Presse et d'Information, 1976). Available on-line at http://xenophongroup.com/mcjoynt/bonnel.htm.

21. N. A. M. Rodger, 347.

22. C. S. Forester, *The Age of Fighting Sail* (Sandwich, MA: Chapman Billies, 1956), 64; John Laffin, *Jack Tar: The Story of the British Sailor* (London: Cassell, 1969), 153–54.

23. David Davies, *Nelson's Navy: English Fighting Ships, 1793–1815* (Mechanicsburg, PA: Stackpole Books, 1996), 60.

24. C. S. Forester, 60.

25. Nathan Miller, *Sea of Glory: A Naval History of the American Revolution* (Charleston, SC: Nautical and Aviation Publishing, 1974), 276.

26. N. A. M. Rodger, 54–60.

27. John Keegan, *The Price of Admiralty: The Evolution of Naval Warfare* (New York: Viking Press, 1988), 6.

28. John Keegan, 6.

29. David Davies, 70.

30. John Creswell, 46.

31. John Creswell, 40.

32. David Davies, 67.

33. N. A. M. Rodger, 55.

CHAPTER 5

1. Gardner W. Allen, *A Naval History of the American Revolution*, Vol. I (Williamstown, MA: Corner House, 1970), 50.

2. Nathan Miller, *Sea of Glory: A Naval History of the American Revolution* (Annapolis, MD: Naval Institute Press, 1974), 56.

3. In what follows the place of each officer on the list will be given as an ordinal number, or marked as unlisted, in parentheses.

4. Samuel W. Bryant, *The Sea and States: A Maritime History of the American People* (New York: T. Y. Crowell, 1967), 78–79.

5. William Bell Clark, *Captain Dauntless: The Story of Nicholas Biddle of the Continental Navy* (Baton Rouge: Louisiana State University Press, 1953), 237.

6. Nathan Miller, 214.

7. Gardner W. Allen, 182.

8. William M. Fowler, Jr., *Rebels under Sail: The American Navy during the Revolution* (New York: Charles Scribner's Sons, 1976), 295n.

9. Nathan Miller, 118–19.

10. Quoting General Peleg Wadsworth in Chester. B. Kevitt, *General Solomon Lovell and the Penobscot Expedition, 1779* (Weymouth, MA: Weymouth Historical Society, 1976), 146.

11. Nathan Miller, 93.

12. See "Naval Service of Captain John Barry," Navy Office of Information, 1969, John Barry ZB file, box 12, Navy Department Library, Washington D.C.; and William Bell Clark, *Gallant John Barry, 1745–1803: The Story of a Naval Hero of Two Wars* (New York: Macmillan, 1938).

13. John Laffin, *Jack Tar: The Story of the British Sailor* (London: Cassell, 1969), 131.

14. Philip Haythornthwaite, *Nelson's Navy* (London: Osprey, 1993), 7.

15. N. A. M. Rodger, *The Command of the Ocean: A Naval History of Britain, 1649–1815* (New York: W. W. Norton, 2004), 129.

16. G. J. Marcus, *The Formative Centuries: A Naval History of England* (Boston: Little, Brown, 1961), 355.

17. Quoted in Stanley Weintraub, *Iron Tears: America's Battle for Freedom, Britain's Quagmire, 1775–1783* (New York: Free Press, 2005), 187.

18. See *The Commissioned Sea Officers of the Royal Navy, 1600–1815* (No author. London: Navy Records Society, 1994).

19. Nathan Miller, 408.

20. N. A. M. Rodger, 389.

21. Quoting John Blankett, Flag Lieutenant on *Victory* from N. A. M. Rodger, 337.

22. The *Belle Poule* built in 1768 should not be confused with the 1828 frigate of the same name that returned Napoleon's remains to France from the island of St. Helena.

23. Henry B. Culver, *Forty Famous Ships* (New York: Garden City, 1938), 134.

24. Nathan Miller, 393–94.

25. Nathan Miller, 393–94.

CHAPTER 6

1. Nathan Miller, *Sea of Glory: A Naval History of the American Revolution* (Annapolis, MD: Naval Institute Press, 1974), 56.

2. See Nathan Miller, 84–99.

3. Nathan Miller, 93–94.

4. Barbara W. Tuchman, *The First Salute: A View of the American Revolution* (New York: Alfred A. Knopf, 1988), 47.

5. Nathan Miller, 93.

6. William M. Fowler, Jr., *Rebels under Sail: The American Navy during the Revolution* (New York: Charles Scribner's Sons, 1976), 92.

7. While this is celebrated as the birth of the U.S. Marines, American colonials had made amphibious landings during the French Wars—in particular the landing at Louisburg under William Pepperell during the War of Austrian Succession.

8. Nathan Miller, 115.

9. Nathan Miller, 217.

10. Howard I. Chapelle, *The History of the American Sailing Navy* (New York: W. W. Norton, 1949), 73.

11. Richard Buel, Jr., *In Irons: Britain's Naval Supremacy and the American Revolutionary Economy* (New Haven: Yale University Press, 1998), 89.

12. J. Lawrence Pool, *Fighting Ships of the Revolution on Long Island Sound, 1775–1783* (Torrington, CT: privately printed, 1990), 74.

CHAPTER 7

1. Paraphrasing a letter from Robert Morris to Captain Nicholas Biddle in December 1776.

2. John Creswell, *British Admirals of the Eighteenth Century* (London: Anchor Books, 1972), 15–16.

3. See David Wells, *Our Merchant Marine: How It Rose, Increased, Became Great, Declined, and Decayed* (New York: G.P. Putnam's Sons, 1890), 15–16. Shipbuilding in the colonial American South is often ignored; however, some of the best designs for eighteenth-century vessels developed in the Chesapeake Bay area of Maryland and Virginia.

4. The author has attempted to be consistent in the forms that are used. However, prime sources such as journals, diaries, and traditional reference works—worthy of citation—may use slightly different methods to convey this information. The author has decided to leave such material in the form found in the original works.

5. William Hutchinson Rowe, *The Maritime History of Maine: Three Centuries of Shipbuilding and Seafaring* (Freeport, ME: Bond Wheelwright, n.d.), 39.

6. Charles Nordhoff, *Sailor Life on Man-of War and Merchant Vessel* (New York: Dodd, Mead, 1884), 66.

7. Howard I. Chapelle, *The History of the American Sailing Navy: The Ships and Their Development* (New York: W. W. Norton, 1949), 84–85.

8. American live oak from the Southern colonies was not considered as a marine raw material until used by the U.S. Navy. The USS *Constitution*, "Old Ironsides," had a keel of white oak from New Jersey, timbers of live oak and red cedar from Georgia, and white pine masts and spars from Maine. See Frances D. Robotti and James Vescovi, *The USS Essex* (Holbrook, MA: Adams Media, 1999), xvii.

9. In 1804 the Admiralty built and launched seven 32-gun fir-built frigates in less than five months. In 1805 an additional five were built. See Nicholas Blake and Richard Lawrence, *The Illustrated Companion to Nelson's Navy* (Mechanicsburg, PA: Stackpole Books, 2000), 31–35.

10. William Hutchinson Rowe, 135–36.

11. Richard Buel, Jr., *In Irons: Britain's Naval Supremacy and the American Revolutionary Economy* (New Haven: Yale University Press, 1998), 94.

12. Modern ship displacement does not use this system.

13. Charles Nordhoff, 58–66.

14. Try drawing a simple diagram of a three-masted ship with four sails on each mast.

15. It is not the purpose of this work to give the reader a complete knowledge of the hundreds of terms and their derivations which can be found in this topic. However, a diligent person can expect to gain a layman's knowledge about the most characteristic sailing vessels after carefully reading these sections and referring to the accompanying illustrations.

16. Tom McGregor, *The Making of C. S. Forester's Horatio Hornblower* (New York: Harper-Collins, 1999), 60.

17. Charles G. Davis, *American Sailing Ships: Their Plans and History* (New York: Dover, 1984), 44.

18. Howard I. Chapelle, 16.

19. Recorded in N. A. M. Roger, *The Command of the Ocean: A Naval History of Britain, 1649–1815* (New York: W. W. Norton, 2005), 608. See Jan Glete, *Navies and Nations: Warships, Navies, and State Building in Europe and America, 1500–1860* (Stockholm, Sweden, 1993).

20. Gerald S. Graham, *The Royal Navy in the War of American Independence* (London: Her Majesty's Stationery Office, 1976), 7.

21. Ulane Bonnel, *The French Navy and the American War of Independence* (New York: Ambassade de France Service de Presse et d'Information, 1976), 4. Available on-line at http://xenophongroup.com/mcjoynt/bonnel.htm.

22. Nathan Miller, 326. See also Gerald S. Graham, 4.

23. Howard I. Chapelle, 10.

24. Theodore Roscoe and Fred Freeman, *Picture History of the U.S. Navy: From Old Navy to New, 1776 to 1897* (New York: Charles Scribner's Sons, 1956), 71.

25. Marjorie Hubbell Gibson, *HMS Somerset, 1746–1778: The Life and Times of an Eighteenth-Century British Man-o'-War and Her Impact on North America* (Cotuit, MA: Abbey Gate House, 1992), ix.

26. Howard I. Chapelle, 64.

27. G. J. Marcus, *Heart of Oak: A Survey of British Sea Power in the Georgian Era* (London: Oxford University Press, 1975), 342–43.

28. Admiral Sir George Anson quoted in G. J. Marcus, 342–43.

29. Theodore Roscoe and Fred Freeman, 72.

30. Howard I. Chapelle, 30.

31. Theodore Roscoe and Fred Freeman, 73. Howard I. Chapelle, 30.

32. Howard I. Chapelle, 102.

33. Neil R. Stout, 129.

34. Howard I. Chapelle, 28.

35. Nicholas Blake and Richard Lawrence, 44–47.

36. John G. Rogers, *Origin of Sea Terms* (Mystic, CT: Mystic Seaport Museum, 1985), 19.

37. See Paul H. Silverstone, *The Sailing Navy, 1775–1854* (Annapolis, MD: Naval Institute Press, 2001), Chapter 1.

38. Howard I. Chapelle, 57–58.

39. John Fitzhugh Millar, *Early American Ships* (Williamsburg, VA: Thirteen Colonies Press, 1986) 146.

40. Howard I. Chapelle, 61.

41. Howard I Chapelle, 59.

42. John Fitzhugh Millar, 150.

43. Quoted in Howard I. Chapelle, 72.

44. William Bell Clark, *Captain Dauntless: The Story of Nicholas Biddle of the Continental Navy* (Baton Rouge: Louisiana State University Press, 1953), 171.

45. Quoted in Howard I. Chapelle, 77.

CHAPTER 8

1. John Creswell, *British Admirals of the Eighteenth Century* (London: Anchor Books, 1972), 93.

2. G. J. Marcus, *The Formative Years: A Naval History of England* (Boston: Little, Brown, 1961), 348.

3. John Creswell, 23; Nicholas Blake and Richard Lawrence, *The Illustrated Companion to Nelson's Navy* (Mechanicsburg, PA: Stackpole Books, 2000), 30; James M. Volo, "The War at Sea," *Living History Journal* (January, 1987), 3.

4. See Adam Ward Rome, *Connecticut's Cannon: The Salisbury Furnace in the American Revolution* (Hartford: American Revolution Bicentennial Commission of Connecticut, 1977); and Robert B. Gordon, *A Landscape Transformed: The Ironmaking District of Salisbury, Connecticut* (New York: Oxford University Press, 2000).

5. See James A. Dibert, *Iron, Independence, and Inheritance: The Story of Curttis and Peter Grubb* (Cornwall, PA: Cornwall Iron Furnace Associates, Inc., 2000), 38.

6. The 32 pounders cast for the frigates of the Federalist Era navy such as "Old Ironsides" (USS *Constitution*) were made at Salisbury Furnace. See Howard I. Chapelle, *The History of the American Sailing Navy* (New York: W.W. Norton, 1949), 91–93.

7. James A. Dibert, 39.

8. Erna Risch, *Supplying Washington's Army* (Washington, DC: United States Army Center of Military Studies, 1981), 359–62. This work will provide most students with an exhaustive study of the development of the Quartermaster's Department.

9. Dorothy Denneen Volo and James M. Volo, *Daily Life during the American Revolution* (Westport, CT: Greenwood Press, 2003), 222.

10. Dorothy Denneen Volo and James M. Volo, 62.

11. Quoted in George Athan Billias, *General John Glover and His Marblehead Mariners* (New York: Henry Holt, 1960), 93.

12. Chester A Hearn, *George Washington's Schooners: The First American Navy* (Annapolis, MD: Naval Institute Press, 1995), 55.

13. Nathan Miller, *Sea of Glory: A Naval History of the American Revolution* (Annapolis, MD: Naval Institute Press, 1974), 75.

14. John Muller, *A Treatise of Artillery* (London: n.p., 1780), 97.

15. The shipment was aboard *L'Amphitrite*, which landed its cargo in Portsmouth, New Hampshire, in April.

16. Thereafter the incredibly short carronade became popular, and many new naval guns were made shorter to facilitate loading.

17. John Muller, xviii.

18. James M. Volo, "The Acquisition and Use of Warlike Stores during the American Revolution, Part II." *Living History Journal* No. 15 (Fall, 1986), 10–13.

19. Erna Risch, 358.

20. Quoted in Stanley Weintraub, *Iron Tears: America's Battle for Freedom, Britain's Quagmire, 1775–1783* (New York: Free Press, 2005), 49. Also see Erna Risch, 344–45.

21. Erna Risch, 345.

22. Erna Risch, 345.

CHAPTER 9

1. Quoted in Chester A. Hearn, *George Washington's Schooner: The First American Navy* (Annapolis, MD: Naval Institute Press, 1995), 107.

2. William Bell Clark, ed., *Naval Documents of the American Revolution,* Vol. 1 (Washington, DC: U.S. Government Printing Office, 1964), 1120.

3. Quoted in Chester A. Hearn, 107.

4. Chester A. Hearn, 106.

5. William Bell Clark, ed., *Naval Documents,* 257–58.

6. William Bell Clark, *George Washington's Navy* (Baton Rouge: Louisiana State University Press, 1960), 63.

7. William P. Cumming and Hugh Rankin, eds., *The Fate of a Nation: The American Revolution through Contemporary Eyes* (London: Phaidon Press, 1975), 49.

8. William Bell Clark, *George Washington's Navy*, 3.

9. The variety of spellings found in eighteenth century documents is truly remarkable. This includes various spellings of proper names, sometimes in the same document. As examples, Broughton is sometimes found without the "r," and Manly is sometimes written with an "ley." The author has chosen to use the most common of these variations unless quoting a primary source and to standardize other spelling variations found in the secondary sources used herein.

10. The *London Chronicle*, December–January 2, 1776, as reported by William Bell Clark, *George Washington's Navy*, 61.

11. Chester A. Hearn, 238.

12. An American prize court was located at Norwalk, Connecticut. During a major amphibious attack by Loyalist forces in 1779 many of the town records were burned—among them the court's papers—almost completely erasing the existence of this prize court from written maritime history.

13. Quoted in Chester A. Hearn, 106.

14. Quoted in Stanley Weintraub, *Iron Tears: America's Battle for Freedom, Britain's Quagmire, 1775–1783* (New York: Free Press, 2005), 75.

15. Arthur Bowler, *Logistics and the Failure of the British Army in America, 1775–1783* (Princeton: Princeton University Press, 1975), 53. Also see Robert W. Neeser ed., *The Dispatches of Molyneux Shuldham, Vice Admiral of the Blue and Commander in Chief of His Britannic Majesty's Ships in North America: January–July 1776* (New York: Naval Society Publications, 1913).

16. John Sewall quoted in Chester A. Hearn, 108.

17. William Bell Clark, *George Washington's Navy*, 62–63.

18. Hearn incorrectly states, "[H]eadquarters believed enemy transports would stop at Halifax before continuing on to Boston. None of them did...."

19. Gardner W. Allen, *A Naval History of the American Revolution*, Vol. I (Williamstown, MA: Corner House, 1970), 83–84.

20. Nathan Miller, *Sea of Glory: A Naval History of the American Revolution* (Charleston, SC: Nautical and Aviation Publishing, 1974), 67.

21. William Bell Clark, *George Washington's Navy*, 6–7.

22. At this time Bromedge was listed in admiralty documents as a master, but by 1778 he had been made post-captain.

23. William Bell Clark, *George Washington's Navy*, 21.

24. Russell W. Knight, "'Headers in Life and Legend," *Marblehead Magazine*, 22: 1–11. Available online at http://www.legendinc.com/Pages/MarbleheadNet/MM/Headers/Headers22.html.

25. Chester A. Hearn, 56.

26. Chester A. Hearn, 56.

27. Chester A. Hearn, 53.

28. Chester A. Hearn, 55–56.

29. Nathan Miller, 72.

30. *Jenny, Little Hannah, Sally* (i), *Betsey, Polly* (i), *Concord*, and *Nancy* were all condemned in mid April at Ipswich, Massachusetts; *Polly* (ii), *Industry, Happy Return, Norfolk, Sally* (ii), and an unnamed schooner were condemned shortly thereafter at Plymouth; and five more prizes including *Henry and Ester, Susannah, Elizabeth*, and the cargo from *Stakesby* were still awaiting action on May 20.

31. Chester G. Hearn, 158.

32. William Bell Clark, *George Washington's Navy*, 228.

33. See John H. Sheppard, *Life of Commodore Samuel Tucker* (Boston: n.p., 1868).

34. Gardner W. Allen, 87.

35. Newspaper sources suggested that he may have been shot through the body with a musketball.

36. Gardner W. Allen, 87.

37. John Skimmer was killed in battle later in the war.

CHAPTER 10

1. Douglas Southall Freeman, *George Washington: A Biography* (New York: Scribner's, 1954), Vol. 4: 127.

2. The City of New York was not incorporated until the nineteenth century. Contemporaries called it New York town to discriminate between the city and the colony as a whole.

3. Simon Schama, *The Embarrassment of Riches: An Interpretation of Dutch Culture in the Golden Age* (New York: Vintage Books, 1997), 76.

4. Quoted in Barnet Schecter, *The Battle for New York: The City at the Heart of the American Revolution* (New York: Penguin Books, 2002), 74.

5. Thomas Jefferson Wertenbaker, *Father Knickerbocker Rebels: New York during the Revolution* (New York: Charles Scribner's Sons, 1948), 69.

6. Barnet Schecter, 67.

7. Quoted in Thomas Jefferson Wertenbaker, 78.

8. The last three galleys are identified by name without further information by Bruce Blivens, Jr., *Under the Guns: New York, 1775–1776* (New York: Harper and Row, 1972), 237.

9. Bruce Blivens, Jr., 239.

10. Bruce Blivens, Jr., 250.

11. Douglas Southall Freeman, Vol. 4: 127.

12. Quoted in Thomas Jefferson Wertenbaker, 88.

13. J. Lawrence Pool, *Fighting Ships of the Revolution on Long Island Sound, 1775–1783* (Torrington, CT: Rainbow Press, 1990), 6. Pool states that the fleet contained 52 warships and 470 transports, but he does not provide a documentary source for his numbers. The author has followed the more convincing estimates of Gerard S. Graham, *The Royal Navy in the War of American Independence* (London: Her Majesty's Stationery Office, 1976), 8.

14. Quoted in Thomas Jefferson Wertenbaker, 88.

15. Barnet Schecter, 111.

16. Thomas Jefferson Wertenbaker, 89.

17. Thomas Jefferson Wertenbaker, 72.

18. George Athan Billias, *General John Glover and His Marblehead Mariners* (New York: Henry Holt and Company, 1960), 97.

19. Barnet Schecter, 98.

20. Barnet Schecter, 113.

21. John Charles Phillip Von Krafft, *Journal of Lieutenant Von Krafft* (New York: Arno Press, 1968), 103.

22. Thomas Jefferson Wertenbaker, 89.

23. William Bell Clark, ed., *Naval Documents of the American Revolution*, Vol. 5 (Washington, DC: U.S. Government Printing Office, 1964), 805.

24. Gardner W. Allen, 87

25. Gardner W. Allen, 88.

26. Gardner W. Allen, 88.

27. Reported in Thomas Jefferson Wertenbaker, 89.

28. Quoted in Barnet Schecter, 126–27.

29. Quoted in Brendan Morrissey, *Boston 1775: The Shot Heard Around the World* (London: Osprey Publishing, 1995), 22.

30. William P. Cumming and Hugh Rankin, eds., *The Fate of a Nation: The American Revolution through Contemporary Eyes* (London: Phaidon Press, 1975), 106.

31. William P. Cumming and Hugh Rankin, 110–11.

32. William P. Cumming and Hugh Rankin, 110.

33. Quoted in Barnet Schecter, 166–67.

34. Thomas Jefferson Wertenbaker, 79.

35. The American lines ran along rising ground overlooking the present W. 125th street. Visitors to the uptown campus of the City College of New York can view the amazing drop from Morningside Terrace into the park below running between W. 129th and W. 141st streets. Tactically the position is all but impregnable to assault.

36. Quoted in George Athan Billias, 112. General Washington wrote to Congress on October 12 noting "the great number of sloops, schooners, and *nine* ships ... full of men."

37. Barnet Schecter, 222.

38. Barnet Schecter, 222.

39. Barnet Schecter, 222.

40. George A. Billias, "Pelham Bay: A Forgotten Battle," *Narratives of the Revolution in New York* (New York: The New York Historical Society, 1975), 105–19.

41. George A. Billias, 105–19.

42. George A. Billias, 116.

43. George A. Billias, 119.

44. George A. Billias, 119.

45. A model of *Turtle* built in 1976 from Bushnell's plans as a Bicentennial project functioned as intended confirming the ingenuity of its inventors. It can be viewed at the Connecticut River Museum in Essex, Connecticut.

CHAPTER 11

1. Erna Risch, *Supplying Washington's Army* (Washington, DC: United States Army Center of Military Studies, 1981), 138. Lt. John Twiss of the Royal Engineers, who appears later in this chapter, is said to have devised a landing craft with a drop front ramp very much like those used in World War II. However, they do not seem to have been adopted by the Royal Navy at this time.

2. PT (Patrol Torpedo); PBR (Patrol Boat, River).

3. Peter Force, ed., *American Archives* (Washington, DC: Self-published, 1840), 436.

4. J. Lawrence Pool, *Fighting Ships of the Revolution on Long Island Sound, 1775–1783* (Torrington, CT: privately printed, 1990), 37.

5. John T. Hayes, *Connecticut's Revolutionary Cavalry: Sheldon's Horse* (Chester, CT: Pequot, 1775), 32. This book is part of the series of excellent monographs produced for the Bicentennial of the American Revolution.

6. John T. Hayes, 51–52.

7. John T. Hayes, 64.

8. North Callahan, *Royal Raiders: The Tories of the American Revolution* (New York: Bobbs-Merrill,1963), 77.

9. James Kirby Martin, *Benedict Arnold, Revolutionary Hero: An American Warrior Reconsidered* (New York: New York University Press, 1997), 10 and 2.

10. These were Crown Point (with both a British and French fort), Fort Carillon at Ticonderoga, Fort Independence, Fort Edward, Fort Ann, and Fort William Henry.

11. The title of this book really refers to seawater, which appears blue. Lake water appears green, and some purists might find the inclusion of the Lake Champlain fleet in this work unusual. Yet due to the importance of the role that it played in the outcome of the war, the author could not omit the lake navy from this study.

12. For a first-person account of the battle see Horatio Rogers, ed., *Hadden's Journal and Orderly Books: A Journal Kept in Canada and Upon Burgoyne's Campaign in 1776 and 1777, by Lieut. James M. Hadden, Roy. Art.* (Albany, NY: Joel Munsell's Sons, 1884).

13. Quoted in Nathan Miller, 179.

14. Erna Risch, 132.

CHAPTER 12

1. Nathan Miller, *Sea of Glory: A Naval History of the American Revolution* (Charleston, SC: Nautical and Aviation Publishing, 1974), 128.

2. Nathan Miller, 128.

3. Reported by Nathaniel Fanning, *The Memoirs of Nathaniel Fanning, an Officer of the American Navy, 1778–1783* (Bowie, MD: Heritage Books, 2003), 99.

4. Nathan Miller, 365–66.

5. Nathan Miller, 369–70.

6. Miller points out that it was much earlier in the battle than is normally thought that this famous phrase was uttered.

7. Nathaniel Fanning, 50.
8. Nathan Miller, 384–85.
9. Nathaniel Fanning, 48.
10. See Dorothy Denneen Volo and James M. Volo, *Daily Life in the Age of Sail* (Westport, CT: Greenwood Press, 2002), 265–81.
11. Nathaniel Fanning, 9–10.
12. Nathaniel Fanning, 13.
13. Nathaniel Fanning, 64.
14. Nathaniel Fanning, 162.
15. Nathaniel Fanning, 173n.
16. Nathaniel Fanning, 179–80. For clothing details, see Dorothy Denneen Volo and James M. Volo, p. 93–117.
17. Nathan Miller, 373–74.
18. Nathaniel Fanning, 165.
19. Nathaniel Fanning, 184.

CHAPTER 13

1. Quoted in G. J. Marcus, *The Formative Centuries: A Naval History of England* (Boston: Little, Brown, 1961), 413.
2. Johnathan R. Dull, *The French Navy and American Independence: A Study of Arms and Diplomacy, 1774–1787* (Princeton: Princeton University Press, 1975), 33.
3. Unfortunately, a large number of its trading vessels fell prey to British cruisers in 1778 (and again in 1779), forcing the company into bankruptcy. Ironically, Basmarein was forced to flee to England to escape his creditors.
4. Johnathan R. Dull, 118–20.
5. Johnathan R. Dull, 139. Gibraltar is named for the eighth-century Moorish leader known as Jabal Tariq, who invaded Spain in A.D. 711.
6. Alfred Thayer Mahan, *The Influence of Sea Power Upon History, 1660–1805* (Englewood Cliffs, NJ: Prentice Hall, 1980), 198.
7. Michael Lewis, *The History of the British Navy* (Fairlawn, NJ: Essential Books, 1959), 140–41.
8. Johnathan R. Dull, 105.
9. Johnathan R. Dull, 263.
10. For a wider discussion of naval strategy in this regard, see Johnathan R. Dull, 188–225.
11. Gerald S. Graham, *The Royal Navy in the War of American Independence* (London: Her Majesty's Stationery Office, 1976), 13.
12. Johnathan R. Dull, 239.
13. De Ternay had died in Newport in December 1780. Commodore Charles Rene Destouches replaced him.
14. Michael Lewis, 145.
15. Dorothy Denneen Volo and James M. Volo, *Daily Life in the Age of Sail* (Westport, CT: Greenwood Press, 2002), 214–15.
16. The author was amazed when visiting St. Kitts for the first time that the Dutch island was so close by and clearly visible from the fort.

17. Among those killed was the man who developed the signal codes for the French, Captain du Pavillon, who was serving aboard the *Triomphant,* the flagship of Vice Admiral Marquis de Vaudreuil. The French code, like the British, was employed to great advantage throughout the American war.

18. Johnathan R. Dull, 239.

19. Richard B. Morris and James Woodress, eds., *Voices from America's Past: The Times That Tried Men's Souls, 1770–1783* (New York: McGraw-Hill, 1961), 56.

20. Richard B. Morris and James Woodress, 56.

21. Nathaniel Fanning, *The Memoirs of Nathaniel Fanning, an Officer of the American Navy, 1778–1783* (Bowie, MD: Heritage Books, 2003), 228–29.

22. Nathaniel Fanning, 228–29.

23. Johnathan R. Dull, 11.

24. Johnathan R. Dull, 228.

CHAPTER 14

1. Frank Moore, *Documentary Account of the American Revolution* (New York: Columbia University Press, undated), 1:194. See also Danske Dandridge, *American Prisoners of the Revolution* (Baltimore: Genealogical Publishing, 1911).

2. Thomas J. Wertenbaker, *Father Knickerbocker Rebels* (New York: Scribner's, 1948), 163.

3. Larry Bowman, *Captive Americans: Prisoners during the American Revolution* (Athens: Ohio University Press, 1976), 54.

4. Frank Moore, 329.

5. John Fiske, *The American Revolution,* 2 Vol. (New York: Houghton, Mifflin, 1896), 2:3.

6. Larry Bowman, 3.

7. Edmund Burke, *Speeches on Conciliation with America* (Boston: Ginn, 1897), 34.

8. Russell F. Weigley, *The Age of Battles: The Quest for Decisive Warfare from Breitenfeld to Waterloo* (Bloomington: Indiana University Press, 1991), 211.

9. Edward Hale, *Franklin in France* (Boston: Roberts, 1887), 195.

10. Russell F. Weigley, 211.

11. William M. Fowler, Jr., *Rebels under Sail: The American Navy during the Revolution* (New York: Scribner's, 1976), 257.

12. Geoffrey Regan, *Snafu* (New York: Avon Books, 1993), 25.

13. Don Higginbotham, *The War of American Independence: Military Attitudes, Policies, and Practice, 1763–1789* (Boston: Northeastern University Press, 1983), 198.

14. Thomas J. Wertenbaker, 153–54.

15. Larry Bowman, 129–30.

16. Edmund Burke, 33–34.

17. Thomas J. Wertenbaker, 163.

18. Richard M. Ketchum, "New War Letters of Banastre Tarleton—Edited." *Narratives of the Revolution in New York* (New York: Kingsport Press, 1975), 180.

CHAPTER 15

1. Alfred Thayer Mahan, *The Influence of Sea Power Upon History, 1660–1783* (New York: Dover Publications, 1987), 209.

2. Stanley Weintraub, *Iron Tears: America's Battle for Freedom, Britain's Quagmire, 1775–1783* (New York: Free Press, 2005), 128.

3. Johnathan R. Dull, *The French Navy and American Independence: A Study of Arms and Diplomacy, 1774–1787* (Princeton: Princeton University Press, 1975), 105.

4. Johnathan R. Dull, 239.

5. Michael Lewis, *The History of the British Navy* (Fairlawn, NJ: Essential Books, 1959), 145.

6. Johnathan R. Dull, 273.

7. Gerald S. Graham, *The Royal Navy in the War of American Independence* (London: Her Majesty's Stationery Office, 1976), 14.

8. Johnathan R. Dull, 294–344.

9. Claude Halstead Van Tyne, *The Loyalists in the American Revolution* (Ganesvoort, NY: Corner House Historical Publications, 1999), 182.

Selected Bibliography

Allen, Gardner W. *A Naval History of the American Revolution.* Williamstown, MA: Corner House, 1970.

Bowler, Arthur. *Logistics and the Failure of the British Army in America, 1775–1783.* Princeton: Princeton University Press, 1975.

Bowman, Larry. *Captive Americans: Prisoners during the American Revolution.* Athens: Ohio University Press, 1976.

Buel, Richard, Jr. *In Irons: Britain's Naval Supremacy and the American Revolutionary Economy.* New Haven: Yale University Press, 1998.

Callahan, North. *Royal Raiders: The Tories of the American Revolution.* New York: Bobbs-Merrill, 1963.

Chapelle, Howard I. *The History of the American Sailing Navy: The Ships and Their Development.* New York: W. W. Norton, 1949.

Clark, William Bell. *Ben Franklin's Privateers: A Naval Epic of the American Revolution.* Westport, CT: Greenwood Press, 1969.

———. *Captain Dauntless: The Story of Nicholas Biddle of the Continental Navy.* Baton Rouge: Louisiana State University Press, 1953.

———. *George Washington's Navy: Being an Account of His Excellency's Fleet in New England Waters.* Baton Rouge: Louisiana State University Press, 1960.

———, ed. *Naval Documents of the American Revolution.* Washington, DC: U.S. Government Printing Office, 1964.

Creswell, John. *British Admirals of the Eighteenth Century: Tactics in Battle.* Hamden, CT: Archon Books, 1972.

Davis, Charles G. *American Sailing Ships: Their Plans and History.* New York: Dover Publications, 1984.

Dickerson, Oliver M. *The Navigation Acts and the American Revolution.* New York: A. S. Barnes, 1963.

Dull, Johnathan. *The French Navy and American Independence: A Study of Arms and Diplomacy, 1774–1787.* Princeton: Princeton University Press, 1975.

Fanning, Nathaniel. *The Memoirs of Nathaniel Fanning, an Officer of the American Navy, 1778–1783.* Bowie, MD: Heritage Books, 2003.

Forester, C. S. *The Age of Fighting Sail.* Sandwich, MA: Chapman Billies, 1956.

Fowler, William M., Jr. *Rebels under Sail: The American Navy during the Revolution.* New York: Charles Scribner's Sons, 1976.

Gibson, Marjorie Hubbell. *HMS Somerset, 1746–1778: The Life and Times of an Eighteenth-Century British Man-o'-War and Her Impact on North America.* Cotuit, MA: Abbey Gate House, 1992.

Graham, Gerald S. *The Royal Navy in the War of American Independence.* London: Her Majesty's Stationery Office, 1976.

Hearn, Chester A. *George Washington's Schooners: The First American Navy.* Annapolis, MD: Naval Institute Press, 1995.

Mahan, Alfred Thayer. *The Influence of Sea Power Upon History, 1660–1783.* New York: Dover Publications, 1987.

McCusker, John J., and Russell R. Menard. *The Economy of British America, 1607–1789.* Chapel Hill: University of North Carolina Press, 1991.

Millar, John Fitzhugh. *Early American Ships.* Williamsburg, VA: Thirteen Colonies Press, 1986.

Miller, Nathan. *Sea of Glory: A Naval History of the American Revolution.* Annapolis, MD: Naval Institute Press, 1974.

Morison, Samuel Eliot. *Sources and Documents Illustrating the American Revolution, 1764–1788, and the Formation of the Federal Constitution.* New York: Oxford University Press, 1965.

Risch, Erna. *Supplying Washington's Army.* Washington, DC: U.S. Army Center of Military Studies, 1981.

Rodger, N. A. M. *The Command of the Ocean: A Naval History of Britain, 1649–1815.* New York: W. W. Norton, 2004.

Silverstone, Paul H. *The Sailing Navy, 1775–1885.* Annapolis, MD: Naval Institute Press, 2001.

Stark, Francis R. *The Abolition of Privateering and the Declaration of Paris.* New York: Columbia University Press, 1897.

Stout, Neil R. *The Royal Navy in America, 1760–1775.* Annapolis, MD: Naval Institute Press, 1973.

Tuchman, Barbara W. *The First Salute: A View of the American Revolution.* New York: Alfred A. Knopf, 1988.

Van Tyne, Claude Halstead. *The Loyalists in the American Revolution.* Ganesvoort, NY: Corner House Historical Publications, 1999.

Volo, Dorothy Denneen, and James M. Volo. *Daily Life during the American Revolution.* Westport, CT: Greenwood Press, 2003.

———. *Daily Life in the Age of Sail.* Westport, CT: Greenwood Press, 2002.

Weintraub, Stanley. *Iron Tears: America's Battle for Freedom, Britain's Quagmire, 1775–1783.* New York: Free Press, 2005.

Credits

p. 4: Unknown ephemera, author's collection.

p. 14: "Smugglers," painted by George Moreland (1792). Print in author's collection.

p. 17: Unknown ephemera, author's collection.

p. 19: "The Bostonians paying the excise-man or tarring and feathering," by D. C. Johnston from a print published in London 1774, Library of Congress. Print in author's collection.

p. 23: "A Naval Brigantine in a Calm Sea," painted by John Celeley (1752).

p. 34: "Boston Tea Party," Currier and Ives. Print in author's collection.

p. 36: Author's table.

p. 40: Unknown ephemera, author's collection.

p. 44: Author's table.

p. 68: Unknown ephemera, author's collection.

p. 81: "The *Victory* Raking the Spanish *Salvador del Mundo* at the Battle of Cape St. Vincent," painted by Robert Cleveley (1798). Print in author's collection.

p. 83: "Battle of Negapatam," painted by Dominic Serres (1786). Print in author's collection.

p. 109: Author's table.

p. 113: Author's table.

p. 114: Author's table.

p. 117: Unknown ephemera, author's collection.

p. 119: Author's original illustration.

p. 123: Unknown ephemera, author's collection.

p. 127: Unknown ephemera, author's collection.

p. 140: Author's collage and original artwork.

p. 143: Author's photo.

p. 145: Author's photo.
p. 152: Author's table.
p. 164: Author's photo.
p. 165: Author's table.
p. 187: "Phoenix and Rose passing Fort Washington," U.S. Naval Academy Library.
p. 196: "British landing at Ft. Lee," watercolor by Thomas Davies, New York Public
    Library.
p. 203: Unknown ephemera, author's collection.
p. 211: Author's table.
p. 220: Unknown ephemera, author's collection.
p. 238: Author's collage and original artwork.
p. 242: "Battle of the Saints," painted by Thomas Mitchell (1782). Print in author's
    collection.
Appendix I: Author's table.
Appendix II: Source is already listed (Jack Coggins, etc.).
Appendix III: Author's table.
Map 1: Author's original artwork.
Map 2: Unknown ephemera, author's collection.
Map 3: Unknown ephemera, author's collection.
Map 4: Author's original artwork.
Map 5: Author's original artwork.
Map 6: Yorktown Map, Library of Congress.

Index

Schuyler, Philip (General), 209
Sea officers, 87–99, 151–54, 176
Searle, John (mutineer), 156
Sears, Isaac, 25
Selman, John (Captain), 152, 158–59
Serle, Ambrose, 153, 182, 183, 189
Seven Years War, 1, 21, 52, 63, 70, 88,
  97, 124, 177, 234
Sherbrook, Miles (Loyalist), 203–4
Shipbuilding (shipwrights), 2, 6,
  45–46, 48, 88, 99, 115–24, 215,
  234
Shuldham, Molyneaux (Admiral), 42,
  154, 166, 199
Silliman, Benjamin (General), 204
Simpson, Thomas (Lieutenant), 91,
  218–19
Skenesboro (Whitehall), New York,
  208–9
Skimmer, John (Captain), 152, 174
Slade, Sir Thomas, 128–29
Small-boat navy, 199–200
Smith, James, 30
Smith, Richard, 18
Smuggling, 2, 14–15, 19
Snider, Christopher, 31
Sons of Liberty (Liberty Boys), 19, 25,
  26, 178
Sons of Neptune, 19, 25
South Carolina, 27, 38, 54–55, 68–69
Spain, 3, 8, 45, 69, 76, 77, 231, 233,
  234, 252, 253
Spanish Navy, 125
Spuyten Duyvil (Cox Hill Fort), New
  York, 185
Stamp Act (1765), 5, 21–28
Stanhope, John (Captain), 161
State navies, 6, 47, 52–57
Staten Island, New York, 183, 184,
  186
Stephens, Philip (Admiralty Board
  Secretary), 62–63
Sterling, Walter, 18, 26–27
St. Eustatius, 49, 82, 103, 147, 237
St. John, Henry, 25
Strategy, 6, 8, 51, 57, 66, 67–76, 151,
  178–79, 190, 214, 235, 240, 248

Submarine warfare (Turtle), 197–98
Suffern, Saint Tropez (Admiral), 238,
  240
Sugar Act (1764), 3–4, 14, 15, 35
Sullivan, John (General), 170, 180,
  200, 215, 235, 249

Tactics, 44–45, 78–85, 190, 193, 195,
  235, 238
Talbot, Silas, 47
Tallmadge, Benjamin (Major), 192, 204
Tappan Sea (Zee). See Hudson River
Taxes, 16, 21–22, 27, 33
Thomas, John (General), 208–9
Throg's (Frog's) Neck, New York, 182,
  192, 194–95
Townsend, Charles, 28
Townsend Revenue Act (1767, 1769),
  3, 28
Trade, 2–3, 11–13, 28–29, 177–78
Trenton, New Jersey, 214, 249, 252
Trescott, Lemuel (Major), 205
Triangular trade, 11–12
Troop ships (British transports), 152,
  154, 182, 229
Tryon, William, 15, 144, 178, 180,
  206–7
Tucker, Samuel (Captain), 152, 162,
  164, 171–72, 173
Tupper, Benjamin (Lieutenant Colonel),
  187
Turtle (submarine), 197–98
Twiss, William (Lieutenant of
  Engineers), 210

Uniforms. See Clothing

Valcour Island, 207, 210–12
Valley Forge, Pennsylvania, 250
Vandeput, George (Captain), 178–79
Varage, Joseph (Captain), 219
Vergennes, Charles Gravier (French
  Minister), 76, 232, 233, 241–42,
  244, 253
Vernon, William, 61
Vice-Admiralty Court, 15, 21, 88, 92,
  207